CRIME AND
SOCIETY IN ENGLAND,
1750–1900

Clive Emsley

LONGMAN GROUP UK LIMITED
Longman House, Burnt Mill, Harlow,
Essex CM20 2JE, England
and Associated Companies throughout the world.

*Published in the United States of America
by Longman Inc., New York*

First published 1987

BRITISH LIBRARY CATALOGUING IN PUBLICATION DATA
Emsley, Clive
   Crime and society in England, 1750–1900.——
   (Themes in British social history)
   1. Crime and criminals——England——
   History 2. Punishment——England——
   History
   I. Title II. Series
   364′.942   HV6943
   ISBN 0-582-49399-4

LIBRARY OF CONGRESS CATALOGUING-IN-PUBLICATION DATA
Emsley, Clive.
   Crime and society in England, 1750–1900.
   (Themes in British social history)
   Bibliography: p.
   Includes index.
   1. Crime and criminals——England——History——18th century.
   2. Crime and criminals——England——History——19th century.
   I. Title. II. Series.
   HV6949.E5E47 1987   364′.942   86–20827
   ISBN 0-582-49399-4 (pbk.)

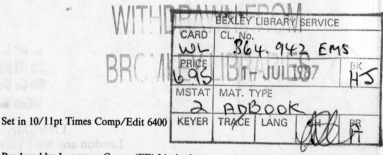
Set in 10/11pt Times Comp/Edit 6400

Produced by Longman Group (FE) Limited
Printed in Hong Kong

CONTENTS

LIST OF TABLES AND FIGURES

PREFACE AND ACKNOWLEDGEMENTS

During the eight or nine years that my historical interest has concentrated on questions of crime and policing I have benefited enormously from exchanges with many colleagues at conferences, seminars, and through correspondence. I should single out the regular colloquia of the International Association for the History of Crime and Criminal Justice, which enabled me to air material now in Chapters 4 and 8, and the CESDIP/University of Paris VIIe seminar, organised by Michelle Perrot and Philippe Robert, which, with its concentration on France and continental Europe, sharpened my perception of English peculiarities. Among the individuals who have responded to my queries and/or who have generously allowed me to read and make use of their research, I would like to take this opportunity to thank Anne Bryson, Shirley Chase, Jennifer Davis, David Englander, David Foster, Janet Gyford, Joanna Innes, Peter King, Roger Ryan, Simon Stevenson and Steve Wilson. Jim Sharpe and John Styles have always been generous with advice and they both kindly commented on a draft of the book. John Stevenson, the series editor, performed the same chore. My thanks to them for their corrections and suggestions; needless to say, the remaining errors are my own. A variety of archivists and librarians have assisted me, particularly the staff of the Bedfordshire County Record Office and the staff of the Open University Library. I am grateful for permission to consult and to cite manuscript material held in the record office of Bedfordshire, Nottinghamshire, Wiltshire, Leeds City, and in University College London. Crown Copyright material is reproduced with acknowledgement to the Controller of H.M. Stationery Office.

Lastly, my apologies to Mark and Kathryn for their father's disappearances into his study when he could have been helping with homework or driving them to various concerts, sports, music practices, or teenage social gatherings. My thanks to my wife, Jennifer, for running the family taxi service during these disappearances, and my thanks to her for a great deal more – hence the dedication.

ABBREVIATIONS USED IN NOTES

C.C.C.S.P.	*Central Criminal Court Sessions Papers*
E.H.R.	*English Historical Review*
H.J.	*Historical Journal*
H.O.	Home Office Papers in Public Record Office
M.E.P.O.	Metropolitan Police Papers in Public Record Office
O.B.S.P.	*Old Bailey Sessions Papers*
P and P	*Past and Present*
P.P.	*Parliamentary Papers*
R.O.	Record Office, as in Beds. R.O.
T.R.H.S.	*Transactions of the Royal Historical Society*
U.C.L.	University College London

For Jenny

Chapter 1

INTRODUCTION: CRIME AND THE LAW

The growth of crime in recent years has been unprecedented[1]; so too, has been the recent growth of academic research and publication particularly in the history of crime. Marx, with his usual intellectual penetration, commented: 'the criminal produces not only crimes, but also criminal law, and with this the professor who gives lectures on criminal law'.[2] Academic historians have been slow to recognise these insights and, until recently, most history books dealing with crime tended to be 'popular' rather than narrowly 'academic' and have concentrated on particular, notorious events or personalities; many have depended largely upon anecdotal or literary sources. More general textbook surveys – political, economic and social – rarely addressed the problem of crime. However in the last ten or fifteen years historians have increasingly turned their attention to crime and how former societies understood it, and sought to deal with it. They have begun searching among court and police records seeking to assess changes over time and to relate such changes to different economic, political and social contexts. This research is another aspect of 'history from below'. From exploring crowds and their motives social historians have swung, perhaps inevitably, to other kinds of 'lawbreaker' and have sought to estimate crime and to understand at least some of its causes, within different contexts.

This book is an attempt to synthesise recent work on crime and English society from roughly the middle of the eighteenth until the close of the nineteenth century. There is a reference to crime in Wales where the legal system was indistinguishable from that of England; but Scotland, with a different legal system, and Ireland, with its rural and nationalist rebels together with a para-military police, receive little attention. The book addresses itself to four key questions: what did contemporaries understand as crime during the eighteenth and nineteenth centuries? What patterns of crime were detected, and have been detected subsequently by historians? Who committed crime? What remedies were attempted to prevent crime and to handle offenders?

A definition of crime which embraces all of its different perspectives and which satisfies every generalisation and nuance is probably impossible. The simplest definition describes crime as behaviour which violates the criminal law, behaviour which 'if detected, would lead to prosecution in a court of law or summarily before an accredited agent of law enforcement'.[3] There are problems with this definition. Some public order legislation gives citizens and law officers, particularly police officers, discretionary powers which can be used if they consider it necessary. Among the most obvious examples are 'threatening, abusive or insulting words or behaviour with intent to provoke a breach of the peace, or whereby a breach of the peace may be occasioned'; and, of course, 'resisting or obstructing a constable in the execution of his duty'.[4] This kind of discretionary power increased with the growth of the new police during the nineteenth century, and it even became possible for men to be arrested by the police and then to be given periods of imprisonment by magistrates for being 'suspicious persons'; the 1869 Habitual Criminals Act, for example, provided for a maximum of twelve months imprisonment on such a charge. Most people would differentiate between such 'offences' and what they consider to be 'real crime' such as murder, rape and theft; but as far as the offender was concerned the result – arrest, trial, punishment – was the same. Nevertheless the definition of crime as behaviour violating the criminal law has the advantage for the historian of relating behaviour to laws in force at a particular time; thus 'criminal' behaviour is tied firmly to its historical context. It is this definition which informs this volume.

Some historians have used the term 'social crime' to differentiate between 'real crime' and those offences which had a degree of community acceptance or which can be linked with social protest. The inhabitants of mid nineteenth-century Manchester had to get their water from taps or pumps in the street or courtyard. Reporting for the *Morning Chronicle* Angus Reach noted:

> Where standpipes or public taps are erected, the charge by the water company is about 10s. a year for every house the inmates of which use the convenience. Of all the petty thefts which occur in Manchester, however, none – although they do not appear in the police returns – are so common as larcenies from taps and pumps.[5]

Probably very few of the water thieves ever considered their behaviour as criminal: even if the water company provided a facility, was not water a man's right and free in the rain and in the rivers? A very small number of offenders set out to justify their behaviour as actions in a kind of class struggle. At the Norfolk Summer Assizes in 1839 William Watts was sentenced to his second term of transportation after having been found guilty of shooting six horses and cattle. Watts declared from the dock that:

> he was perfectly satisfied with his sentence but to such a state had they brought the poor of this country by oppressing them with taxes, poor

rates, and other things, that it was impossible for a poor man to live by
honest means, and all this was to support big-gutted relieving officers, and
other folks connected with them and the [Poor Law] unions.[6]

John Rule has suggested that it is useful to think of two main types of
social crime during the late eighteenth and early nineteenth centuries:
first, those crimes which drew collective legitimation from their explicit
protest nature, and second, crimes which, although actions against the
law, were not regarded as criminal by those who committed them. Wary
of the limitations he includes poaching, illicit distilling, wrecking and
smuggling among social crimes.[7] It is also possible to include rioting –
particularly over the high cost of food, over enclosures, recruiting,
turnpike tolls and so forth – and the appropriation of some perquisites
from the workplace as social crimes; 'perks' seem to have been
increasingly the objects of criminal prosecution by employers during the
eighteenth and nineteenth centuries. Food riots, or disorders over the
appropriation of common land, and perks, in particular, demonstrate
that there could be different perceptions of justice from that enshrined in
the law. Furthermore the language of the law can obscure the protest
nature of some crimes as where, for example, individuals making an
attack on an enclosure were indicted on charges of 'forcible entry';
though, by the same token, it must be noted that some prosecutions in
summary courts for the offence of 'trespass' were often prosecutions for
the theft of growing crops.[8]

While few serious historians would now dismiss eighteenth- and
nineteenth-century riots as the work of the dregs of society lacking in any
motives other than the desire for drink, plunder and, perhaps, rape, the
concept of social crime has its drawbacks. The poor may not have
regarded poaching as a crime; 'they almost universally look upon game,
when in a wild state, as not being the property of any individual',
declared a Bedfordshire Justice before a Parliamentary Select Committee
in 1826.[9] But poaching did not merely involve poor men taking game to
eke out their meagre diet. There were plenty of gentlemen poachers who
were prosecuted under the Game Laws; in the spring of 1796, for
example, the Reverend Francis Barstow was fined £20 by Lincolnshire
justices for shooting game without a proper certificate.[10] Moreover from
the mid eighteenth century until the legislation of 1831 which greatly
reduced its profitability, poaching was increasingly a business carried on
by organised gangs. In spite of laws forbidding the sale of game there
was a ready and expanding market among poulterers, innkeepers and
victuallers to provide for the dietary demands of urban gentlemen and
well-to-do tradesmen; while the landed gentry's creation of large new
game preserves gave poachers, as well as sportsmen, new opportunities.[11]
Whether members of an organised gang, pursuing a business and
satisfying a large market, can be adequately described as social criminals
is, to say the least, a moot point.

Along the coasts, wreckers believed that they had a right to whatever was thrown up on their shores as a result of storm or misadventure, though legislation prohibiting such activity went back to Edward I. Local sanction of this offence could stretch to Methodist lay preachers, who appear to have participated, and to local parsons, who might receive wine or brandy liberated from wrecks.[12] But what of that other coastal crime – smuggling? The gangs had support from local communities; but they were not averse to violence and intimidation to ensure support. An excess of violence could be counter productive, as in the case of the savage murder of a revenue officer and his informant in West Sussex in February 1748.[13] Furthermore, smuggling could be big capitalist business. This was especially the case with tea smuggling in the two decades between the end of the Seven Years War and the Commutation Act of 1784 which reduced the duty of tea by more than three quarters. During these years wealthy merchants with far-flung interests replaced many of the small-scale smugglers and encroached massively on the legal tea market. Tea was smuggled in large, well-armed vessels; the illicit cargoes were even insured. In the end the smugglers were too efficient. They provided the public with an inexpensive, widely available beverage; at the same time they generated vigorous counter action by legal tea merchants, the East India Company, and the government, culminating in the 1784 legislation which dramatically reduced the rewards to be gained from smuggling. Perhaps these smugglers were social criminals, but their actions also promoted 'the international and domestic trade of the kingdom, which, in turn, contributed to the growth of the British economy in the latter part of the eighteenth century'.[14]

During the 1760s there was widespread coining in the West Riding which received considerable support from all sections of the local community. This support was not grounded in an appeal to customary rights or widespread and long-standing hostility to the monopoly of the Royal Mint. Rather it was the result of the failure of the Mint to produce gold coinage of sufficient quality and quantity which provided the coiners with their opportunity; at the same time the offence 'provided a widely diffused source of income during a period of acute depression in the local staple [textile] industry'. Thus, according to John Styles, rather than emerging as a challenge to a new economic order, popularly condoned money-making in the West Riding involved the commercial exploitation of an opportunity which was partly the product of a local economic crisis.[15]

Other offences might be tacitly condoned by social groups or communities. At Greystoke in Cumberland in 1827, Mary Kirkbride died of poisoning. The overdose of laudanum which killed her appeared to have been administered by a group of local women, including the wife of one of the overseers of the poor. A wall of silence descended around the case; Mary Kirkbride came from a family notorious for burdening the parish with illegitimate children and for bringing trouble to the community.[16] Six years later the new Metropolitan Police broke up a political demonstration in Calthorpe Street, London; during the fracas a police constable was mortally wounded by a knife thrust. A significant proportion of artisan London believed that the police had acted in a 'ferocious and brutal' manner quite 'unprovoked by the people'. This attitude was reflected in the verdict of the coroner's jury – 'justifiable homicide' – and the subsequent feting of that jury by the populace.[17] Just over half a century later Captain Thomas Dudley and one of his ship's crew, Edwin Stephens, were tried for murdering cabin boy Richard Parker. Dudley had stabbed Parker in the throat with his penknife and bled him to death over his ship's chronometer case. Dudley, Stephens and another seaman, Ned Brooks, then drank the blood and feasted off the body for five days. The incident is horrific; but so too were the circumstances in which Dudley and his crew found themselves. They had been shipwrecked in the South Atlantic and adrift in an open boat for nineteen days with scarcely any food – two tins of turnips and a small turtle caught on the fourth day. Dudley gave a full statement when he was rescued, and was astonished when he and Stephens were arrested; Brooks was a Crown witness. Dudley's defence was that he had observed a custom of the sea; public opinion appears to have acquiesced, though there was disquiet that Dudley and the others had selected the weakest among their unfortunate group rather than drawing lots. Defence counsel argued that Dudley and his crew were outside the jurisdiction of any court as well as of civilised society. The different courts hearing the case over a seven-month period fudged and hedged over the legal and ethical problems. Dudley and Stephens were found guilty and sentenced to death for murder; but, in the event, they were only required to serve a token period of hard labour.[18]

The killings of Kirkbride, Culley and Parker have not been described as 'social crimes' yet, to the extent that each was condoned or excused by different social groups, the label would not be entirely inappropriate. This underlines some of the problems in using the term: if the armed poacher or armed smuggler was a social criminal, why not the killer of P.C. Culley? and if the killer of P.C. Culley, why not the killers of Kirkbride and Parker, save that the former were well-to-do and, apparently, acting in cold-blooded premeditation while their victim was poor and unfortunate; while Parker was not killed in the context of class struggle. The value of the concept of social crime is that it draws attention to the fact that laws were not universally accepted and that some offences, on some occasions, could be legitimised by social groups and communities. But used as a blanket term for certain offences rather too many lawbreakers are cloaked in the mantle of Robin Hood; as E. P. Thompson warned 'there is not 'nice' social crime here and 'nasty' antisocial crime there'.[19]

Radical criminologists have fulminated about modern legal systems in the western world which drag hundreds of poor, petty offenders through the courts but which allow large-scale corporate offences to go unprosecuted.[20] This issue has been little explored in an historical context, yet it is clear that considerable sums were embezzled and otherwise fraudulently appropriated in the late Hanoverian and Victorian periods, and that employers sometimes flouted laws or cut metaphorical corners and real costs which cheated their workforce and endangered life. Herbert Spencer believed that fraud was endemic in railway companies a decade after the beginning of the 'railway mania' of 1844 to 1847. It was not that the company directors were morally lower than the community as a whole but that:

> there is the familiar fact that the corporate conscience is ever inferior to the individual conscience – that a body of men will commit as a joint act, that which every individual of them would shrink from did he feel personally responsible.

In addition there was a remoteness from the effects of corruption:

> Hence in railway affairs a questionable share transaction, an exorbitant charge, a proceeding which brings great individual advantage without apparently injuring any one, but which, even if analysed in its ultimate results, can but very circuitously affect unknown persons living no one knows where, may be brought home to men who, could the results be embodied before them, would be shocked at the cruel injustices they had committed – men who in their private business where the results *can* be thus embodied, are sufficiently equitable.[21]

Sixty years later Judge Edward Parry warned how 'knaves' running building societies, investment schemes and similar organisations took money from the poor, but structured their contracts in such a way that they were legally immune from prosecution even when the poor man's savings were squandered or lost. Often it was a matter of class and education:

> Fraud is a more complicated offence than larceny, and defrauders sometimes get the better of the law. Cheating is not always a crime, and successful cheating is a question of better education.[22]

Nineteenth-century gentlemen were aware of corporate crime and of legal, but reprehensible, corporate behaviour, yet it was not these kinds of offences which much vexed either theorists of crime or legislators. The law was very slow to act against abuses in the commercial world; and while, for example, the 1844 Company Act required that auditors examine a company's books before it could function legally, there was no requirement that 'auditors' be accountants. It was not until the twentieth century that balance sheets and profit and loss accounts had to be published, and only after the Second World War did investors get any real protection. Legislation against abuses in factories and mines, and against the truck system for paying wages, was passed in the first half of the nineteenth century; but the inspectorate established to enforce the factory legislation was few in number and limited in powers. Furthermore the inspectors were discouraged from prosecuting offenders. In 1876 Alexander Redgrave looked back over more than thirty years as clerk to the factory inspectorate:

> In the inspection of factories it has been my view always that we are not acting as policemen ... that in enforcing this Factory Act, we do not enforce it as a policeman would check an offence which he is told to detect. We have endeavoured not to enforce the law, if I may use such an expression, but it has been my endeavours ... that we should be the advisors of all classes, that we should explain the law, and that we should do everything we possibly could do to induce them to observe the law, and that a prosecution should be the very last thing we should take up.[23]

Of course it is unlikely that the rulers of a state will legislate against their own interests or supporters; it might, therefore, be argued that the nineteenth-century state, dependent on a new economic order involving a new level of capitalist investment, a burgeoning factory system and a massive exploitation of coal and iron, would not act against the financiers, owners and employers in this new order except when compelled by the most flagrant abuses. This is not an argument that can be either proven or disproved; it depends very much on a pre-determined attitude to the state and the society which emerged during the industrial revolution. It might better be argued, and with a greater reference to the evidence, that the policy of state intervention in these areas was complex, fluctuating and often tentative. Tightening up on financial fraud is an exceedingly difficult task for legislators and, subsequently, for the courts. What, for want of a better term, can be called laissez-faire ideology probably also had a role; there was a fear that too much legislation and too much inspection would inhibit Britain's industrial development. Inspectors and inspections cost money, and no nineteenth-century treasury minister, let alone parliament, would have been prepared to sanction the kind of expenditure necessary to check a significant proportion of abuses on the factory floor or at the coal face. There were other restraints also; in the case of some chemical processes, the unchecked side effects of which destroyed vegetation and harmed the health of the workforce, there was simply insufficient expertise to enable the control of noxious and dangerous vapours until well into the nineteenth century; and the noxious vapours of the Alkali Industry, like the general pall of smoke which hung over industrial cities and also endangered health, were seen as signs of Britain's progress and a mark of full employment. Such feelings were to be found as much among the workers, whose health was threatened, as among the employers, whose factories did the threatening.[24] Further-more the illegal use of juvenile labour was connived at by some of the workforce, and safety precautions were resented by workers if they slowed up the work process, especially if this might consequently have an impact on wages rates. It was even suggested, during the 1890s, that female workers discarded the respirators and protective clothing given by more reputable employers 'because they hide the charms of the wearers'. A lack of adequate education and preparation of the workforce was the more likely reason.[25]

Given that corrupt, dangerous, fraudulent and otherwise reprehensible activities did not become crimes until the law decreed, this raises another series of questions about who makes the law, who administers it, and what legislators and agents of the law think they are doing. In the middle of the eighteenth century Adam Smith could suggest to students at the University of Glasgow that:

> when ... some have great wealth and others nothing, it is necessary that the arm of authority should be continually stretched forth, and permanent laws or regulations made which may protect the property of the rich from the inroads of the poor ... Laws and governments may be considered in this and in every case as a combination of the rich to oppress the poor, and preserve to themselves the inequality of the goods which would otherwise be soon destroyed by the attacks of the poor, who if not hindered by the government would soon reduce the others to an equality with themselves by open violence.[26]

Observing England during the early 1830s Alexis de Tocqueville concluded that the law was, indeed, functioning in such a fashion:

> The English have left the poor but two rights; that of obeying the same laws as the rich, and that of standing on an equality with them if they can obtain equal wealth. But those two rights are more apparent than real, since it is the rich who make the laws and who create for their own or their children's profit, the chief means of getting wealth.[27]

Few Victorian gentlemen would have agreed with such assessments. In 1865 *The Times* published a leading article on the case of a Mr Payne, treasurer of the Manchester Relief Fund, who had pocketed £2,400 from the fund. It noted how Payne had avoided prosecution because the law was simply not geared to cope with such an offence. The legislation regarding embezzlement, 'that is, of receiving money and not accounting for it', passed in the reign of George III, applied only to clerks and servants. *The Times* was highly critical of the way in which the law had been framed, but it did not perceive that one class had seen crime as emanating only from another class, rather the problem was that the law did not yet reach the desired national consensus; 'in many respects [it] still lags behind the dictates of true morality and the moral sense of the people'.[28] It was this view that the law derived from consensus, and that, while the process might be long and drawn out, abuses, as they were detected, were reformed, which dominated in the nineteenth century. In 1898 the Attorney General could assure members of parliament that everyone, prisoners included, had confidence in the administration of justice in England.[29] A consequence of this, at least in part, was that criminals could be portrayed as a separate class, outside consensual society and making war upon it.

But, as was noted in the discussion of social crime, laws were not universally accepted during the eighteenth and nineteenth centuries. In a seminal essay Douglas Hay has portrayed the eighteenth-century English criminal law as one of the 'chief ideological instruments' of the ruling class:

> It was easy to claim equal justice for murderers of all classes, where a universal moral sanction was more likely to be found, or in political cases, the necessary price of a constitution ruled by law. The trick was to extend that communal sanction to a criminal law that was nine-tenths concerned with upholding a radical division of property.

> [The law] allowed the rulers of England to make the courts a selective instrument of class justice, yet simultaneously to proclaim the law's incorruptible impartiality and absolute determinacy.[30]

Hay's challenging thesis has not gone uncriticised. John Langbein has insisted that 'the criminal law is simply the wrong place to look for the active hand of the ruling classes' and he emphasises the fact 'that gentlemen prosecutors were few and far between'.[31] This latter point has been developed more fully by Peter King arguing that:

> the criminal law may more fruitfully be described as a multi-use right within which the various groups in eighteenth-century society conflicted with, cooperated with and gained concessions from each other.[32]

The simple division which posits a ruling class making and administering the law, and a ruled class on the receiving end, obscures the often marked differences between agents of the law and prosecutors.

It might also be urged, against Hay, that there was no systematic attempt to plug every loophole in the defences of property during the eighteenth century. Some of the legislation was catch all; the Black Act 1723 is the most notorious example.[33] However a preliminary analysis of the legislation comprising the Bloody Code suggests that parliament was perceived as having, and indeed did have, important administrative functions during the eighteenth century which historians have generally ignored. Furthermore a reconstruction of how eighteenth-century parliaments actually made criminal statutes challenges the image of an undifferentiated ruling class legislating in its own interest. The debates were real and heated; the interests represented in these debates were not confined to the landed gentry; and there were positive notions advanced of propriety and public interest. When, in 1751, Henry Bankes introduced a bill to protect the owners of mines from theft and robbery he met considerable opposition; yet here was a supporter of the government and the brother of a gentleman who was a leading member of a consortium running the only graphite mines in Britain, mines which were constantly being invaded by the local population of Borrowdale.

What concerned the members of parliament who opposed the bill was a matter of legal principle; was it right to make illegal taking from the ground a felony? A second, much narrower bill was eventually passed in 1752, but its passage was difficult and the offence was not made capital.[34]

No-one has produced an hypothesis for the law in nineteenth-century England which parallels the complexity, power and subtlety of Hay's for the preceding century. The traditional, some might say anodyne, view has it that humanitarian reformers like Sir Samuel Romilly and Sir James Mackintosh, through tireless efforts, brought an awareness both inside and outside parliament, that the criminal justice system needed reform and particularly that the two hundred or so capital statutes of England's Bloody Code, required drastic surgery. While such men stressed the barbarity of the legal code, other reformers like John Howard paved the way for improvements in the prison system which, it was believed, would give offenders the opportunity and the time to reflect upon their evil ways and, in consequence, reform themselves. Change, or rather reform and improvement, was thus the product of the humanitarianism inherent in the Enlightenment and its perception of man as a rational being. In Britain the picture fitted well with the all pervading Whig interpretation of history as progress.

The Whig view of progress in the criminal justice system was frontally assaulted by Georg Rusche and Otto Kirchheimer.[35] They linked different systems of punishment with different social structures: thus, under feudalism, there was an increase in corporal punishments since, in most cases, the body was the only property accessible; the mercantile system saw a change to forced labour and the penitentiary; the industrial system required a free market in labour and, in consequence, corrective detention gradually replaced forced labour. Change during the Enlightenment stemmed less from an altruistic desire to make punishment more humane than from the twin desires to protect the rising bourgeoisie from arbitrary punishment from above and from social upheaval from below brought about by brutal and unequal punishment. More recently the French philosopher-historian, Michel Foucault, has described within the Enlightenment a growing desire to establish a disciplined society which he does not see as related specifically to changing economic and social structures. The savage punishments of the old regime often created a bond between the offender and the crown assembled around the scaffold; punishment might engender feelings of revulsion, but it did not necessarily frighten and consequently it did not deter. What was needed was a new system of punishment which would: '[H]omogenize its application. Reduce its economic and political cost by increasing the effectiveness and by multiplying its circuits'.[36] Foucault's aim was much wider than explaining changes in the criminal justice system. He sought to describe a whole pattern of cultural change involving the relationship between new forms of knowledge and the shifting strategies and institutions through which power was and is exercised. Prisons were a key element here, but so too were asylums, barracks, factories, hospitals and schools. Together with these institutions went new forms of expert knowledge, notably in medicine and psychiatry, which could also be used to enclose and restrict the body.

In the last analysis all of these hypotheses are unproveable; they are also deterministic. The Whig view sees change as rational and progressive; opponents of reform thus become blinkered and re-actionary. The idea that alternative developments were possible and might have been equally rational and progressive is implicitly denied. The Rusche and Kirchheimer hypothesis is more apparently deter-ministic: no matter what men do as individuals the economic and social structure within which they labour would seem to determine all. Foucault's assessment is stimulating in the questions which it poses and in the last few years it has generated considerable debate, discussion and research.[37] But, ultimately, Foucault's theory of new forms of knowledge seems to deny the possibility of alternative visions within a given period of history.

It is difficult to see how changing ideas about crime and criminals, and changing practices in criminal justice and punishment during the eighteenth and nineteenth centuries could not have been related to changing ideologies and economic and social structures. The question is whether the links were quite as one way as Rusche and Kirchheimer and Foucault suggest; or whether, as Gordon Wright has argued with reference to France:

> It is more likely that the relationship between values and socioeconomic base, then as now, was reciprocal – that base and value-system combine to shape society's view of men and the world.[38]

The economic, political and social structure of a society creates a framework in which the criminal justice system functions and men may draw parallels between that system and new modes of production. Michael Ignatieff has shown how the rhetoric which equated men with machines was common to both prison reformers and industrialists in early nineteenth-century England.[39] But the framework created leaves room for a variety of alternatives, and many pressures ranging from perceptions of a nation's traditions to financial stringency can combine to ensure that ideals are not realised by legislators let alone their agents.

Eighteenth-century parliaments tended to legislate for local problems, even the Black Act addressed a local problem; but gradually, and increasingly, legislators began to see crime in a national context. Peel's reorganisation of the criminal law during the 1820s was itself symptomatic of this change. Yet laws passed in the context of perceiving a national problem still had to be implemented by local agents on the streets and in the courts who may have had a different perception from that of the majority at Westminster. The law may have been deemed impartial and, increasingly, the product of consensual values by members of the judiciary, by legislators, theorists and so on, but the law had to be interpreted and enforced by local agents who had their own assumptions, interests, and prejudices, and who could be, on occasions, at odds with each other.[40]

Offenders could be brought before three principal kinds of court during the eighteenth and nineteenth centuries. The least serious offences could be dealt with summarily by magistrates sitting alone, or in pairs in petty sessions; the petty sessions became increasingly formal and regularised during the period. The county magistrate was, technically, a royal appointment; in practice he was selected by the Lord Lieutenant of a county for the approval of the Lord Chancellor. He had to be a man of some wealth and social standing to have his name entered on a county's commission of the peace in the first place; he then had to be of sufficient public spirit to take out his *dedimus potestatem*, which involved travelling to the county town, swearing an oath before the clerk of the peace, and paying the appropriate fees. Corporate boroughs also had magisterial benches generally composed of some combination of the mayor and aldermen; borough corporations were usually self-perpetuating oligarchies of the principal inhabitants until the Municipal Corporations Act of 1835 established a common system of election for town councils. This act also sought to separate the executive arm of town administration (the town council) from the judicial arm (the magistrates), and required that borough magistrates be supervised by a recorder, a barrister appointed by the Crown; but throughout the nineteenth century town councillors continued to be selected as borough magistrates. The number of offences which could be tried summarily increased during the eighteenth century and even more markedly during the nineteenth, particularly with the passage of the Juvenile Offenders Acts 1847 and 1850 and the Criminal Justice Acts 1855 and 1879. In the larger towns and cities stipendiary magistrates, acting in what were increasingly referred to as 'police courts' took on more and more of the burdens of summary jurisdiction. The first stipendiaries were appointed in London in 1792. But these paid professionals, like their unpaid associates and predecessors, were gentlemen; after 1835, however, they had to have served a minimum of five years at the bar as a barrister.

More serious offences were prosecuted on indictment and were heard at Quarter Sessions which met four times a year in both counties and corporate towns and which, in theory, though rarely in practice, all serving magistrates in the respective county or town could attend. The most serious indictable offences were tried before judges at assizes. During the eighteenth and early nineteenth centuries there were two assizes each year held in the major county towns of most counties at Lent and during the summer; Northumberland, Cumberland, Westmoreland and Durham were the exceptions, each having only one assize a year. Emergencies, such as serious food riots in Sussex in 1795 and the Luddite troubles, could lead to special assizes being held. The nineteenth century saw experiments with different numbers of assizes in different counties. The metropolitan equivalent of the assizes was the court meeting at the Old Bailey which was holding eight sessions a year during the 1750s; in 1834 the Old Bailey was enlarged and rehoused in the new Central Criminal Court.

Edward Parry recognised the possibility of judicial bias:

> In every age your judge will be tinged with the prejudices of his time and his class, and I cannot see how you can expect to grow middle-class judges in hot-beds of middle-class prejudices without the natural formation of a certain amount of middle-class bias in the thickness of their middle-class wood.[41]

But Parry did not regard this as a problem for the enforcement of the law and for attitudes towards offenders. How far magistrates and judges acted as much because of assumptions and prejudices is an issue which will recur below. What the working-class accused made of the gentlemen who sat as magistrates and judges, particularly the latter in their sumptuous and increasingly archaic garb, will remain an open question. It is clear, however, that 'gentlemen' monopolised the judicial benches, and a brief glance through any court records will show that, in general, people from another social class monopolised the dock. But that said, while one class may have made the law and administered it in the courts, this was by no means the only class to use the law for redress and it was not unknown for the law to protect the poor against the well-to-do.[42] It is also clear that, as a group, the ruling class believed its own rhetoric concerning equality before the law and the need for impartiality and independence in the judicial process. Such beliefs dictated behaviour.

Magistrates and judges were not the only agents of the law who were called upon to interpret the law. The nineteenth century saw the creation of the new police in Britain. While histories of the police in Britain have tended to ignore the issue, it is clear that the policeman on his beat had discretion in identifying some behaviour as criminal or not and in deciding what action to take. He could take the offender into custody occasionally, if he so wished, using a discretionary charge; he could warn him or her, ignore him or her, or even administer summary chastisement with fist, truncheon, cape, or whatever else came to hand.[43] It was largely victimless offences which were open to such discretion – drunkenness, prostitution, street gaming and, especially on Sunday, street selling. If a crime, a theft for example, was reported to a policeman and the offender was identified or subsequently detected then, probably, an arrest and prosecution would result. But the reporting of a crime and the identification of an offender by witnesses in itself required a perception on the part of victim and/or witnesses that a crime had been committed and that legal action should follow. Discretion in matters relating to crime began well before the legislators and the courts; and policemen were not, generally, the initiators of the processes designed to control criminal behaviour.

Teasing out perceptions and the use of discretion are as central to the historian's understanding of crime as studying legislation and enforcement. In the narrowest sense Langbein may be correct in insisting that the criminal law is 'the wrong place' to seek out 'the active hand' of the ruling class; but perceptions of crime and of the criminal, discretion in using the law, new legislation and new systems of enforcement, are all important issues for the historian approaching relationships within a given society and assessing how different societies functioned and evolved.

Rather than attempting a chronological survey of crime and the various developments in the criminal justice system together in short, meaningful chunks, the book is divided thematically. Roughly, the first half explores perceptions and, as far as they are ever ascertainable, the realities of crime from several angles: the statistical evidence, class perceptions, the perceived differences between urban and rural crime, the extent of crime at the workplace. Chapter 6 is designed as a kind of coda, rounding off the first half with a discussion of the usefulness of the concepts of a 'criminal class' and 'professional criminals'. The second half of the book looks at developments in the pursuit, the prosecution, and the treatment of offenders: the courts, the police, and punishment. The final chapter attempts to pull the whole together with some conclusions.

REFERENCES AND NOTES

1. **Sir Leon Radzinowicz** and **Joan King**, *The Growth of Crime: The International Experience*, Penguin, Harmondsworth, 1979, p. 15.
2. Quoted by **Paul Phillips**, *Marx and Engels on Law and Laws* Martin Robertson, Oxford, 1980, p. 161.
3. **J. A. Sharpe**, *Crime in Early Modern England 1550–1750*, Longman, London, 1984, p. 4.
4. For modern discretionary offences see **David J. Smith** and **Jeremy Gray**, *Police and People in London*, Gower, Aldershot, 1985, pp. 13–15.
5. **J. Ginswick** (ed.), *Labour and the Poor in England and Wales 1849–51: The letters to the Morning Chronicle*. 8 vols, Cass, London, 1983, i, 25.
6. Quoted by **John E. Archer**, ' "A fiendish outrage"? A study of animal maiming in East Anglia 1830–70', *Agricultural History Review*, **33** (1985), pp. 147–57 (at p. 154).
7. **John G. Rule**, 'Social crime in the rural south in the eighteenth and early nineteenth centuries', *Southern History*, **1** (1979) 135–53: see also the 'Conference Report' in *Bulletin of the Society for the Study of Labour History*, **25** (1972), pp. 5–12.

8. **John Bohstedt**, *Riots and Community Politics in England and Wales 1790–1810*, Harvard U.P., Cambridge, Mass. 1983, p. 197; **Janet Gyford**, ' "Men of Bad Character": Property crime in Essex in the 1820s', unpublished M.A., University of Essex, 1982, p. 64.

9. *P.P.* 1826–27 (534) vi, *Select Committee on Criminal Commitments and Convictions*, p. 34.

10. Lincs, R.O. Kesteven Quarter Sessions Minute Books, Epiphany 1796–Easter 1802, f.19. The Minute Book gives a tantalising glimpse of what may have been some kind of feud developing between Barstow and the two magistrates who fined him for his Game Law Offence – the Reverend John Myers and John Hutchin. The preceding November these same magistrates had fined him £20 for wearing hair powder without a licence (f.4).

11. **P. B. Munsche**, *Gentlemen and Poachers: The English Game Laws 1671–1831* Cambridge U.P., 1981 *passim*.

12. **John G. Rule**, 'Wrecking and coastal plunder', in **Douglas Hay, Peter Linebaugh, E. P. Thompson** *et al., Albion's Fatal Tree: Crime and society in eighteenth-century England*, Allen Lane, London, 1975, pp. 184–5.

13. **Cal Winslow**, 'Sussex smugglers' in Hay, Linebaugh Thompson *et al., Albion's Fatal Tree*, pp. 136–39 and 159, note 1.

14. **Hoh-Cheung** and **Lorna H. Mui**, 'Smuggling and the British tea trade before 1784', *American Historical Review*, lxxiv (1968), pp. 44–73 (at p. 73).

15. **John Styles**, ' "Our traitorous money-makers": The Yorkshire coiners and the law, 1760–83', in **John Brewer** and **John Styles** (eds.), *An Ungovernable People: The English and their law in the seventeenth and eighteenth centuries*, Hutchinson, London, 1980, pp. 247–8.

16. **Virginia Berridge** and **Griffith Edwards**, *Opium and the People: Opiate use in nineteenth-century England*, Allen Lane, London, 1981, p. 82.

17. **Sir Charles Reith**, *British Police and the Democratic Ideal*, London, 1943, p. 143; **Gavin Thurston**. *The Clerkenwell Riot: The killing of Constable Culley*, Allen and Unwin, London, 1967.
(Both Reith and Thurston completely miss the point of the popular hostility to the police on this occasion.)

18. **A. W. Brian Simpson**, *Cannibalism and the Common Law*, Chicago University Press, 1984, *passim*.

19. 'Conference Report', *Bulletin of the Society for ... Labour History*, 1972, p. 10.

20. **David M. Gordon**, 'Capitalism, class and crime in America', *Crime and Delinquency*, xix (1973), pp. 163–86 argues that the loss resulting from 'Index Crimes' (i.e. robbery, burglary, larceny etc.) is only a fifth of the loss resulting from unreported commercial theft, embezzlement and fraud, yet the criminal justice system is almost entirely concerned with the former. See also inter alia, **Steven Box**, *Power, Crime and Mystification*, Tavistock, London, 1983.

21. **Herbert Spencer**, 'Railway morals and railway policy', *Edinburgh Review*, C (1854) pp. 420–61 (at pp. 426–7).

22. **Edward Abbot Parry**, *The Law and the Poor*, London, 1914, pp. 154–56 and 201.

23. Quoted by **W. G. Carson**, 'The institutionalization of ambiguity: Early

15

British Factory Acts', in **Gilbert Geis** and **Ezra Stotland** (eds.), *White-Collar Crime: Theory and research*, Sage, Beverley Hills, 1980, p. 168.

24. **Colin A. Russell, Noel G. Coley** and **Gerrylynn K. Roberts**, *Chemists by Profession: The origins and rise of the Royal Institute of Chemistry*, Open University Press, Milton Keynes, 1977, pp. 42 and 102; **A. E. Dingle**, ' "The monster nuisance of all": Landowners, alkali manufacturers, and air pollution, 1828–64', *Economic History Review*, xxxv (1982), pp. 529–48.

25. Carson, 'Institutionalization of Ambuigity', pp. 159–60; **Brian Didsbury**, 'Cheshire Saltworkers' in **Raphael Samuel** (ed.), *Miners, Quarrymen and Saltworkers*, RKP, London, 1977, pp. 156–58; **Anthony S. Wohl**, *Endangered Lives: Public health in Victorian Britain*, Dent, London, 1983, pp. 270–72 and 275 especially.

26. **Adam Smith**, *Lectures on Jurisprudence* R. L. Meek, D. D. Raphael and P. G. Stein (eds.), Oxford U.P., 1978, p. 208.

27. **Alexis de Tocqueville**, *Journeys to England and Ireland* (ed. J. P. Mayer) Anchor Books, New York, 1968, p. 78.

28. *The Times* 14 January 1865.

29. **Graham Parker**, 'The prisoner in the box – The making of the Criminal Evidence Act, 1898', in **J. A. Guy** and **H. G. Beale** (eds.), *Law and Social Change in British History*, Royal Historical Society, London, 1984, p. 163.

30. Douglas Hay, 'Property, authority and the criminal law', in Hay, Linebaugh, Thompson *et al., Albion's Fatal Tree,* pp. 26, 35 and 48.

31. **John H. Langbein**, 'Albion's fatal flaws', *P and P*, **98**, (1983), pp. 96–120 (at pp. 102 and 119).

32. **Peter King**, 'Decision makers and decision-making in the English criminal law, 1750–1800', *H.J.* **27** (1984), pp. 25–58 (at p. 53).

33. Sir Leon Radzinowicz, *A History of English Criminal Law*, 5 vols. Stevens, London, 1948–86, i, 49–79; **E. P. Thompson**, *Whigs and Hunters: The origins of the Black Act*, Allen Lane, London, 1975, *passim*. Both Radzinowicz and Thompson categorize the Black Act as typical of the eighteenth-century Bloody Code, and Thompson explains the legislation in terms of the ruthless Hanoverian ruling class acting in its own interest against the foresters who were resisting that class's assault on customary rights. However recent research has identified a crucial and narrowly political motive behind the legislation, namely the Jacobite connection of the foresters, and this does put a very different complexion on the issue. E. **Cruikshanks** and H. **Erskine–Hill**, 'The Waltham Black Act and Jacobitism', *Journal of British Studies*, xxiv (1985), pp. 358–65.

34. While Bankes wanted to make the taking of black lead from mines a felony, it is not clear that he wanted to make the offence capital. The problem is that eighteenth-century bills never included the intended punishment; the punishment was left blank for the committee to fill in after the second reading. Unless ancillary documentation survives, which it does not seem to in this case, the precise intentions of the bill's promoters remain unclear. For the problems in assessing the legislation which went into the Bloody Code see **Joanna Innes** and **John Styles**, 'The crime wave: Recent writing on crime and criminal justice in eighteenth-century England', *Journal of British Studies*, xxv (1986); idem, 'The "Bloody Code" in context: Eighteenth-century criminal legislation

reconsidered. A report on work in progress', unpublished paper, December 1984. My thanks to the authors for permission to read and to cite the latter.

35. **Georg Rusche** and **Otto Kirchheimer**, *Punishment and Social Structure*, Russell and Russell, New York, 1968, *passim*.

36. **Michel Foucault**, *Discipline and Punish: The origins of the prison*, Penguin, Harmondsworth, 1978, p. 89.

37. See especially **Michelle Perrot** (ed.), *L'Impossible Prison: Recherches sur le système au XIXe siècle*, Seuil, Paris, 1980.

38. **Gordon Wright**, *Between the Guillotine and Liberty: Two centuries of the crime problem in France*, Oxford U.P., New York, 1983, p. 22. Wright implies, however, that Foucault sees a precise relationship between the socio-economic base and his changing forms of knowledge which I do not take to be the case; and this lack of relationship is very much the criticism of Jacques Leonard who describes Foucault's theory as 'machinery without the machinist' or 'strategy without generals'. Jacques Leonard, 'L'historien et le philosophe', in Perrot, *L'Impossible Prison*, p. 14 especially.

39. **Michael Ignatieff**, *A Just Measure of Pain: The penitentiary in the Industrial Revolution 1750–1850*, London, Macmillan, 1978, *passim*.

40. For example Norma Landau has described the antagonism of certain eighteenth-century magistrates towards the officers of His Majesty's Customs and Excise which led to them frequently diminishing statutory fines imposed on offenders prosecuted by the officers. **Norma Landau,** *The Justices of the Peace, 1679–1760*, University of California Press, Berkley and Los Angeles, 1984, pp. 223–26.

41. Parry, *The Law and the Poor*, pp. 100–1.

42. For example David Englander has shown how the wage-earner knew how to use the law to advantage against the landlord. **David Englander**, *Landlord and Tenant in Urban Britain 1838–1918*, Oxford U.P., 1983, p. 38 and (for Scotland) pp. 39–44.

43. **Clive Emsley**, ' "The thump of wood on a swede turnip": Police violence in nineteenth-century England', *Criminal Justice History*, VI (1985), pp. 125–49.

Chapter 2

THE STATISTICAL MAP

Many of the key questions, certainly many of the most popular questions about crime, are quantitative. How much was there? Was it increasing or decreasing? Which types of crime were most prevalent at particular periods or in particular places? Even the central question: did economic and social change foster different kinds of criminality requires statistical evidence to hazard an answer. Yet the statistical evidence of crime is fraught with dangers and difficulties.

Criminologists who engage in statistical debates often employ criminal statistics adjusted to take account of population growth or decline, and of changes in age structure. Some historians of crime in the eighteenth and nineteenth centuries have also used this kind of data, though there is the obvious problem of reliable population figures for the period before 1801. The statistics discussed in this chapter are raw figures, nevertheless, as will be explained below, the enormous population changes of the two centuries must always be borne in mind in any assessment of the statistical pattern of crime.

The period of this volume can be divided roughly into three given the kinds of statistics available to the historian. Before 1805 there are no national crime figures. Historians of the eighteenth century, seeking to tackle the questions which require quantifiable answers, have to do their own counting of indictments, trials and convictions in the judicial records – either in the fragmentary assize records at the Public Record Office, or in the quarter sessions records in County Record Offices. Generally speaking there is little surviving evidence from eighteenth-century petty sessions; even though sentences passed at petty sessions were meant to be filed at quarter sessions, the surviving records suggest that few were. In 1827, when the Home Office requested that county clerks of the peace send returns for Game Laws convictions over the preceding seven years, an active magistrate counselled Peel:

> I fear those returns must necessarily be so deficient as to give a most erroneous impression as to the enormous increase of offences of that nature, it being the practice of magistrates out of sessions or at petty

sessions to omit returning such convictions so generally that in many cases not a tenth part, perhaps not a twentieth part of the actual number of convictions which have led to imprisonment and its pernicious consequences have been sent to the Clerks of the Peace to be recorded.[1]

In 1810 the government published figures of committals for indictable crime in England and Wales going back to 1805; and from then on these statistics were published annually. It was the controversy over the Bloody Code which appears to have first occasioned the collection and publication of these statistics. The 1830s and 1840s witnessed the flowering of the statistical movement in Britain and from 1834, thanks to Samuel Redgrave, the Criminal Registrar, the published criminal statistics were reorganised under six main types of offence – a classification which has survived, more or less unchanged, to the present:

1. Offences against the person (ranging from homicide to simple assault);
2. Offences against property involving violence (robbery, burglary, etc);
3. Offences against property not involving violence (larceny, etc);
4. Malicious offences against property (arson, machine breaking, etc);
5. Offences against the currency;
6. Miscellaneous offences (including riot, sedition, and treason).

From 1836 the statistics of commitments to prison began to be systematised and published in an annual digest. Statistics had a quantitative connotation during these years, but this was generally subsidiary to the main concern of collecting and arranging facts illustrative of the condition and resources of the state; indeed it was not until the twentieth century that statistics came to mean solely numbers and the methods of analysing them. The early statistical movement generally took statistical facts to be pure and uncontroversial; by deploying these facts social investigators sought to stand aside from party but, nevertheless, to push for reforms. Reforming ideals guided the statistical movement, and 'moral statistics' lay at its heart with a concentration, primarily, on education, then on crime and, less frequently still, on religion. These reformers urged greater accuracy and greater sophistication in the collection of criminal statistics and pointed to what they took to be the superiority of the French in this respect.[2] In 1856 the government put an appendage to its County and Borough Police Act which established the modern tripartite split in British criminal statistics, and from 1857 these statistics consisted of: first, indictable offences reported to the police which had not necessarily resulted in an arrest or been 'solved'; second, committals for trial, both on indictment and before summary jurisdiction; and third, the number of persons convicted and imprisoned.

While the 'criminal class' is not the concern of this chapter it is worth noting, tangentially, another variety of statistics prepared by policemen and regularised from 1857. These were the figures of 'known thieves and depredators' in a particular police district. The major problem with these statistics is that it was not until the close of the century that any form of guidance was given as to what this category should contain. One stalwart of the Statistical Society lamented in 1860:

> What is meant by 'known thieves and depredators', is not, so far as I know, *anywhere defined*. Nor do the police in the different parts of England attach the same meaning to the term. In Yorkshire, and generally throughout the North of England, they profess to return no one as a known thief who is ever known to do any 'honest work'. In the South, with the exception of the large towns, every man is entered as a 'known thief', who had ever been known to steal.

Thus Birmingham had one thief to every 134 honest men, but one committal for every 246 inhabitants, while Liverpool had one thief to every 1155 honest men and one committal for every 55 persons.[3] An analogous problem exists with the numbers of 'habitual criminals' collected following the Habitual Criminals Act 1869 and the Prevention of Crimes Act 1871. This legislation gave the police considerable supervisory powers over those who had been convicted of more than one offence and could therefore be considered as 'habitual' criminals. Policemen could arrest habituals on suspicion and it was then incumbent on the accused to show that he was not intending mischief when apprehended, or else he could be sentenced to a maximum of twelve months' imprisonment. The difficulty with the statistics of habitual criminals, as recorded by the Criminal Registrar, is that they seem to contradict the evidence of other sources about crime: London appears to have been the scene of most crime, and certainly it was metropolitan crime which created the most scares, but in the lists of habitual criminals London comes a long way down the list. The cause of this discrepancy seems principally to stem from the reluctance of the stipendiary magistrates in the metropolis to accept the way in which the police wished to use the legislation and they exploited loopholes in the law to this end on the grounds that 'we cannot punish a man merely for being in the streets, although he may be a convicted thief and the well-known associate of bad characters'. In this respect the independent, professional magistrates of London acted very differently from many of their lay brethren in the provinces.[4]

Leaving aside the problem of defining members of the criminal class and known thieves and depredators, the chief difficulty with the principal forms of criminal statistics is the 'dark figure', that is the number of offences committed of which there is no record because no-one bothered to, wished to, or was able to report a particular offence. Committals or indictments leave an even bigger gap between themselves and what might be hypothesised as 'the actual amount of crime' since they necessitate an accusation against a particular, identified individual. Experts were aware of the dark figure at least from the end of the eighteenth century. In his *Treatise on the Police of the Metropolis*, Patrick Colquhoun noted: 'Under the present system there is not above one offence in one hundred that is discovered or prosecuted'.[5] Edwin Chadwick and his colleagues investigating crime and policing during the 1830s:

> found that in respect to the crimes against property and other classes of crime, that the number of cases pursued bore little or no relation to the cases of crime actually committed. We found large masses of crime with scarcely any pursuit at all ... [6]

In 1867, after ten years of the more detailed tripartite criminal statistics, James T. Hammick, a barrister and member of the council of the Statistical Society, declared:

> It is certain that the actual amount of crime committed can never at any time be ascertained. Robbery is sometimes carried on for years without detection; and the unwillingness of persons to make known and to prosecute frauds by servants and others will always render the returns on this head [i e crimes reported to the police] incomplete.[7]

The statistics of committals and indictments which form the basis of the criminal statistics for some two thirds of the period covered by this volume are obviously some way from any measurement of actual crime. They are the end product of a variety of filters and require, at the very least a victim prepared to prosecute or someone prepared to report an offence, and an individual who has been accused and apprehended. But individual prosecutions were also the product of a social, economic and political context which changed from decade to decade, even from year to year. In some years the context may have provoked a ferocious response to a particular offence, in others the response could have been far more lenient. Over two hundred prosecutions for sedition have been counted for the years 1792 to 1801. This was probably two hundred more than in the preceding decade; it reflects the growth of Painite radicalism in England during the decade of the French Revolution; it also reflects the panic of many men of property and their determination to crush Jacobinism at home as well as abroad.[8] A Mancunian who cursed the King, his chief minister and the latter's policies following the severe impact of the 1784 Fustian Tax may have been cautioned or completely ignored. The same man damning the King, his chief minister and the latter's policies a decade later, as the cost of the Revolutionary Wars demanded more and more sacrifices in men and money, was much more likely to find himself before the courts charged with seditious words. Of course, such a narrowly 'political' offence as speaking sedition is only likely to occur in public before an audience which can provide a witness or two. Yet similar variations can be suggested with reference to the prosecution of other crimes. A statistical increase in indictments for petty theft during the years of dearth in the eighteenth and early nineteenth centuries may reflect a genuine increase in theft brought about by necessity. It may also reflect some farmers and gentlemen determined to make examples by a prosecution, rather than by an admonition, so as to dissuade anyone else who might also be tempted to offend because of the severity of the time; though, conversely, some gentlemen appear to have been inclined to more leniency towards property offenders in times of distress. In other instances the fear of increased crime might, of itself, have generated an increase in prosecutions. In November 1765 the printer of the *Chelmsford Chronicle* appears consciously to have used one or two robberies and some reports of robberies both to boost his sales and to assert his newspaper's claim to being the key organ of information in Essex. His emphasis on these offences, in turn, generated arrests on flimsy evidence which, in turn, generated more copy. The stereotype bandit gangs described in the newspaper were never apprehended.[9] The London garotting panic of 1862 appears to have provoked an increase in prosecutions for street robbery. Once press, police and private individuals were aware of the offence they began to see it all around. Hugh Pilkington M.P. was 'garotted' in Pall Mall on 17 July 1862. There had been only fifteen robberies with violence in the metropolis in the first six months of the year but as the panic gathered momentum in the aftermath of the attack on Pilkington and as *The Times* orchestrated a press attack on philanthropists for being too soft on the kind of 'habitual criminals' who became 'garotters', so the number of reported incidents, and prosecutions, increased: in September there were two alleged garottings, in October twelve, in November thirty-two.[10]

Changes in policing could also affect the statistics of crime. In 1828 two parliamentary select committees agreed that most of the apparent increase in crime manifested in the committal figures before them was the result of better enforcement and changes in classification.[11] The establishment of the new police forces from the 1830s invariably produced local increases in the numbers of individuals committed for public order offences: drunk and disorderly, drunk and incapable, obstructing the highway, vagrancy. These offences were essentially public and arrests were relatively easy. Directives to individual police forces to clamp down on any one of such offences could produce a sudden peak in local statistics. In October 1869, for example, the Chief Constable of Bedfordshire reported that for the year ending in September his men had apprehended 291 vagrants as opposed to only 105 the preceding year. The increase was 'accounted for by the Police receiving instructions last January to apprehend all Vagrants offending.' The year ending in September 1870 appears to have seen things get back to normal with a mere 117 such arrests.[12] It was less easy to yield such dramatic results following instructions to clamp down on house breaking, burglary and robbery, yet changes or differences in the way that such offences were recorded affected the figures. A sub-committee of Manchester City Council contrasted the incidence of 'highway robbery' in Liverpool and Manchester for the year 1866. The figures were as follows (Table 2.1). On the surface there appeared to be a major difference in the incidence of the crime and in the police clear-up rate. But the sub-committee went on to note:

> In Manchester every robbery from the person, accompanied by violence, in the street or elsewhere ... is classified as highway robbery; whilst ... in Liverpool, as well as in other places, those robberies only which are committed in the streets and highways, and accompanied by violence, are thus classed in the return.[13]

TABLE 2.1 The incidence of 'highway robbery' in Liverpool and Manchester, 1866

	Highway robberies	Apprehensions	Percentage of apprehensions to offences
Liverpool	56	10	17.7%
Manchester	217	136	62.6%

It must be recognised further, that the perceptions of victim and of police could influence the labelling of an offence. The difference between robbery and larceny from the person was technically that violence was employed in the former; but the two offences overlap and the eventual way in which a crime was recorded could depend on how the victim and/or police wished to conceive of 'violence'. A similar problem existed with burglary and some larceny; the decision to proceed with a summary prosecution under the Criminal Justice Act, or with an indictment at assizes, could rest with the police perception of the accused's character and whether or not he had previous convictions, it would seem that, if the accused was 'known' to the police then the police would opt for the more serious charge.[14]

In 1879 the Metropolitan Police found itself under attack in the press because of what appeared to be an increase in offences against property; the statistics showed 735 burglaries and breakings reported in 1877; and 2,429 the following year. In a confidential memorandum prepared for the Home Secretary the police responded that the *Pall Mall Gazette* had taken as its base-line the year 1871 – a year of prosperity, and a year in which, the police insisted, there was less 'crime' than any other during the decade. But in addition there had been a recent change in the way certain serious crimes were recorded, and this, it was argued, exacerbated the distortion:

From the establishment of the Metropolitan Police down to October 1877 it was the practice to classify offences against property according to the practical rather than the exact legal standard. An entry into a dwelling house by day was not described as a house breaking, nor by night as a burglary unless there was a clear breaking by force. Therefore entrances effected by false keys, by open or unfastened doors and windows were set down as 'larcenies by this or that method' and not as housebreaking or burglary ... That this change [in October 1877] was legally right there may be little doubt, but the effect of its being suddenly carried out was disastrous ... To it a very large – fully three quarters – proportion of the additional burglaries and housebreakings occurring in 1878 over 1877 may be attributed.[15]

The following decade, within two years, the number of women convicted of soliciting in London fell by more than fifty per cent: from 3,233 in 1886 to 1,475 in 1888. 'This enormous decrease ... ', commented a leading contemporary criminologist, 'is not due to a diminution of the offence, but to a change in the attitude of the police'.[16]

Changes in the law also affected criminal statistics. The succession of acts, beginning in the mid eighteenth century, which allowed prosecutors and witnesses expenses, probably had some impact on indictment levels.[17] New laws also meant new crimes. The creation of income tax to help finance the Revolutionary and Napoleonic Wars led to the new crimes of income tax evasion and making false declarations of income.[18] Raising the age of consent to 13 years in 1875 and to 16 years ten years later, brought men with proclivities for sex with young, teenage girls within the category of offenders. But sexual assaults were always notoriously under-reported. During the nineteenth century there appears to have been a reluctance among women and girls to report sexual offences because of embarrassment within the strict legal mores of the Victorian era. Also many working-class women were probably discouraged by the reluctance of male officials to take such charges seriously, especially when a man from a higher social group was involved; and if a trial did take place the woman's 'virtue' and 'fantasies' were as much at issue as the man's actions. In some cases middle-class women were able to conceal sexual assaults under prosecutions for breach of promise.[19] The creation of income tax and changing the age of consent probably had an imperceptible impact on the overall crime figures. The Elementary Education Act 1870, however, resulted in 96,601 parents being brought before the courts in the first year and, allegedly, half a million were prosecuted in the first twenty years of the legislation.[20] Of course, many would deny that these offenders were 'criminals' in the sense that thieves, rapists and murderers were 'criminals'; as one contemporary put it:

Few people ... would say that 'crime' was increasing and civilisation demoralising us because we now compel parents to send their children to school, and hale before the magistrates those who fail to do so, not having yet been accustomed to accept the new law.[21]

Yet theft and assault figures were also affected by legislation particularly when indictable offences were shunted into summary jurisdiction categories. This happened, for example, with a succession of acts passed in the middle years of the nineteenth century: 1847, the Juvenile Offenders Act; 1850, a second Juvenile Offenders Act; 1855 the Criminal Justice Act. The consequent fall in committals on criminal indictments was erroneously taken by one of the pioneers in the use of statistics in the history of crime, as a real fall in crime.[22] However when the statistics of convictions at both quarter sessions and under the summary legislation are considered there appears a marked increase in crime. This seems best understood not as an increase in crime *per se*, but as an increase in prosecutions before summary courts which were greatly facilitated by the legislation.[23]

The succession of problems with criminal statistics led J. J. Tobias to despair of their utility in his *Crime and Industrial Society in the Nineteenth Century*. The only firm relationship which, he believed, existed was 'that changes in chief constable produce changes in one series of figures.' He preferred to rely on literary analyses for assessing the pattern of criminality, and this while noting that it was common for nineteenth-century assertions 'on the topic of crime to be backed up with statistics, either taken from official or other publications or drawn from personal investigations'.[24] In fact some of the nineteenth-century experts did rather more than 'back up' their assertions with statistics; the Reverend William Douglas Morrison 'proved' that there was virtually no link between destitution and crime by a tortuous statistical analysis involving a variety of different figures.[25] Tobias generally accepted Morrison's perception of a 'criminal class' lurking in the big cities. As David Philips has pointed out in his telling criticisms of Tobias, the use of literary evidence, albeit from 'powerful authorities' (Tobias's term) are 'useful and instructive in showing what people thought about these subjects; they do not establish the truth of these questions'.[26]

Tobias's concern was, simply, that crime statistics were just too dangerous and too unreliable for any value to be made of them. Rather different warnings have emanated from others. Some criminologists argue that the further a criminal record is from an original act, the less use it has for any analysis of the pattern of criminality.[27] Thus the figures of crimes reported to the police are more significant than those of cases processed by the courts; for the eighteenth century, when there was no police, the indictments presented in the courts provide the surviving record closest to a criminal act. Yet the police too are bureaucratic agents involved in the control of crime and in consequence some radical criminologists have insisted that since all criminal and judicial statistics are the products of the decisions and purposes of those responsible for the control of crime, they can never be used as a measure of actual criminal activities.[28] Historians who seek to use crime figures have to confront these challenges.

The initial response must emphasise the obvious: historical evidence is, of its very nature, fragmentary. It cannot give the historian his conclusions, it requires his interpretation; and few historians worth their salt would seek to base general conclusions on one set of source material, least of all, perhaps, on the statistical evidence of something whose definition is as elusive as is that of crime. It would be indefensible to accept these statistics as a measure of actual levels of crime. It would be foolish, without considering other evidence and without considering the origins of the statistics, to accept them as precise guides to the pattern of crime; in the same way that the dark figure remains a mystery, so too must be the variation between the dark figure and the number of crimes reported and/or prosecuted. The statistics, used with caution, provide a starting point, a hypothesis, for patterns of both criminal activity and responses to perceptions of that activity.

J. M. Beattie and Douglas Hay, who have produced the most cogent statistical work on eighteenth-century crime, have both urged the value of counting indictments to assess overall patterns. For Beattie:

> if the forces governing the selection of cases to be tried worked roughly the same way from year to year, or at least did not change randomly and wildly, then changes in the number of indictments might be expected to derive from changes in the number of offences ... Some would argue ... that until we learn what the relationship is between the known and the unknown by a study of pre-trial processes and arrangements it will be impossible to interpret changes in the levels of prosecuted offences. In that case we will wait for ever.[29]

Hay pushes the case one stage further suggesting that the argument for abandoning criminal statistics in favour of assessing the criminal justice system alone is 'logically untenable':

> Unless one proves that control is overwhelmingly, irresistably determinant of indictment levels ... then officially recorded crime must be the net result of both the behaviour of those subject to the law and those controlling it. In short, if changes in levels of behaviour likely to be prosecuted are said to be unknowable, then the causes of sequential changes in the legal response (or precipitant) are also unknowable.

Moreover he suggests that the eighteenth-century indictment might give a more accurate picture of the pattern of crime than the statistics amassed by the modern bureaucratic police since eighteenth-century prosecutions were initiated by private individuals and 'there was no equivalent to the effect of police practice and attitudes, usually considered the most serious biasing influence on present statistics'.[30] Beattie's and Hay's general arguments inform the statistical aspects of the, as yet unpublished, studies of eighteenth-century Essex and Somerset.[31]

The most significant study of nineteenth-century judicial statistics for England and Wales is that of V. A. C. Gatrell. He argues that the national figures, taken over a long term, iron out regional idiosyncracies and freak periodic fluctuations to give a general picture of the pattern, though naturally not the level, of crime. While admitting that control reactions to some lesser offences might be 'highly unstable, irregular, and even whimsical' he emphasises that:

> in respect of the more serious and traditional thefts and acts of violence, the actions of the controllers will be very much more, even if not absolutely, constrained by a long-standing and traditional consensus as to the heinousness of the criminal act and the unquestionable desirability of as direct an action against it as possible, and also by public expectation that the law be evenly and efficiently enforced and that justice appear to be done.[32]

Furthermore, he points out, while working-class suspicion of the new police never died out during the nineteenth century, the working class were ever more inclined to use the processes of the police and the law when they were the victims of a crime. This, he suggests, in the long-term, served to narrow the gap between actual indictable crime and recorded crime, while the statistics, which show a decline in theft and violence after the 1840s, tend to support his arguments since this decline occurred at the very time when police and court activity, and public co-operation with this activity, were increasing.

Taking the various forms of raw crime statistics over the whole period from 1750 to 1900 the following pattern emerges: a gradual increase in theft and assault during the second half of the eighteenth century, becoming much steeper in the second decade of the nineteenth century and continuing at a steady rate until the close of the 1840s. For the second half of the nineteenth century the figures show a gradual decline in theft and violence, though housebreaking and burglary remain at a constant, and thus at a proportionately greater level. Within this overall pattern there are marked annual fluctuations, as well as peaks and troughs extending over slightly longer periods than one year. Second the statistics suggests that the most common crime – well over half and often more than three-quarters – throughout the whole period was small-scale theft. Third, the great majority of offenders – generally three in four – were male, and there was a strong concentration of young men in their teens and early twenties.[33] These latter points fit well with what is known of crime in contemporary society; while the overall pattern of crime during these 150 years can readily be accommodated within historical understanding of the development of English society during the period.

The gradual increase in eighteenth-century crime might be accounted for, at least in part, by the increase in population. It might also partly be explained with reference to increasing possessions, urbanisation and the capitalisation of industry. There was more to steal in an expanding town, but also, given the looser ties between urban and capitalist employers and their workforce, the desire to settle offences without recourse to the law may have diminished. Beattie's research on Surrey and Sussex has revealed more indictments in the urban parishes in, and on the fringe of, the metropolis. Peter King's study of Essex presents a similar picture though it also suggests that the convenience of a local court was, of itself an encouragement to prosecution, for those small towns with their own courts have greater levels of crime recorded in the proceedings of these courts than those towns whose individuals had to trek to county quarter sessions to conduct a prosecution. As noted in the introduction, the eighteenth century saw an increase in the number of capital statutes, giving rise to the descriptive phrase 'the Bloody Code'; but the great majority of capital prosecutions – ninety-five per cent or more – in the second half of the century were based on statutes enacted before 1742, and many of which went back to the Tudors.[34] The periodic fluctuations in theft during the century have been explained with reference to war and dearth, though not by the simplistic assumptions that dearth automatically led to more theft, and that massive demobilisation also, automatically, led to more theft as former soldiers and sailors, thrown on to the labour market, were compelled to steal for want of money and employment.

Analyses of the statistics, and the content of indictments and surviving depositions, taken together with a variety of other evidence suggests two things. First, enlistment in time of war removed those persons from the community who most commonly were indicted for property offences in times of peace, namely young men in their late teens and early twenties. Such young men seem to have been particularly vulnerable to the temptation of criminal activity for a variety of reasons. During the eighteenth century young men in their late teens and early twenties were often living-in apprentices or servants of different sorts. Some may have been tempted into crime to acquire money to support their leisure activities and to establish a degree of independence alongside their peers in these difficult waiting years before full independence as a labourer or artisan; in 1797 John Crow, aged sixteen, admitted to Constable Joseph Putt of the Borough Police Office that he had taken three bushels of coal from a barge 'to get a few shillings to keep the holidays with'.[35] Some absconded or were thrown out by their masters and were, in consequence, unable to use the local employment market; their existence became, at least for a while, marginal; they were forced to move on looking for work, vagrants were invariably eyed with suspicion and the labelling process of 'vagrant' equals 'thief' could become self-fulfilling. The fact that war removed such young men was not lost on contemporaries. As the American War of Independence closed George III expressed concern that 'the number of idle persons that this peace will occasion' would increase the number of highwaymen; and in the summer of 1795 the *Leicester Journal* commented: 'At Lincoln there is but one prisoner for trial [at the Assizes]; at Cambridge not any; and at Norwich during the last year, there have been but six persons. This, at least, is one benefit arising from the war [against Revolutionary France]'.[36] Secondly, it was often only when these young men were removed from the community that the impact of dearth becomes really apparent in the figures for theft; in years of dearth, which coincided with war, figures for indictments for property crime can be seen to go up and married men and women, for whom wheat prices were of vital importance to the family budget, became more evident among the accused.[37] Yet there is a problem, as yet scarcely analysed, which may undermine this war/theft relationship, namely the number of young men who were apprehended in wartime but who, before any indictment was preferred against them, were encouraged or pressurised to enlist. Figures are fragmentary, yet there appear to have been very large numbers recruited in this way, indeed numbers quite possibly sufficient to account for the drop in indictments for theft in wartime.[38] Lastly, while it would be difficult to prove or to quantify, it is possible that the eighteenth-century newspaper press played a role at least in reinforcing concern about crime at the end of wars. When peace came the newspapers found themselves with space to fill because of a decline in exciting, foreign, war news; crime stories were exciting and possibly increased reporting of crime helped to generate increased fears which, in turn, generated decisions to launch prosecutions against offenders as a warning to others. Significantly the Colchester 'crime wave' of 1765, which was certainly reinforced by press reporting, came in the aftermath of war.[39]

The sharp increase in the crime figures for the period following the Napoleonic Wars, and which continued until the middle of the century, is well known, though not thoroughly explained. The committal statistics published by the government show an increase of nearly seven times between 1805 and 1842 – the latter year seeing the peak of committals for the period, 31,309 of them. The increase in population was enormous during these years but, at about eighty per cent, it was well below the increase measured in the crime statistics.[40] Moreover the crime increase seems to have been as marked in predominantly rural counties, like Bedfordshire and Sussex, as it was overall (Figure 2.1). The statistics show a steady level until 1811, followed by an upward trend especially marked by the post-war peaks in 1817 and 1819. After a brief decline there is a steady upward movement resuming in the mid 1820s to the peak in 1832. Again there is a brief decline followed by another upswing to the all-time peak of 1842, then a further decline followed by an upswing to the lesser peak of 1848. What is especially noticeable about the peaks of committals in the first half of the nineteenth century is how they coincide with years marked by economic depression and political unrest. Several historians and social scientists have commented on the way in which crime appears to increase during

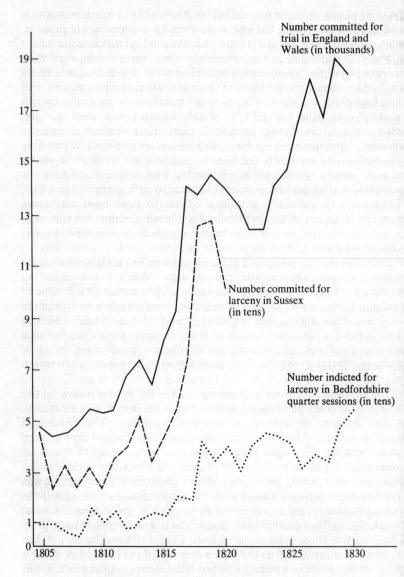

Based on figures in Parliamentary Papers, Sussex gaol calendars (my
thanks to Steve Wilson for these) and Bedfordshire indictments.
For the increasing trend 1805–18, county by county, see
P.P. 1819 (585)VIII *Select Committee on Criminal Laws*, Appendix I, vii

FIGURE 2.1   Crime patterns in the early nineteenth century

imes of concern about popular disorder.[41] The correlation suggests first, that victims might have been more ready to prosecute because of the general feeling of insecurity, second, that offenders were more inclined to steal because of economic hardship, and possibly, third, that the political unrest momentarily weakened some of the usual inhibitors which discouraged theft. None of these hypotheses can be proved, but they warrant some further discussion. A further element also merits some consideration: the end of the eighteenth and the beginning of the nineteenth centuries saw a marked increase in the number of dedimuses obtained annually by magistrates in England and Wales. In part this increase may be accounted for by new commissions of the peace issued to each county following the accession of a new monarch; but from about 150 dedimuses a year from the mid 1760s to the end of the 1780s, the annual average increased generally to over 200 with peaks of about 300 at the accession of George IV and 400 at the accession of William IV. More active justices meant more men available to hear complaints and issue warrants.[42]

A new level of awareness and concern about popular disorder can be detected amongst the propertied classes in the aftermath of the Gordon Riots of 1780; it continued through the years of war against Revolutionary and Napoleonic France – years punctuated by rioting in response to food shortages, high prices and recruiting demands. The concern among the propertied was aggravated, probably, by lurid reports of street massacres and guillotinings in France as well as by the demands, and less often, the menaces of British Jacobins; this concern did not end with the defeat of France. The thirty years following Waterloo were themselves punctuated by rioting sparked by both economic and political motives; they also witnessed mass demonstrations calling for a variety of reforms, and peaceful or not, these demonstrations provoked fears. Also after the wars Britain's propertied classes peered with fascinated horror at the burgeoning slums of, particularly, the new industrial cities. The late 1830s and the 1840s were the years of the most acute anxiety; it fed on economic depression as well as the radical and industrial agitation which culminated in 1842 with the second Chartist petition and the Plug Plot. H. A. Frégier coined the term 'les classes dangereuses' in 1840; and while the Parisian poor may, in the event, have been far more dangerous to the bourgeoisie than any of their British counterparts, Frégier's term was rapidly anglicised and taken over by British men of property as much to define their fears as any social group lurking in the city slums.[43] Alongside the concern about disorder there were changing attitudes to the poor and irritation among the propertied at having to dig deeper into their pockets to find money to finance, first the wars against France, and second the poor rates which were aggravated by the wars. Peace brought an end to income tax, but the rapid demobilization of the armed forces and the restructuring of major sectors of the economy from war to peace, meant little reduction

31

in the poor rates and often quite the reverse. It was during the wars that the Reverend Thomas Malthus had published his *Essay on the Principle of Population as it affects the Future Improvement of Society*. The *Essay*, running through several editions and an enlargement, presented a pessimistic picture of the poor implying that it was their own improvidence and immorality which led to problems of over population, food shortages and, consequently, to high poor rates. While Malthus's arguments did not go unchallenged, they manifestly convinced many.[44] However any simple equation that prosecutions were greater in times of popular unrest because gentlemen of property were increasingly concerned about such unrest and increasingly suspicious of, and irritated by the poor, falls down on the evidence of the very large number of humble prosecutors. A combined anxiety involving popular disorder and crime in the first half of the nineteenth century, does not appear to have stopped at class divides.

The debate on the standard of living of the early nineteenth-century working class is a historical controversy that has run and run; but whether or not the overall standard of living declined or improved, there is no question that there were periods of serious distress for large numbers of the population. Around a quarter of a million men were demobilised on to a contracting labour market at the end of the wars in 1814 and 1815. The wartime boom in agriculture came to an abrupt end while unemployment became acute in industrial districts which, like the coal and iron districts of Shropshire, had been geared up for war production. Matters were compounded by the repeal, in 1814, of the Elizabethen Statute of Artificers and Apprentices. Legislation over the preceding half century had whittled away at the statute; the repeal removed the last protection for artisans against the employment of cheap labour.[45] The years up to the middle of the century witnessed cycles of economic booms and slumps. The slump of the late 1830s and early 1840s was the nadir; 1842 was possibly the worst year for unemployment in the entire century with thousands, especially in the urban areas of the northern industrial districts, compelled to sell or pawn their possessions and to rely on charity, soup kitchens or the New Poor Law. On the land the agricultural worker, increasingly distanced from his employer, was in at least as unfavourable a situation as his urban counterpart in the succession of crises. The decline of protection for, and supervision of, young males which resulted from the repeal of the Statute of Artificers and the continuing decline of living-in conditions for both urban and rural workers, probably strengthened the forces pushing young men into a marginal existence in their early years of adulthood. But the peaks of committals, coinciding with the depths of the economic depressions, suggest that some offenders stole to keep body and soul together. David Philips noted among those committed in the Black Country during the 1830s and 1840s, an increase in the numbers of adults in their late twenties and thirties in the depression years, which suggests people turning to illegal activity when jobs and money were short.[46] A confession which protested hunger and poverty in mitigation quite probably was an attempt to get more lenient treatment, but it might still have been the truth and the incidence of such confessions is striking. At the Old Bailey in December 1816, for example, sixteen-year old William Dennison admitted stealing a coat: 'I do not wish to add falsehood to fraud, I own I took the coat, but it was from mere distress.' John Waldon, who worked from time to time for a cabinet maker admitted stealing a stool which he had been instructed to deliver: 'The distress of my family caused me to act as I did. I was going along with the stool as my master had desired, and the gentleman asked me if I would sell it, and I did.' Twenty years later Sarah Field admitted pawning some of her widowed landlady's possessions: 'It was through distress – I meant to take them out the next day.'[47] In rural Bedfordshire in the spring of 1819, as the worst of the post-war depression came to an end, Thomas Parkins was indicted for stealing two faggots from the property of the Honorable William Waldergrave of Cardington: 'I was in great distress, my Wife near lying in, I went to get a faggot, to make her a bit of fire.' The following year two men and a boy were indicted for stealing fowls, ten bushels of soot, and a bridle from a farmer. 'I was in distress' protested William King, 'I had neither money nor victuals, and was forced to do something ... I was going about the country to look for work.' 'I could get no work,' declared fellow offender John Gascoigne, 'nor any victuals and was driven to it ... we were to have ten pence a bucket for the soot ... we roasted one of the fowls under a hedge.' In 1822, John Stone of Leicester was prosecuted for stealing a watch:

> I am a poor Stocking Weaver in distress. I was travelling into
> Leicestershire, after having been to London to offer myself for a soldier;
> but was not tall enough. My parents are in distress, my Father out of
> employment. I have eight brothers and sisters ...

The voluntary statements of two of the three men charged in 1830 with stealing two smock frocks from a Dunstable draper put another slant on the motives of such petty offenders – John Morgan: 'I was very much distressed and I done it for the purpose of being taken up'; James Lilburn: 'I was very much distressed and did it to be taken up.'[48]

The incidence of this kind of protest by the accused and the known plight of poor labourers in the early nineteenth century has prompted George Rudé to suggest that historians divide crime into three main categories for analysis: '(1) *acquisitive* crime; (2) "social" or "survival" crime; and (3) *protest* crime, or protest made in breach of the law'.[49] There are several problems with this. Rudé himself notes the difficulty of fitting '*some* violent crimes' (my italics) into the scheme. But the squalid nature of, and apparent petty causes of the overwhelming majority of violent crimes raise the question as to whether the scheme is at all applicable to crime against the person with the exception of poaching

33

affrays and other major disorders which could fit under the 'protest' crime category. But even applied solely to property crime the scheme has problems. It has already been suggested that a plea of poverty may have been true; it may also have been false. Can a historian always determine whether a crime is either 'acquisitive' or 'survival' in origin? Is it not possible for an offence to be both? In January 1766 Sarah Plint, otherwise Anne Price, was prosecuted at the Old Bailey by William Thompson, an engraver, for stealing bed linen and other property from the room where she lodged. A single woman living alone in a single lodging room in eighteenth-century London was likely to be on the margin of existence, but Plint/Price was noted in court for having a string of aliases and for having been twice tried for similar offences; she was found guilty and sentenced to seven years transportation. In January 1801 John Brand was prosecuted at the Old Bailey by John Gregory, his master a potato merchant, for stealing 63 lbs of potatoes. Brand protested:

> I have a large family, and every necessary of life is excessively dear; and it is in the habit of the trade to allow men potatoes for their family's use; I was taking these home for that purpose.

Gregory responded: 'I paid him sixteen shillings a week, besides potatoes for his family's use, whenever he asked for them.' On the occasion of the theft Brand made no such request; the jury accepted Gregory's word. Rudé himself gives several examples of men and women accused of petty thefts – thefts which, at first glance, might appear to have been 'survival crimes' – who, when they were apprehended, had pockets full of pawn tickets; of course 'survival' may have prompted their action but this suggests that for some petty offenders the practice of stealing and pawning was becoming a habit.[50]

If hard times on occasions, prompted people to steal, they might also have prompted the poorer victim to lash out with a prosecution when, in better times, he or she might have been prepared to compound the offence or even ignore it. The working man who lost his tools, some clothing, foodstuffs, or money through theft was, like the offender, unquestionably more vulnerable to economic pressure in lean years.

Much crime during the first half of the nineteenth century was, without question, 'acquisitive'; even some of that which might, at first glance, be presumed 'protest' or 'survival'. Some sheep theft, for example, was well organised and involved large numbers of animals over large distances,[51] all of which suggests enterprise and planning rather than simply the promptings of hunger and unemployment or a desire for revenge on a particular farmer. Furthermore, one of the few seasonal studies of crime has shown that while there was a peak in both summary and indictable crime in the dead season of winter when little employment was available for agricultural workers and groups like building workers, there was also an August and autumn peak at precisely the moment when employment was at its peak: the indictable offences for the August and autumn peak were less than those for winter, but summary offences were about equal. Summary offences generally encompassed the theft of growing crops and such crops were, of course, most available in the late summer and autumn; but some indictable offences were also of this type.[52] The mobility of summertime fairs and of harvest time also provided opportunities for petty theft; and the fear of criminality among mobile workers encouraged the possessors of property to be wary of itinerant strangers.

Overall the larceny statistics for the second half of the nineteenth century also show some correlation between the peaks of offences known to the police and the years of high unemployment and need. But V. A. C. Gatrell has pin-pointed a significant structural change between the two halves of the century. After the 'hungry forties' the working class rarely had to contend with the coincidence of high food prices and economic depression which so marked certain years of the late eighteenth and early nineteenth centuries. This was due, in part, to a rise in the export market for industrial goods which enabled firms to off-set short-term contractions in the home market. At the same time stable, even declining, food prices helped many sections of the working class to ride out short-term periods of unemployment. Together, Gatrell suggests, these elements help to explain the overall decline in theft and violence in the second half of the nineteenth century: put at its simplest, during this period the poor became less habituated to theft because they were less subjected to periods of severe unemployment coinciding with serious subsistence problems. In addition, the growth and the professionalisation of the new police probably had some deterrent effect; the destruction of the rookeries for urban improvements removed some of the most impenetrable Alsatias; the Vagrancy Acts meant a stricter supervision of the casual poor.[53] It might also be urged here that, if indeed there is a link between people's fear of popular disorder and the fear about crime which, in turn, leads to more prosecutions, then a decrease in such fears might, in turn, lead to less prosecutions for petty crime. While there may have been periodic concerns about the dangerous classes during the second half of the nineteenth century, the anxieties never appear to have been as acute as in the preceding half century.

The statistics discussed so far have generally been those relating to property offences. It was offences against the person, sometimes involving robbery and sometimes not, which provided the most spectacular and terrifying images of criminality during the eighteenth and nineteenth centuries: the Ratcliffe Highway murders, which left two families gashed and bludgeoned to death in the East End of London in December 1811 and which sent ripples of fear throughout the country; the metropolitan garotting panics of the mid 1850s and 1862, which set a trend for describing a variety of robberies in London and the provinces as 'garottings' – on one occasion, even an attempted suicide was so described; the butchery of Jack the Ripper in East London in the autumn of 1889, which also reverberated in the provinces.[54] Yet few incidents of violence against the person were as dramatic as these and few were tried on indictment; often an assailant was required by a magistrate to enter into a recognisance to keep the peace either towards the victim, or the monarch's subjects in general. Table 2.2 gives a breakdown of the assaults taken before the Bedfordshire magistrates every five years between 1750 and 1840 noting where the assailant was indicted and where he or she was simply required to enter into a recognisance to keep the peace; it must be noted that in the latter instances the 'assault' may simply have been verbal. Most striking here is the very high number of assaults on women, only one third of which were prosecuted on indictment; nineteen of these sixty-one assaults were by husbands on their wives. Understandably perhaps, and in contrast to the attacks on women, about eighty-five per cent of attacks on authority, in the shape of constables or overseers of the poor, were indicted. In all, offences against the person constituted rather more than one-tenth of the statistics of crime available for the nineteenth century: about ten per cent of the committals made on indictments between 1834 and 1856; just over ten per cent of crimes known to the police between 1857 and the end of the century; and about fifteen per cent of summary committals in the second half of the century. Assaults on authority, in the shape of policemen formed a significant percentage of nineteenth-century assaults and declined at a slower rate than common assault; they constituted about fifteen per cent of summary prosecutions for assault in the 1860s and about twenty-one per cent in the 1890s. Probably, however, the majority of these assaults were simply for resisting or obstructing the police in their duty.[55]

While people were concerned about homicide throughout the period this never appears to have been statistically a prominent offence. Anxiety about murder and a perceived increase in violent robbery in London led to more severe legislation in 1752, but there were only ten convictions for murder during that year and this was exceptional; the annual average for murder convictions in London and Middlesex between 1749 and 1771 was four.[56] Analysis of the Wiltshire coroners' bills between 1752 and 1796 reveals that murder as part of robbery was very rare in the county, and even when the enormous number of infanticides are removed from the figures, most homicides can be seen to have been committed within the family, and among people known to each other (Table 2.3). In Victorian England the homicide rate reached 2 per 100,000 of the population only once, in 1865; generally it hovered around 1.5 per 100,000 falling to rarely more than 1 per 100,000 at the end of the 1880s and declining even more with the new century. In round figures this meant that between 1857 and 1890 there were rarely more than 400 homicides reported to the police each year, and during the

TABLE 2.2 Assaults in Bedfordshire based on indictments and recognizances every five years, 1750–1840.

VICTIMS	ASSAILANTS																Total assailants
	Gentry		Professional		Farmer		Tradesman/ artisans		Husbandman/ gardener		Labourer/ servant		Women		Unknown		
	I.	R.*	I.	R.	I.	R.	I.	R.	I.	R.	I.	R.	I.	R.	I.	R.	
Gentry	—	2	—	—	1	—	—	2	—	—	—	5	—	—	—	—	10
Professional	1	—	—	—	1	—	—	—	—	—	—	2	—	—	—	—	3
Farmer	—	—	—	—	1	1	—	1	—	—	1	8	—	—	—	2	12
Tradesman/artisan	—	—	—	—	—	—	1	6	—	1	3	6	2	—	1	2	22
Husbandman/gardener	—	—	—	—	—	—	—	—	—	1	—	2	—	—	—	—	
Labourers/servants (including gamekeepers)	1	—	—	—	—	1	1	2	—	—	10	7	2	—	6	1	31 (19 indictments)
Constables/overseers	1	—	—	—	—	1	3	1	—	—	18	2	6	—	2	—	34 (29 indictments)
Women	1	—	1	—	—	3	3	8	1	—	10	17	2	7	3	4	61† (20 indictments)
Children	—	—	—	—	—	—	—	1	—	—	2	—	1	—	—	—	4
Unknown	2	—	—	—	—	—	3	2	—	—	15	19	—	2	22	6	72
Total indictments/ recognizances	8	—	1	—	2	6	11	23	1	4	59	67	11	11	34	13	

*I. indicates Indictment, R. indicates Recognizance.
†19 of these 61 cases specified husbands assaulting wives; there is one incident recorded in these years of a woman brought to court for assaulting her husband.

TABLE 2.3   Homicides in Wiltshire, 1752–96*

Homicides committed:

(a)	by parent(s)	42 (33.3%)	(includes 31 infanticides of illegitimate offspring)
(b)	by spouse	4 (3.1%)	(includes 1 wife killing husband)
(c)	by other member of family	7 (5.5%)	
(d)	by person(s) clearly known to victim	11 (8.7%)	(includes 7 apprentices dying as a result of treatment received from master or mistress)
(e)	as a result of fighting	14 (11.1%)	
(f)	during robbery	4 (3.1%)	
(g)	during riot	3 (2.3%)	
(h)	by person unknown	17 (13.4%)	(12 of which appear to involve the murder of unwanted illegitimate babies)
(j)	in unspecified situation	24 (19%)	(though fighting or acquaintance between the victim and the perpetrator appears probable in several instances)
	Total	126	

*Based on the evidence in R. F. Hunnisett, ed. *Wiltshire Coroner's Bills 1752–1796*, Wiltshire Record Society, xxxvi (1981)

1890s the average was below 350. Moreover a closer look at Victorian homicides reveals that, while the fear may have centred around being murdered by a burglar or a similarly ferocious member of the 'dangerous classes', in most homicides assailant and victim were known to each other, and often they were related; the very high arrest rate in cases of malicious wounding reported to the police would appear to stem partly from the same cause.[57] Figure 2.2 is a breakdown of all the homicides and attempted homicides reported in *The Times* for England and Wales during the years 1850 and 1860. The years have significance to the extent that they both witnessed grisly murders carried out by robbers, murders which prompted many column inches in the press. The Reverend G. E. Hollest was murdered in his house at Frimley, Surrey, by burglars in the autumn of 1850; an incident which prompted considerable concern and was instrumental in the creation of the Surrey Constabulary. In August 1860 Mary Emsley, a seventy-year old widow, was murdered by George Mullins, a former policeman, subsequently a plasterer who had done some work for the victim and who robbed her after the murder.[58] Yet such murders, by strangers and by persons out

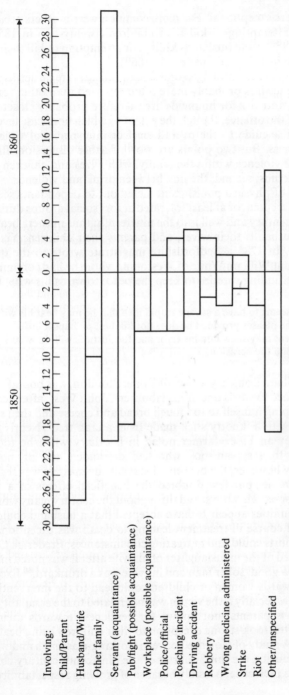

FIGURE 2.2 Homicides and attempted homicides 1850 and 1860

for gain, were exceptional. Far more common were mothers accused of killing, or attempting to kill their children (twenty-two in 1850 and eighteen in 1860) and husbands killing, or attempting to kill their wives (twenty-two in 1850 and nineteen in 1860).

It is generally acknowledged that since homicide is regarded as a most serious offence it is probably more often reported than other forms of crime. The statistics for homicide are therefore probably closer to the real level of the offence, though the extent to which homicide levels can be taken as a guide to the overall level of inter-personal violence is anyone's guess. But two points are worth further discussion: first the incidence of violence within the family, with wives and children as the principal victims; second, the link between drink and violence.

A degree of physical punishment meted out to dependants seems to have been accepted, or at least tolerated across social groups during the eighteenth century and well into the nineteenth; thus masters beat their servants, husbands their wives, and parents their children. Yet there were limits. In 1786 a Bedfordshire magistrate wrote to the quarter sessions about William White of Westoning whom he had committed to gaol for not finding sureties to keep the peace towards his wife, Mary:

> the Man seems to have a savage stupid idea that he may beat his wife as much as he pleases provided he does not kill her: perhaps a little confinement may shew him his error and the Justices will do what is proper upon the occasion.

In 1802 William Long, a yeoman of Upper Stondon, was bound over to keep the peace towards one of his labourers, John West, after accusing West of helping himself to too much bread and cheese and then setting about him with a 'knotty stick made from a crab tree'. Nearly half a century later an Essex farmer noted in his diary when he took his horse-whip to a servant-boy who had defrauded him of money.[59] Increasingly however, the beating of servants by masters was regarded as unacceptable, but few doubted the beneficial effects of a sound thrashing for naughty boys, and throughout the century many working-class communities appear to have accepted that a husband could beat his wife. Of course ill-treatment leading to death was exceptional but even here courts could find mitigating circumstances: Frederick Gilbert was acquitted of the manslaughter of his wife after it was noted in court that he was a good, sober man and his wife was a drunkard.[60] Excessive violence towards women or children could lead to the intervention of others, and especially if the victim was not related to the assailant; some working-class parents, not known for gentleness towards their own children, often took strong exception to their children being beaten by teachers.[61] A study of violence between working-class men and women in London during the third quarter of the nineteenth century charts a decline in its incidence, possibly because of growing respectability, and rising living standards which reduced stress on the male as the principal economic provider. Perhaps also the cult of respectability made wives even less likely to complain since such assaults were shameful; and in the growing suburbs they were less public, less likely to disturb the neighbours, while the bruising was less visible than on the crowded stair of a tenement.[62] The question remains, of course, as to what extent the pattern of violence between working-class men and women in London can be taken as typical for England and Wales. In Birmingham for example, the evidence for 1860s and 1870s suggests that wives here were more, rather than less inclined to prosecute husbands for assault. In Wales, however, policemen and magistrates nearly always refused to accept the word of a beaten wife unless supported by other witnesses.[63]

The cult of respectability itself may have contributed to one variety of homicide; of those children allegedly killed by their mothers, at least four in 1850 and at least seven in 1860 died immediately after their birth and were illegitimate. These deaths, however, probably constituted only a tiny percentage of the incidence of infanticide during these years. Though, in general, homicide might be one of the best-reported crimes, infanticide was notoriously under-reported and rarely came before the criminal courts. It was difficult to get coroners to hold inquests on dead infants, and even when a coroner did register a verdict of murder the assize jury, which heard the subsequent criminal case, was generally reluctant to return a verdict indicating culpability on the mother's part. Eliza Higgins, a twenty-one-year-old domestic servant lodged in a London workhouse, was tried for the wilful murder of her baby daughter in 1857; the Old Bailey jury hearing the case found her guilty of manslaughter, recommended mercy, and commented 'that the bastardy laws had a strong tendency to increase this class of crime'.[64] Juries often decided that the accused was only guilty of 'concealment of birth' in these cases. But, of course, infanticide and/or concealment of birth were by no means offences new to the nineteenth century. Other cases, involving the deaths of older children, reveal appalling instances of neglect and ill-treatment, as in the case of Maria Hook who, aged four years, allegedly weighed only six pounds when she died after months of dreadful treatment by her stepmother.[65] The cases of family violence which reached the press and the courts were, almost certainly, the most unpleasant tip of a very nasty iceberg.

Drink was often remarked upon as a cause of violence in the family. In May 1850 Patrick Barry returned home drunk to his rooms in Jennings Buildings, Kensington, and proceeded to kick his wife to death.[66] Drink could be seen as a mitigating circumstance for the violent offender as in the case of Frederick Gilbert noted above and, more remarkably, in the prosecution of three men at York following the death of Mary Duggan 'a woman of abandoned character'. One February night Duggan had left a pub with Richard Farrar, George Coates and James Oates and all four had gone into a field. The following morning Duggan was found dead 'with her person exposed and much bruised'. The judge directed the jury to acquit the defendants since:

> these facts did not amount to the crime of manslaughter. The woman, being intoxicated, had voluntarily accompanied the prisoners; and she was not like an infant who, unable to take care of itself, had been left exposed to the cold and died inconsequence.[67]

Some earnest Victorian temperance reformers gave drink as a fundamental cause of all crime. The Reverend James Nugent, a chaplain of Liverpool Borough Prison, informed the House of Lords Select Committee on Intemperance in 1877 that nine out of ten of the convicts in that prison were there 'directly or indirectly through drink'. William Hoyle, a Lancashire cotton manufacturer and pillar of the temperance community had published *Crime in England and Wales in the Nineteenth Century: an Historical and Critical Retrospect* the year before he appeared before the committee; he deployed statistics to demonstrate a direct correlation between the increase in crime and the increase in beer shops and public houses. Other witnesses were less zealous and suggested only a connection between crimes of violence and drink,[68] a connection explored in some detail in the sober historical analysis of Gatrell and Hadden. Placing the figures for assault and drunkenness alongside the business cycle they have shown slight increases in these offences during years of prosperity suggesting that high wages and high employment led to a greater consumption of alcohol which, in turn, contributed to more violent crime. However for the last quarter of the century in particular the overall trend in the statistics of both violent crime and drunkenness is markedly downwards. This may be explained, in part, by what contemporaries perceived as the civilization or moralization of the population. Perhaps also there was a decrease in anxiety about small-scale, drink-related violence.[69] Such a decrease would link with the diminishing fears about the dangerous classes from the mid nineteenth century which, it has been suggested above, contributed to a decline in the reporting, and the prosecuting, of small-scale theft.

While there seems to be an interplay between criminal statistics and periodic fears of crime and disorder, it is also probable that the collection and publication of national crime statistics led to the perception of crime as a national and impersonal problem. During the eighteenth century, when there were no such statistics, crime was essentially a personal problem for victims and accused. Statistics made crime national and made the criminal a national bogeyman. Crime could now be shown to be offences perpetrated on a large scale against respectable people by a group which, by being measured statistically – whatever the faults of the statistics – could be defined collectively as criminals or as the criminal class. This perception of criminals as a group is the subject of the next chapter.

REFERENCES AND NOTES

1. Quoted in **Eric Stockdale**, *A Study of Bedford Prison 1660–1877*, Phillimore, London, 1977, p. 130. The Revd Philip Hunt who sent this warning to Peel might be considered as having been at least an accessory to what some would consider as one of the greatest thefts of the early nineteenth century; as chaplain to Lord Elgin he played a key role in the removal of the Elgin Marbles from the Acropolis.

2. **M. J. Cullen**, *The Statistical Movement in Early Victorian Britain: The foundations of empirical social research*, Harvester, Brighton, 1975, especially pp. 1–16 and 72–74. For a detailed introduction to nineteenth-century criminal statistics see **V. A. C. Gatrell** and **T. B. Hadden**, 'Criminal statistics and their interpretation', in **E. A. Wrigley** (ed.), *Nineteenth-century society: Essays in the use of quantitative methods for the study of social data*, Cambridge U.P., 1972.

3. **T. Barwick Lloyd Baker**, 'Abstract and inferences founded upon the official returns of England and Wales for the years 1854–59, with special reference to the results of reformatories', *Journal of the Statistical Society*, xxiii (1860), pp. 427–54 (at pp. 436–37).

4. **S. J. Stevenson**, 'The "Criminal Class": Legislation, labelling and prosecution in the late nineteenth century.' Paper presented to Urban History Group, Economic History Society Conference, Cheltenham, 4 April 1986. For a more extended treatment see idem, 'The "Criminal Class" in the mid-Victorian city: A study of policy conducted with special reference to those made subject to the provisions of 34 & 35 Vict. c.112 (1871) in Birmingham and East London in the early years of registration and supervision,' unpublished D. Phil, Oxford University, 1983.

5. **Patrick Colquhoun**, *A Treatise on the Police of the Metropolis*, 3rd edn., 1796, p. vii.

6. U.C.L. Chadwick MSS 'Police Memoranda etc., undated (post 1850)', probably referring to the 1836–39 Royal Commission on Constabulary.

7. **James T. Hammick**, 'On the judicial statistics of England and Wales with special reference to recent returns relating to crime', *Journal of the Statistical Society* xxx (1867), pp. 375–426 (at p. 392).

8. **Clive Emsley**, 'An aspect of Pitt's "terror": Prosecutions for sedition during the 1790s', *Social History*, **6** (1981), pp. 155–84; see also idem, 'Repression, "terror" and the rule of law in England during the decade of the French Revolution', *E.H.R.*, C (1985), pp. 801–25.

9. **Peter King**, 'Newspaper reporting, prosecution practice and urban crime: The Colchester crime wave of 1765'. Paper presented to Urban History Group, Economic History Society Conference, Cheltenham, 4 April 1986.

10. **Jennifer Davis**, 'The London garotting panic of 1862: A moral panic and the creation of a criminal class in mid-Victorian England', in **V. A. C. Gatrell, Bruce Lenman** and **Geoffrey Parker** (eds.), *Crime and the Law: The social history of crime in Western Europe since 1500*, Europa, London, 1980 p. 205.

11. Cullen, *Statistical Movement*, p. 14. The committees were: the Select Committee on Criminal Commitments and Convictions and the Select

Committee on the Police of the Metropolis.

12. Beds. R.O. QEV 4.
13. 'Discrepant criminal statistics', *Journal of the Statistical Society*, xxxi (1868), pp. 349–52 (at p. 352).
14. See the discussion in **Jennifer Davis**, 'Law breaking and law enforcement: The creation of a criminal class in mid-Victorian London', unpublished Ph.D. Boston College, 1984, pp. 137–39, 152–58 and 246–51.
15. H.O. 45.9755. A60557.
16. **William Douglas Morrison**, *Crime and its Causes*, London, 1891, p. 6.
17. For this legislation see below pp. 145–6.
18. Perhaps the first such offender to be prosecuted was Micah Gibbs, a gentleman of Wellow who was found guilty by the Somerset quarter sessions in October 1800 of producing fraudulent certificates to the tax commissioners at Bath. He was fined £200 and sentenced to four months in Ilchester Gaol where he was to remain until the fine was paid. Somerset R.O. QS Minute Book CQ2 2/4(3).
19. **Susan S. M. Edwards**, 'Sex Crimes in the nineteenth century', *New Society*, 13 September 1979, pp. 562–63.
    Before 1875 it was a felony to have sexual intercourse with a child aged ten or under, but only a misdemeanour with a child between ten and twelve years.
20. **E. G. Du Cane**, 'The decrease of crime', *Nineteenth Century*, xxxiii (1893), pp. 480–92 (at p. 485); William Douglas Morrison, 'The increase of crime', *Nineteenth Century*, xxxi (1892), pp. 950–57 (at pp. 951–52).
21. Du Cane, 'The decrease of crime', p. 485.
22. **K. K. Macnab**, 'Aspects of the history of crime in England and Wales between 1805–60', unpublished Ph.D. University of Sussex, 1965, p. 347. Macnab does remark that the decline is 'rather suspicious'.
23. **David Philips**, *Crime and Authority in Victorian England*, Croom Helm, London, 1977, pp. 132–35 and 146.
24. **J. J. Tobias**, *Crime and Industrial Society in the Nineteenth Century*, Penguin edn. Harmondsworth, 1972, chap. 2 and appendix; quotations from pp. 25 and 19 respectively.
25. Morrison, *Crime and its Causes*, chap. 4.
26. Philips, *Crime and Authority*, p. 20.
27. **Thorsten Sellin**, 'The significance of the records of crime', *Law Quarterly Review*, lxv (1951), pp. 489–504.
28. See, inter alia **Jason Ditton**, *Contrology: Beyond the new criminology*, Macmillan, London, 1979, especially chap. 2. For the most prolonged and sophisticated argument in favour of using statistics for the study of eighteenth-century crime see **J. M. Beattie**, *Crime and the Courts in England 1660–1800*, Oxford U.P., 1986.
29. **J. M. Beattie**, 'Judicial records and the measurement of crime in eighteenth-century England', in **Louis A. Knafla** (ed.), *Crime and Criminal Justice in Europe and Canada*, Wilfred Launier U.P., Waterloo, Ontario, 1981, p. 138.
30. **Douglas Hay**, 'War, dearth and theft in the eighteenth century: The record of the English courts', *P and P*, **95** (1982), pp. 117–60: quotation at pp. 159 and 151 respectively.
31. **P. J. R. King**, 'Crime, law and society in Essex 1740–1820', unpublished

Ph.D. Cambridge University, 1984, (a revised version, *Crime, Justice and Discretion: Law and society in Essex and the South East counties 1740–1820*, is forthcoming from Oxford U.P.); **S. R. Pole**, 'Crime, society and law enforcement in Hanoverian Somerset', unpublished Ph.D. Cambridge University, 1983. For a critical view of Hay's and Beattie's use of statistics see **Joanna Innes** and **John Styles**, 'The crime wave: Recent writing on crime and criminal justice in eighteenth-century England', *Journal of British Studies*, xxv, (1986).

32. **V. A. C. Gatrell**, 'The decline of theft and violence in Victorian and Edwardian England', in **Gatrell, Lenman** and **Parker** (eds.), *Crime and the Law*, p. 248.

33. **J. M. Beattie**, 'The criminality of women in eighteenth-century England', *Journal of Social History*, viii (1975), pp. 80–116; idem, *Crime and the Courts*, pp. 243–48; **David Jones**, *Crime, Protest, Community and the Police in Nineteenth-Century England*, RKP, London, 1982 pp. 132–34; idem, 'The Welsh and crime, 1801–91' in **Clive Emsley** and **James Walvin** (eds.), *Artisans, Peasants and Proletarians 1760–1860*, Croom Helm, London, 1985, p. 92; King, 'Crime, Law and Society', pp. 82–4, and 141; Macnab, 'Aspects of crime', especially pp. 59 and 341–48; Philips, *Crime and Authority*, pp. 147–50, 151–52.

34. Hay, 'War, Dearth and Theft', p. 146 and note 78; King, 'Crime, Law and Society', pp. 335–37.

35. *O.B.S.P. 1796–97* no. 335, p. 321.

36. **Sir John Fortescue** (ed.), *The Correspondence of George III*, 6 vols. London, 1928 vi, p. 387; *Leicester Journal*, 24 July 1795. *The Gentleman's Magazine* commented in November 1772: 'It is worthy of observation, that during the two last years of the last war, viz. 1759, 1760, the number of criminals condemned at the Old Bailey amounted to 29 only, and the days of the Judges' attendance to 46; but that during the two last years of peace, viz. 1770, 1771, the number of criminals condemned have amounted to 151, and the days of the Judges' attendance to 99.' (xlii, 541). For similar contemporary concern see Hay, 'War, Dearth and Theft', pp. 138 and 142.

37. Hay, 'War, Dearth and Theft', *passim*.

38. **P. J. R. King**, 'War, judicial discretion and the problem of young adulthood 1740–1815', paper presented to the Social History Society Conference on 'War and Society', 4–6 January 1984; Clive Emsley, 'The recruitment of petty offenders during the French Wars 1793–1815', *Mariner's Mirror*, **66** (1980), pp. 199–208 deals only with those offenders who were brought before the courts rather than those weeded out before indictment. I am grateful to John Styles for his critical comments on this point.

39. King, 'Newspaper reporting, prosecution practice and urban crime'.

40. Macnab, 'Aspects of Crime', especially appendices 1 and 2.

41. **T. R. Gurr**, *Rogues, Rebels and Reformers: A political history of crime and conflict*, Sage, Beverly Hills, California, 1976, p. 10; **Abdul Lodhi** and **Charles Tilly**, 'Urbanisation, crime and collective violence in nineteenth-century France', *American Journal of Sociology*, **79** (1973), pp. 296–318 (at p. 296); **J. A. Sharpe**, *Crime in Early Modern England 1550–1750*, Longman, London, 1984, pp. 182–87.

42. **Norma Landau**, *The Justices of the Peace, 1679–1760*, University of California Press, Berkley and Los Angeles, 1984, p. 395.

43. See the discussion in **Gertrude Himmelfarb**, *The Idea of Poverty: England in the early Industrial Age*, Faber and Faber, London, 1984, pp. 393–97.

44. **Clive Emsley**, *British Society and the French Wars 1793–1815*, Macmillan, London, 1979; Himmelfarb, *The Idea of Poverty*, especially pp. 100–44; **Joseph Lowe**, *The Present State of England in Regard to Agriculture, Trade, and Finance*, 2nd edn., London, 1823, pp. 210–24.

45. **John Rule**, *The Experience of Labour in Eighteenth-Century Industry*, Croom Helm, London, 1981, pp. 95–96 and 114–19.

46. Philips, *Crime and Authority*, pp. 145–46 and 163–64.

47. *O.B.S.P. 1816–17*, no. 20, p. 11 and no. 73, p. 38; in both instances the jury recommended mercy: in Dennison's case judgment was respited; Walden was fined 1 shilling and discharged. *C.C.C.S.P. 1836–37* no. 64, pp. 80–81; Field, also recommended to mercy, was imprisoned for one month.

48. Beds R.O. QSR 24/271; QSR 24/229; QSR 25/324; QSR 1830/409.

49. **George Rudé**, *Criminal and Victim: Crime and society in early nineteenth-century England*, Clarendon Press, Oxford, 1985, p. 78 and chap. 5 *passim*.

50. *O.B.S.P. 1765–66*, no. 84; *O.B.S.P. 1800–1*, no. 105, p. 77; Rudé, *Criminal and Victim*, p. 93.

51. **John Rule**, 'The manifold causes of rural crime: sheep-stealing in England c. 1740–1840', in **John Rule** (ed.), *Outside the Law: Studies in crime and order 1650–1850*, Exeter Papers in Economic History no. 15, University of Exeter, 1982; **R. A. E. Wells**, 'Sheep-rustling in Yorkshire in the age of the Industrial and Agricultural Revolutions', *Northern History*, xx (1984), pp. 127–45.

52. **Janet Gyford**, ' "Men of Bad Character": Property crime in Essex in the 1820s', unpublished M.A. University of Essex, 1982, pp. 63–65.

53. Gatrell, 'Decline of Theft and Violence', pp. 305–16; Gatrell expresses scepticism about that area upon which 'the Victorians were prone to congratulate themselves ... most' when noting a decline in crime, namely the assault on juvenile crime from the 1850s (pp. 305–7).

54. **T. A. Critchley** and **P. D. James**, *The Maul and the Pear Tree: the Ratcliffe Highway Murders 1811*, Constable, London, 1971, pp. 79 and 96–97. Davis, 'London garotting panic', p. 205; **R. S. Sindall**, 'Street violence in the Victorian city and its effects on the law and system of punishment', unpublished Ph.D. University of Leicester, 1984, especially chap. 4 which emphasises the metropolitan nature of the garotting panic and the role of the press in fostering this panic; Sindall also notes that the statistics indicate a greater incidence of street violence in the north west rather than in London.

    Sir Robert Anderson publicly blamed 'the sensation-mongers of the newspaper press' for the scare created by Jack the Ripper in 'Our absurd system of punishing crime', *Nineteenth Century*, xlix (1901), pp. 268–84 (at p. 269). However Anderson's own role in the Ripper affair (as head of the C.I.D.) was hardly distinguished. **Stephen Knight**, *Jack the Ripper: The final solution*, Panther Books, London, 1977, pp. 247–49 and 251, argues that Anderson was deeply involved in the establishment and masonic cover-up of the affair; the result, perhaps, of the contemporary pursuits of new 'Watergate' scandals.

55.   Gatrell and Hadden, 'Criminal statistics', pp. 269–71; Gatrell, 'Decline of theft and violence', pp. 284–95 and appendix A5.

56.   **John H. Langbein**, 'Shaping the eighteenth-century criminal trial: A view from the Ryder Sources', *University of Chicago Law Review*, **50** (1983), pp. 1–136 (at pp. 44–46). For a discussion of homicide during the eighteenth century see Beattie, *Crime and the Courts*, pp. 77–124.

57.   Gatrell, 'Decline of theft and violence', pp. 286–95 and appendices A1 and A2.

58.   See inter alia *The Times* 2, 3, 5, 8, 14, 19 October 1850; 18, 20, 22, 23, 25, 27 August 1860, and 24, 26, 27 October 1860; **T. A. Critchley**, *A History of Police in England and Wales*, 2nd edn. Constable, London, 1978, p. 98. Although her murder was shocking Mary Emsley was manifestly not everyone's favourite old lady. Detective Inspector Thornton, in charge of the murder investigation reported that she 'was possessed of considerable house property situated in very low neighbourhoods of Bethnal Green, Ratcliffe, Stratford, Barking, Dagenham etc, and she was in the habit of personally collecting the greater portion of her rents on a Monday and in consequence of her frequent litigation with her tenants, her very plain way of dressing and living, she became well known at the East End of London'. According to her solicitor she had been threatened by tenants. Nor was she popular with her own family having told them that she intended to make a will leaving all her money to build almshouses. MEPO 3/62.

59.   Beds R.O. QSR 15/191; QSR 18/67; Essex R.O. D/DBs F 38, Bretnall's Diary, entry for 10 November 1847 (quoted in Gyford, 'Men of Bad Character', p. 15).

60.   *The Times* 7 April 1850.

61.   **Barbara Weinberger**, 'Law breakers and law enforcers in the late Victorian city: Birmingham 1867–77', unpublished Ph.D. University of Warwick, 1981, p. 222; **Stephen Humphries**, *Hooligans or Rebels? An oral history of working-class childhood and youth 1889–1939*, Basil Blackwell, Oxford, 1981, pp. 82–89.

62.   **Nancy Tomes**, 'A "torrent of abuse": Crimes of violence between working-class men and women in London 1840–75', *Journal of Social History*, xi (1978), pp. 328–45.

63.   Weinberger, 'Law breakers and law enforcers', pp. 219–20; Jones, 'Welsh and crime', p. 93.

64.   **Lionel Rose**, *Massacre of the Innocents: Infanticide in Great Britain 1800–1939*, London, RKP, 1986, chaps. 7, 8. *C.C.C.S.P. 1856–57*, no. 597 p. 47.

65.   *The Times*, 14 August 1850.

66.   *The Times*, 23 May 1850.

67.   *The Times*, 16 March 1850.

68.   P.P. 1877 (418) xi, *Select Committee of the House of Lords on Intemperance Third Report* qq. 8327 and 8401–11. The Earl of Onslow for one was not convinced by Hoyle's use of statistics and asked him: 'Do you not think it would be no very difficult matter to prove almost anything you wished to prove by judiciously manipulating statistics from various parts of the country?' (q. 8411).

69.   Gatrell and Hadden, 'Criminal statistics', pp. 370–71; Gatrell, 'Decline of theft and violence', pp. 291 and 300.

Chapter 3
CLASS PERCEPTIONS

When Peel proposed the consolidation and rationalisation of the criminal law to parliament in 1826 he announced that he would begin with laws relating to felony:

> because I consider the crime of theft to constitute the most important class of crime. There are acts no doubt of much greater malignity, of a much more atrocious character than the simple act of robbery; but looking at the committals and convictions for crime, it will at once be seen, that those for theft so far exceed the committals and convictions for any other species of offence, that there can be no question of its paramount importance in the catalogue of offences against society.

He explained that, in 1825, 14,437 persons had been charged with various crimes; some 12,500, or six-sevenths of those persons, had been charged with theft.[1] Throughout the eighteenth and nineteenth centuries theft of various sorts was the principal offence which occupied the time of the different courts. Most thefts were petty; only a very few involved large sums of money or objects of great monetary value; only a very few involved violence. It was the quantity rather than the quality of the offences which concerned people and, arguably, this has always been the case. But once the decision had been made, albeit unconsciously, to concentrate on quantity, rather than what might be termed 'quality' crime, other things followed. Most of the offenders brought before the courts for these crimes came from the poorer sections of society and, as a consequence as the discourse of 'class' became more and more central to the analysis and perception of society, so criminality tended to be seen as, essentially, a class problem.

Counterfactual history is fraught with danger, yet, if legislators and commentators on crime had concentrated on the few big thefts or embezzlements as their bench mark for crime, rather than on the very many small thefts and incidents of disorders, then the overall perception of criminality and of the criminal class would have been very different. This is not to say that there was a middle-class conspiracy during the nineteenth century when these perceptions developed. Concern about the poor and their 'immoral' or 'disorderly' behaviour went back a long way; Jim Sharpe well chronicled the criminalisation of the poor in the early modern period.[2] But, as has already been argued, fear of the poor reached a new peak in the aftermath of the French Revolution and with the experience of the fast-growing and teeming cities in the early nineteenth century. Crime was often perceived as another problem, like sanitation, within the burgeoning urban sprawls.

Of course it was recognised that men of wealth and social standing also committed offences. From time to time there were outcries against various forms of white-collar crime and corruption. At the close of 1843 the *Illustrated London News* gloomily predicted:

> If we progress at the same rate for half a generation longer, commercial dishonesty will become the rule, and integrity the exception. On every side of us we see perpetually – fraud, fraud, fraud.[3]

Half a century later the author of an article on limited companies in the journal *Nineteenth Century* lamented that such organisations placed 'a premium upon dishonesty'.[4] But such offenders, however widespread, were rarely perceived as members of a criminal class and then not until the close of the nineteenth century when biological discourse began to rival class discourse in the analysis of crime and criminality. The illegal and/or immoral actions of white-collar offenders set a bad example to their social inferiors, but these offenders were 'rotten apples' within their social class.[5] It was a consoling distinction to which the middle and upper classes clung; offenders within their social milieu were exceptions and the criminal class was to be found located elsewhere. Poor clerks caught embezzling their employer's money were similarly not regarded as part of a criminal element with society. Public debate on such offences during the 1860s and 1870s concentrated on examining employer-clerk relations. The employers were criticised for not having a proper sense of business management and ensuring that their books balanced, for not providing a better system of surveillance over the clerks who could so easily be tempted by the large sums with which they often had to deal, and for paying the clerks a 'beggarly pittance' hardly commensurate with the trust and responsibility expected of them. 'We can't for a moment dispute the right of merchant princes paying what salaries they deem fit to their clerks', declared a Manchester journal, 'but we would ask, is the system of paying low salaries likely to conduce a high moral tone in the young men employed?'[6]

But if low wages and poverty were regarded as contributing to crime among clerks, this was rarely the case within lower social groups. Throughout the period 1750 to 1900 most experts and commentators went out of their way to deny any relationship between low wages, poverty and the bulk of crime. The main causes of crime were given as moral weakness, luxury, idleness, corrupting literature, parental neglect, and lack of education; any one, or any permutation of these were discussed and debated at length and given different emphases depending upon the prejudices and aspirations of the individuals concerned, and also upon the changing economic and social climate within which they were being presented.

Henry Fielding, novelist and Bow Street magistrate, believed that trade had changed the face of the nation. The old bonds of society had broken down and produced a dramatic alteration in:

> the Manners, Customs, and Habits of the People, more especially of the lower Sort. The Narrowness of their Fortune is changed into Craft; their Frugality into Luxury; their Humility into Pride, and their Subjection into Equality.[7]

The increase in crime which prompted his *Enquiry* in 1751 was simply one manifestation of this. The too frequent and too expensive diversions among the lower sort had led to idleness which, in turn, led 'the more simple and poor spirited betaking themselves to a State of Starving and Beggary, while those of more Art and Courage became Thieves, Sharpers, and Robbers'.[8] Besides proposing changes in the system of prosecution and punishment, Fielding included among his remedies tougher regulations for the drink trade and for drunkenness, for pawnbrokers, and to control vagabondage. He divided the poor into three categories; 'Such . . . as are able to work. Such as are able and willing to work. Such as are able to work, but not willing'.[9] The last category was the largest and Fielding was all for compelling this group to work. But if the idle and immoral poor committed most crimes, Fielding did not see crime simply in class terms. Crime was the result of immorality, but rich and poor occupied the same moral universe and a glance at any of Fielding's novels reveals that he perceived the wealthy and well-to-do to be as guilty of immorality and vice as the poor. In his novels Fielding could describe model magistrates like the honest and benevolent Squire Allworthy in *Tom Jones*; he also often included central characters whose very unworldliness left their virtue and dignity unassailable. Parson Adams, in *Joseph Andrews*, might be comic and quixotic but his virtues were those which an increasingly luxurious and sophisticated society were leaving further and further behind. Like John Gay in *The Beggar's Opera* before him, Fielding could satirize the King's leading minister by paralleling his career with that of a criminal. Sir Robert Walpole was known as 'The Great Man'; Fielding's Jonathan Wild was also 'Great' and one who, early on in the novel, compares the behaviour of the thief with that of the statesman:

> how easy is the reflection of having taken a few shillings or pounds from a stranger, without any breach of confidence, or perhaps great harm to the person who loses it, compared to that of having betrayed a public trust, and ruined the fortunes of thousands, perhaps of a great nation.[10]

Such a comparison was to become possible only for radicals in the following century.[11] For Fielding, most crime was committed by the poor led astray by luxury; but crime, with its contributory drunkenness, idleness and poverty, were only symptoms of a deeper lying problem – a new kind of society with a value system rooted in self-interest and individualism. Not every eighteenth-century magistrate or minister agreed with his assessment of the deeper problems yet, in practical terms, control and supervision of the poor who committed crime seemed a possibility.

Fielding believed that the robber:

> being too lazy to get his Bread by Labour, or too voluptuous to content himself with the Produce of that Labour, declares War against the Properties, and often against the Persons of his Fellow Subjects.[12]

Sir John Fielding, who took over as Chief Magistrate of Bow Street on Henry's death, was much concerned with the practicalities of fighting this 'war' – crime was located among a certain section of society and the fight had to be carried to them. When giving evidence before a House of Commons committee enquiring into burglaries and robberies in London in 1772 Sir John stated that the present 'gang' of housebreakers were the sons of 'unfortunate people, and of no trade'. He believed that they had started their criminal careers as child pickpockets and had graduated to housebreaking as they grew older 'in order to procure a greater income to supply their increased expenses'. He urged a strict regulation of ballad singers, 'a greater nuisance than Beggars, because they give opportunity to Pickpockets, by collecting people together'. These singers were capable of real work; their songs, moreover were 'generally immoral and obscene'. Even more important was a tighter control of public houses some of which were kept by 'the most abandoned characters, such as bawds, thieves, receivers of stolen goods'; and all manner of offences were hatched in these establishments.[13]

In the same year that Sir John Fielding addressed the Commons Committee, Jonas Hanway, an influential London philanthropist, published his *Observations on the Causes of dissoluteness which reigns among the low Classes of the People*. Crime was not the chief concern of this pamphlet, nor of its much larger successor, *The defects of police, the cause of immorality and the continual robberies committed particularly in and about the Metropolis*, published in 1775. Hanway was alarmed by what he thought was an overall moral decline among all classes in what he termed as an 'age of pleasure'. Crime was one of the ways in which this lack of morality manifested itself among the lower classes. Like Henry Fielding, Hanway saw rich and poor as inhabitants of the same moral universe; if the former set a bad example, what could be expected of the latter? 'Whether in high life, or in low, if the desire for money rages in the breast, it is like a dropsy, increased by the gratification of a

51

thirst'.[14] 'Concubinage' and the '*promiscuous commerce* of the sexes' was spreading downwards from those at the top of society who should have been setting a moral example; so also was a weakening of the bonds of 'filial piety'. People of all classes now disdained frugal fare and gorged themselves; the abuse of the liberty of the press by which newspapers printed 'falsehoods and nonsense', together with drinking and gambling all served to make matters worse. Sadly also the county gentry were declining as gentlemen brought their families to London and indulged in extravagant expense rather than supervising their local poor. Hanway noted that most of those who were executed were young men; they had been 'either bred [as] thieves, or [had contracted] a habit of idleness, and following the example of men in superior life, [had grown] expensive'.[15] The problem here was that apprentices were being given too much freedom by their masters. '*Reading* and *thinking*, when they are not at work, and the habit of sober discipline, are much out of fashion'[16]:

> I have good reason to believe there is scarce an *apprentice boy*, turned of fifteen years of age, who, contrary to the practice of our forefathers, is not suffered to go abroad almost every night, as soon as the shop is shut. These boys, and young men, challenge it as a kind of *right*; and if the master is as dissipated as his servant, which is often the case, he takes no thought, till he finds himself *robbed*; which I believe happens more oftener than he discovers. You will easily conceive it next to impossible the apprentice should wander abroad, without learning to drink strong liquors: some go further, and game: many keep bad company: the society of each other is dangerous. They neglect their Bible, and have as little relish for a Common Prayer Book. Numbers become a prey to prostitutes, and accelerate their ruin. Vice is costly: money must be supplied, let it come from what quarter it may.[17]

Henry Fielding's *Enquiry* continued to be warmly recommended as the best analysis of crime, its causes and remedies during the 1780s, particularly as the close of the American War of Independence appeared to result in an increase in crime; it certainly resulted in an increase in indictment and capital convictions. 'If robbers continue to increase, as they have done for some time past', lamented the *St James's Chronicle* in November 1784, 'the number of those who rob will exceed that of the robbed'. Martin Madan, who quoted the *Chronicle* in his *Thoughts on Executive Justice*, believed that:

> No civilized nation ... has to lament, as we have, the daily commission of the most dangerous and atrocious crimes, in so much that we cannot travel the roads, or sleep in our houses, or turn our cattle into our fields, without the most imminent danger of thieves and robbers. These are increased to such a degree in numbers and audaciousness, that the *day* is now little less dangerous than the *night* to travel in ... [18]

It was not to be until more than forty years after Henry Fielding's *Enquiry* that another major analysis of crime in London was attempted. Patrick Colquhoun, former Lord Provost of Glasgow and one of the first stipendiary magistrates to be appointed under the Middlesex Justices Act of 1792, first published his *Treatise on the Police of the Metropolis* anonymously in 1795. He shared Fielding's and Hanway's belief that gaming among the young men of the 'middle and higher stations' set a bad example to the 'lower ranks', an argument which recurred throughout the nineteenth century. Colquhoun saw crime rooted in the luxurious living and the improvidence of the poor. Unlike the more sensible 'middle ranks' the poor indulged themselves with, for example, exotic seafood even when prices were high; they had no notions of frugality and care. They spent too much time in public houses, gaming and generally squandering more than they could afford:

> Were we to examine the history of any given number of these our
> miserable fellow-mortals, it would be discovered that their distresses,
> almost in every instance, have been occasioned by extravagance, idleness,
> profligacy, and crimes: – and that their chief support is by gambling,
> cheating, and thieving in a little way.[19]

But if Colquhoun's image of the poor was, at first glance, reminiscent of Fielding's, his perception of society and the ultimate cause of the poor's behaviour was very different. Colquhoun had trade connections himself and the protection of commerce on the Thames was one of his prime interests; it prompted his other significant study of crime and police, *A Treatise on the Commerce and Police of the River Thames*. He gloried in the wealth and prosperity which trade had brought to the Thames, and thus to London and to the nation as a whole. Admittedly this wealth brought temptation, but the real problem was the breakdown of religion and moral rectitude among the poor. Some of this he attributed to deliberate subversion and, while he named no names, he clearly had the popular radicals and free thinkers among the English Jacobins in mind.[20] The remedy was to be found in better control and supervision of lower orders. He insisted that in parts of Europe there were not the burglars and highwaymen who could be found in England; the reason was to be found in:

> a more correct and energetic system of Police, joined to an early and
> general attention to the employment, education, and morals of the lower
> orders of the people; a habit of industry and sobriety is thus acquired ... [21]

Between 1795 and 1807 Colquhoun's Treatise on the *Police of the Metropolis* went through seven English editions and was considerably enlarged.[22] If such a publication history is a mark of success then, indeed, the book was a tremendous success. Colquhoun had his critics, notably over his assertion that moral deterioration and crime were getting worse; and others winced at what one critic termed his 'prudish political puritanism' which would seek to control the poor with an un-English system of police.[23] Yet he struck a chord with the propertied classes of the metropolis and elsewhere. Colquhoun had sympathy for people in dire distress and he organised soup kitchens for the 'industrious' poor of Spitalfields in the famine years of the 1790s, but the poor's problems in his estimation had no connection with a changing society; the poor suffered largely because of their own idleness and improvidence. 'Idleness is a neverfailing road to criminality. It originates generally in the inattention and the bad example of profligate parents.'[24]

During the half century following the first edition of Colquhoun's *Treatise on the Police* questions of crime and police became key concerns of successive governments. Select committees of parliament presented reports on different aspects of the policing of London in 1812, 1816, 1817, 1818, 1822, 1828, 1833 and 1834; and between 1836 and 1839 the Royal Commission on the Rural Constabulary held its deliberations and drew up its report and recommendations.

Those select committees meeting before the creation of the Metropolitan Police in 1829 heard some witnesses who challenged Colquhoun's belief that the morals of the poor were deteriorating. But all saw crime as a problem emanating from the poorer sections of society; it was the mass of petty offences which gave cause for concern, since the more 'atrocious offences' like highway robbery were considered to be in decline.[25] The committees of 1816 and 1828 were particularly concerned at what seemed to be an increasing number of juvenile offenders; witnesses blamed first indigent, or vicious and abandoned parents who ignored their offspring, and second, and to a lesser extent, shopkeepers and stall-holders who foolishly exposed their wares unprotected in front of their shops or stalls.[26] Echoing the argument of Sir John Fielding, something of a consensus emerged that juvenile offenders started with petty theft and then progressed to more serious offences; incarcerating them with older, hardened offenders served only to accelerate the process. The 1816 committee was obsessed with drink as a contributory factor to crime and with public houses harbouring prostitutes, thieves and vagabonds; witnesses who appeared unconcerned, or who played down the significance of public houses, were questioned with rigour and persistence.[27] Ten years later two M.P.s suggested in the House of Commons that unemployment and poverty may have been contributing to crime.[28] Several witnesses made a similar link before the 1828 committee; but Sir Richard Birnie, the chief magistrate of the Bow Street police office, insisted that if there was less depravity among them then more of the poor would find employment, and increasingly this kind of assertion became the most popular except among those of a radical persuasion.[29]

John Sayer, a Bow Street police officer, agreed in 1816 that he was acquainted with 'a great number of the dangerous characters or suspect persons who are constantly about London'.[30] Birnie and another stipendiary magistrate, John Rawlinson, told the 1828 committee that the police knew who the thieves infesting London were.[31] In this they followed a tradition among 'professional policemen' going back at least as far as Henry Fielding, that much crime was the work of 'professional', readily identifiable, criminals. Henry Fielding wrote of an organised gang of about 100 carrying out robberies; they were well practised at using disguises; they rescued colleagues who were caught, bribed prosecutors and used corrupt lawyers and false witnesses.[32] Colquhoun, never a man to conjure with small figures when confronted with a problem, estimated that there were 115,000 persons living in London wholly or partly by different forms of crime. Among these were a hard core of 2,000 'Professed thieves, Burglars, Highway Robbers, Pickpockets, and River Pirates'; and these numbers, he feared, would increase when peace threw back into society the criminals syphoned off by the armed forces in wartime.[33] Such thinking informed the beliefs of the Metropolitan Police from its creation. The Royal Commission on the Rural Constabulary sought information from the divisional commanders of the Metropolitan Police and it received precise figures. The superintendent of P division, for example, was particularly thorough declaring that his jurisdiction contained, '2 burglars. 2 housebreakers. 1 highway robber. 14 pickpockets. 48 common thieves. 4 obtainers of goods by false pretences. 1 receiver of stolen goods. 1 horse stealer. 3 dog stealers and 4 utterers of base coin'.[34] What these figures actually represented is an open question, but the Report of the Royal Commission was able to present statistics of 'Depredators, Offenders and Suspected Persons' for the Metropolitan Police District, for Liverpool, Bristol, Bath, Hull and Newcastle-upon-Tyne. It insisted that the figures were meaningful and were among the benefits of properly organised police systems.[35] As was noted in the preceding chapter, from the late 1850s figures such as these were published in the Judicial Statistics, though without any guidance being given to the individual constabularies as to what they should include. The collection and publication of these statistics, in themselves, helped give a further reality to the perceptions of the existence of a criminal class.

The Report of the Royal Commission on the Rural Constabulary sought to give an explanation for crime across the whole of England and Wales. It was largely drafted by Edwin Chadwick, but he did not dominate the Commission as has sometimes been assumed. Criminality, according to the Report, was rooted in the poorer classes, particularly those who roamed the country: 'the prevalent cause [of vagrancy] was the impatience of steady labour'.[36] Chadwick, and by implication his fellow commissioners, were either unaware of, or simply ignored the seasonal nature of much nineteenth-century employment and the consequent need for many, even urban dwellers, to spend time moving from place to place and from job to job.[37] Poverty and indigence, insisted the Report, did not lead to crime; criminals suffered from two principal vices – 'indolence or the pursuit of easy excitement', and they were drawn to commit crimes by 'the temptation of the profit of a career of depredation, as compared with the profits of honest and even well paid industry'.[38] Criminals then, made a rational decision to live by a life of crime because of its attractions; furthermore they knew that the lack of a preventive police would probably enable them to get away with any offence.

What Chadwick had done was to identify a criminal group within the working class, a group which possessed those habits which, to his mind, were the worst habits of the class as a whole. These habits were then given as the causes of crime. Other experts and reformers who investigated and analysed crime in the middle years of the century subconsciously performed much the same sleight of hand: they identified criminals as a group within the working class, ascribed to that group the habits and vices of which they most disapproved, or the disadvantages which they most sought to alleviate. These habits and/or disadvantages then became the prime causes of crime. Such an analysis had been embryonic in Colquhoun, perhaps even in Fielding, but to achieve its full shape the moral fervour of early Victorian reformers was required, coupled with the frightening spread of urbanisation and the perception of a society irrevocably divided into social classes.

Seven of the expert witnesses who were called before the 1828 Select Committee on Police in the Metropolis had given drink as a contributory factor in crime. In 1834 a Select Committee enquiring into drunkenness concluded that the 'vice' was declining among the middle and upper classes, but increasing among the labouring classes with a notable impact on crime. 'The spread of Crime' the Committee declared, in a sentence as notable for its purple prose and passion as its length:

> in every shape and form, from theft, fraud and prostitution in the young,
> to burnings, robberies and more hardened offences in the old; by which
> the gaols and prisons, the hulks and convict transports are filled with
> inmates; and an enormous mass of human beings, who, under sober habits
> and moral training, would be sources of wealth and strength to the
> country, are transformed, chiefly through the remote or immediate
> influence of Intoxicating Drinks, into excrescences of corruption and
> weakness, which must be cut off and cast away from the gangrenous
> contamination of its whole frame, leaving the body itself in a constant
> state of that inflammatory excitement, which always produces exhaustion
> and weakness in the end; and thus causing the country to sacrifice every
> year a larger portion of blood and treasure than the most destructive wars
> occasion; the innocent population thus made criminal, being, like the
> grain subjected to distillation, converted from a wholesome source of
> strength and prosperity into a poisoned issue of weakness and decay.[39]

In the sense that employment and good wages led to greater consumption of liquor which, on occasions, contributed to a greater incidence of offences against the person, the statistics of crime suggest that the committee in one respect were groping in the right direction, but the thinking behind their equation was far more crude and simplistic and, clearly, offences against property were as much their concern as violence. The problem, as the committee perceived it, was the poor's lack of morality.

The 'lack of moral training' was not a new issue in 1834, but it was taken up and emphasised by a clutch of educational reformers over the next two decades particularly as concern grew about juvenile delinquency.[40] Individuals like Mary Carpenter, Joseph Fletcher, James Kay-Shuttleworth, Jelinger Symons and John Wade urged that proper education would lead to a diminution of crime; but it was not secular education merely involving reading, writing and arithmetic which they wanted. Symons explained that:

> when the heart is depraved, and the tendencies of the child or the man are unusually vicious, there can be little doubt that instruction *per se*, so far from preventing crime, is accessory to it.[41]

Better education might simply produce better-educated criminals; already there were complaints that the reading matter of the working classes was 'decidedly reprehensible in their moral tone, pandering to the worst passions of their readers, and regularly venting forth nauseous details of seduction, crime and horror'.[42] What was needed was essentially Christian and moral education which would explain to the working classes their true station in life. John Glyde, a self-educated artisan who dabbled in Owenism and Chartism and who published extensively on his native Suffolk, urged:

> It is to our low neighbourhoods, and to the neglected children roaming the streets, that we must look, if we would check the current of crime ... It is in the dwelling-place of the poor that the zealous must labour for the dissemination of Christian principles, and teach men the value of their relative duties as members of society. This is the fountain head of crime, and it is here that the evil must be grappled with.[43]

This education had to instill in the young habits of industry, and if bad parents or the efforts of ragged schools or Sunday Schools failed to do this, then reformatory schools would have to take over, substituting for the parents and preparing juvenile offenders for a moral adulthood. Symons summed the situation up as follows:

> [Labour] is the backbone of reformation. No one can attach more weight than I do to the agencies of religion and kindness. They touch the heart and soften the asperities of a vicious nature, even if they fail to Christianise. But there must be a change of habit as well as of mind, and the change of habit mostly needed is from some kind of idleness to some kind of industry. *We are dealing with a class whose vocation is labour; and whose vices and virtues are infallibly connected with indolence or industry.* There is no penitence either in man or lad who shirks hard work; nor is there any better evidence of the reality of the conversion of a criminal than the sweat of his brow. [my italics][44]

Of course it was difficult for even the most respectable member of the working class to work up a sweat by hard physical labour if he was unemployed. Even the most provident of the working class who, for example, delayed a marriage until they had amassed what they felt to be sufficient capital to set up home together, could find their nest-egg consumed by a sudden spell of unemployment.[45] Contemporary gentlemen recognised that the want of regular employment could contribute to crime, but this was because the working class lacked moral fibre as a result of their ignorance, idleness, dissoluteness and drunkenness – habits which the young often picked up from bad parents. Thomas Plint, the Leeds reformer, explained that the working class had difficulty in withstanding 'the fiery ordeal of protracted idleness, and its inevitable concomitant, protracted temptation'. The longer an economic crisis continued, the greater the temptation:

> The occasional act becomes a constant habit; principle is overlaid, and conscience drugged and stupified ... Nor does the return to prosperity obliterate the evil which a long cycle of distress has produced. Work may be resumed, and the former comforts gladden the household, but the *trail and slime* of the moral evil which has dwelt in the heart and ruled there, remains, and will evidence itself in a thousand forms.

Yet it remained the individuals within 'the operative classes' who were at fault rather than the system.[46] For Plint's contemporaries, like the Reverend John Clay, the Chaplain of Preston Gaol, and Matthew Davenport Hill, the Recorder of Birmingham, it was possible to argue that times of economic prosperity linked with the moral weakness of the working class to tempt them into crime.[47]

The 1830s and, particularly, the 'hungry forties' witnessed apocalyptic visions of society shared by men at opposite ends of the political spectrum. Engels asserted that 'the incidence of crime has increased with the growth of the working-class population and there is more crime in Britain than in any other country in the world'. Crime was an aspect of the new social war which worsened with every passing year. Sir Archibald Alison, the Tory Sheriff of Lanarkshire, perceived:

> destitution, profligacy, sensuality and crime [advancing] with unheard-of rapidity in the manufacturing districts, and the dangerous classes there massed together combine every three or four years in some general strike or alarming insurrection, which, while it lasts, excites universal terror.[48]

It was during the 1840s that the Chartist G. W. M. Reynolds began publishing *The Mysteries of London*, which, with its sequel, were 'probably the longest, best-selling fiction of the time'.[49] The former was inspired by Eugene Sue's *Les Mystères de Paris*, the best selling novel in France during the 1840s, and with scenes of appalling savagery and violence as well as sexual titilation, Reynolds gave his readers a frightening portrait of a brutalised, savage poor – a truly dangerous class.

The middle classes in England readily accepted H. A. Frégier's term 'the dangerous classes' as descriptive of the creatures inhabiting the most squalid districts of the burgeoning cities. The French historian, Louis Chevalier, built on Frégier's perception to describe early nineteenth-century Paris as a pathological city in which the labouring classes merged into the dangerous classes while frightened bourgeois conceived of themselves like pioneers in the frontier-America portrayed by James Fenimore Cooper – men surrounded by savages.[50] While many aspects of Chevalier's analysis are open to criticism, his description of how the middle classes perceived their social inferiors strikes a chord with the English experience: if nothing else the poor looked very different in physique as well as dress.

In 1862 the Reverend H. W. Holland writing on 'professional thieves' in the *Cornhill Magazine* described how any visitor entering a thieves' district would be struck by the inhabitants' strange dress and physiognomy; the adults were 'seedy and sleepy' while the children 'lounge about, looking very suspicious and preternaturally sharp'. He went on to explain that:

> Nearly all habitual thieves, male and female, die of consumption, and under or about thirty-five years of age. Drink, debauchery, irregular hours, the sudden transitions from luxuries to a low prison diet – these things soon kill them off.[51]

The question immediately posed by such descriptions is, what was the difference between the life-style and life expectancy of these 'professional thieves' and those of the poorer sections of the working class? Whatever the early statisticians may have argued about improvements in life expectancy, the tables published during the middle years of the nineteenth century revealed a significant difference between the life expectancy of the working class and that of their social superiors; and very large numbers of the working class died before the age of thirty-five. Tuberculosis, 'the Captain of the Men of Death', the 'White Plague', was a remorseless killer of the urban poor, and while it declined during the nineteenth century it still accounted for perhaps one third of all deaths from disease during the Victorian period.[52] Poor nutrition, in the context of long hours and hard physical labour, together with appalling and unchecked industrial diseases, ensured that even if the adjectives 'seedy' and 'sleepy' might be questioned, the physiological differences between the working class, particularly the poorer sections, and the middle class were certainly real.

In another article on thieves in the *Cornhill Magazine* Holland who claimed to have lived among them for two years, noted that even 'the worst of them' spoke gloomily of their future given the efforts of policemen, prisons, ragged schools and reformatories – the metaphor he used was telling and typical – 'just as a Red Indian would complain of the dwindling of his tribe before the strong march of advancing civilization'.[53] During the 1850s to 1870s a succession of intrepid explorers picked up their notebooks, as often as not found trusty guides among the stout-hearted, blue-uniformed, helmeted, guardians of law and order, and penetrated the dark and teeming recesses of poor working-class districts. They then wrote up their exploits for the vicarious delight of the reading public as journeys into criminal districts where the inhabitants were best compared with Red Indians or varieties of black 'savages'. Among the first of these explorers was Angus Reach who, reporting on the manufacturing districts for the *Morning Chronicle*, accompanied a sub-inspector of the Manchester Police into the depths of Angel Meadow. They entered a 'low lodging house':

> Hot as the place was, most of the women had shawls about their heads. They were coarse looking and repulsive – more than one with contused discoloured faces. The men were of that class you often remark in low localities – squalid hulking fellows, with no particular mark of any trade or calling on them. The women were of the worst class of prostitutes, and the men their bullies and partners in robberies.

Continuing their journey Reach and the inspector visited a pub, well-known as the haunt of thieves. The inspector challenged a boy pickpocket: 'The light from a lamp fell upon his face and I never saw a worse one – little, deep-sunk eyes and square bony jaws, with a vile expression'.[54] Dickens went 'On Duty with Inspector Field' into the depths of the Saint Giles Rookery:

> We stoop low, and creep down a precipitous flight of steps into a dark close cellar. There is a fire. There is a long deal table. There are benches. The cellar is full of company, chiefly very young men in various conditions of dirt and raggedness. Some are eating supper. There are no girls or women present. Welcome to Rats' Castle, gentlemen, and to this company of noted thieves![55]

When another explorer took a day trip down the Thames to see a bare-knuckle boxing match his adventure became 'A Day's Pleasure with the Criminal Classes'.[56] Such literature reached its apogee with Henry Mayhew.

Mayhew revived, possibly unknowingly, Henry Fielding's differentiations of the poor when in the first of his eighty-two reports for the *Morning Chronicle*, he divided the London poor into 'they [that] *will* work, they [that] *can't* work, and they [that] *won't* work'.[57] Mayhew's reports showed sympathy for the plight of the poor and an awareness of the problems of the casual nature of so much of the labour in the metropolis, but when it came to crime he insisted that poverty and casual labour were causes only in so far as they destroyed 'all habits of prudence and where there is no prudence, the present affluence cannot be made to provide for the future want'. He visited a lodging house in dockland reporting the inmates' description of their hard lives and their problems in getting work; yet his report finished with his 'experienced guide' emphasising that few of these men could be made honest. 'I have known a few in my time that have been reclaimed, but they are the exceptions, and certainly not the rule.' Mayhew accepted the analysis of the Constabulary Commissioners a decade before: criminals were essentially the idle and the vagabond'. Young thieves, he explained, 'love idleness', and while pickpockets rarely drank (it would impede their dexterity) they were 'libidinous ... and spend whatever money they can spare upon the low prostitutes'.[58] Drink was, nevertheless, a powerful contributor to crime: following some dubious statistical reasoning which set figures for drunkenness alongside figures for larceny and assault, Mayhew demonstrated that the labouring classes were more drunken and consequently more criminal.[59]

Just over a third of the letters for the *Morning Chronicle* were incorporated into Mayhew's massive *London Labour and the London Poor: A Cyclopaedia of the Condition and Earning of those that will work, those that cannot work, and those that will not work*, the first volume, and other sections of which, first appeared in 1851. Here Mayhew began by noting the different physical and mental characteristics of the nomadic street people:

there is a greater development of the animal than of the intellectual or moral nature of man ... they are more or less distinguished for their high cheek-bones and protruding jaws – for their use of a slang language – for their lax ideas of property – for their general improvidence – their repugnance to continuous labour – their disregard of female honour – their love of cruelty – their pugnacity – and their utter want of religion.

In short these exotic tribes – 'costermongers strongly resemble the North American Indians in their conduct to their wives' – lacked all of the virtues which respectable middle-class Victorian society held dear. Lurking among these tribes was a separate 'class' of thieves. They were mainly young, they were idle and vagrant, they enjoyed the literature which glorified pirates and robbers, notably Dick Turpin and Jack Sheppard, and, of course, many looked different. Mayhew organised a 'meeting of vagrants' in Shadwell to inquire into their way of life; the gathering was given the sub-heading 'Meeting of Thieves':

... never was witnessed a more distressing spectacle of squalor, rags and wretchedness ... Many were not only good-looking, but had a frank, ingenuous expression that seemed in no way connected with innate roguery. Many, on the other hand, had the deep-sunk and half-averted eye which are so characteristic of natural dishonesty and cunning.[60]

The fourth volume, which first appeared in its entirety in the enlarged edition of 1861–62, concentrated on 'the Non-Workers, or in other words, the Dangerous Classes of the Metropolis'. This was a work by several hands; Mayhew himself set out to define crime and the 'criminal class'. Crime, he argued, was the transgression of social laws in the same way that sin and vice were, respectively, the transgression of religious and moral laws. The crime of theft, however, transgressed all three varieties of laws. There were two different kinds of criminals 'the professional and the casual'. The latter committed their crimes 'from some accidental cause' such as malice, lust, shame, temptation, cupidity, want or political prejudice. The professional criminals were 'those who object to labour for their living' and who preferred to live by plundering others. The crimes of 'professional criminals' were 'regular crafts, requiring almost the same apprenticeship as any other mode of life'. These crafts consisted of burglary, various forms of robbery from the person, poaching, coining, smuggling, and working illicit stills.[61] Mayhew gave an extensive breakdown of thieves and their dependants: there were 5 major headings, 20 sub-headings and over 100 categories, most with exotic slang titles. Under the sub-heading of ' "Sneaksmen", or those who plunder by means of stealth', for example were:

iv 'Till Friskers', or those who empty tills of their contents during the absence of the shopmen.

v 'Sawney-Hunters', or those who go purloining bacon from cheesemongers' shop-doors.

vi 'Noisy-racket Men', or those who steal china and glass from outside of china-shops.

vii 'Area Sneaks', or those who steal from houses by going down the area steps.

viii 'Dead Lurkers', or those who steal coats and umbrellas from passages at dusk, or on Sunday afternoons.

ix 'Snow Gatherers', or those who steal clean clothes off the hedges.[62]

Whether it was conceivable that a 'Sawney-Hunter' was so wedded to his own trade that he would not indulge in a bit of 'Snow Gathering', should the opportunity arise, was not allowed in Mayhew's categorisation. The question might also have been posed: was there really a living to be made in specialising as a 'Noisy-racket man'? It seems possible that, in some instances at least, he took the slang for a particular offence and then made a criminal trade out of it. Furthermore it was contradictory for Mayhew to list among 'those who will not work': 'embezzlers or those who rob their employers' and dishonest servants who 'make away with the property of their masters'. Did it make sense to argue that the 'accidental causes' of temptation or want did not contribute to these latter offences, or even to some of the professional crimes such as burglary and poaching? Yet such questions do not appear to have vexed either Mayhew or his readers.

The Reverend William Tuckniss who wrote the introduction to Mayhew's fourth volume refused to commit himself on the overall trend of crime:

  although the criminal statistics of some localities exhibit a sensible
  diminution in certain forms of vice, we must not forget that an increase of

education and a growing intelligence bring with them superior facilities for the successful perpetration and concealment of crime.[63]

But from the middle of the century many commentators were confidently asserting that crime was being checked. James Greenwood, a journalist with experience of the poor districts of London and the police courts, believed that in 1869 there were some 20,000 thieves in the metropolis, yet their numbers had decreased in recent years.[64] The advocates of the reformatory system emphasised the important role that their brain-child was playing in reducing juvenile crime. There remained an irredeemable, incorrigible residuum, which, with the cessation of transportation, could no longer be shipped out of the country. This group was increasingly referred to as the criminal class; the backbone of this class were those defined by Mayhew as 'professional' and by the legislators as 'habitual' criminals. Such men, declared *The Times* in a leading article in 1870:

> are more alien from the rest of the community than a hostile army, for they have no idea of joining the ranks of industrious labour either here or elsewhere. The civilized world is simply the carcass on which they prey, and London above all, is to them a place to sack.[65]

In spite of the 'progress of the nation' and the apparent advance of civilization the question had to be posed: why did this residuum remain?

Greenwood noted that many juveniles resorted to crime because of hunger,[66] yet, in general, habitual criminals were rarely perceived as being brought to crime by poverty. Bad, uncaring parents, drink, the corrupt literature which glamorised offenders, and a general lack of moral fibre continued to be wheeled out as causes of crime. Poverty remained the hallmark of most criminals in the literature of the second half of the nineteenth century, but this was not so much because poverty was regarded as a cause of crime, but rather because crime could not be held to pay. 'Thieving is always a losing game', explained Holland. 'The money they get never does them any good; it never stays with them. It all goes in gambling, debauchery and law expenses.'[67] *The Times*, commenting on the conviction of seven thieves in 1865, believed that they had taken property valued at between £11,000 and £12,000 in six months; of course, it went on, they would not have realised anything like this sum when they fenced it, but, more importantly:

> None of them were living in other than mean houses, and some tawdry jewelry about the women seems to represent the extent of their luxury. In fact, they dare not spend much, or they would attract the attention of the police, and they are thus condemned to enjoy their spoil with the same stealthy fear with which they seize it.[68]

Greenwood, in turn, emphasised:

> There can be no question that that of the professional thief is a bitterly severe and laborious occupation, beset with privations that moral people

have no conception of, and involving an amount of mental anxiety and torment that few human beings can withstand through a long lifetime.[69]

Even if for many the incidence of crime appeared to be decreasing, the problem was how to explain the persistence of crime in spite of the advantages and opportunities provided by the advance of civilization and the expansion of the mid-century panacea of education. In addition to the old standbys of corrupting literature, drunkenness, uncaring and criminal parents, and the mixing of first-time offenders with recidivists in prisons, concepts of heredity and ideas drawn from developments in medical science began to be enlisted for explanation. Early in the nineteenth century phrenologists had visited prisons to make case studies of convicts in the belief that inordinate mental faculties led to crime. They detected irredeemables from the shape of their heads, their desperate and fixed expressions and their 'mental bravado'.[70] Visitors to the penal colonies in Australia often declared that the convicts had an unmistakable 'peculiarity of the visage [making them look] different from all other men'.[71] While a schoolmaster with experience of Newgate in the early 1830s noted that the features of prisoners were 'strongly marked with animal propensities'; and this seemed particularly so among some of the boys who had 'an approximation to the face of a monkey'.[72] From the middle of the century British doctors, like James Thompson who worked in Perth Prison, began collating biological analyses of convicts, thus providing an academic underpinning to these perceptions of 'animal propensities' by the supposedly foolproof means of empirical research. In the majority of the inmates of the juvenile wing of one English prison Dr Forbes Winslow discovered the boys to have 'the cerebrum ... badly organised, the crown of the head was nearly flat, the posterior region full. In other words, there was little or no intellect, the moral sentiments were small and the propensities large'. Forbes Winslow shared his findings with the readers of the *Morning Chronicle*.[73] In the last quarter of the century these developments were given a sharper focus by, on the one hand, the housing problem in London and the studies of the great social investigators, and, on the other, the gradual filtering into Britain of the physiological and psychological theories of the European students of the new science of criminology or, to use the more common contemporary term, criminal anthropology.

At the bottom of the social scale in London Charles Booth found Social Class A: 'occasional labourers, loafers and semi-criminals'. This was a:

> savage semi-criminal class of people [which] had its golden age in the days when whole districts of London were in their undisputed possession. They mainly desire to be left alone, to be allowed to make an Alsatia of their own. Improvement in our eyes is destruction in theirs. Their discontent is the measure of our success.[74]

In meticulous detail Booth detailed the squalor and poverty in which this group lived, and the little-different surroundings of Social Class B, only marginally above it. Such revelations fuelled the arguments of those critics of the system of outdoor relief who maintained that mistaken humanitarianism and charity were creating, rather than alleviating, the problem of the unpleasant residuum in the slum districts of cities: charity merely fostered idleness and improvidence. At the same time the work of Booth, and others, with its exposures of bad housing and inadequate diet, encouraged a perception of the residuum as the product of the inevitable workings of social Darwinism. Arnold White, who in the aftermath of the Boer War was a central figure in warning the public about the degeneration of the British race, first expressed some of these concerns during the 1880s. He lamented the exodus from the bracing countryside, which produced fit and sturdy men, to the unhealthy cities where half of the poor were so mentally, morally and physically unfit, that the best thing for the nation to do was to leave them alone to die out. The problem was that the 'criminal and pauperised classes with low cerebral development renew their race more rapidly than those of higher nervous natures'.[75] Yet while criminals could still be seen as part of the residuum, lurking in their slums and, by implication, eager and ready to prey on the respectable, the increasingly popular biological explanation of crime meant that it was no longer necessary to define criminality simply in class terms.

The mass of petty thefts and the large number of crimes committed by juveniles continued to be the main objects of concern, but it began to be publicly acknowledged by experts that crime was not simply a problem rooted in the poorer sections of the urban working class. Charles Booth noted that 'every social grade has its criminals, if not by conviction, at least by character'.[76] The new criminal anthropology with its 'scientific' physiological and psychological theories enabled the criminal to be studied as an individual rather than simply part of a class, and provided an understanding of the criminal as an individual. Reduced to the simplest formula, the criminal was someone who was not 'normal'; normal individuals did not assault, murder, rape, or steal from others. L. Gordon Rylands explained:

> the active causes of all kinds [of crime] are these: Defective training or total absence of any; immoral associates and bad example in prison as well as out of it; drink; idleness, and the hereditary transmission of evil tendencies. These causes, however, frequently overlap, and one is often found to be the effect of another, the only perfectly simple and absolutely final division is into two main heads, Heredity and Environment, which comprise all others.

Yet, under the heading of environment Rylands seemed to have little more in mind than the lack of good and caring parents, the lack of a decent home environment (more the fault of parents than anyone or anything else), bad company in the slums and in prisons. These problems, he believed, might be alleviated by the state taking control of all children found on the streets 'without visible means of subsistence, or who seemed to be neglected by their parents'; the 'inherited tendencies' of 'embryo criminals' might thus be nipped in the bud. Theft, suicide and 'homicidal monomania' were, nevertheless all hereditary failings in Ryland's perception.[77] In 1890, for a series of 'Contemporary Science' books, Havelock Ellis published a critical survey of the work of the criminal anthropologists of Europe and the United States; the book went through four editions in twenty years. Ellis explained that research into the physical characteristics of criminals revealed that they were individuals incapable of living by the standards recognised as binding by a community:

> By some accident of development, by some defect of heredity or birth or training, [the criminal] belongs as it were to a lower and older social state than that in which he is actually living.

Research into the physical characteristics of the criminal moreover, demonstrated that:

> [I]n the criminal ... there is an arrest of development. The criminal is an individual who, to some extent, remains a child his life long – a child of larger growth and with greater capacity for evil.

But this did not mean that the criminal was 'an idiot' or even 'merely weak-minded'. The criminal was far more dangerous. 'The idiot and the feeble-minded, as we know them in asylums, rarely have any criminal or dangerous instincts'.[78] Ellis's fervent advocacy of 'social hygiene', by which, civilization 'at a certain stage ... is compelled to continue its own course, and to preserve, perhaps to elevate, the race' was a logical development from these ideas.[79]

Like Ellis, the Reverend William Douglas Morrison popularised for a British audience the work of men like Enrico Ferri, Cesare Lombroso and Gabriel Tarde; indeed he wrote the introduction for an English translation of Lombroso's *The Female Offender*. Morrison deployed the Europeans' conclusions alongside his personal experience as chaplain of Wandsworth Prison. He continued to accept many of the old moral perceptions: crime was rarely prompted by poverty or destitution:

> the habitual criminal, as he will very soon tell you if you possess his confidence absolutely, declines to work. He never has worked, he does not want work; he prefers living by his wits.

The habitual beggar and the vagrant were one and the same. But Morrison was emphatic that crime was not simply a problem found in the lowest recesses of the working class. The debtor was sometimes 'a worse criminal ... than the thief who snatches a purse'. Furthermore if imprisoned debtors were included in the tally of convicts,

> and if all cases of drunkenness and assault were punished with imprisonment instead of a fine, it would be found that the well-to-do showed just as badly in the statistics of crime as their poorer neighbours.

The fundamental problem was not class but 'degeneracy', and heredity and urban environment were the keys to understanding. 'Degeneracy' was inherited 'when the criminal is descended from insane, drunken, epileptic, scrofulous parents'. It could be acquired when an individual 'adopts and deliberately persists in a life of crime'.[80] The problem was augmented by the highly concentrated population of cities which led to 'the creation of a large degenerate caste'. Morrison believed that there was a separate 'class' of habitual criminals, but it was 'not to be confounded with the working or any other class' since it was separate and quite distinct from 'the rest of the community'.[81] Yet the prime focus of concern for Morrison, as for Ellis, Rylands and others, remained the 'degenerate' residuum within the urban slums.

There are two implicit elements about the perceptions of the criminal class explored so far in this chapter which warrant some explicit emphasis: first, the criminal class was perceived overwhelmingly as male; second, the perceptions discussed were those of middle-class commentators who had in mind, if not a middle class, at least a respectable audience. There were occasional references to women committing crimes, even to them being afflicted by criminal 'diseases'; the clergyman writing on 'Thieves and Thieving' for the *Cornhill Magazine*, for example, declared:

> Probably, kleptomania is no imaginary disease ... The writer has now one particular instance of it in his mind, in which a young lady of good sense and most respectable station could never be trusted in a shop alone. If this disease can happen in the upper classes, why may it not exist in the lower strata of social life?[82]

But, in general, women were seen as appendages to thieves and, of course, as Mayhew emphasised, the exotic tribes of the cities treated their women in different ways from those expected in civilised society. To the extent that, statistically, women appear to have committed fewer thefts and fewer assaults it might be argued that some of this concentration on the male 'criminal' was justified. But it is significant that for women transported for theft in the early nineteenth century the description 'hardened offender' and 'abandoned prostitute' were almost synonymous. This stereotype emerged from the gap which existed between the expectations of the middle class and the mores of the poorer sections of the working class for whom cohabitation was cheaper and sometimes more convenient than marriage.[83] Furthermore there is a parallel between the perceptions of the male criminal and the female prostitute. Prostitution in itself was not a criminal offence, but there was growing concern about 'the Great Social Evil' and, at least from the middle of the nineteenth century there were determined attempts at control. One aspect of the concern was the belief that prostitutes indulged in petty theft between themselves or upon clients, and that they consorted with thieves. Several of the social investigators who studied prostitution noted economic hardship as a spur to some women to take up the 'profession', yet even among the most sympathetic investigators economic causes – like the economic causes of some criminal actions – were invariably submerged in generalisations about the prostitute's family environment, her impulsive nature, her restlessness, her desire for quick money and love of luxury. The prostitute's gaudy and fashionable clothing was, perhaps, the most blatant manifestation of 'luxury' among the poorer sections of society. Dr William Acton's *Prostitution, Considered in its Moral, Social, and Sanitary Aspects, In London and Other Large Cities* has been hailed as among the most humane and sympathetic studies published during the Victorian period. He did not see prostitution as the slippery slope to damnation automatically, noting that young women often became prostitutes only for a short while, subsequently returning to more acceptable work and mother-hood. But among Acton's list of the causes of prostitution are those which have significant echoes of what others proposed as the causes of crime among the criminal and/or dangerous classes:

> Natural desire. Natural sinfulness. The preferment of indolent ease to labour. Vicious inclinations strengthened and ingrained by early neglect, or evil training, bad associates, and an indecent mode of life. Necessity, imbued by the inability to obtain a living by honest means consequent on a fall from virtue. Extreme poverty. To this blacklist may be added love of drink, love of dress, love of amusement.[84]

Of course members of the working class were aware of crime and criminals; they were more commonly the victims of crime and they both prosecuted and persecuted offenders of different types. Probably, as in some contemporary inner city areas, members of the working class felt more insecure and more likely to be the victims of some form of crime, than members of the middle class.[85] But working-class perceptions of criminality are less easy to grasp than the confident conclusions of experts or the equally confident descriptions of journalists aimed at a predominantly middle-class audience. The terminology of 'class', aside from the public and written pronouncements of the labour movement, does not appear to have figured much in the language of the working class itself. The late Victorian and Edwardian working class generally referred to themselves as 'the likes of us', 'the labouring sort', or 'working people'. Their social superiors were 'collar-and-tie men', 'the gentry', 'the higher ups', 'the likes of they'. Criminals, when spoken of as a group, may also have been 'the likes of they'.[86] The working class had no need to intellectualise criminals either as a class or as a group acquiring or inheriting degenerate characteristics; though this is not to deny the use of such colloquialisms as 'like father, like son', nor is it to deny the possibility of the working class perceiving those that they recognised as 'criminals' in the terms of the stereotypes depicted in literature.

Some offences, as was noted in the introduction, were not perceived as crimes either by the perpetrators or the communities in which they lived. Poaching is an obvious example. But hostility to the Game Laws was not confined to a single class and spread across social groups, particularly when the creatures defined by the law as protected game were regarded by communities as vermin. During the early 1750s men of all classes combined to dig up Lord Uxbridge's rabbit warrens which were ruining the commons of Cannock Chase.[87] Over the century later when Sussex court convicted Robert Dickinson of trespass in search of game, he protested: 'I do not call conies game, I call them vermin, according to the Bible'.[88] Nineteenth-century gentlemen feared that poaching was the first step on the road to a life of crime. Possibly a few did follow such a route, but the problem is ascertaining at what point a poacher who gravitated to another form of crime was rejected by his community. In his study of poaching on Cannock Chase, Douglas Hay concluded that cottagers who poached were seldom active thieves; after all, if a man stole from gentlemen and wealthy farmers he was unlikely to be entirely above suspicion among his neighbours. However evidence from the sixteenth and seventeenth centuries suggests that villagers were prepared to tolerate a degree of petty theft among known members of the community; and the case of William Herring, a 'yeoman' of East Wilton in Yorkshire, who was transported for sheep-stealing in 1793, suggests that it was possible for certain tough individuals to terrorise local communities without opposition or public complaint for several years.[89] Yet even with a 'social crime' like poaching attitudes did change, and changes in the law probably contributed to this change. The most extreme inequalities of the Games Laws were swept away in 1831; but the Poaching Prevention Act 1862, which empowered police to stop and search suspects, together with the Ground Game Act 1880, which gave tenant farmers inalienable rights over hares and rabbits on their property, seem to have had the side effects of reducing sympathy for the poacher and making him appear more of a 'criminal'.[90]

At the same time that some crimes were not perceived as such by certain social groups or communities, several nineteenth-century authors, generally liberals or radicals of various hues, did urge, contrary to the overall picture given in this chapter, that poverty could lead to crime. *The Poor Man's Guardian* even went so far as to suggest that the laws of the country were made by rich men to protect the great evil – property.[91] Yet there was never any suggestion that gaoled 'criminals' were, in any sense, political prisoners. There was violent hostility to the political disfranchisement which went with admission to the workhouse or with receipt of poor relief. Admission to the workhouse or the resort to relief was a constant threat hanging over a significant percentage of the poor and one of the chief condemnations of the New Poor Law was, in Disraeli's words, that 'it announces to the world that in England poverty is a crime'.[92] However no radical group called for the political enfranchisement of men in gaol. Indeed from the corresponding societies of the 1790s to the Chartists and beyond, conviction and imprisonment for a crime meant the forfeiture of political rights. This may be explained by the notions of morality which pervaded the thought of nineteenth-century working-class activists as well as the Victorian middle class – criminals, unlike paupers, made a conscious, positive and immoral decision when they committed a crime. At the same time it may also have been a recognition by the radical activists that the working class were as much the victims of crime as the perpetrators – political reform, and parliaments chosen by universal manhood suffrage, would remove the vestiges of inequality within the law.

The literature dealing with criminals which was aimed at the working class was both moralistic and titillating as was much of that aimed at their social superiors; indeed as the nineteenth century wore on there was an increasing overlap between the reading matter of the middle class and the respectable working class. The 'last dying words', with cheap woodcuts at the top of a sheet, which were hawked at public executions throughout the eighteenth, and well into the nineteenth centuries, were infused with a moralistic tone as the condemned was made to repent and to warn others against following in his, or her, footsteps. Some ballads took a similar line, like 'A Shining Night, or Dick Daring, the Poacher':

> Be advised then ye young be advised too ye old,
> To soberness honesty, industry hold,
> For stealing and murder may rise it is clear
> From a shining night if 'tis our delight in the season of the year.[93]

The criminals portrayed in such ballads were stereotypes of a pedigree which went back at least as far as the Tudors and Stuarts. In Dick Daring's case poaching led to more serious crimes, but generally speaking it was drinking and whoring which was held to have put the offender on the slippery slope to perdition. There were some ballads, however, which romanticised the 'criminal'. If 'Dick Daring' was a warning, 'Keepers and Poachers' portrayed the poacher William Taylor as a veritable Sydney Carton:

> The judge and the jury unto him did say
> 'If you wil confess, your sweet life shall be saved.'
> 'Oh no,' then said William, 'that won't do at all,
> For now you have got me I'll die for them all'.[94]

Ballads such as this were rooted in an oral tradition and the notion that poaching was no 'real crime'. Other 'corrupting' material was not. John Gay's *The Beggar's Opera* had rapidly acquired a notorious reputation for leading young men astray, and cheap books telling of the adventures of Jack Sheppard, Dick Turpin and others were similarly looked at askance by middle-class gentlemen; though, of course, the original novels *Rookwood* (1834), which both created and immortalised Turpin's ride to York, and *Jack Sheppard* (1839) were written by the son of a respectable lawyer from the neighbourhood of Manchester, William Harrison Ainsworth. Moreover, while Ainsworth is now relegated to the rank of second-class or 'popular' novelist he was, at the time, a friendly competitor of Dickens and the two even considered collaborating. Physique, physiognomy and geography are all tokens of class in Ainsworth's novels; critics were worried by what they considered as immorality in his novels, yet the popularity of his characters was seized on by others to produce a variety of imitations in the form of ballads, 'memoirs' and plays as well as novels.[95] Increasingly, with the developments in printing and publishing, and with the growth of literacy in the second half of the nineteenth century, the availability and the amount of this literature became greater. Printers and publishers found an appreciative audience for both adventure stories and lurid tales of ''orrible murder'; all the better if they had a basis in fact. In 1868 a man could defend his sons' behaviour before a court on the grounds that literature romanticising criminals has corrupted them. While in 1884 it was said of Ernest Castles, a nineteen-year old who shot a police constable in Oldham, that his 'mind has been corrupted by the reading of trashy literature'.[96] The following year a London magistrate declared that:

> there is not a boy or a young lad tried in our Courts of Justice whose position there is not more or less due to the effect of this unwholesome literature upon his mind.

Publishers, naturally, insisted that 'a moral and healthy tone may be maintained in conjunction with the boldest fiction'.[97] But the power of such literature either to improve or corrupt is not really ascertainable. Most probably it was read primarily for fun and escapism. Probably it reinforced stereotype perceptions of criminals. But members of the working class reacted to individual offenders essentially according to the offences which they committed: petty pilferage at work was often not seen as a crime, theft from a friend or neighbour more generally was; a public house argument which led to blows, or striking a policeman interfering with such as argument outside a pub, might not be perceived as crime, but extreme violence and murder, whatever the circumstances, generally was.

The argument here is not to deny the existence of a criminal class, or at least a group of professional criminals. There were individuals and groups who made a significant part of their living from activities which lay outside the law; probably however, as will be argued below in Chapter 6, the word 'class' implies a large number, and a more homogeneous group than actually existed. But while these individuals may have effected most of the very spectacular and large-scale thefts during the eighteenth and nineteenth centuries, the overwhelming majority of offences were not of this variety. Nineteenth-century experts and commentators looked at who were being processed by the police, the courts and the prisons, never seriously questioned the idea that the multitude of petty thefts (sometimes with the addition of assaults and disorderly conduct) should be the benchmark of criminality, and they then set out to find the causes of this criminality. Since the great majority of offenders came from one social class it was logical to locate the causes of crime within what were generally perceived as the vices of this class. There would be many today who would accept some of the Victorian notions of links between vice and crime: strong drink does appear to have contributed to some incidents of disorder and inter-personal violence; a poor man may have yielded to temptation because of his poverty, yet not every poor man stole, and it might be argued that such nebulous concepts as strength of character and morality do come into play here. The problem was that most nineteenth-century analysts of crime ignored the seasonal and uncertain nature of much employment, and the gruelling aspects of the working-class existence; these certainly contributed to physiological differences between the classes and they probably encouraged the 'vices' (drink, cheap crime literature, rowdiness, consorting with prostitutes) when times were good and when the poor had money in their pockets.

REFERENCES AND NOTES

1. *Hansard*, new series, xiv (1826), cols. 1218–19.
2. J. A. Sharpe, *Crime in Early Modern England 1550–1750*, Longman, London, 1984, especially chap. 5.
3. *Illustrated London News*, 2 December 1843.
4. S. F. Van Oss, 'The "Limited-Company" Craze', *Nineteenth Century*, xliii (1898), pp. 731–44 (at p. 736); see also Alfred Emden, 'The crying need for reforms in our company law', *Nineteenth Century*, xxxv (1894), pp. 1033–50.
5. It has been argued that the enforcement of the 1833 Factory Act was guided by the 'rotten apple' thesis and that factory inspectors made the consoling distinction between a majority of respectable employers who would never break the law (though they did) and 'rotten apples'. W. G. Carson, 'The institutionalization of ambiguity: Early British Factory Acts', in Gilbert Geis and Ezra Stotland (eds.), *White-Collar-Crime: Theory and research*, Sage, Beverley Hills, 1980, pp. 166–67.
6. Gregory Anderson, *Victorian Clerks*, Manchester U.P., 1976, pp. 37–40.
7. Henry Fielding, *An Enquiry into the Causes of the late Increase of Robbers*, 2nd. edn., London, 1751, p. xxiii.
8. Ibid., p. 7.
9. Ibid., p. 69.
10. Henry Fielding, *The History of the Life of the late Mr Jonathan Wild the Great*, Everyman Edition, p. 18.
11. *Punch* for example, commented: 'It is true that the criminal may have been

led by the example of aristocratic sinners to disregard the injunctions of revealed religion against the adulterer, the gamester, and the drunkard; and having imitated the "pleasant follies" of the great without possessing the requisite means for such enjoyments, the man of pleasure has degenerated into the man of crime. It is true that the poor and ignorant may have claims upon the wealth and intelligence of the rich and learned; but are we to pause to inquire whether want may have driven the destitute to theft, or the absence of early instruction have left physical desires of the offender's native superior to its moral restraints. Certainly not, whilst we have the gallows.' *Punch*, vol. 1, 20 November 1841.

12. Fielding, *An Enquiry*, p. 169.

13. *P.P.* 1812 (127), ii, *Select Committee on the Nightly Watch of the Metropolis*, appendix 8, pp. 34–39. The belief that small offences led inexorably to big ones was already common in the seventeenth century, see J. A. Sharpe, *Crime in Early Modern England*, pp. 152–56 and 160–66.

14. **Jonas Hanway**, *The Defects of Police, The Cause of Immorality and The Continual Robberies Committed, Particularly in and about the Metropolis*, London, 1775, p. 273.

15. Jonas Hanway, *Observations on the Causes of the Dissoluteness which reigns among the lower Classes of the People; the Propensity of some to Petty Larceny: and the Danger of Gaming, Concubinage, and an excessive Fondness for amusement in high life*, London, 1772, p. 38.

16. Ibid., p. 15.

17. Hanway, *The defects of police*, p. 241.

18. **Martin Madan**, *Thoughts on Executive Justice, with respect to our Criminal Laws, particularly on the Circuits*, London, 1785, pp. 4–5 and 123. Madan's recommendations of Fielding's *Enquiry* is on p. 78; there is a similar recommendation in **William Blizard**, *Desultory Reflections on Police: With an essay on the means of preventing crimes and amending criminals*, London, 1785, p. 76.

19. **Patrick Colquhoun**, *A Treatise on the Police of the Metropolis*, 3rd edn., London, 1796, p. 33.

20. Patrick Colquhoun, *A Treatise on the Commerce and Police of the River Thames*, London, 1800, pp. 37–38 and 40.

21. Colquhoun, *Treatise on the Police*, p. 88. Colquhoun's argument here was highly questionable. It was generally accepted that the most 'correct' and 'energetic' police of the eighteenth century were to be found in France, yet the pre-Revolution rural police, the *maréchaussée*, had problems with brigands, the like of which simply did not exist in Britain. Furthermore the revolutionary wars, during which Colquhoun was writing, witnessed an increase in brigandage in France, the Low Countries and the Rhineland.

22. For the popularity of the *Treatise on the Police* see **Sir Leon Radzinowicz**, *A History of English Criminal Law*, 5 vols, Stevens, London, 1948–86, iii, pp. 221 note 2, and 227–28.

23. 'Reflections occasioned by the perusal of a recent treatise on Indigence, etc.': *Monthly Magazine*, xxvi (1808) pp. 108–12 (at p. 111).

24. Colquhoun, *Treatise on the Police*, p. 88.

25. *P.P.* 1816 (510) v, *Report on the State of the Police of the Metropolis*, pp. 29, 143–44 and 212.

26. Ibid., pp. 29–30 (for comments on shopkeepers) and pp. 42, 56 and 63 (for comments on parents); *P.P.* 1828 (533) vi, *Select Committee on the Police of the Metropolis*, p. 57 (shopkeepers) and pp. 48, 59, 85 and 145 (parents).
27. *P.P.* 1816 (510) v, *Report on the State of the Police of the Metropolis*, pp. 18–21, 38–41 and 48–49.
28. *Hansard*, new series, xiii (1825), col. 300; *Hansard* new series, xiv (1826), col. 1243. Though it probably needs to be emphasised that in each of these instances the discussion was centred on rural, rather than urban crime.
29. *P.P.* 1828 (533) vi, *Select Committee on the Police of the Metropolis*, p. 38; for suggestions that unemployment and poverty may have contributed to crime see pp. 56, 84, 134 and 226.
30. *P.P.* 1816 (510) v, *Report on the State of the Police of the Metropolis*, p. 215.
31. *P.P.* 1828 (533) vi, *Select Committee on the Police of the Metropolis*, pp. 40 and 63.
32. Fielding, *An Enquiry*, p. 4.
33. Colquhoun, *A Treatise on the Police*, p. vii.
34. U.C.L. Chadwick MSS 11 f.2.
35. *P.P.* 1839 (169) xix, *Royal Commission on Constabulary*, pp. 7, 10.
36. Ibid., p. 68.
37. **Raphael Samuel**, 'Comers and goers', in **H. J. Dyos** and **M. Wolff** (eds.), *The Victorian City*, 2 vols. R.K.P., London, 1973, chap. 5.
    For similar statements about vagrancy being a cause of crime see *P.P.* 1852–53 (71) xxxvi, *Select Committee on Police*, qq. 844–45, 1416, 1423–24, 1775, 3004–7 and 3722.
38. *P.P.* 1839 (169) xix, *Royal Commission on Constabulary*, pp. 34 and 67.
39. *P.P.* 1834 (599) viii, *Select Committee on Inquiry into Drunkenness*, p. vi.
40. **Susan Magarey** has written of the 'invention' of juvenile delinquency between 1820 and 1850 ('The invention of juvenile delinquency in early nineteenth-century England', *Labour History*, **34** (1978), pp. 11–27). While it probably is true to note a growth in the concern about juvenile offenders during this period it must be remembered that eighteenth-century commentators like Henry Fielding and Jonas Hanway also expressed anxiety about criminal activities committed by boys and young men.
41. **Jelinger C. Symons**, *Special Report on Reformatories in Gloucestershire, Shropshire, Worcestershire, Herefordshire and Monmouthshire, and in Wales* (Printed in the Minutes of the Parliamentary Committee on Education, *P.P.* 1857–58), p. 236.
42. **John Glyde**, jun., *The Moral, Social and Religious condition of Ipswich in the Middle of the Nineteenth Century*, Ipswich, 1850, reprinted S. R. Publishers, Wakefield, 1971, p. 66. The same point was made by Lord Brougham: 'Those who had the mere power to read perused only the narratives of banditti, of swindlers, of thieves; they filled their minds with that species of information which only polluted'. *Hansard*, 3rd series, xc (1847), col. 200.
43. Glyde, *Moral Condition of Ipswich*, p. 111.
44. Symons, *Special Report on Reformatories*, p. 223.
45. **David Vincent**, *Bread, Knowledge and Freedom: A study of nineteenth-century working class autobiography*, Europa, London, 1981, p. 49.
46. **Thomas Plint**, *Crime in England: Its relation, character, and extent as*

developed from 1901 to 1848, London, 1851, pp. 84–85. For similar explanations about crime in Suffolk see John Glyde, jun. *Suffolk in the Nineteenth Century: Physical, social, moral, religious and industrial*, London, 1856, pp. 132–33 and 156–58.

47. **John Clay**, 'On the effect of good or bad times on committals to prison', *Journal of the Statistical Society*, xviii (1855), pp. 74–79; **M. D. Hill**, *Suggestions for the Repression of Crime, Contained in Charges Delivered to Grand Juries of Birmingham*, London, 1857, p. 109.

48. Both quotations are in **David Philips**, *Crime and Authority in Victorian England*, Croom Helm, London, 1977, pp. 13–14.

49. **Gertrude Himmelfarb**, *The Idea of Poverty: England in the early Industrial Age*, Faber and Faber, London, 1984, p. 435.

50. **Louis Chevalier**, *Classes Laborieuses et Classes Dangereuses à Paris pendant la Première Moitié du XIXe Siècle*, Librarie Plon, Paris, 1958 (English translation, RKP London, 1973). For a critique of Chevalier see **George Rudé**, *Debate on Europe 1815–50*, Harper and Row, New York, 1972, pp. 78–87.

51. **H. W. Holland**, 'Professional thieves', *Cornhill Magazine*, vi (1862), pp. 640–53 (at p. 653).

52. **Anthony S. Wohl**, *Endangered Lives: Public health in Victorian Britain*, Methuen, London, 1984, pp. 130–31.

53. **H. W. Holland**, 'Thieves and thieving', *Cornhill Magazine*, ii (1860) pp. 326–44 (at p. 339).

54. **J. Ginswick** (ed.), *Labour and the Poor in England and Wales*, 8 vols., Frank Cass, London, 1983, i, p. 79.

55. **Charles Dickens**, 'On Duty with Inspector Field', in *Reprinted Pieces*.

56. **J. Ormsby**, 'A day's pleasure with the criminal classes', *Cornhill Magazine*, ix (1864), pp. 627–40.

57. **Henry Mayhew**, *The Morning Chronicle Surveyor of Labour and the Poor: The metropolitan districts*, Caliban Books, Firle, 1980, i, p. 40. The first letter in the series was published in the *Morning Chronicle* 19 October 1849, the last 12 December 1850.

58. Ibid., i, pp. 90, 94, 102 and 107.

59. Ibid. ii, pp. 239–40.

60. Henry Mayhew, *et al, London Labour and the London Poor*, 4 vols., London, 1861–62, i, pp. 2–3, 43 and 148.

61. Ibid., iv, pp. 29, 30.

62. Ibid., iv, p. 25.

63. Ibid., iv, p. xii.

64. **James Greenwood**, *The Seven Curses of London*, London, 1869 (reprinted, Basil Blackwell, Oxford, 1981), p. 57.

65. *The Times*, 29 March 1870.

66. Greenwood, *Seven Curses*, pp. 42 and 83.

67. Holland, 'Professional thieves', p. 653.

68. *The Times*, 14 April 1865.

69. Greenwood, *Seven Curses*, p. 59.

70. **David de Guistino**, *Conquest of Mind: Phrenology and Victorian social thought*, Croom Helm, London, 1975, pp. 145–53.

71. Quoted in **Richard White**, *Inventing Australia: Images and identity 1688–1980*, Allen and Unwin, Sydney, 1981, p. 66.

72. Quoted in **Philip Priestley**, *Victorian Prison Lives: English prison biography*, Methuen, London, 1985, p. 78.
73. *Morning Chronicle*, 11 March 1850.
74. **Charles Booth**, *Life and Labour of the People in London 1st series, Poverty*, 4 vols., London, 1902, i, p. 174.
75. **Arnold White**, *Problems of a Great City*, London, 1886, p. 47.
76. Booth, *Life and Labour, Poverty*, i, p. 175.
77. **L. Gordon Rylands**, *Crime: Its causes and remedy*, London, 1889, pp. 46 and 92.
78. **Havelock Ellis**, *The Criminal*, London, 1890, pp. 206, 214 and 229.
79. Idem, *The Task of Social Hygiene*, London, 1912, p. 2.
80. **W. D. Morrison**, *Crime and its Causes*, London, 1891, pp. 85, 140 and 199.
81. Idem, 'The increase of crime', *Nineteenth Century*, xxxi, (1892), pp, 950–57 (at p. 957); idem, *Crime and its Causes*, pp. 141–42.
82. Holland, 'Thieves and Thieving', p. 340.
83. **Michael Sturma**, 'Eye of the beholder: The stereotype of women convicts, 1788–1852', *Labour History*, **34**, (1978), pp. 3–10.
84. Quoted in **Frances Finnegan**, *Poverty and Prostitution: A study of Victorian prostitutes in York*, Cambridge U.P., 1979, p. 7. See also **Judith R. Walkowitz**, *Prostitution and Victorian Society: Women, class and the state*, Cambridge U.P., 1980, pp. 25, 38–39 and 41–45. Acton drew much of his inspiration from the pioneering work in Paris almost half a century earlier, of A. J. B. Parent-Duchâtelet. For an excellent introduction to the latter see **Jill Harsin**, *Policing Prostitution in Nineteenth-Century Paris*, Princeton U.P., 1983.
85. For the contemporary concerns see **David J. Smith** and **Jeremy Gray**, *Police and People in London*, Gower, London, 1985, p. 32.
86. **Bernard Waites**, 'The effects of the First World War on aspects of the class structure of English society', unpublished Ph.D. The Open University, 1983, pp. 56–57.
87. **Douglas Hay**, 'Poaching and the Game Laws on Cannock Chase', in **Douglas Hay, Peter Linebaugh, E. P. Thompson** *et al, Albion's Fatal Tree: Crime and society in eighteenth-century England*, Allen Lane, London, 1975.
88. *Sussex Express*, 1 March 1879.
89. Sharpe, *Crime in Early Modern England*, chap. 4, pp. 79–80 especially; **R. A. E. Wells**, 'Sheep-rustling in Yorkshire in the age of the Industrial and Agricultural Revolutions', *Northern History*, xx, (1984), pp. 127–45 (at p. 139).
90. **David Jones**, *Crime, Protest, Community and Police in Nineteenth-century Britain*, RKP, London, 1982, pp. 78–79 and 83–84.
91. Himmelfarb, *The Idea of Poverty*, p. 234.
92. Quoted in ibid., p. 182.
93. **V. de Sola Pinto** and **A. E. Rodway**, *The Common Muse: Popular British ballad poetry from the fifteenth to the twentieth Century*, Chatto and Windus, London, 1957, p. 236.
94. Recorded on *Waterloo-Peterloo: English folksongs and broadsides 1780–1830*, by the Critics Group, Argo Record Company, 1968.
95. Himmelfarb *The Idea of Poverty*, chap. xvii. It is interesting to note how time gave respectability. The *Athenaeum's* reviewer of Ainsworth's Jack

Sheppard condemned it as a 'bad book' because it contained all the 'inherent coarseness and vulgarity of the subject'. He drew a contrast with **Fielding**'s *Jonathan Wild* and **Gay**'s *The Beggar's Opera* whose effect was to 'raise the public in the moral and intellectual scale'. (Quoted in ibid., p. 428). The reviewer was clearly ignorant of the obloquy heaped on *The Beggar's Opera* at least until the end of the eighteenth century and the accusations that the character of Macheath was so glamorous that many young men were seeking to emulate him as highwaymen. See **Percy A. Scholes**, *The Oxford Companion to Music*, 10th edn., Oxford U.P., 1970, pp. 95 and 101, plate 18,6.

96. *Illustrated London News*, 30 May 1868; *The Times*, 23 May 1884. Summing up the case of a soldier in the Rifle Brigade who had attempted to kill his girl friend as part of a suicide pact, the judge commented: 'He supposed these people had been reading novels'. *The Times*, 18 July 1860.

97. Both quotations in **Patrick Dunae**, 'The penny dreadfuls: Boy's literature and crime, 1870–1900', *Social History Society Newsletter*, vol. 2, no. 1, p. 6.

Chapter 4

ENVIRONMENTAL PERCEPTIONS

Contemporaries who thought and wrote about crime in England between 1750 and 1900 perceived it largely as an urban problem. London, the largest city in western Europe, was the focus for the concerns of both Henry Fielding and Patrick Colquhoun. The former lamented that:

> Whoever ... considers the Cities of London and Westminster, with the late vast Addition of their Suburbs; the great Irregularity of their Buildings, the immense Number of Lanes, Alleys, Courts and Byeplaces; must think that, had they been intended for the very Purpose of Concealment, they could scarce have been better contrived.

Colquhoun described London as:

> not only the grand magazine of the British Empire, but also the general receptacle for the idle and depraved of almost every Country, and certainly from every quarter of the dominions of the Crown; – where the temptations and resources for criminal pleasures – gambling – fraud and depredation, as well as for pursuits of honest industry almost exceed imagination.[1]

Most of the more alarming, and certainly the best publicised of nineteenth-century crimes were committed in London.[2] Yet, in spite of the dominance of London, during the nineteenth century, students of criminal behaviour and the criminal class looked beyond the metropolis and found crime in the burgeoning urban environments with their teeming, anonymous populations and their uneducated, nomadic poor living in insanitary slums. Thomas Plint fused the assessments of Fielding and Colquhoun when he declared that:

> The pickpocket and the thief can find no nesting-place amongst the statesmen of Cumberland and Westmoreland, or the miners of Durham and Cornwall. They fly to Birmingham, London, Manchester, Liverpool, Leeds. They congregate where there is plenty of plunder, and verge enough to hide in.

In 1867 James T. Hammick emphasises 'that the criminal classes are, for the most part, congregated in the towns.' For the Reverend William Douglas Morrison it could 'easily be ascertained without the aid of any figures' that cities were 'the nurseries of modern crime'. Implicit in what Hammick and Morrison had to say, and explicit in Plint, was the notion that crime in rural society was not as serious. This was an idea shared by many and articulated most powerfully by opponents of the new police in the 1830s and 1840s. 'In cities', according to the Reverend Charles Brereton:

> the majority of thieves exist in gangs, practise fraud by profession, and live by a constant series of depredations ... criminals in the country only occasionally once or twice a year steal a sheep, pig, corn, hay, wood, turnips, poultry as the case may be.

This was just one of the many reasons why, according to Brereton, the Metropolitan Police model was inapplicable to rural England. Towards the end of the century such ideas had been developed by enthusiasts for the Settlement Movement who urged young gentlemen to spend time doing 'good works' in slum areas like London's East End. What was lacking in these districts, according to Canon Barnett, the founder of Toynbee Hall, was 'a leisured class ... who will see that the laws are carried out and generally keep the social life going'. Canon Henry Scott Holland, an early enthusiast for Oxford House, summed this perception up with his call to young gentlemen to 'Come and be the squires of East London'.[3] All of this can best be understood in terms of the vision of a contented rustic England which developed during the nineteenth century and in which the stability and tranquillity of rural society were emphasised to compensate for the terrors of urbanisation and recurrent concern about the effects of the industrial economy.

The attempts of various sociologists and social anthropologists to explain the differences between rural and urban life styles has given a theoretical underpinning to the belief that rural crime and urban crime are markedly different. Most notable in this respect is the *Gemeinschaft-Gesellschaft* dichotomy put forward by the German sociologist Ferdinand Tönnies: in traditional society, generally equated with rural society, people live in a face to face community where social mobility is low, customs and actions are legitimated in terms of custom and precedent; modern society, in contrast, is impersonal and a variety of voluntarily formed associations regulate different aspects of social life.[4] *Anomie*, or social instability particularly resulting from the disruption, or disappearance of value systems in the teeming new cities of the nineteenth century, has also been popular in explaining a growth of crime during the great period of industrialisation and urbanisation. At the close of the nineteenth century some European criminologists and social investigators, notably Émile Durkheim, were concerned that the city, together with the spread of 'modern civilisation', was destabilising the 'equilibrium' of certain individuals and prompting degeneracy and deviance. In the words of Havelock Ellis: 'Like insanity, criminality flourishes among migrants, and our civilisation is bringing us all, more or less into the position of migrants'.[5] These concepts implicitly, though perhaps not always consciously, inform the comments of a variety of historians. J. J. Tobias, for example, concluded that:

> The large towns during much of the nineteenth century failed to provide the support which former country dwellers had known in the smaller communities from which they came. Entry into the criminal class was a means of finding suport; it was entry into an association, informal but none the less, members of which could be found almost everywhere.[6]

Obviously environment to some extent dictates the forms and styles of crime. White-collar crime depends on particular forms of economic and social structure generally rooted in a bureaucratic and urbanised society. Street robbery, by definition, could not happen in a corn field or forest; similarly poaching and sheep-stealing, common offences in the eighteenth and nineteenth centuries, could only be rural offences, though not necessarily committed by rural dwellers; several large towns in the Midlands and East Anglia had poachers working from their suburbs in the nineteenth century.[7] Some London gangs were suspected of secretly killing other animals, notably horses, and then offering to buy the carcasses from the owners for horse meat.[8] Sheep-stealers and rustlers were drawn similarly from both town and country, as well as from a variety of social groups; and motives were varied. Rural and urban poverty could be a spur, though it seems possible that in some districts there was almost a tradition of periodically improving the family diet with stolen mutton. Sometimes resentment or revenge appears to have motivated the rural sheep stealer; and, on occasions, as in the case of poaching, sheep were taken to provide butchers with illicit meat for the urban market.[9]

Arson, while it was occasionally employed as a weapon during trade disputes,[10] was primarily a rural offence, and environment was a contributory element. The farmer's house was known and it was unlikely to be in a distinct, middle-class district; his barns and ricks, like his sheep and other livestock were vulnerable on dark nights in ways which factories, or workshops in tolerably lighted streets, subject to increasing police patrols, were not. A casual agricultural labourer, angered or victimised by a farmer, could exact prompt revenge and the chances of getting away with it seemed reasonable. At the very end of 1841 the Reverend Henry Owen, a magistrate living at Haveringham in Suffolk, saw £80-worth of his corn go up in flames. The Chief Constable believed that the outrage was committed 'in consequence of the Revd Mr Owen having punished some persons of bad character in the neighbourhood'.[11] In 1845 William Grange set fire to the hay and corn stacks of John Handysides, a farmer of Ackham in the North Riding, when Handysides dismissed him without payment. Grange declared at his trial that he intended to show Handysides 'an example that farmers should treat their labourers with respect and not clandestinely as he had done'. He was found guilty and transported. The Chief Constable of the East Riding reported to the quarter sessions in January 1864 that the 'illiterate rustic' was easily offended and that:

> the majority of these evil-doers, of course, are those who have been discharged from their employments, or punished for offences, or refused favours, or warned to be on their good behaviour, or deluded into an idea of wrong or an insult to their families.[12]

Insurance companies rightly recognised that the problem was not one-sided and warned their agents to enquire whether farmers were deemed 'obnoxious' in their locality before undertaking to offer their services; in addition they surcharged unpopular farmers who were already policyholders.[13]

About half of those arrested for arson in the East Riding during the 1860s were agricultural labourers and several of these were itinerants, locally known as Wolds Rangers – defined by a prosecuting counsel as 'a man who travels the Wolds getting work from day to day and consequently being fully conversant with the district'.[14] Vagrants were much involved with a wave of arson in north Wales, the border countries and the Midlands during the 1860s and, according to one contemporary, from then until the closing years of the century arson remained 'a favourite method of [vagrants] venting spite'.[15]

But rural arson was not always the work of isolated individuals and it was not unknown for villagers to give support to the arsonists' activities by impeding the efforts of fire-fighters.[16] Furthermore it would be erroneous to seek to understand every instance of rural arson in terms of the class war. Henry Clapham set fire to his brother's stack at Burton Pidsea in the East Riding as part of a family feud.[17] George Serle, alias Edwin Serle, alias Walter Tomlinson, alias Cockayne, alias Thompson, born in Belper, Derbyshire, and a horse-trimmer by trade, had a long career of starting fires. In 1854 he was sentenced to one year's hard labour for arson in Derbyshire; five years later he was sentenced to five years' penal servitude for setting fire to stacks of wheat and hay at Biggleswade, Bedfordshire. Shortly after the expiration of this sentence the Nottinghamshire Lent Assizes of 1866 gave him fifteen years' penal servitude for a similar offence.[18] Serle appears to have delighted in lighting fires. More prosaically, some fires were started by property owners in the attempt to defraud their insurance companies, while others were simply the result of children playing with matches.[19]

Animal maiming was also overwhelmingly a rural crime, for obvious reasons; and it had other similarities with arson. Personal feuds between members of the same social class, revenge, and elements of social protest can be detected among the motives. The brutal, grisly, often very bloody and messy injuries inflicted on the sexual organs of a few of the animal victims suggest that some of the perpetrators were seeking other kinds of gratification.[20]

The availability of shot-guns in rural areas, combining with the greater problems of surveillance, meant that pot-shots were sometimes taken at informants and policemen, probably to a far greater degree than in urban areas. This was especially the case in Suffolk during the rural disorders of the 1840s. In March 1844 Charles Grimmer, a farmer of Pakefield near Lowestoft, heard two shots outside his house and on going to a window he received a shot-gun blast in the shoulder. 'Mr Grimmer', noted the Chief Constable:

> has on several occasions taken an active part with Police to detect a gang of thieves that reside near him which is the cause assigned for the attempt upon his life.[21]

Rural communities, however, as explained below,[22] were not the only ones in which informers and certain types of offender could find themselves set upon or ostracised.

The level of sophistication might also contribute to both types of crime and responses to crime. The rural poor often did not see Christianity and Paganism as mutually exclusive. They combined the two in their own distinctive world view, though Paganism became less significant as the nineteenth century wore on.[23] Girls in rural districts, anxious to discover future husbands or to attract particular young men, sometimes butchered and mistreated animals in ways which sickened rational and sensitive Victorians. In February 1848 Mary Brice, Jane Matthews and Sarah Page were brought before Bletsoe Petty Sessions by the Bedfordshire Constabulary under 5 and 6 William IV cap. 59 for torturing a cat. They were fined and sentenced to short periods of hard labour in the house of correction. The prison chaplain was appalled by their offence:

> The three females ... had the barbarous cruelty – a cruelty that sickens the very heart, to open up with a pair of scissors the body of a *living cat*, and take out her *heart* ... the motive was most ignorant and superstitious. It was the belief that, by *sticking pins* in the poor animal's heart, and then *burying* it in the earth, they would *bring back* their *lovers*. This happened in a *village* in Bedfordshire in the year 1848![24]

When crimes were committed against them, at least up until the middle of the nineteenth century, the rural poor seem to have been as inclined to go to 'cunning' or 'wise' men as to constables or policemen. It was even alleged that an escaped thief in Norfolk consulted a 'cunning' woman for a 'safe conduct'. These 'cunning' men and women were professionals who charged fees and whose expertise could be purchased to thwart witches and tell fortunes in addition to identifying thieves and finding stolen, or lost, property.[25] There were other ways of dealing with witches, but in the eyes of the law these could constitute assault. The

Reverend R. M. Healey was asked by a wheelwright to say a few words over a sow which, the wheelwright believed, was being 'overlooked' by a witch. The traditional way of dealing with a witch who 'overlooked' a victim or an animal, was to stick pins in her chair, or otherwise draw her blood and thus render her powerless. The wheelwright confessed that he had not done this as the witch would take him before the Spilsby magistrates, and Victorian magistrates were 'that iggnerant' that they would have fined him. At Cromer in 1847 a group of boys were brought before the magistrates for stoning the poor woman who carried the local letter bag; they wanted to draw the blood 'of the old witch'.[26]

Some historians, though not specifically with reference to Britain, have detected more significant differences between rural and urban crime. Rural society, it has been argued, being more primitive, had a higher incidence of inter-personal crime than urban areas. In the latter the disorganisation created by urban growth, or simply the greater opportunity for theft provided by the urban environment, led to a greater incidence of property crime.[27] Such conclusions fit comfortably with both Marxian and Modernization theories of social and economic development, though they have received a severe battering directed primarily at the data bases upon which they were constructed. Furthermore it has been emphasised by Jim Sharpe, that property crime, as measured by indictments and executions for such offences, fell markedly between the early seventeenth and early eighteenth centuries, namely during the period generally portrayed as so significant for the rise of English capitalism.[28]

Towns and cities appeared to both eighteenth and nineteenth-century social commentators as anonymous, dangerous and dirty, particularly those areas where the poorer sections of the community lived. When the poor had only one room for the family then the courtyard, the street and the pub became centres for leisure and recreation, for meeting and arguing; the courtyard and the street became sites for displaying wares, selling hot food and dumping rubbish. Many streets, in consequence, appeared to be owned by the poor; and the elite could never know these teeming, jostling masses in the way that they knew retainers on their estates or supposed that their predecessors had known whole communities. The poor became exotic 'wandering tribes' to be described by a Mayhew; they also became objects of social policy to enable the respectable among them to prosper, and to make the residuum among them respectable. At the same time there emerged a romantic view of a passed Golden Age: for Fielding this was before the corruption of society, and especially the poor, by the luxury and wealth created by trade; for William Cobbett it was before the development of 'the thing' and 'the infernal wen' of London. The Golden Age was to be found in a romantic Merrie England, and even before Joseph Strutt had published his *Glig Gamena Angel-Deod, or the Sports and Pastimes of the People of England* (1801) or William Thomas had coined the word 'folklore',[29] gentlemen were in pursuit of the popular recreations of rural England so as to preserve them in 'Calendars' or 'Everyday Books'. Historians critical of the shape of the industrial revolution and what it meant for the working class, once implied that it saw the destruction of a reasonably contented rural society. More recently, historians of the customs and rituals of the old rural community have followed a similar tack; the new economic order of industrialising Britain, in its attempt to establish a rational and compliant workforce, battered away remorselessly at the old popular culture with its undeniable brutality, horseplay and lack of deference. The reconstruction of custom and ritual in rural, or 'pre-industrial' communities, has been invaluable; yet some of the conclusions drawn about the criminalisation of aspects of traditional behaviour, might tend to mislead.

Largesse was a customary rural practice at harvest time. It was, according to Bob Bushaway, a way 'in which harvest wages were supplemented'. In some areas the chosen chief of a gang of labourers would request money from any person passing a field wherein harvesting was in progress. Elsewhere labourers solicited largesse by going from door to door in a neighbourhood. The behaviour had an implicit element of threat, but it was also a levy 'made on the whole community, as a recognition of and reward for the labourer's work during harvest'.[30] The key questions here are where, if at all, can a line be drawn between largesse and extortion and what the precise difference was between largesse, which folklorists could find acceptable in a rural community of the past, and extortion which was repugnant? The notion of largesse manifestly did not enter into Lord Fortescue's condemnation of 'sturdy beggars' infesting parts of Devonshire in the 1850s:

> Numbers of sturdy beggars, particularly in summer, invade our farmhouses and cottages and in the absence of the men extort money or provisions from the women who they find at home. Indeed in this house I have for some years kept at my own expense an assistant constable in the shape of a trusty labourer to repel the above class of visitors, some of whom when they have been saucy I have committed to Bridewell where they have almost invariably been recognised as old offenders.

Fielder King, a substantial landholder in Hampshire and Sussex spoke similarly of 'vagrants ... alarming the females in the house and obtaining alms from fear rather than charity'.[31]

To switch momentarily from a problematic concept taken from the study of rural life to an unpleasant event which occurred in the urban world and which created a major stir in newspaper columns: on 3 August 1874 Richard Morgan, a twenty-five year old warehouse porter in Liverpool, was on his way home from a day out with his wife and brother, when he was accosted on the corner of Tithebarn Street and Lower Milk Street. John McCrave, alias Quinn, Michael Mullen and Peter Campbell asked him for sixpence; when he refused they set about him. Samuel Morgan sought to defend his brother. A crowd gathered and urged on the assailants; the crowd cried out a warning when the police appeared, and impeded Samuel Morgan's pursuit of the attackers. Richard Morgan died as a result of his beating; the doctors called it 'nervous shock', finding his heart 'to a slight extent fatty and large, though scarcely to the extent of disease'. Morgan's death brought the phenomenon of the Liverpool 'Cornermen' dramatically to public notice. The Recorder of Liverpool called for more police; his colleagues elsewhere, and a succession of newspapers, expressed outrage at the level of violence. McCrave and his fellows were arrested, tried and executed. They were not harvesters demanding recognition and reward for their work, they came from a community of casual labourers who eked out their existence on Liverpool's docks. That community backed them against both the victim and the police; it would appear to have considered outsiders at least as fair game for the urban equivalent of largesse. The attack on Morgan was not an isolated event.[32]

Mumming was another way of extracting money or goods in the rural community. The mummers performed their plays for all ranks of people and thus, according to Bushaway, emphasised the social cohesion of the old society. Mumming became increasingly obsolete as the nineteenth-century progressed.[33] At New Year in Bradford during the 1860s, however, mummers – men and boys with blackened faces – crossed into middle-class districts and even forced their way into middle-class homes demanding money and drink.[34] In 1887 a correspondent of *The Times* expressed alarm about 'the increasingly aggressive character of the roughs' who were to be found in London's suburbs:

> At Essex Villas, Kensington, yesterday, upon my wife reaching home with a box outside her brougham, a rough who had followed, waiting until the coachman drove off, forced his way into the hall, and refused to leave until he was given something. While the police were being sent for he, during 10 minutes, indulged in the most loathsome abuse, evidently hoping to terrify the lady into acceding to his demands. He only left when the policeman appeared in the street, and then he only strolled away, for, as he stated, he did not care for all the police in London. The policeman would take no action, merely seeing him down the street in a leisurely fashion. At the police station I am informed my only remedy is by summons.[35]

The Kensington rough described above appears to have made no attempt to act as a mummer or to offer any service, other than his departure, for his payment. But several questions are posed by each variety of urban extortion described here, especially, when money was demanded in the form of largesse or to reward mumming. Obviously Liverpool Cornermen and Bradford Mummers, and London 'roughs' did not see themselves as reinforcing community cohesion; they wanted something, and were prepared to use coercion, intimidation and physical violence to get it. But what did the rural practitioners of largesse and mumming think that they were doing? Their behaviour may, at one time, have reinforced community solidarity. Yet recent historical research has pushed unified village communities further and further back in time; there are doubts about their existence in the mid sixteenth century;[36] and whether the average, typical mummer or harvest gang leader (whatever such a being was) ever consciously thought in such terms is highly debatable. Furthermore, even in the second half of the eighteenth century, much harvesting was being done by itinerant labouring gangs, and any demands for largesse on their part would hardly have been reinforcing local communities. Unquestionably during the eighteenth and nineteenth centuries there was an assault on such forms of popular culture as largesse and mumming; the question remains as to when such institutions were ever accepted by all participants in the ritual in the ideal form which was allegedly destroyed by the assault on popular culture. Richard Cobb once queried whether research into rioters and their behaviour was not tending to make them rather too respectable.[37] The same question might be posed with reference to the custom and rituals of rural plebeians; it is surely not just cynicism or class prejudice to suggest that some of the men who sought alms and/or largesse in the late eighteenth and early nineteenth centuries were just as nasty and unscrupulous as Fortescue and King implied.

Urbanisation did not destroy the ability of groups bound by work, ethnic, religious or other ties, from existing as communities; nor did it leave the new urban dweller as an isolated individual among a society of strangers. Irish immigrants, and their descendants, remained in readily identifiable enclaves. New migrants sometimes came with recommendations to those from their villages who had gone before. These immigrants brought practices from their rural backgrounds with them, which, like keeping pigs and faction fights were often ill-suited to their cramped urban dwellings. Such behaviour, while it concerned and alienated the native population, may have served to reinforce the communities' Irishness. The smaller levels of immigration by Jews from Holland and Germany in the eighteenth century and from Eastern Europe at the end of the nineteenth century reveals similar communal solidarity. But a comparison of Irish and Jewish immigrants in nineteenth-century British cities also provided an object lesson against the simple notion of immigrant ghetto areas equating with criminal areas. The Irish were notorious for alleged criminality, though their offences were primarily of the public order variety as is evidenced by a cursory glance at the headlines of any nineteenth-century urban newspaper produced in a town with a significant Irish population, as well as by court records.[38] Jews were singled out as criminal in late eighteenth and early nineteenth-century London. There was particular outrage in the 1770s following the murder of a servant who tried to resist a gang of Jewish burglars in Chelsea in 1771. Jews appear to have played prominent roles as coiners and receivers in Georgian London; Dickens's Fagin had at last one well-known original in Ikey Solomons. The Jewish community had its share of pickpockets and petty thieves, and the poorer members were known to fight and riot in the same kinds of ways as the poorer classes of London; however they were never as closely indentified with drink as the Irish. The reputation of Jewish criminals prompted a reforming campaign by respectable, well-to-do Anglo-Jewry. Partly because of this reforming campaign and also the strict regulations imposed on tenants in the tenements built for immigrants by Jewish philanthropists, the East European Jews who entered the country towards the end of the nineteenth century acquired a reputation (generally, and not always deserved) for keeping out of trouble. This was even the case when the tenements were sited in what were formerly notorious districts.[39] Turning away from the special case of immigrants, Robert Roberts who was brought up in 'the classic slum' in Salford at the beginning of the twentieth century, recalled how his community was a village with his parents' corner shop one of the focal points. The 'village' had man-made boundaries: railway tracks to the north and south, a different slum village to the east and, to the west, 'lay the middle classes, bay-windowed and begardened'.[40]

The principal problem with the urban-rural division in seeking to understand crime is that it is simply too crude. Urban and rural are opposite ends of a spectrum and however the extremes are defined, there is a vast area between them. Indeed for much of the eighteenth and nineteenth centuries most Englishmen lived in neither big industrial cities nor on the land, but in small towns, some of which, like Exeter and York, boasted the title of city. These small towns were centres for rural society, and had been for centuries: they had markets and fairs; some were the meeting places for Quarter Sessions and Assizes; and some, as boroughs, had their own courts. The focus of these towns remained essentially rural. But, at the same time, there were areas which, while rural in setting, were essentially focussed on burgeoning economic and industrial development. The industrial villages of the West Riding provide one example; the pit villages in the coalfields of Durham and Northumberland provide another.

Urban and rural also break down significantly at the extremes. No two cities are entirely similar and different economic structures and different functions provide opportunities for different types of crime. Seaports and garrison towns offered wider opportunities for the 'victimless crime' of prostitution. Ipswich was a garrison town and, with a population of nearly 33,000 in the mid-nineteenth century, it was alleged to have fifty-two brothels.[41] Seaports also generated other forms of crime. In 1811 the magistrates of the Thames Police Office reported:

> In our District and Experience ... we find Riots and dangerous affrays among foreign seamen (many of whom continue on shore until they are

destitute and then seek a support by plunder) the most prevalent offences and most difficult to be prevented.[42]

Discharged merchant seamen, their pockets bulging with pay, encouraged other forms of offences. 'Street robberies and particularly larceny from the person (chiefly committed on seafaring people)' appeared the most prevalent forms of crime in the Whitechapel district of Regency London; the perpetrators, according to the magistrates, were 'pickpockets and prostitutes'.[43] The docks and warehouses of major ports provided greater opportunities, if not greater rewards than the much smaller canal wharfs of, for example, Manchester and Birmingham. The prevalence of small metal trades, together with the employment of boys to take unfinished goods from one small workshop to another, was considered a key element contributing to the scale of juvenile offences in mid nineteenth-century Birmingham.[44]

But if different towns and cities provide different opportunities for crime, the Chicago 'School' of Human Ecology urged, half a century ago, that it is possible to generalise about urban social structure particularly with reference to the zonal arrangements of land-use, physical conditions and demographic structure. Drawing on such conclusions R. N. Davidson has suggested an 'eclectic typology of the urban environment' for portraying urban neighbourhoods in terms of their crime characteristics; 'eclectic because of the stubborn refusal of the ecological dimensions to provide a neat framework to the classification'.[45] While it is not possible for the historian to amass the data of the modern criminologist and thus parallel all of Davidson's nuances, a rough division of the city into centre, commercial and industrial zones, inner-city residential districts and suburbs is of immense value in helping to comprehend the criminal characteristics of urban neighbourhoods in the past.

The city centre attracts crowds to its shops and its entertainments. These crowds provide opportunities for the pickpocket and the prostitute. Shops provide opportunities for shoplifting and, together with offices, for burglary. Entertainments provide the possibilities for affrays and minor assaults. The commercial and industrial zones, often near the centre, provide opportunities for theft and embezzlement though, because the number of people permitted legitimate access is fewer, the level of personal victimisation is also less. However much they structured their perceptions of criminality within contemporary ideology both Fielding and Colquhoun saw the wealth of the metropolis as fostering crime. Colquhoun was particularly concerned about thefts from warehouses and ships on the Thames. Court records, and Arthur Harding's recollections of East End dockers bringing home tea and selling it to corner shopkeepers, reveal such depredations continuing throughout the nineteenth century.[46] In mid nineteenth-century Manchester the Chief Constable denied that the factory system had encouraged theft, but 'the warehousing system, from the value and the portable nature of the property left lying about in great ranges of rooms, was to a certain degree prolific of theft'.[47] John Rawlinson, a London Police Magistrate, told the Select Committee on the Police of the Metropolis in 1828, that the increasing exposure of goods in shop doors encouraged theft. A decade later the Superintendent of D Division of the Metropolitan Police noted:

> the too frequent practice of shopkeepers exposing their goods for sale outside of their shops [which] affords an easy facility to plunder, together with the ready mode of disposing of such plunder at Marine store shops, old clothes shops etc.

In 1865, echoing the comments of Colonel James Fraser, the Commissioner of the City of London Police, *The Times* expressed amazement at 'the unsuspecting confidence of the commercial, or, at least, the shopkeeping world'. As for pilfering from industrial areas, the Superintendent of K Division of the Metropolitan Police informed the Constabulary Force Commissioners that:

> Robberies to an immense extent are daily occurring by workmen at large Factories, but I am informed by the Principals, that the men would not submit to be searched indiscriminately and continually, and that the combination amongst them is so strong that a strike would be the result.[48]

It is apparent that there was a vast amount of theft from the workplace in mid nineteenth-century London, but it is impossible to put a figure on how much was taken, where from, or by whom.

In contemporary society there is a high concentration of crime and of offenders in certain inner-city residential areas. Davidson divides these areas into two basic sub-types: residual areas, in which there is an element of social cohesion and a degree of balance in the demographic structure; and transitional areas with high turnovers of population and few family units. There was tremendous mobility in the nineteenth-century city, even among the respectable working class; indeed moving could be a mark of respectability with a move being the only way in which a family could get into lodgings which did not require immediate repairs.[49] But, that said, movement was often not very far within the city and it remains possible to detect both residual and transitional districts.

Not every residual district appeared prone to crime, but some were notorious. Irish districts were singled out as particularly criminal: the Bedern in York, Caribee Island and Stafford Street in Wolverhampton offer good examples during the thirty or forty years following potato famine. But criminality here was, primarily, in respect of public order.[50] Some, and not simply Irish districts, became virtual 'no-go areas' for the police and, more particularly, for the rent collector and landlord.[51] It may be that there was a high level of theft within such districts which, because of the inhabitants' antipathy to the police, was never reported. Victims might also be intimidated into not bringing charges and this,

David Jones has suggested, could be one reason why the statistics might belie the undoubted criminality of the 'China' district of mid nineteenth-century Merthyr Tydfil, a 'frontier town of the industrial revolution'. While respectable society rejected the population of 'China', that population itself reveals bonds of family, self-respect, independence, and a unity of self interest.[52] The bonds uniting the community of 'China' would seem similar to those which brought the Liverpudlians of Tithe Barn Street and Lower Milk Street to the defence of McCrave and his fellow Cornermen, and which united the population of the Jago, or Nicol, in Arthur Harding's childhood. The police, and others, stigmatised such areas as the aphorism 'guarding St James by watching St Giles' testifies of itself; until its destruction in the mid-nineteenth century, notably by the cutting of New Oxford Street, the St Giles 'rookery' was regarded with horror by respectable Londoners and the Reverend Thomas Beames explicitly compared it with the Faubourg St Antoine of Paris, notorious for its plebeian revolutionaries. Other residential areas stigmatised as criminal were to be found elsewhere in London and in provincial towns and cities at the end of the nineteenth century; as one area was cleared, so the mantle of most criminal district or street, was passed on to another.[53]

In some respects certain residual areas, especially those where the landlords and rent collectors dare not go and repairs were never made, may have been worse in respect of poverty and squalor than transitional districts with their lodging houses – at least after the creation of the system of lodging house supervision in the mid-nineteenth century. Transitional areas were probably the worst centres of anomie, though there are problems in employing this concept to explain crime; there is no justification for seeing crime as the result of an ill-defined 'social disorganisation' when crime might just as well be considered as a fundamental component of such disorganisation.

Lodging houses with their rootless, generally single, populations were suspect at least from the 1750s when Fielding quoted his friend and colleague, Saunders Welch, High Constable of Holborn, at length on the subject. Welch considered that some of the worst of such houses were to be found in St Giles and in St George, Bloomsbury:

> with miserable Beds from the Cellar to the Garret, for ... Twopenny Lodgers ... in these Beds, several of which are in the same Room, Men and Women, often Strangers to each other, lie promiscuously, the Price of a double Bed being no more than Threepence, as an Encouragement to them to lie together ... as these Places are thus adapted to Whoredom, so are they no less provided for Drunkenness, Gin being sold in them all at a Penny a Quartern ... in the Execution of Search Warrants. Mr Welch rarely finds less than Twenty of these Houses open for the Receipt of all Comers at the latest Hours ... in one of these Houses, and that not a large one, he hath numbered 68 Persons of both Sexes, the Stench of whom was so intolerable, that it compelled him in a very short time to quit the Place.[54]

Such images recur throughout the nineteenth century and further illustrate the concerns about itinerants and those with no permanent employment, as well as the determination to equate criminality with physical ugliness. Angus Reach, whose description of a 'low lodging house' in Angel Meadow, Manchester, was quoted in the preceding chapter, reported the city's chief constable as speaking warily of 'a considerable floating population, and a smaller number of persons who are known both to work and steal'.[55]

It is clear that the police stigmatised certain lodging house districts as criminal and, while these were generally the cheapest and poorest, the labelling may have become to some extent self-fulfilling with those who could avoid lodgings in a stigmatised area making every effort so to do. At the same time, given that the 'crime' problem was understood as centring on the mass of petty thefts, a majority of the offenders responsible for these activities probably were to be found in these districts.

Low lodging houses in St Giles and other poor districts of London, in Angel Meadow and in Deansgate, Manchester, and those in Thomas Street, Birmingham, had notorious reputations. The inhabitants of all such districts were doubly vulnerable: on the one hand, having been defined as what a modern sociologist has called 'police property',[56] they suffered regular police searches; on the other, unlike the Irish or the people of Merthyr's 'China', their lack of community cohesion militated against any resistance or unity of self interest. The property of anyone staying in such a lodging house, which obviously would not have been much, was also at risk for most things could be pawned; any property too meagre for the pawn broker could be taken to the dolly shop, and there was always the second hand clothes dealer and the rag and bone man. Again estimates of crime within the transitional neighbourhood, and especially one stigmatised as criminal, are impossible given the relationship between the inhabitants and the police.

Many of the poorer inner-city residential areas became even less salubrious as cities expanded and new transport systems fostered the spread of suburban residential districts. The better districts have much lower offender and offence rates in contemporary society; during the nineteenth century, in comparison with residual and transitory areas of the inner city, public order offences in the suburbs appear to have been tiny. Thefts from gardens and burglaries seem to have been the typical offences. The spread of suburbs may have contributed to the fact that the statistics of burglary and housebreaking resisted the general overall decline in crime from the middle of the nineteenth century. Indicative that suburban districts were the more likely target of the professional, calculating house burglar is the fact that it was in these districts of metropolitan London where, from the mid 1880s, policemen on night beats were authorized to carry revolvers. This authorization came in the wake of two particular burglaries by armed men in Islington and

Wimbledon in the summer of 1883 and because of concern over the availability of cheap revolvers manufactured in Germany. It is, however, also true that policemen in the exterior districts of London had been allowed from early on to carry edged weapons: cutlasses for the men on foot and sabres for those who were mounted. These weapons were countenanced because of the large size and lonely nature of the beats in these districts, often in the countryside, and the consequent inability of a man to get speedy assistance from the constable on a neighbouring beat should he be attacked.[57]

Suburban residential districts, like the elegant and fashionable areas which were still to be found in the centre of some cities, had their own kinds of offenders. The different kinds of white-collar offenders were often to be found living here, and these districts contained a high proportion of domestic servants among whose numbers lurked some who filched from their employers and, occasionally, even illicitly pawned pieces of their employer's property.

The smaller towns and cities also had their mixture of respectable housing and narrow squalid courts harbouring different kinds of offender and providing the opportunities for different kinds of offence. The respectable inhabitants of mid nineteenth-century Horncastle, Lincolnshire, for example, with a population just reaching 4,500 in 1841, were concerned about their 'lawless and immoral' inhabitants. Dog Kennel Yard in particular was notorious for its brothels and prostitution. During the 1840s the town was plagued by two gangs: Frank Kent led a group of adolescents who specialised in aggressively harassing country people and vagrants; Jack Sharpe, a labourer, and Maskell Spencer, a blacksmith, led a different group known as 'The Gang', whose offences included poaching and robbery.[58]

Similar gangs, or at least groups of young men in persistent and varied trouble with the authorities, were to be found in what were, more obviously, rural villages. In the summer of 1825 two young men, James Redman, aged 20 and James Grummet, aged 23, were charged with stealing pistols from troopers of the Bedfordshire Yeomanry Cavalry; the troopers had stopped at the Royal Oak public house in the village of Houghton Conquest on their way home from a training exercise and, foolishly, they had left their pistols in the holsters on their saddles. The local constable had considerable difficulty in hanging on to his prisoners; villagers assaulted him and there were attempts to break the prisoners out of the village cage. At the Midsummer Quarter Sessions Grummet alone was convicted; he was actually seen to take a pistol, Redman it appeared was not. Grummet was sentenced to three months' hard labour, but he was no stranger to Bedford Gaol: in May 1818 he had been sentenced to three months for game law offences, and he had received a similar sentence for similar offences in December 1819. On each occasion the gaoler has cause to describe his behaviour as 'indifferent'. Redman had also been in trouble before. At the Epiphany

Sessions in 1822 the Grand Jury had thrown out a bill of indictment for theft brought against him; eighteen months later he was sentenced to one month's hard labour for stealing a duck. In 1824, with two others, he was bound over to keep the peace towards Thomas Sharp of Wilstead. While visiting Houghton Conquest, Sharp had gone into the Royal Oak; showing rather more valour than discretion he suggested to Redman that he moderate his language, upon which Redman ferociously assaulted Sharp aided by the two others. When William and James Page were arrested in 1823 for stealing stockings from a draper's stall at Silsoe Fair, William Page bemoaned that there were seven or eight in Houghton Conquest far worse than him and that 'it was the first time that he had ever got into the Gang'. James Page protested: 'I am not the worst', and named seven who, he believed, were worse, including James Redman and James Grummet. A few weeks after his acquittal for the theft of the yeomanry pistol, Redman was committed for trial on a charge of housebreaking, together with John Hosler, aged 19, and Joseph Redman, aged 26. Hosler was also on James Page's list and had received a sentence of two months' hard labour for wood theft in 1825. At the Bedfordshire Lent Assizes in 1826 all three were found guilty and sentenced to death. All three were reprieved: Joseph Redman's apparent previous good behaviour told in his favour since he was given only one year's hard labour; James Redman and John Hosler were transported for life.[59]

Houghton Conquest, where the Redmans, Grummet and Hosler resided, was notorious. During the late sixteenth and early seventeenth centuries it had been a thriving and important country village; over the following century, it had declined but in the second and third decades of the nineteenth century its population soared from 507 and 505 recorded respectively in the censuses of 1801 and 1811, to 651 in 1821 and 796 in 1831. The sudden growth of the parish, far above that for Bedfordshire as a whole, possibly led contemporary gentlemen to view it with suspicion; though it should be emphasised that the Parish Register of Houghton Conquest records Grummets and Redmans from the end of the sixteenth and beginning of the seventeenth centuries respectively.[60] According to the Reverend J. W. Burgon, vicar of St Mary's Oxford and subsequently Dean of Chichester, who wrote a brief history of the village during the 1870s, there was a popular saying that 'Bedford gaol would fall when it did not contain a Houghton man'. The streets were said to be unsafe after dark; the roads were impassable in winter. Burgon maintained that the reason for the village's unsavoury nature was the lack of any stable and responsible gentry. The gentry families in the village during its heyday had died out in the seventeenth and early eighteenth centuries. Houghton Park had repeatedly changed hands. The church living became increasingly undesirable; Dr William Pearce, the Master of Jesus College, Cambridge, who held the living between 1786 and 1820, was non-resident. Burgon dated the beginning of a slow improvement from the appointment of the Reverend Thomas Barber as rector in 1821. Barber enforced order in church 'by the power of his lungs' and on the streets 'by the weight of his arm'. He carried a stick, and sometimes used it; and, as a magistrate, Burgon declared, he succeeded in getting some of the worst offenders transported.[61] Of course Barber could not have sentenced men to transportation alone, but he was the magistrate who committed the Redmans, Grummet and Hosler.

Burgon's analysis of why Houghton Conquest became so notorious says as much about his, and his contemporaries' perception of rural life, as it does about the village itself. John Glyde came to what he believed was a startling conclusion after analysing the residences of criminals in mid nineteenth-century Suffolk: about one third of the county population were urban dwellers, yet they committed only about one-fifth of the crime. 'The simplicity and innocence of peasant life exists only in imagination.' The poor criminal villagers, he concluded, had been left 'morally and physically a prey to their passions' by land-owners, clergy and employers.[62]

Both Burgon's and Glyde's conclusions fit with the nineteenth-century image of two kinds of village – 'open' and 'closed'; a perception which emerged with the Poor Law investigations conducted at the first half of the century. In the closed village, control was firmly in the hands of a single landowner, or a small group of like-minded gentlemen. Their aims were to keep poor rates to a minimum and to preserve their personal amenities such as the views over their country houses or parks. To these ends they bought up land and enclosed commons to make larger agricultural units, game reserves and parks; they also limited settlement and building. Their control meant that they exercised a powerful influence over the local population; only hard-working, deferential, and moral labourers were allowed settlement and the consequent relief in hard times. Open villages had no such controls. They were usually very much larger and sprawling; shopkeepers and independent artisans built cottages for rent which often turned into rural slums. The occupants of these slums provided labour for local farmers in both open and closed villages.[63] Some open villages might be squatter settlements providing labour for a nearby town. Headington Quarry, formerly a waste area on the edge of Shotover Common on the outskirts of Oxford, provides a good example. Many of the men here worked as quarrymen or brickmakers. Physical toughness was regarded as a virtue in the village. Disputes were settled without recourse to the police who patrolled Headington in pairs. Outsiders gave the village a wide birth.[64] Other open villages were viewed with similar horror and were accused of being centres of rural immorality and vice and, in consequence, the havens of burglars and other dangerous criminals. In 1848, Francis Howells was one of the investigators sent by the Poor Law Commissioners to study how the law of settlement and removal was unctioning. In his report Howells explained how, about 1840, Lord Manvers had pulled down several cottages at Laxton in Nottinghamshire o as to be rid of the occupants. The evicted families found temporary helter in the workhouse:

> I think it is right to say ... that these people had become troublesome as poachers and as idle dissolute characters; and I believe that Lord Manvers was considered to have done a good thing when he broke up this gang of bad characters. They did not remain long in the [work]house, but went out and took up their abode in the neighbouring village of Egmanton, where Mr Barrow told me he thought they were the foundation of a gang of burglars. Mr Barrow adds 'We have broken up two different gangs of burglars in Egmanton', an open parish. And this perhaps, is one of the worst evils that the open parishes suffer from the close parishes, that they receive into them the bad characters to whom the owners of close parishes are naturally unwilling to give shelter, and whom they wish to get rid of if they can.[65]

The open-closed village dichotomy was not as clear-cut as the poor aw literature, and nineteenth-century commentators who worried about idle, disorderly and criminal rural labourers, implied.[66] Detailed analysis of closed villages with resident gentry reveals that these could also contain frequent offenders. Westfirle is a case in point: the Gage family owned ninety-eight per cent of the available acreage in the village and were the largest single employer, yet over one-third of those prosecuted for criminal offences between 1820 and 1850 were prosecuted on more than one occasion and some of the offenders had criminal careers not unlike the men from Houghton Conquest described above.[67] At the same time research into rural protest suggests, not surprisingly perhaps, that it was the larger villages – the 'open' villages – with their greater proportion of agricultural labourers to employing farmers, and their distinctly higher percentage of independent artisans, which were more likely to participate in such behaviour.[68] Though, occasionally, a few magistrates and gentlemen might sympathise, the machine-smashing, the incendiarism, the destruction of game and of property, and the riotous assemblies which popular protest involved, were all criminal actions by law. Moralising contemporaries had little difficulty in making an intellectual leap at this point: if the idle and immoral poor participated in these crimes, then they would also participate in others; poaching thus became the first step on the road to a life of crime. To the extent that they probably contained proportionally more poachers, open villages were more criminal; few permanent labourers seem to have been convicted of poaching on the land of their employer.[69] Also poaching gangs could benefit from the services which certain independent villagers could offer; butchers, for example, were useful to a variety of poachers and sheep stealers; innkeepers might purchase game themselves, or to be able to pass it on to, or via, their clientele.

Some industrial villages were 'closed' inasmuch as they were built and run by the employer and his immediate subordinates. While the employer might look to his workforce's moral and intellectual improvement by restricting strong drink and providing schools for children and a mechanics' institute for his men, he could also enforce discipline through evictions and dependence by establishing his own store; given that the village could be remote such stores could be a boon it was the requirements and restrictions that went with it which made the truck system so hated by workers. When the employer was also the local magistrate, his power was complete. 'If the men took any measure against the masters they would not be employed' commented Thomas Jones Phillips, clerk of the peace at Bedwellty, while explaining to a parliamentary committee in 1842 that there had been no prosecutions in Monmouth under the Truck Act since the iron masters were also the magistrates.[70] But not all industrial villages functioned in this way. In some instances building development was left to independent tradesmen within the village. Furthermore mining, which was probably the most common reason for the creation of new industrial villages during the late eighteenth and nineteenth centuries, was an industry which was far less susceptible to rigorous regulations and supervision of the labour force than factory work. Miners were feared as notoriously unruly during the eighteenth century; the image stayed with many mining communities well into the nineteenth century. In 1847 Jelinger Symons told a parliamentary committee that the mining district of Monmouthshire contained 'a larger proportion of escaped criminals and dissolute people of both sexes than almost any other populace'.[71] Thousands poured into County Durham in the second quarter of the nineteenth century to meet the requirements of industry, especially the demand for miners. The pit strike of 1831–32 was noted for its ferocity. After the creation of the county constabulary, policemen were commonly assaulted in pit villages; in 1842 it was argued that the relatively crime-free agricultural districts of the county were financing the police presence in the colliery districts. Yet for all that contemporaries branded the Durham miners as dangerous and criminal, theft does not appear to have been much of a problem in pit villages. In his reports to the *Morning Chronicle* Angus Reach found that the mining districts of Northumberland and Durham contradicted 'the theories generally entertained upon the connection of ignorance with crime by presenting the least criminal section of the population of England'. Statistically Reach found that there was a smaller proportion of offenders in the mining districts of Cornwall, Cumberland and Staffordshire. He concluded that the small amount of theft in the north east was probably due to the power of Methodism:

> aided by the comparatively isolated condition in which the mining population lives – seldom or never coming in contact with the members of any industrial class except their own, and little exposed to the influences and excitements of great towns.[72]

It might also have been the case that, in the event of a theft, the mining communities were reluctant to involve the authorities, especially the police who guarded blacklegs and assisted at evictions during strikes. Justice for theft in a pit village, at least during the first half of the nineteenth century, may have been rougher and speedier than that sanctioned by the state, but responses probably varied with the nature of the incident.[73]

Environment did have an inter-relationship with crime, but not simply along the lines that the urban-rural division might suggest. During the eighteenth and nineteenth centuries industrialization and urbanization changed communities, but the experience was not so shattering that people, especially poor immigrants spreading to cities or sprawling open villages, ceased to live in, and to perceive themselves as part of, communities. Some communities tended to be more law abiding than others, but theorists of crime, policemen and the respectable classes in general tended to perceive any areas where the poor teemed and where there was no visible form of elite control and surveillance, as haven for the dangerous classes. Popular disorder, even when it had recognisable and even modest aims – food at a fair price, the traditional right to use common land – was increasingly perceived as dangerous and criminal. Popular exuberance at fairs and wakes, the noise and 'disorder' which spilled over from pubs, crowded courts, tenements and streets, was perceived similarly, even though it was condoned by the immediate community in which it occurred and, occasionally, might have involved the meting out of popular justice. Some of this disorder and exuberance was criminal in a narrow sense of the word, even if tolerated by both the rural and urban communities in which it occurred. But it seems to have been difficult for those contemporaries fired by 'respectability' and ideas of progress, fortified by Malthusian theory, and recognising that they lived in a society which was changing at a frighteningly rapid rate under the twin impact of urbanization and industrialization, to perceive continuities in community behaviour and the difference between different forms of offence.

REFERENCES AND NOTES

1. **Henry Fielding,** *An Enquiry into the Causes of the Late Increase of Robbers,* 2nd edn., London, 1751, p. 116; **Patrick Colquhoun,** *A Treatise on the Police of the Metropolis,* 3rd end., revised and enlarged, London, 1796, pp. xi–xii.

2. See above pp. 35–6. Among the exceptions to the predominance of London crimes in creating fear was the grisly murder of four-year old Francis Saville Kent at Road, Wilts, in January 1860. The fascination with the case was partly due, however, to the difficulties experienced by the authorities in identifying the murderer – Francis's sister, Constance. The

case generated columns of newspaper comment throughout the year, and see also the comments in **J. F. Stephen**, 'The criminal law and the detection of crime', *Cornhill Magazine*, ii (1860), pp. 697–708. For the report of the Metropolitan Police officer sent to investigate the murder see MEPO 3/61.

3. **Thomas Plint**, *Crime in England: Its relation, character, and extent as developed from 1801 to 1848*, London, 1851, p. 19; **James T. Hammick**, 'On the judicial statistics of England and Wales with special reference to recent returns relating to crime', *Journal of the Statistical Society*, (1867) xxx, pp. 375–426 (at p. 391); **William Douglas Morrison**, 'The increase of crime', *Nineteenth Century*, (1892) xxxi, pp. 950–57 (at p. 956); **C. D. Brereton**, *A Refutation of the First Report of the Constabulary Force Commissioners*, 3 parts, London, n.d. Part 1, p. 73; Barnett and Scott Holland are quoted in **Mandy Ashworth**, *The Oxford House in Bethnal Green*, Oxford House, London, 1984, p. 7.

    Angus Reach was something of an exception. In his mid century reports for the *Morning Chronicle* he noted that 'where great bodies of people, the vast proportion of them labouring poor, are crammed together, crime must abound'. But he also emphasised that there was far more rural crime than many people imagined, indeed the amount was 'of startling magnitude to the many who naturally connect rustic beauties with rural innocence, and take but little account of the fact that the agricultural labourer endures more habitual and more pinched hunger and cold amid his fair fields and woods, than the factory operative amid the dust and smoke of his alley and his mill'. **J. Ginswick** (ed.), *Labour and the Poor in England and Wales*, 8 vols., Frank Cass, London, 1983 i, 6.

4. **Ferdinand Tönnies**, *Community and Society*, trans. and supplemented by Charles P. Loomis, RKP London, 1955. *Gemeinschaft* is generally translated as 'community'; *Gesellschaft* as 'association', 'organisation' or even 'society'.

5. **Havelock Ellis**, *The Criminal*, London, 1890, p. 297. For a useful introductory critique see **Howard Zehr**, *Crime and the Development of Modern Society*, Croom Helm, London, 1976, pp. 20–29; see also **Robert A. Nye**, *Crime, Madness and Politics in Modern France: The medical concept of national decline*, Princeton U.P., 1984, especially pp. 149 and 171.

6. **J. J. Tobias**, *Crime and Industrial Society in the Nineteenth Century*, Penguin, Harmondsworth, 1972, p. 108.

7. **David Jones**, *Crime, Protest, Community and Police in Nineteenth-Century Britain*, RKP, London, 1982, p. 66.

8. **John E. Archer**, ' "A fiendish outrage"? A study of animal maiming in East Anglia 1830–70', *Agricultural History Review*, 33 (1985), pp. 147–57 (at p. 153 and note 32).

9. **John G. Rule**, 'The manifold causes of rural crime: Sheep-stealing in England c. 1740–1840', in John Rule (ed.), *Outside the Law: Studies in crime and order 1650–1850*, Exeter Papers in Economic History, no. 15, University of Exeter, 1982; **R. A. E. Wells**, 'Sheep-rustling in Yorkshire in the age of the industrial and agricultural revolutions', *Northern History*, xx (1984), pp. 127–45. See also **K. P. Baun**, 'Social protest, popular disturbances and public order in Dorset, 1790–1838', unpublished Ph.D. University of Reading, 1984, pp. 136–138.

0. E. J. **Hobsbawm**, 'The machine breakers', *P. and P.* no. 1 (1952), pp. 57–70; for an example of arson apparently linked with a trade dispute in early nineteenth-century Liverpool see H.O. 40.18.53–56, Messrs. Gregson and Bury to Peel, and Charles Lawrence to Peel, both 22 March 1824. In July 1842 the board of the Norwich Union resolved to discontinue cotton mill insurance as renewals fell due because of incendiarism in the north west, though it must be remembered that the Norwich Union's strength lay in the insurance of farm stock. Norwich Union Fire Insurance Society Board Minutes, 18 July 1842. My thanks to Dr Roger Ryan for this reference and for general information on this point.

11. Suffolk R.O. (Ipswich Branch) 2577/1, Chief Constable to Home Secretary, 2 January 1842; **R. P. Hastings,** *Essays in North Riding History 1780–1850*, North Yorkshire County Record Office Publications no. 28, (1981), p. 101.

12. Humberside R.O. Chief Constable to quarter sessions, 5 January 1864. I am grateful to David Foster for his quotation and for permission to use and cite his unpublished material on arson in East Yorkshire.

13. Norwich Union Fire Insurance Society, Board Minutes, 31 August 1835, 12 July 1841, 4 December 1843, 4 January 1847. Once again I am indebted to Dr Ryan for references and information on this point.

14. *York Herald*, 26 March 1864. Dr Foster has information on the occupation of eighteen of the forty-two persons arrested for arson between 1863 and 1870; the largest group – eight – were agricultural labourers and/or Wold Rangers.

15. C. J. **Ribton-Turner,** *A History of Vagrants and Vagrancy*, London, 1887, p. 313. For this, and the arson outbreak in North Wales, the border counties and the Midlands see Jones, *Crime, Protest, Community,* pp. 202–3.

16. Jones, *Crime, Protest, Community*, p. 48; **Michael J. Carter,** *Peasants and Poachers: A study in rural disorder in Norfolk*, Boydell Press, Woodbridge, 1980, pp. 28–29.

17. *Beverley Guardian*, 22 October 1864.

18. Beds. R.O. QGV 10/4/13.

19. A. J. **Peacock**, 'Village radicalism in East Anglia 1800–50', in **J. P. D. Dunbabin,** *Rural Discontent in Nineteenth-century Britain*, Faber and Faber, London, 1974, pp. 32–33. Beds. R.O. QEV 4, Chief Constable's letter 15 October 1844 reports eight accidental fires 'two of which occurred by children playing with Lucifer matches'. Four of the eighteen arrested in East Yorks. for whom occupations are given, were children.

20. Archer, ' "A Fiendish Outrage"?'.

21. Suffolk R.O. (Ipswich Branch) 2577/1, Chief Constable to Home Secretary, 16 March 1844.

22. See below pp. 138–40.

23. **James Obelkevich,** *Religion and Rural Society: South Lindsey 1825–75*, Clarendon Press, Oxford, 1976, chap. 6 passim; **J. F. C. Harrison,** *The Second Coming: Popular millenarianism 1780–1850*, RKP, London, 1978, chap. 3 passim, esp. pp. 41–42.

24. Beds. R.O. QGR 1/23 Prison Chaplain's report 4 April 1848; *Bedford Times* 11 March 1848; for similar behaviour in South Lincolnshire see Obelkevich, *Religion and Rural Society*, p. 292.

25. **John Glyde,** *The Norfolk Garland,* London, 1872, pp. 58–59; Beds. R.O. QSR 1824/384 and 1827/368; Obelkevich, *Religion and Rural Society*, pp 287–91; **John Rule,** 'Methodism, popular beliefs and village culture in Cornwall 1800–50' in **Robert D. Storch** (ed.), *Popular Culture and Custom in Nineteenth-Century England,* Croom Helm, London, 1982, p. 63.

26. Obelkevich, *Religion and Rural Society*, pp. 275 and 286; Glyde, *Norfolk Garland*, pp. 50–51.

27. For a useful introduction to the *vol-violence* theory, especially popular with French historians of eighteenth-century crime see **Iain A. Cameron,** *Crime and Repression in the Auvergne and the Guyenne, 1720–90,* Cambridge U.P., 1981, chap. 6 passim. For the nineteenth-century, again with reference to France see **A. Q. Lodhi** and **Charles Tilly,** 'Urbanization, crime and collective violence in nineteenth-century France', *American Journal of Sociology,* **79** (1973), pp. 296–318; and see **Zehr,** *Crime and the Development of Modern Society.*

28. **David Cohen** and **Eric Johnson,** 'French criminality: Urban-rural differences in the nineteenth century', *Journal of Interdisciplinary History,* XII (1982), pp. 477–501; **Herbert Reinke,** 'Violence in the age of criminal statistics: Nineteenth-century Germany', paper presented at the Second International Conference on the History of Crime and Criminal Justice, Maastricht, 17–19 May 1984; **J. A. Sharpe,** *Crime in Early Modern England 1550–1750,* Longman, London, 1984 chap. 2 *passim* and p. 177.

29. In a letter printed in *Athenaeum,* 22 August 1846.

30. **Bob Bushaway,** *By Rite: Custom, ceremony and community in England 1700–1880,* Junction Books, London, 1982, pp. 131–32.

31. H.O. 45.4609 Fortescue to Palmerston, 17 January 1853; **P.P.** 1852–53 (71) xxxvi *Report of the Select Committee on Police* q. 415.

32. *The Times,* 16 and 18 December 1874, 8 January 1875; and for reports of similar cases 8 and 12 January 1875.

33. Bushaway, *By Rite,* p. 158.

34. Storch, *Popular Culture,* pp. 1–2.

35. *The Times,* 21 October 1887.

36. Sharpe, *Crime in Early Modern England,* p. 74.

37. **Richard Cobb,** *The Police and the People: French popular protest 1789–1820,* Oxford U.P., 1970, p. 89.

38. **Frances Finnegan,** *Poverty and Prejudice: A study of Irish immigrants in York 1840–75,* Cork U.P., 1982, chap. 9 passim; **R. E. Swift,** ' "Another Stafford Street Row": Law, order and the Irish presence in mid Victorian Wolverhampton', *Immigrants and Minorities,* **3** (1984), pp. 5–29.

39. **Todd M. Endelman,** *The Jews of Georgian England 1714–1830: Tradition and change in a liberal society,* Jewish Publication Society of America, Philadelphia, 1979, especially chap. 8: **Jerry White,** *Rothschild Buildings: Life in an East End tenement block 1887–1920,* RKP, London, 1980; **V. D. Lipman,** 'Jewish settlement in the East End of London 1840–1940: The topographical and statistical background', in **Aubrey Newman** (ed.), *the Jewish East End 1840–1939,* The Jewish Historical Society of England, London, 1981, pp. 25–26 and 32.

40. **Robert Roberts,** *The Classic Slum: Salford life in the first quarter of the century,* Penguin, Harmondsworth, 1973, p. 16.

41. **John Glyde, jun.,** *The Moral, Social and Religious Condition of Ipswich in*

the Middle of the Nineteenth Century, Ipswich, 1850, reprinted S.R. Publishers, Wakefield, 1971, p. 57.

42. H.O. 42.114.147–48.

43. H.O. 42.114.178–80.

44. Tobias, *Crime and Industrial Society*, p. 173; *P.P. 1847*, vii, *Select Committee on Juvenile Offenders* q. 227; **Barbara Weinberger**, 'Law breakers and law enforcers in the late Victorian city: Birmingham 1867–77', unpublished Ph.D. University of Warwick, 1981, pp. 136–40, notes an apparent decline in theft from employers by the 1870s.

45. **R. N. Davidson**, *Crime and Environment*, Croom Helm, London, 1981, p. 89; for the whole 'typology' see pp. 89–93.

46. See below p. 113.

47. Ginswick (ed.), *Labour and the Poor*, i, 39.

48. *P.P. 1828*, (533) vi, *Select Committee on the Police of the Metropolis*, p. 57; U.C.L. Chadwick MSS 11 f. 2; see also ff. 4–5, response of the Superintendent of K Division; *The Times* 25 March and 14 April 1865; U.C.L. Chadwick MSS 11 f. 27.

49. **David Englander**, *Landlord and Tenant in Urban Britain 1838–1918*, Oxford U.P., 1983, pp. 7–9.

50. See above note 38. Violent criminality has been noted as high among the foreign born in eastern Germany and in France during the nineteenth century see Cohen and Johnson, 'French criminality', pp. 486–89 and **Vincent E. McHale** and **Eric A. Johnson** 'Urbanization, industrialization and crime in Imperial Germany', *Social Science History,* **1** (1976), pp. 45–78 and 210–47 (at pp. 326–37).

51. Englander, *Landlord and Tenant*, pp. 34–36; **Timothy Cavanagh**, *Scotland Yard Past and Present: Experiences of thirty-seven years*, London, 1893, pp. 24–27. See also Charles Dickens's fulminations in 'On an Amateur Beat' in *The Uncommercial Traveller*.

52. Jones, *Crime, Protest, Community*, pp. 108–9.

53. **Thomas Beames**, *The Rookeries of London, Past, Present and Prospective*, 2nd edn., London, 1852, pp. 65–68 and see also pp. 25, 26. White, *Rothschild Buildings*, pp. 131–32; Lipman, 'Jewish settlement', pp. 25–26; Weinberger, 'Law breakers and law enforcers', pp. 243–44.

54. Fielding, *An Enquiry*, pp. 141–42. Thirty years later William Blizard described similar dwellings constituting 'a sort of distinct town, or district [of London], calculated for the reception of the darkest and most dangerous enemies to society ... the owners of these houses make no secret of their being for the entertainment of THIEVES!': **William Blizard**, *Desultory Reflections on Police*, London, 1785, pp. 30–31.

55. Ginswick (ed.), *Labour and the Poor*, i, 39.

56. 'A category becomes police property, when the dominant powers of society (in the economy, polity, etc.) leave the problems of social control of that category to the police'. **J. A. Lee**, 'Some structural aspects of police deviance in relations with minority groups', in **C. Shearing** (ed.), *Organisational Police Deviance*, Butterworth, Toronto, 1981, pp. 53–54.

57. **Clive Emsley**, ' "The thump of wood on a swede turnip": Police violence in nineteenth-century England', *Criminal Justice History*, VI (1985), pp. 125–149 (at pp. 136–138).

58. **B. J. Davey**, *Lawless and Immoral: Policing a county town 1838–57*, Leicester U.P., 1983.

59. *Cambridge and Hertford Independent Press*, 16 July 1825; Beds. R.O. QGC 10/1; QSR 25/1823/330; QSR 25/1824/248; QSR/1825/309–16 and 367–72.

60. The population of Bedfordshire increased as follows: 1801 – 63,393; 1811 – 70,213; 1821 – 83,716; 1831 – 95,400. Thus between 1811 and 1831 the county population increased by some 36 per cent; the increase in the population of Houghton Conquest for the same period was 57.6 per cent.

61. Beds. R.O. P11/28/2/139–65. The parish register of Houghton Conquest suggests a marked decline of gentry families after 1700. **F. G. Emmison**, *Bedfordshire Parish Registers*, xliv MS vols. (1931–53), xli (1950).

62. **John Glyde, jun.**, *Suffolk in the Nineteenth Century: Physical, social, moral, religious and industrial*, London, 1856, pp. 146–47; John Glyde, 'Localities of crime in Suffolk', *Journal of the Statistical Society*, xix (1856), pp. 102–6.

63. **Dennis R. Mills**, *Lord and Peasant in Nineteenth-Century Britain*, Croom Helm, London, 1980, p. 24. But note that not all agricultural proletarians lived in open villages; some lived in towns and might have a twenty-mile round trip walking to and from work. Finnegan, *Poverty and Prejudice*, p. 64.

64. **Raphael Samuel**, ' "Quarry Roughs": Life and labour in Headington Quarry, 1860–1920', in **Raphael Samuel** (ed.), *Village Life and Labour*, RKP, London, 1975.

65. **Dennis R. Mills**, 'Francis Howell's report on the operation of the Laws of Settlement in Nottinghamshire 1848', *Transactions of the Thoroton Society of Nottinghamshire*, **76** (1972), pp. 46–52 (at p. 51).

66. Mills, *Lord and Peasant*, passim.

67. **Shirley Chase**, 'Crime and policing in a nineteenth-century "closed" village: Westfirle, East Sussex 1820–50', unpublished research paper. My thanks to Ms Chase for permission to read and make reference to this paper. Similar patterns of frequent offenders can be found in other Sussex villages both 'closed' and 'open'.

68. **E. J. Hobsbawm** and **George Rudé**, *Captain Swing*, Lawrence and Wishart, London, 1969, pp. 172–89; **B. Reney**, *The Class Struggle in Nineteenth-century Oxfordshire: The social and communal background to the Otmoor Disturbances of 1830 to 1935*, Ruskin College, Oxford, History Workshop Pamphlet, **3**, 1970.

69. Jones, *Crime, Protest, Community*, p. 74.

70. **P.P.** 1842, ix, *Select Committee on the Payment of Wages*, q. 1584; there were similar comments passed with reference to Batley [qq. 280–84], Bradford [qq. 181–83], Chorley [qq. 1771 and 1774] and Pentwyn Works, Pontypool [qq. 2352–58].

71. *P.P.* 1847, xxvii, part II *Select Committee on Education in Wales*, p. 290.

72. Ginswick (ed.), *Labour and the Poor*, ii, 60–61.

73. **James C. Burke**, 'Crime and criminality in County Durham 1840–55', unpublished M.A. University of Durham, 1980, pp. 123–33. **David Philips**, *Crime and Authority in Victorian England*, Croom Helm, London, 1977, p. 213, shows that Staffordshire miners were prepared to prosecute if workmates stole from each other.

Chapter 5
FIDDLES, PERKS AND PILFERAGE

The focus on crime as something committed by 'criminals' belonging to a particular social group, together with the notion that burgeoning nineteenth-century cities were the refuge of this group, helped to lead contemporaries away from a serious consideration and appreciation of one major centre of criminal activity – the workplace. A study of modern workplace crime has concluded that the phenomenon is widespread and that 'in many jobs ... it [is] often abnormal *not* to fiddle'. The word 'fiddle' is preferred since:

> morally it is relatively neutral. It is ... a 'weasel word'. It allows us to look at part-time crime not so much with complaisance as with empathy. Using the word 'fiddle', we can more readily appreciate the world-view or cosmology of the fiddler.[1]

Contemporary workplace crime, in Gerald Mars's analysis, is determined not by class or social group, but by occupational structure. Every transaction involving commodities has the potential for dishonesty, but the expropriation of a commodity is not always perceived of as 'theft' either by the offender or by the victim. There is an assumption that 'theft', in the form of burglary from a warehouse, is different from 'theft', in the form of pilferage by a warehouseman. At the same time, should the owner of the warehouse send underweight goods from that warehouse to another businessman, then his appropriation is very often termed 'breach of contract' and not a criminal offence. Perhaps fiddling between businessmen is currently the most common form of fraud, and was the most common form of fraud during the eighteenth and nineteenth centuries; unfortunately the topic has been little explored by historians, and the evidence to prove the scale of such fraud would be very difficult to find. While white-collar offenders are not ignored in this chapter, the focus, following the pattern of historical research on crime to date, remains on their social inferiors. The key question for the historian here is to what extent the massive changes wrought on the workplace during the eighteenth and nineteenth centuries brought about changes in workplace crime or even, as some have argued, led to the criminalisation of certain workplace practices which had previously been tolerated?

Workplace crime or 'fiddles' come under a variety of alternative headings, most of which are not neutral words but are those employed by employers or, more commonly, agents of the law concerned with repression. Perquisites or 'perks' can be tolerated by an employer; they can also be the objects of periodic clamp-downs. Generally a 'perk' is regarded by the workforce as an entitlement, though it can sometimes be abused to an extent that few employees could, or would seek to, justify. It is a hazy line that separates perks from pilferage or small scale theft from the workplace. Pilferage can be practised by virtually an entire workforce at a particular workplace or in a particular job; in a few instances it might shade into more organised and more large-scale theft. A third kind of workplace crime can come under the heading of fraud: this can involve deception on the part of both an employer and his employees to profit at the expense of a third party; it can involve deception on the part of an individual selling goods to, or performing a service for, another. Examples of all of these crimes, or 'fiddles' abound throughout the eighteenth and nineteenth centuries.

The largest single employment sector in Britain during the eighteenth, and for much of the nineteenth century, was agriculture. Various labourers and agricultural communities claimed a whole series of allowances or perks which were gradually whittled down or subjected to greater control and supervision. Gleaning was the best known allowance whereby, after the harvest had been gathered, women and children entered the fields and collected the scattered grain which the harvesters had missed.[2] Corn or beans collected in this way could form a significant percentage of the poor rural family's diet or wage. The custom had biblical authority, though it was clearly practised differently from place to place. During the eighteenth century it was known for individuals to object violently to anyone from outside the community seeking to glean in local fields; and farmers who tried to prevent gleaning, or who turned hogs and cattle out to graze on stubble and thus denied access to the poor, were the objects of popular odium and even assault. In *The Farmer's Kalendar* (1771) Arthur Young criticised farmers who denied gleaning to the poor in this way; but Young was also concerned about abuses by the gleaners and, while acknowledging that the custom was generally accepted, he was at pains to point out that the poor had no imprescriptable right to it. A case of theft brought before Bedfordshire Quarter Sessions in 1785 reveals that there were those among the poor who recognised abuses in gleaning. Ann Smith, a pauper widow of Blunham deposed that:

> whilst she and the rest of the ... poor people were gleaning after the cart of Mr Matthew West of the said Parish, Farmer, upon the lands of the said Mr West ... she ... with ... Mary Emery and the other gleaners on

account of a heavy shower or rain which then and there fell, were obliged
to sit down and leave off gleaning. That during this period as they were
lamenting to one another that they must go home without their usual
quantity of grain or gleaning ... the said Mary Emery openly declared that
she would not go home without her bundle, and that there was Barley
enough in the Fields lieing [sic] upon the lands near to them, and that she
would have some before she went home, and not come so far for nothing,
or words to this effect, and that she did in consequence of this resolution
go upon the land of John Wilcher (another farmer in the Parish) adjoining
to them, and thereof took about the quantity of a couple of lapfuls in her
apron of loose or mowed Barley and put it into an open sack (used
occasionally for that purpose of carrying home their grain) which she had
with her ... she appeared to this informant to do it in a felonious
audacious manner in defiance of justice and with a wicked heart purposely
and designedly to defraud the said John Wilcher of his said property, and
not in a wanton jocon [sic] manner or what is commonly called playing
the rogue or in fun.[3]

In 1788 the Court of Common Pleas gave judgment in the case of *Steel v
Houghton and Uxor*; the judges declared that there was no specific right
in common law permitting anyone to glean without the authority of the
farmer who owned the land. 'Though [the farmer's] conscience may
direct him to leave something for the poor,' added one judge, 'the law
does not oblige him to leave anything'.[4] The soil, the seed, the
cultivation and, in consequence, the profits belonged to the farmer to do
with as he thought fit. Here was a vigorous defence of property against
what many considered as custom: such a defence was typical of the
eighteenth century. Yet it was not necessarily acted upon in such a way
in the courts. In Essex a group of farmers set out to put a stop to gleaning
on the basis of this ruling; the magistrates refused to convict at summary
level, and the one case indicted at Quarter Sessions was thrown out by
the grand jury. When the gleaners responded by attempting to prosecute
or otherwise obtain legal redress against farmers who had assaulted
them, once again the magistrates refused co-operation and the matter
did not reach court.[5] Perhaps it was partly because of such difficulties
that many farmers continued to permit gleaning; at the same time some
gleaners continued to abuse what men of property could now term a
privilege rather than a customary right. Matthew Munn was a
wheelwright who held land next to his house in Potton, Bedfordshire. On
31 July 1790 some five and a half acres of rye lay reaped in his field; it
was market day and Munn feared that some of his grain might be stolen
so he hid in a ditch behind a hedge. From this vantage point he saw
Frances Finding and Jane Jinn, the wives of local labourers, enter his
field but they:

did not confine themselves altogether to gleaning or picking up the loose
eares which lay scattered about distinct from the shocks, but every now
and then would steal a handful or so out of the shocks.[6]

Nineteenth-century prosecutions for gleaning reveal that magistrates hearing such cases often acted leniently recognising that some offenders were not aware of having committed a felonious act in gleaning without the landowner's authority. More importantly the cases reveal that landowners did not use the 1788 judgement for a blanket assault on gleaning; the decision to prosecute seems to have depended rather more on farming practice than on the simple desire to preserve property rights. Scarcely anyone was prosecuted for gleaning in a wheat field since, in a four or five crop rotation, gleaning was a way of ensuring that the field was cleared for winter ploughing. Barley and beans were different: these would be used for livestock feed and farmers feared that if labourers kept livestock then, when the gleanings ran out, they might be tempted to pilfer. Additionally barley could be undersown with grass to permit grazing between harvest and autum frosts; cattle and sheep could not be turned into fields when gleaners were present. Most prosecutions involving gleaners tended to involve barley or beans.[7] As the century wore on communities regulated gleaning themselves with the use of gleaning bells which rang to start and to finish daily operations. At Rempstone in Leicestershire a Queen of the Gleaners was appointed to supervise; she proclaimed three 'laws':

1st. My attendant shall ring a bell each morning when there are fields to be gleaned.

2nd. Half-past 8 o'clock shall be the hour of the meeting, at the end of the village, and I will then accompany you to the field.

3rdly. Should any of my subjects enter an ungleaned field, without being led by me, their corn will be forfeited and it will be bestrewed.[8]

Similar monarchs were appointed elsewhere and their appearance in the nineteenth century might best be comprehended within James Obelkevich's concept of 'pseudo-gemeinschaft' by which farmers and the village élite sought to re-establish rural customs, but in a manner that underlined the élite's separateness from, and their paternalism towards, their labourers.[9] Technological change, in the shape of mechanical binders and reapers introduced towards the end of the century, transformed harvesting and eliminated gleaning.

Even after the 1788 ruling by the Court of Common Pleas gleaning continued to be justified in terms of customary rights; the taking of other produce from the land was not open to such justification, though some may have considered that their labour in the fields entitled them to some such 'perks'. Some farmers probably tolerated such behaviour, providing it was only occasional and limited; and, of course, such 'perks' or pilferage were difficult to prove unless a man was caught in the act, or with the produce on him. The evidence from eighteenth-century Essex suggests that summary courts dealt with far more cases of vegetable theft than game offences, though historians and, because of their symbolic importance, contemporaries, tended to concentrate on the latter.[10]

George Edwards, an organiser of agricultural trade unionism and subsequently Labour M.P. for South Norfolk recalled that his 'first experience of real distress' came in the year 1855:

> On my father's return home from work one night he was stopped by a policeman who searched his bag and took from it five turnips, which he was taking home to make his children an evening meal. There was no bread in the house. His wife and children were waiting for him to come home, but he was not allowed to do so.

Edwards's father was sentenced to fourteen days' hard labour; on his release no farmer would employ him and the family spent the winter in the workhouse.[11] It would, of course, be folly to suppose that every incidence of the appropriation of growing produce was prompted by a labourer's need to feed a starving family or by a belief that his sweat and effort justified a 'perk'. Growing crops could only be taken at certain times of the year; there was a peak of summary indictments in the late summer and autumn when such crops were plentiful but also when there was a peak of agricultural employment. Furthermore, on occasions growing crops were taken by organised gangs. In 1822 eight bushels of apples were stolen from farmer John Burr's land on the outskirts of Bedford. Five men armed with bludgeons cowed his night watchmen and took the apples away in a cart.[12]

Wood gathering for fuel, for building, even for a maypole, like gleaning, was perceived as customary right. There was ambiguity here; picking up fallen wood was one thing, cutting down green branches or living trees was another; and when a cart was brought to carry away the timber it suggests that the offenders were as likely to be involved in selling wood for profit as collecting for their own families' use. Legislation was passed during the seventeenth and eighteenth centuries relating to wood theft – the law, of course, spoke in terms of theft and timber was a valuable commodity for fuel, for building and to meet the demands of the Royal Navy. Like the ruling on gleaning this legislation can be interpreted as a further, deliberate move to emasculate the old rural popular culture and to strengthen the defences of private property. But legislation does not act on its own; the laws on wood theft, like the extensions to the Game Laws, gave prosecutors a choice in how they dealt with offenders. Winchester College considered itself plagued by wood stealers during the 1790s: 'near 3,000 trees' were damaged in six or seven years. The Warden and Scholars responded with the full force of the law against five men at the Hampshire Quarter Sessions in 1798; all five were sentenced to seven years' transportation.[13] Yet most offenders still seem to have been brought before magistrates for summary jurisdiction and, if found guilty, sentenced to a small fine or a short term of imprisonment. Prosecutors appear to have considered the nature and frequency of the offence and the character of the accused. The historian cannot consider every single offence and every single offender, but must bear in mind that there were a variety of motives for wood theft. Some undoubtedly did consider that taking wood was a right particularly when pressed by bitter cold and/or penury. At the other extreme a percentage of wood theft was probably the result of pure vandalism. In 1795 Lord Petre gave troops quartered on Warley Common the authority to cut timber for their needs from his land. The timber was carefully marked out, but during their stay the soldiers ripped up several hundred young trees from an unmarked area.[14]

Agricultural work itself provided opportunities for less ambigious offences. Thomas Pedder and James Walduck were employed by Christopher Prior in 1818 to thresh wheat 'and to draw straws for platting [sic] and to sell it for our master to women and others applying'. They confessed that, when they sold the straw, they did not give Prior all the money that they received. Five years later farmer Thomas Wiles employed James Smith to thresh his barley; he observed Smith put some of the barley into his own sack. John Palmer, a miller of Luton, was indicted in 1817 for defrauding William Williams. Palmer had received four bushels of wheat for grinding, but had only returned three and one half bushels of wheat and flour mixed. Agricultural instruments were pilfered from the workplace; occasionally perhaps because they could be used at home:

> I Never Intended Keeping the Spade ... I took the Spade to dig Potatoes again ... I Placed the Spade where any one might See It and It Remained there three hours as the Moon Shone Bright If I Intended Keeping the Spade I should of hid It ...[15]

But some of the implements taken were most likely acquired for what they would fetch when sold.

'Chips' claimed by the workers in the Royal Dockyards constitute the best known example of an eighteenth-century industrial workplace fiddle. The government was involved directly; its attempts to save money in the yards prompted a succession of investigations which, amongst other things, drew attention to the workforce's perquisites and, subsequently, provided historians with such a wealth of detail. Other evidence has been left by the steady trickle of offenders dealt with by the disciplinary procedures of the yards themselves or prosecuted in the courts.[16] Originally chips constituted scrap wood which men were permitted to take home from the yards to use as firewood. By the early seventeenth century the authorities considered that perquisite was being abused, not the least when in 1634 a boat-load of 3,500 one foot long wooden tree-nails was seized at Deptford; the tree-nails had been made by two men out of the chips which they had collected in six years' work in the royal yards. A succession of attempts were made to end or at least to limit the size of chips; a regulation of 1753 stated that they should consist of no more than could be carried, untied, under one arm. But the ambiguity continued until, in 1801, the government succeeded in commuting them to a cash payment. Ambiguity existed also over what constituted a chip and who was permitted to take them from the yards. It was alleged that men spent the last half hour of the working day sawing up new and useful wood to take out as chips. Technically only men working in the yards were allowed to take chips out, yet many others did so such as wives and children who brought in lunch for their menfolk, and even individuals who visited the yards when, for example, the launching of a ship was celebrated. Chips were also stretched in some minds to include nails, paint, ropes, sail-cloth and, indeed, anything which could not be nailed down. During the American War of Independence it was alleged that receivers in Portsmouth were paying 1s.3d for five pounds of used copper nails; this was more than the average daily wage for the unskilled yard labourer. When, in 1801, the skilled men were asked to state how much they would be prepared to accept to forgo their daily bundle, they estimated the value at 8d; the basic daily rate for a skilled shipwright or caulker then stood at 2s.1d., though, because of the exigencies of war, they were probably earning three times that amount. But pay in the royal yards was always in arrears: at the close of the Seven Years War wages were fifteen months late and throughout the war against Revolutionary France they were at least three months late. For this reason, if for no other, chips were essential to the workman's existence and were preserved with tenacity. Yard officials, themselves taking unofficial earnings in the form of fees and indulging in a variety of fiddles, were aware of the financial problems of their workforce and this may have fostered a degree of laxity and toleration. Juries in dockyard areas were reluctant to convict the smaller offenders, partly, it would appear, because they accepted chips as a man's right and partly also, perhaps, because they were aware of the essential nature of the chips to the family economy of the workman. Informers were very unpopular and sometimes were subjected to counter charges. The commutation of chips was accompanied by a more regular system of wage payment, though it was not until July 1813 that the men began to be paid on a regular weekly basis. This, together with stricter supervision and police provision, probably did succeed in reducing dramatically the amount of material taken from the yards, but pilferage was by no means completely eradicated.[17]

Tangentially it should be remembered that the Admiralty was not interested only in reducing expenditure by controlling the perks of its manual labourers in the dock yards. It also sought to rationalize the salary system for its clerical establishment and to abolish their unofficial emoluments. Clerks took fees for making out bills, certificates, contracts, warrants and so forth, tasks which produced between two and three fifths of their annual income. In the Navy Office clerks also performed 'agency business' by which they settled the accounts of contractors, officers and seamen, and used Navy Office stationery and postage in so doing. The commutation of these perks and the new salary scales were ill-considered and prompted much unrest; in 1800 the clerks in the Navy Office embarked on a go-slow so as to obtain overtime payments.[18]

The Royal Dockyards were exceptional during the eighteenth century for the large number of workers employed on a single site. Industrial production in general was dominated by the putting out system whereby men and women worked in their own accommodation using materials received from, and which remained the property of, a master manufacturer. The putting-out system provided opportunities for a variety of fiddles on the part of both masters and outworkers. Clothiers were reported to be using false weights so as to give their weavers greater or smaller quantities for weaving a standard piece at a fixed financial rate; in the former instance they obliged the weaver to weave extra cloth for no extra payment; in the second instance they could reduce the weaver's pay claiming that the cloth which he returned was of insufficient weight. As in the dockyards employers sometimes paid wages in arrears and this could bind the weaver to an employer and force him to live on credit. Pay might also come in tokens, notes of hand or even counterfeit coppers negotiable at a discount or only with specific retailers in a form of truck. Payments of this kind however were not always the result of deliberate fiddles since the English coinage was in a poor state during the eighteenth century; when the war with Revolutionary France compelled the Bank of England to withhold payment in specie in 1798, the problem of finding coinage to pay workers' wages became acute.[19] Outworkers in the textile trades responded to the clothiers' fiddles with a variety of their own by which the employers received back short-length yarn or short-weight cloth; the outworker could then sell off the surplus, or put it to his or her own use. (Most likely *her* own use since short-reeling appears in Quarter Sessions records as predominantly an offence committed by women.) Weavers also insisted on their 'thrums' – the weft ends which were left on a loom after the finished cloth had been removed. Since legally the outworker's materials remained the property of the employer, the retention of thrums constituted an offence: in law this offence was not larceny but embezzlement. Yet employers' attempts to collect thrums as well as finished cloth could lead to trouble. There was a bitter weavers' strike in Essex in the winter of 1757 to 1758 when the Colchester clothiers demanded the return of waste. The intervention of a local M.P., which led to the clothiers' offering 3d for a thrum, reveals the extent to which the custom was acknowledged both within and outside the industry. The Essex weavers initially considered the commutation payment too small but, in the end, they were compelled to accept it. Eighty years later Yorkshire worsted manufacturers were still purchasing thrums from their outworkers.[20]

Perks in eighteenth and early nineteenth-century outwork were not confined to the textile industries. Journeymen tailors took 'cabbage' –

the pieces of cloth left over after cutting out and, on occasions, rather more than simply the waste shreds were acquired. The practice long outlived the heyday of outwork and was commented on by James Greenwood in 1869:

> As with the tailor, so it is with the upholsterer, and the dressmaker, and the paperhanger, and the plumber, and all the rest of them. I don't say that every time they take a shred of this, or a pound of that, that they have before their eyes the enormity of the offence they are about to commit. What they do they see no great harm in. Indeed, point out to them and make it clear that their offence has but to be brought fairly before the criminal authorities to ensure them a month on the treadmill, and they would as a rule be shocked past repeating the delinquency. And well would it be if they were shocked past it, ere misfortune overtake them. It is when 'hard up' times set in, and it is difficult indeed to earn an honest penny, that these rudimentary exercises in the art of pillage tell against a man.[21]

In some trades fiddles did not apply simply to left-overs. Journeymen hatters indulged in 'bugging' by which they substituted cheaper materials for those which master hatters had put out to them. Shoemakers acted similarly buying cheap leather from carriers and substituting it for the more valuable material received from the master; the more valuable leather was then converted to their own use.[22]

Nail-making involved both outwork and production by individual nailers for direct sale. An individual nailer could use up to a ton of iron in a year; the work required little equipment or training, but it was laborious and poorly paid. Nailers not only embezzled iron which was put out, they also provided a ready market for iron pilfered or embezzled by others. By the late eighteenth century there were said to be 40,000 men, women and children working as nailers in the Black Country as well as thousands of others engaged in the different metal trades. Almost any piece of metal, including gate hinges and latches and bits of agricultural machinery, could be reworked in small family forges or by bigger manufacturers who asked no questions of individuals with metal to sell. These practices continued into the nineteenth century, and other metal working centres appear to have had similar problems to the Black Country; in 1854 a Sheffield grand jury complained that one-fifth of the indictments brought before them were for the theft of scrap metal. The decline of outwork did not mean that industrial workers no longer expropriated raw materials or finished goods; far from it. But the definition of the offence did change. An employer's ownership and possession of goods coincided in a factory or workshop, and consequently any expropriation by an employee who had not been given the goods to work on in his or her own home, came under the legal definition of larceny. Embezzlement increasingly was used to refer simply to fraudulent conversion of money.[23]

Nor was it only in the outwork trades that journeymen claimed perks.

At the close of the eighteenth century London's journeymen printers claimed the right to a copy of each book which they printed. In January 1797 George Cawthorne, a printer and bookseller, prosecuted one of his workmen for stealing a book. Reluctantly Cawthorne and two other printers admitted in court that their employees were claiming this 'right'. One printer protested that, if the 'right' was admitted, it would destroy all profits and he personally would stand to lose £20 a week by it. Interestingly, according to the printers, it was the King's printer who was breaking ranks and allowing workmen to take books from the workshop. Sir John Heath, the judge hearing the case, finally stopped the proceedings:

> I think, Gentlemen of the Jury, there can be no occasion to go any further; at the same time, the acquittal of this man must not be understood to decide the right.[24]

Nearly eighty years later, in January 1875, a somewhat similar case was brought before the stipendiary magistrates of the Worship Street Police Court. A workman was prosecuted for taking six copies of a lithographic print from his place of work; unlike Cawthorne, the printer accepted his workmen's right to one proof copy if they wished – but one proof copy was sufficient.[25]

Generally speaking throughout the period coal miners were allowed coal for their own use. In eighteenth-century Staffordshire, however, they appear to have taken much larger amounts which were sold at a profit. There were other fiddles in mining also. If paid by a filled 'corve' miners were known to put large coals at the bottom of a corve leaving plenty of hollow spaces; the top was then filled with smaller coals so that the container merely looked full. In the tin and copper mines of Cornwall tutworkers who sank shafts and drove levels and who were paid by the fathom, allegedly bribed mine captains to over-measure their work. Tributers, who negotiated separate contracts for raising ore in different parts of a mine, were paid according to the value of the ore which they raised; the gangs were known to come to agreements between themselves so that those on a poor pitch, who were earning at a high rate, and those on a good pitch, who were paid at a lower rate, exchanged a little ore and split the resulting profits between them.[26]

Any movement of goods not directly supervised by an employer offered employees an opportunity for fraud or appropriation. In 1800 Richard Pybus was employed by Edward Brumfitt who ran a transport business in Leeds. Among his tasks Pybus had to deliver goods which arrived in Leeds on Brumfitt's waggon. On one occasion he was instructed to deliver a package to a merchant, Richard Sissons, and to collect a fee of 9s.11d. Pybus decided to augment the fee to 13s.6d. and, upon discovery, was prosecuted for fraud. Jane Hartwell was 'the letter carrier from Harrold [Bedfordshire] to Bozeat [Northants]'. In 1816 she was prosecuted for taking a £10 banknote from a letter given to her by a

Harrold shopkeeper to post in Bozeat. Twenty years later the Metropolitan Police gave the Constabulary Commissioners several examples of individuals absconding when entrusted with money by their employers.[27] Probably Pybus, Hartwell and others were only prosecuted when the scale of the offence was regarded as sufficiently large to merit anything other than a warning or a dismissal. But continual very small pilferage could eventually mount up to a significant theft: Frederick Huggins was employed as a porter by Richard Hellaby; one of his tasks was to load the trap of Hellaby's commercial traveller and he regularly took a neck-tie while engaged in this task until, in November 1856, Hellaby prosecuted him for the theft of forty-eight such ties.[28] In large-scale movements of goods the opportunities for fiddling were much greater and could be developed by teams of men into something reminiscent of a perk. The building of and the growth of railways provided wide opportunities for railway staff, generally respectable and skilled men, to appropriate goods in transit,[29] but probably the most notorious examples of this behaviour were to be found on the docks.

Both Patrick Colquhoun and John Binney, one of Mayhew's collaborators, reported dock workers pilfering from cargoes as they unloaded them, as well as taking ships' equipment. The pilfered goods were smuggled out of the docks in bags or strings worn under clothing, or simply in hats and pockets. They could be used by the dockers themselves, or sold to small grocers, publicans, dealers in old iron and anyone else who was in the market.[30] Arthur Harding described a similar pattern existing in the 1890s; Harding's Aunt Liza, who ran a corner shop, bought tea, sugar and whisky taken by dockers, repackaged and then resold it. Everyone involved could profit from such an arrangement: the dockers, Aunt Liza, and Aunt Liza's customers who were able to buy the repackaged goods at less than the usual market price.[31] Colquhoun was appalled that the dockers 'consider it as a kind of right which attaches to their situation, to plunder wherever opportunity offers'. Moreover he insisted that:

> above sixty of these plunderers meet regularly, and subscribed a certain sum
> for establishing a general fund; out of which the penalty of 40s. adjudged
> under the Bum-boat Act, to be paid by every person convicted of
> conveying goods pilfered from vessels, is regularly discharged; by which
> means the delinquents, instead of going to gaol, are enabled to return to
> their former criminal pursuits. Some of the members of this club, although
> apparently common labourers, are said to have their houses furnished in a
> very superior style and to be possessed of property in the funds to the
> extent of from £1,500 to £3,000.[32]

It seems unlikely that these extremely wealthy dockers existed outside Colquhoun's fertile imagination, yet clubbing together to pay the fine of a workmate unlucky enough to be caught, prosecuted and convicted, was practised at least much later in the century.[33]

The Constabulary Force Commissioners received evidence of

continuous pilferage on the canals. The boatmen removed cloth, ironmongery, liquor, sugar, tea, indeed anything which could be turned to their own use or sold off to a receiver. Some receivers were grocers like Harding's Aunt Liza; others were master manufacturers who took the goods from the boatmen and subsequently sold them as if their own. A variety of dodges were employed to ensure that the loss of goods was not discovered until the boatmen were well clear.[34] The replacement of canal transport by the railway did not abolish such pilferage, it simply changed its location, changed the problems of the fiddlers and of those whose task it was to prevent them. The Constabulary Commissioners noted that carrying firms were 'immediately interested only in the prevention of those depredations in which the losses admit of distinct specification, and for which they can be made accountable'.[35] The firms whose goods were carried were, as their evidence to the Commissioners testifies, well aware of the potential for loss through pilferage and probably made allowance. During the eighteenth century coal-mine owners often loaded more coal into canal boats than was listed on manifests; this was not simply because of the difficulties involved in gauging a boat's weight but also because they were well aware that the boatmen sold coal on route and paid off lock-keepers and other officials for an easy, unimpeded journey.[36] Other employers tolerated fiddles which did not hit them personally, but which could be passed on to the purchaser. At the end of the nineteenth century dairy owners admitted that they took the dishonesty of their milkmen into account when calculating wages. The most common fiddle was 'bobbing', or watering the milk and selling the surplus at a profit; such adulteration of milk by milkmen, however, was probably the least of the causes for the atrocious quality of cheap milk in the cities.[37] James Greenwood maintained that the London General Omnibus Company was able to keep their conductors' pay at 4s. for a seventeen-hour day because of an understanding by the employers and their employees that the latter were pocketing a percentage of the daily takings. It was, according to Charles Booth, 'almost as though the omnibus had been hired from the company, and was run by the men on their own account'.[38] An increase in wages and the introduction, not without opposition, of the bell punch finally put an end to this or at least limited the conductor's opportunities for perks.

In general the workplace offences discussed so far were those committed by employees. Several historians have sought to slot their perception of such offences into changes in the economic structure. It has, for example, been urged that the shift to centralised, factory-based manufacture was less the result of this system's proven technical superiority and more because of concern about embezzlement and labour discipline under the out-work system.[39] More cogently it has been argued that a criminalisation of perks took place in the eighteenth century and that this was another aspect of the destruction of a vital artisan culture and of the alienation of the worker from the product of his labour. This was mirrored in rural areas where farmers increasingly distanced themselves socially from their labourers and where notions of property were strengthened by enclosure with the poor rural dweller being reduced to a wage labourer denied the right to graze animals, to pick up fallen wood, to glean from the fields which he had sown and reaped with his labour – the land was property: using it, or taking things from it when not sanctioned by the owner, was an offence against that property:

> Since property was a thing, it became possible to define offences as crimes against things, rather than as injuries to men. This enabled the law to assume, with its robes, the postures of impartiality: it was neutral as between every degree of man, and defended only the inviolability of the ownership of things. In the seventeenth century labour had been only partly free, but the labourer still asserted large claims (sometimes as perquisites) to his own labour's product. As, in the eighteenth century, labour became more and more free, so labour's product came to be seen as something totally distinct, the property of landowner or employer, and to be defended by the threat of the gallows.[40]

Such analyses have considerable attractions in that they draw together and relate changes in society and the economy and concurrent changes in the law, in its interpretation and enforcement. There is evidence of a close link between industrial development and prosecution for industrial theft in some areas. In early nineteenth-century Wigan, for example, the law appears to have been administered humanely and impartially by the local magistracy, except when it was involved with reference to industry. Employers were scarcely prosecuted, and if convicted were only moderately fined, for operating the truck system; on the other hand heavy sentences were imposed even for first offences of industrial theft. Workers, including children, were commonly prosecuted for breach of contract in leaving work without proper notice, and the sentence in this case was also a heavy fine:[41] the Master and Servant Act 1823 worked explicitly in the employer's favour in that he could only be prosecuted in civil law for breach of contract, the employee was liable to criminal prosecution for the same offence. Prosecutions for industrial theft rose markedly in the Black Country between 1835 and 1860: from about fifteen per cent of all larcencies prosecuted to about forty per cent or from about ten per cent of all prosecutions in one year to about one third. The increase coincided with a change in the composition of the local magistracy from a majority of landed aristocracy and gentry to one of coal owners and industrialists – the principal local employers. Furthermore the Criminal Justice Act 1855 authorised summary trial for these petty offences; prosecution thus became cheaper and quicker, and there was a qualitative leap in the number of prosecutions during the years immediately following the act.[42] An analysis of prosecutions under this act at eight police courts in mid nineteenth-century London reveals employee theft to have been the most common offence, but equally it reveals that most of these prosecutions were underataken by small tradesmen and masters, not by the larger firms and the bigger employers.[43] At the same time, however, it is apparent that employers did not always resort to the law to control their workforce; even in the late nineteenth century employers tolerated some fiddles, especially when their profits were untouched. They might choose to make an example of a single individual as a warning to others, and only then if his offences were in excess of the generally accepted and tolerated level; such appears to have been the situation in the London Omnibus Company, and even here the employers preferred dismissal to prosecution. Alternatively, as the Superintendent of K Division of the Metropolitan Police informed the Constabulary Commissioners, some employers did not take action because of the solidarity among their workforce, fearing a strike if they did so.[44]

The eighteenth century witnessed a considerable amount of legislation which sought to control the fiddles of the outworker. Yet it is difficult to sustain the argument that this legislation criminalised what had been legal or at most tolerated before. Jim Sharpe has emphasised that, in the half-century before 1640, it was probably easier to regulate industrial production by patent of monopoly rather than by parliamentary statute.[45] During this period parliamentary government was in decline; the events of the 1640s reversed this process and if there appears something of a flood of legislation relating to outwork during the eighteenth century, it must be remembered that, partly owing to the availability of Parliament after 1688 (it now had to meet annually), there was simply very much more legislation of all kinds passed in the eighteenth century. From Tudor times, even before, outworkers could be prosecuted for detaining waste; what the acts of 1749 and 1777 did was to put a time limit on this return – twenty-one days in the first instance, and eight in the second. The Act of 1749 gave magistrates acting summarily the power to punish embezzling outworkers with sentences of prison, and/or corporal punishment from the outset, rather than with the financial penalties for first offences and prison or corporal punishment if the offenders could not pay, as established under earlier legislation. Evidence is fragmentary, yet it appears that a very high proportion of offenders convicted before 1749 could not, or would not pay fines and consequently received corporal punishment. The 1749 Act thus tended to codify the practice of the courts rather than to change the law both in this respect, and also in as much as the receivers of embezzled goods, who were generally from a more well-to-do social background than the outworkers, continued to be subjected to financial penalties; the receivers had generally paid their fines before 1749, and besides it was against legislative practice to subject men who could be of some substance to immediate corporal punishment. But not all legislation relating to embezzlement during the eighteenth century made offenders liable to immediate custodial or corporal punishment. The most common outwork offence was short-reeling and this was the subject of separate legislation in 1774 which led to a small fine, only five shillings for a first offence, rather than prison or whipping, being the most common punishment. There had been modifications in the doctrine that larceny could not be committed by persons to whom goods were temporarily transferred by the owner[46], yet, during the eighteenth century, no-one appears to have contemplated plugging the loop-hole in the security of property provided by outwork; there was no attempt to change the legal situation which rendered outworkers only liable to summary prosecution for embezzlement rather than to indictments for larceny before quarter sessions or assizes.

The view that the period of massive industrialization and capitalization witnessed a deliberate and corresponding criminalisation of certain work practices and that workplace theft is best understood as a defence of customary rights against attempts to impose a new system of wage discipline is open to two further objections. First, it tends to limit workplace crime to one social group and to put a blanket legitimation on their activities. Second there is precious little evidence that the bulk of workplace crime was ever conceived as a protest against a new wage discipline; there is similarly precious little evidence that customary rights were preferred to the new wages. Thrums, chips and cabbage may have been defended as a legitimate right for the workman, yet not necessarily in preference to a regular wage, workplace offences were not always directed against the employer, and the taking of a man's half-finished work, subsequently finished and sold by another as his own – a common offence in the late eighteenth-century metal trades – can hardly be construed as a legitimate perk.[47] When dockers or boatmen or railwaymen 'knocked off' cargo, their actions may have been sanctioned by tradition and protected by communal solidarity, yet they could never have been defended in court as was attempted, not without success or a sympathetic hearing, by weavers who had taken thrums, colliers who had taken coals and rural labourers who had taken wood or gleanings without authority. Furthermore there were other offences committed by employees at their place of work for which the word perk is in no sense applicable: the shopman who took money from the till, or who took anything else that caught his eye; the domestic servant who appropriated his or, more commonly, her employer's property. The number of such cases which came before the courts almost certainly constitute only a tiny fraction of the number of offences which occurred and which were discovered. On occasions an employer might mark his money or his goods to check up on such petty pilfering:

> John Fewkes of Basford in the County of Nottingham, cordwainer, maketh oaths and saith the prisoner William Parnell has worked for me for about 6 months last and during that period I have missed different articles belonging to me. I also keep a Beer Shop which the prisoner

117

frequented and I have lately missed tobacco therefrom ... on the morning of Thursday the 9 August I marked 16 papers of tobacco by putting my name in the inside of them and I put them in the draw where they were usually kept in the Bar.[48]

Domestic servants, and possibly some other employees, might also be 'tested' for honesty with coinage or paper money left where they were likely to see it.[49]. The dismissal of a dishonest servant was, of course, far easier, far cheaper and, perhaps, less demeaning or embarrassing than a prosecution. Lastly, the question might be posed: if fiddling is to be condoned by one social group, why not by another which also took advantage of a lack of workplace supervision? White-collar offences, almost by definition workplace offences, and fiddles by different kinds of tradesmen, were also subjects of controlling legislation, though, admittedly this was often less well structured and, for a variety of reasons less well enforced.

James Greenwood reserved some of his most savage denunciations for the shopkeeper who used false weights and measures or who adulterated food and drink. Such an offender was:

by far a greater villain than the half-starved wretch who snatches a leg of mutton from a butcher's hook, or some article of drapery temptingly flaunting outside the shop of the clothier, because in the one case the crime is perpetrated that a soul and a woefully lean body may be saved from severance, and in the other case the iniquity is made to pander to the wrongdoer's covertous desire to grow fat, to wear magnificent jewellery, and to air his unwieldly carcase annually at Margate.[50]

But such frauds long-predated the tradition of an annual seaside holiday. In the mid eighteenth century they were compounded by regional variations in weights and measures; localities cherished their variations and this impeded the proposals of a parliamentary committee in 1758 that national standards be adopted and that all weights below one pound should be made of gold, silver, brass, copper or bell metal, and all those above a pound should be made of brass, copper, bell metal or cast iron.[51] There was also the problem of laxity among local authorities and/or their officials. A miller who returned short weight of flour could be indicted for fraud, but most traders guilty of market-place offences were dealt with under the common law. Market juries, local magistrates and part-time inspectors of weights and measures were responsible for acting against corrupt practices. This area has been little studied, however, it is conceivable that external events, such as a bad harvest leading to a food shortage and high prices, on the one hand tempted unscrupulous market traders and bakers to maximise their profits by defrauding their customers and, on the other, encouraged men to be on the look-out for such frauds and to prosecute; in April of the famine year of 1795, for example, three men were hailed before Richard Colt Hoare in petty sessions, accused of selling under-weight

118

bread.[52] In 1802, following hard on the heels of another subsistence crisis, Bedfordshire magistrates meeting in petty sessions at Biggleswade reported that, until a recent inspection by the current inspector of weights and measures, there had never been any such thing in the district. The result of the inspection was that eighty-seven persons were summonsed, but the magistrates 'presuming ignorance in all Persons against whom such Informations were exhibited fined each in the lowest Penalties allowable by Law and took away the defective Balances, Weights and Measures'. The role of inspector, like that of constable, did not suit many. The widow of John Kilpin, one of the inspectors in Bedfordshire, explained that her husband had 'dreaded and disliked' his tasks and kept putting them off, hating to leave his family 'to be exposed to the Abusive Insulting language and rough treatment of the People to whom he was sent'.[53] Significantly when the new police were established during the 1830s–1850s, many senior officers were given the tasks of inspectors of weights and measures.

The adulteration of food and drink was an even more difficult offence to police. John Bright, while President of the Board of Trade, maintained that 'adulteration ... arises from the very great and, perhaps, inevitable competition in business; and that to a large extent it is prompted by the ignorance of customers'. He went on to say that it would be quite impossible, as well as intolerable, to have inspectors continually checking goods in shops. These comments made James Greenwood furious; he pointed out that France and Germany had both a better system of inspection and much stiffer penalties.[54] To the extent that an investigation of adulteration required the taking of samples and then analysis, however, Bright had some justification in arguing that inspection was impossible: qualified and competent chemists were not plentiful, while the cost of sufficient inspectors would have been looked at askance by the Treasury, by parliament and by taxpayers. Change came gradually, beginning with the Food and Drugs Act of 1860; but the number of inspectors remained small and the fines inflicted on offenders were trifling – in 1899 4,319 prosecutions were brought for adulterating food and the average fine was £1.16s.8d.[55]

The offenders, of course, were not 'criminals' but 'rotten apples'; among some of their fellows they might simply have been perceived as 'unlucky'.

Some shopkeepers did well out of systems of truck, even after early nineteenth-century legislation sought to put an end to the practice. The problem with truck legislation was that the magistrates who were to enforce it were often the employers who practised it, especially as industrialists became more prominent on magisterial benches. Employer magistrates would not have heard the cases of industrial theft brought against their own employees, nor cases brought against themselves for infringing the Truck Acts: the Victorian élite was not so hypocritical as to have tolerated such behaviour, after all the law was just and impartial and had to be seen as just and impartial.[56] Yet it is difficult to expect that employer magistrates would not have had sympathy for their fellows as victims, or acting as prosecutors, in cases of industrial theft, or as defendants in cases brought under the Truck or Factory Acts.

The expansion of capitalism provided opportunities for more extensive and more profitable workplace fiddles by a variety of company directors, bankers, managers and clerks. Some of the frauds perpetrated in this area involved enormous sums of money. In 1857 it was revealed that Colonel W. Petri Waugh was indebted to the London and Eastern Banking Company for £244,000 which was just £6,000 less than the entire subscribed capital of the bank. The Colonel was a director of the bank, and he had acted with the connivance of J. E. Stephens, the manager. Petri Waugh fled to Spain, where he started a mining company; but his only criminal offence was holding funds while a bankrupt. Stephens had committed no criminal offence.[57] In 1882 Charles Magniac, Liberal M.P. for Bedford, received an urgent summons to London by telegraph. He met one of his partners in Matheson and Jardine on the railway station platform:

> we both agreed that some fraud must have been committed implicating the firm. This I found on my arrival proved to be the case, but the amount is so *gigantic* and *incredible* ... *Over* a million in sterling.

The offence had been so simple for the perpetrator:

> [S]ubject to the general control of one of the managing partners it was the duty of a young man in the office, a nephew of the Mathesons, to withdraw from delivery to replace in the strong room the securities belonging to the firm and partners. He became so entangled with a scoundrel in speculations on the Stock Exchange and from small beginnings has finally abstracted and made away with securities to such an amount that I am positively frightened to think of it.

It was subsequently learned, though never revealed in any court case, that there was more than one 'scoundrel' involved and that they had been involved 'in two similar affairs one [of] which occurred about a year ago – and the other rather more'.[58] Fifteen years later a partner in Baring Brothers' Liverpool house was compelled to resign when it was discovered that he was embezzling large sums. 'William Smith', his real name was never revealed, was suspected by some of his clerks but, fearing for their own jobs, they had never reported their suspicions. Hoping to avoid a scandal, or possibly sympathetic to their partner, Baring Brothers did not prosecute; indeed they gave Smith £150 to pay off some debts and paid his salary for three months after his resignation.[59] During the 1850s respected merchants were prosecuted for using fraudulent dock warrants. Robert Ferdinand Preis used such warrants to prove transactions in the grain trade involving amounts large enough to cause fluctuations in London grain prices. J. W. Cole used a similar, sophisticated system of fraudulent warrants with imported metals. Cole's fraud was suspected by the City Bankers, Overend and Gurney, but they feared for their own capital if Cole was exposed and bankrupted, consequently they said nothing. In the 1870s there was an outcry over the exposure of a member of parliament, J. S. Balfour, following his development of the pyramid building of multi-company business: Balfour used the share capital of one company to pay the premiums of others in what one clergyman branded 'the biggest crime of the nineteenth century'.[60]

Legislation was slow in keeping pace with the opportunities for fraud and fiddling provided by the expansion and development of the business and financial world during the nineteenth century. This might be interpreted as middle-class Victorian society looking after its own, yet more probably and more practically, business and financial fraud was often very sophisticated and complex and its perpetrators cautiously avoided, or trespassed only marginally, on existing legal sanctions. Most nineteenth-century legislators, policemen and jurymen could understand the 'science' of garotting or housebreaking. The science of financial fraud, at least in legal terms, was far more difficult.

Fraud and embezzlement did not occur only at the top of the business and financial world. Clerks were caught taking significant sums from their employers. Of course this was never defended as a perk, but possibly a significant number of these offenders saw themselves as merely 'borrowing' money to tide them over a difficult period. In the second half of the nineteenth century the confidence and security of the position of clerk was seriously eroded by the expansion of the clerical labour force and an influx of women and young men. At the same time the small businessman and other traditional employers of clerks were hit by the great depression and by the growing concentration of capital. Fewer and fewer clerks were able to rise to a partnership with their employers or to establish a business on their own account. Embezzlement, in the modern sense of the word, may have been the only way that some could see to keep up appearances and to maintain themselves at the levels of comfort and respectability expected of the Victorian middle class even at its lower end.[61]

In the same way that legislation did not keep pace with the opportunities for offences in the business and financial world, so too, it did not keep pace with the opportunities for corruption and misconduct in public life which expanded with the growth of bureaucratic organisation and regulation. 'Old corruption', the patronage system by which the Crown and its ministers oiled the cogs of administrative and parliamentary machinery was under attack at least from the early years of George III's reign. Reformers emphasised the importance of public well-being over the profit of the individual holding office and, increasingly, their arguments won the day in public. The system of patronage which reached its apogee under the Whig oligarchy, was in retreat in the early nineteenth century, yet revelations of misconduct by men in public life, of corrupt practices at elections and elsewhere, continued throughout the Victorian period. No nineteenth-century parliament contemplated drafting principles of conduct for men in public life however, nor posing questions about possible procedural or structural weaknesses in administrative and regulatory systems which provided the opportunities for corruption and misconduct. Paradoxically it was probably partly because of the outward dominance of morality that such questions were not posed. Victorian society was confident, proud of its industrial development, of its commerce and of its constitutional system, each of which, it boasted, were models for the world. Such a society was hardly likely to turn it upon itself to contemplate immorality within the structures of which it was so proud. Great store was put by the personal integrity of men in public life and, as in the case of white-collar crime, those who were exposed for transgressing the bounds of the expected, moral conduct were viewed as the exceptional 'rotten apples'. Perhaps they were exceptional; but then again corrupt dealings are secretive and are hard to prove. Anti-corruption legislation, such as the Public Bodies Corrupt Practices Act 1889, arrived on the statute book, it has been argued, 'almost as an aside to the mainstream of legislative activity'.[62] This particular act followed the revelations in the interim report of the Royal Commission enquiring into the Metropolitan Board of Works; several architects holding official positions in London were shown to have been feathering their nests with a variety of practices bordering on blackmail and extortion, as well as profiteering by the secretive acquisition of land scheduled for major development. The Royal Commission put the blame on a weak departmental head and the lack of expert supervision in several key areas. No criminal charges were brought on the grounds of insufficient evidence and because of the immunity offered to witnesses. Ten years later revelations of secret commission payments in many trades and professions prompted the Lord Chief Justice, Lord Killowen, to introduce the Illicit Secret Commissions Bill, which foundered for a variety of reasons, not the least of which was the problem of how to cope with corruption in private activities. A brief, four-clause bill was eventually passed in August 1906.[63]

While some M.P.s, some senior public servants, and some business-men seeking or fulfilling government contracts were involved in corruption and misconduct, functionaries lower down the bureaucratic ladder, particularly those with discretionary authority, also found opportunities for personal profit and not always by overtly breaking the law. The old police collected fees, shared fines and rewards, and might also take a cut from the compounding of an offence. The new police were paid regular wages to prevent such abuses and were forbidden to accept gratuities. But, as one mid nineteenth-century commentator put it:

Policemen are but men, their pay but scanty, their situations precarious, and it would be too much to expect that all are so pure as to decline to make a little money when favourable opportunities present themselves.[64]

Some gratuities did find their way into policemen's pockets, and 'knocking-up' members of the working class early in the morning to enable them to get to work could add a few unofficial pence to the weekly wage. Some detectives picked up extra money by unofficial enquiries or by putting pressure on debtors. Section 16 of the Licencing Act 1872 threatened a fine for any licencee who supplied, either as a gift or for sale, any liquor or refreshment to a police constable on duty, or who offered a bribe to a constable. In April 1897 the Manchester Watch Committee thought it necessary to send a copy of section 16 to all licence holders in the city. Constables collecting 'Christmas boxes' from shopkeepers and 'rents' from market traders slipped closer towards illegality. Some of the new police slipped even further by finding opportunities to profit from close co-operation with thieves – like Constables Jesse 'Juicy Lips' Jeaps and Charles King of London in the 1850s – or with swindlers, like the four London detectives prosecuted in 1877 for assisting in a betting fraud. Some simply acted on their own like the Chief Constable of Coventry who absconded in 1861 with £56 from the police fund.[65] Both the Old and the New Poor Law provided different officials with opportunities for petty profiteering, fraud and embezzlement. Local tradesmen had lucrative contracts for supplying food and clothing to workhouses, and the workhouse master had considerable discretion in these purchases; it can only be guessed at as to what extent some tradesmen won or maintained such contracts by gifts freely given, solicited or extorted. At the same time unscrupulous contractors could, and did, supply shoddy goods and adulterated food to maximise their profits; the paupers themselves were rarely in a situation to complain. Senior officials of the poor law administration were also concerned about profiteering by their medical officers.[66] In 1818 two parish constables were indicted at the Bedfordshire Quarter Sessions after claiming expenses respectively of £2.2s and £3.2s.6d for moving vagrants who had never existed. Nearly half a century later, in 1866, Daniel Harford Cox, an Assistant Overseer, was sentenced to four months in gaol by Bedfordshire magistrates for two separate offences involving Poor Law money amounting to £452.0s.3d.[67] This was small beer compared with some of the amounts which had gone missing in London. During the 1850s there were thirty-three embezzlement and default cases reported in fourteen of the thirty-nine Poor Law Unions and Parishes in the Metropolis. Ten of these offences involved the Assistant Clerk of the City of London Union who, during 1855–56, misappropriated £5,821.13s.8d of which a mere £500 was recovered. Between 1853 and 1856 the collectors of the poor rates in the City Union embezzled £14,342.13s.9d of which only £674.14s.3d was recovered.[68]

In cases of fiddling or pilferage at the workplace it was, as ever, working-class offenders who appeared in court most often. The prosecution of such offenders was less likely to provoke a crisis of confidence in the institution for which they worked than the prosecution of directors, managers or clerks. But, more importantly when it came to prosecution, the workplace crimes of working-class offenders, generally were more easy to detect and, in legal terms, their offences were easier to comprehend and to prove. Even so it would seem that only a tiny percentage of such offences were prosecuted, and only then when other sanctions, such as dismissal, seemed inappropriate, when it was felt that an example must be made to limit such offences, or when a particular offender had chanced his arm beyond the norms regarded as acceptable.[69] Eighteenth and nineteenth-century workplace crime was manifestly not simply the products of industrialisation, the desire of workers to strike back at an employer or at the developing capitalist system, or to preserve their traditional rights and a vibrant popular culture. An understanding of such crime is severely restricted when explained solely as an element of the developing struggle between capital and labour. It was not the new workplace alone which provided opportunities for fiddles; it was not new attempts to control the workforce which alone criminalised practices of long standing. The milkman 'bobbing' the milk, the petty official of the New Poor Law embezzling from the sums in his care, the government official demanding, or the contractor offering, a secret commission, all fall outside the simple class analysis. Most work, from casual labour to professional, provided opportunities for crime or, if legislation had not yet caught up with it, for what might be termed immoral profiteering.

REFERENCES AND NOTES

1. **Gerald Mars,** *Cheats at Work: An anthropology of workplace crime*, Unwin Paperbacks, London, 1983, pp. 18 and 164. The concept of a 'weasel word' is drawn from **Jason Ditton**, 'Perks, pilferage and the fiddle: The historical structure of an invisible wage', *Theory and Society*, **4** (1977) pp. 39–71.
2. **Bob Bushaway,** *By Rite: Custom, ceremony and community in England 1700–1880*, Junction Books, London, 1982, pp. 138–48; **David H. Morgan**, 'The place of harvesters in nineteenth-century village life', in **Raphael Samuel** (ed.), *Village Life and Labour*, RKP, London, 1975, pp. 53–61.
3. Beds. R.O. QSR 15/1785/81.
4. Quoted in Bushaway, *By Rite*, p. 141.
5. **P. J. R. King**, 'Crime, law and society in Essex 1740–1820', unpublished Ph.D. Cambridge University, 1984, pp. 287–89.
6. Beds. R.O. QSR 16/1790/46.

7.   Morgan, 'The place of harvesters', p. 57.

8.   Quoted in **Alasdair Clayre** (ed.), *Nature and Industrialization*, Oxford U.P., 1977, p. 23.

9.   **James Obelkevich,** *Religion and Rural Society: South Lindsey 1825–75*, Clarendon Press, Oxford, 1976, p. 60.

10. King, 'Crime, law and society', pp. 264–68.

11. Quoted in Clayre, *Nature and Industrialization*, pp. 19–20.

12. Beds. R.O. QSR 25/1825/345. For the August and autumn peak of summary convictions see above, pp. 34–5.

13. Bushaway, *By Rite*, pp. 222–23.

14. *The Times* 23 October 1795.

15. Beds. R.O. QSR 23/1817/423; QSR 23/1818/245 and 249; QSR 25/1823/304; QSR 1827/321.

16. **R. J. B. Knight**, 'Pilfering and theft from the dockyards at the time of the American War of Independence', *Mariner's Mirror*, **61** (1975), pp. 215–25; **Roger Morriss,** *The Royal Dockyards during the Revolutionary and Napoleonic Wars*, Leicester U.P., 1983 especially pp. 93–96; **John Rule,** *The Experience of Labour in Eighteenth-Century Industry*, Croom Helm, London, 1981, pp. 128–30.

17. A colleague at the Open University recalls that during his boyhood in Plymouth in the Second World War, his next-door neighbour, who worked in the Royal dockyard, successfully removed from the yard, piece by piece, a lathe. The lathe was then reassembled at his home.

18. Morriss, *The Royal Dockyards*, pp. 129–35.

19. **John Styles**, 'Embezzlement, industry and the law in England, 1500–1800' in **Maxine Berg, Pat Hudson** and **Michael Sonenscher** (eds.), *Manufacture in Town and Country before the Factory*, Cambridge U.P., 1983, pp. 183–84; **Clive Emsley,** *British Society and the French Wars 1793–1815*, Macmillan, London, 1979, pp. 57–58, 120–21 and 151.

20. Rule, *Experience of Labour*, pp. 126–7 and 130–33; Styles, 'Embezzlement, industry and the law', p. 204.

21. **James Greenwood,** *The Seven Curses of London*, London 1869 (reprinted, Basil Blackwell, Oxford, 1981), p. 109.

22. Rule, *Experience of Labour*, pp. 125–6 and 130; see also 'Conference Report', *Bulletin of the Society for the Study of Labour History*, **25** (1972), p. 13.

23. **Douglas Hay,** 'Manufacturers and the criminal law in the later eighteenth century: Crime and "Police" in South Staffordshire', *Past and Present Society Colloquium: Police and policing*, 1983, pp. 13–15; **David Philips,** *Crime and Authority in Victorian England*. Croom Helm, London, 1977, p. 182; 'Conference Report', *Bulletin of the Society for Labour History*, p. 7. As for the continuance of pilferage by industrial workers after the decline of outwork see the quotation from the Superintendent of K Division of the Metropolitan Police, p. 89 above, and **David Jones,** *Crime, Community, and Police in Nineteenth-Century Britain*, RKP, London, 1982, p. 157.

24. *O.B.S.P. 1796–97*, no. 108, pp. 155–56.

25. **Jennifer Davis,** 'Law breaking and law enforcement: The creation of a criminal class in mid-Victorian London', unpublished Ph.D. Boston College, 1984, p. 279.

26. Rule, *Experience of Labour*, pp. 127–28; see also Philips, *Crime and Authority*, pp. 182–84.
27. Leeds City Archives LC/QS 1/2 f. 117; Beds. R.O. QSR 22/1816/160 and 228–29; U.C.L. Chadwick MSS 11 answers to q. 10.
28. *C.C.C.S.P. 1856–57* no. 13, pp. 14–15.
29. Davis, 'Law breaking and law enforcement', pp. 99–103.
30. **Patrick Colquhoun**, *A Treatise on the Police of the Metropolis*, 3rd edn. London, 1796, chap. 3 passim; idem, *A Treatise on the Commerce and Police of the River Thames*, London, 1800, chap. 2 passim; **Henry Mayhew** *London Labour and the London Poor*, 4 vols., London, 1861–62, iv, pp 366–70.
31. **Raphael Samuel** (ed.), *East End Underworld: Chapters in the life of Arthur Harding*, RKP, London, 1981, pp. 16–17.
32. Colquhoun, *A Treatise on the Police*, p. 64.
33. Davis, 'Law breaking and law enforcement', pp. 84–99.
34. *P.P.* 1877 (418) xi, *Select Committee on the House of Lords on Intemperance, Third Report*, qq. 8256–58.
35. *P.P.* 1839 (168) xix, *Royal Commission on Constabulary* pp. 48–54.
36. **Harry Hanson,** *The Canal Boatmen 1760*–1914, Manchester U.P., 1975, p 37.
37. Jennifer Davis, 'Criminal Prosecutions and their context in late Victorian London', paper presented to the Conference on the History of Law Labour and Crime, at the University of Warwick, 15–18 September 1983, p. 7; **Anthony S. Wohl,** *Endangered Lives: Public health in Victorian Britain* Dent, London, 1983, pp. 20–21.
38. Greenwood, *Seven Curses*, pp. 94–107; **Charles Booth,** *Life and Labour o the People of London, 2nd series Industry* (5 vols.) 1903, iii, p. 311.
39. **S. A. Marglin**, 'What do bosses do? The origins and functions of hierarchy in capitalist production', *Review of Radical Political Economies*, **6** (1974) pp. 46–55.
40. **E. P. Thompson,** *Whigs and Hunters: The origin of the Black Act*, Allen Lane, London, 1975, p. 207; see also the paper by Peter Linebaugh in 'Conference Report', *Bulletin of the Society for Labour History*, pp. 11–15
41. **P. C. Barrett**, Crime and punishment in a Lancashire industrial town Law and social change in the borough of Wigan, 1800–50', unpublished M.Phil. Liverpool Polytechnic, 1980, pp. 84–86 and 191–95.
42. Philips, *Crime and Authority*, pp. 190–91.
43. Davis, 'Law breaking and law enforcement', pp. 267–70 and 283–84.
44. Davis, 'Criminal prosecutions', pp. 5–6; and see note 24 above.
45. **J. A. Sharpe,** *Crime in Early Modern England 1550–1750*, Longman London, 1984, pp. 149–50. For the statutes which sought to control the outwork see Styles, 'Embezzlement, industry and the law', pp. 209–10.
46. Styles, 'Embezzlement, industry and the law', p. 188, and passim.
47. Hay, 'Manufacturers and the criminal law', p. 15. At the Labour History Society Conference on Industrial Crime one contributor noted from 'his own experience in the mining industry, [that] the most politically and industrially conscious workers were not sympathetic to pilfering, whereas the less conscious would steal a fellow worker's tools if they would filch something from an employer'. 'Conference report', *Bulletin of the Society for Labour History*, pp. 7–8.

48. Notts. R.O. QSD/1836; for a similar example, on this occasion of a confectioner marking money in his till and catching his shopman see *O.B.S.P. 1796–97*, no. 87.

49. **Stephen Humphries**, *Hooligans or Rebels? An oral history of working-class childhood and youth 1889–1939*, Basil Blackwell, Oxford, 1981, pp. 170–72.

50. Greenwood, *Seven Curses*, p. 97.

51. **Avril D. Leadley**, 'Some villains of the eighteenth-century market place' in **John Rule** (ed.), *Outside the Law: Studies in crime and order 1650–1850*, Exeter Papers in Economic History, no. 15, University of Exeter, 1982, p. 24.

52. Wilts. R.O. Stourhead Archive 383/955 Justice Book of R. C. Hoare 1785–1815.

53. Beds. R.O. QSR 18/1802/13; QSR 20/1808/170.

54. Greenwood, *Seven Curses*, pp. 101–2.

55. Wohl, *Endangered Lives*, p. 54.

56. **D. C. Woods**, 'The operations of the Master and Servants Act in the Black Country 1858–75', *Midland History* vii, (1982), pp. 93–115 (at p. 94); and see below pp. 156–7.

57. **Rob Sindall**, 'Middle-class crime in nineteenth-century England', *Criminal Justice History*, iv (1983), pp. 23–40 (at p. 32); and for more detail see R. S. Sindall, 'Aspects of middle-class crime in the nineteenth-century', unpublished M.Phil, University of Leicester, 1974, pp. 103–7.

58. Beds. R.O. Whitbread MSS (uncatalogued) Magniac to Whitbread 15 September and 12 October 1882.

59. **Gregory Anderson**, *Victorian Clerks*, Manchester U.P., 1976, pp. 35–36.

60. Sindall, 'Middle-class crime', pp. 31–32; idem, 'Aspects of middle-class crime', pp. 106–8, 143–47 and 156–60; **Rev J. Stockwell Watts**, *The Biggest Crime of the Nineteenth Century and what the Churches say to it*, London, 1893.

61. Sindall, 'Middle-class crime', p. 34; see also in general Anderson, *Victorian Clerks*, and **Geoffrey Crossick**, 'The emergence of the lower-middle class in Britain: A discussion', in Geoffrey Crossick (ed.), *The Lower Middle Class in Britain* Croom Helm, London, 1977.

62. **Alan Doig**, *Corruption and Misconduct in Contemporary British Politics*, Penguin, Harmondsworth, 1984, p. 69.

63. **Phil Fennell** and **Philip A. Thomas**, 'Corruption in England and Wales: An historical analysis', *International Journal of the Sociology of Law*, **11** (1983), pp. 167–89; **David Owen**, *The Government of Victorian London 1855–89*, Belknap Press, Cambridge, Mass. 1982, chap. 8 and 9.

64. **W. H. Watts**, 'Records of an old police court', *St. James's Magazine* xii (1865), pp. 499–506 (at p. 506). On occasion, however, members of the new police were permitted to take gratuities and rewards. At the Nottinghamshire Epiphany Sessions in 1856, for example, three police constables from the county force were commended for apprehending a sheep stealer and were rewarded out of county funds; one man received £3, the others £1 each 'which appears to this court to be a reasonable compensation for their expenses, exertions and loss of time'. Notts. R.O. QSM 1856–60, adjournment sessions 7 March 1856.

65. **Clive Emsley**, *Policing and its Context 1750–1870*, Macmillan, London,

1973, pp. 128 and 159; **Phillip Thurmond Smith,** *Policing Victorian London: Political policing, public order, and the London Metropolitan Police,* Greenwood Press, Westport, Conn. 1985, pp. 53–54, 69 and 71; Manchester Police Museum, Watch Committee Minutes 1895 onwards, vol. 3, f. 83; **Barbara Weinberger,** 'Crime and police in the late nineteenth century: A case study from the Coventry area', unpublished M.A. University of Warwick, 1976, p. 34.

66. **M. A. Crowther,** *The Workhouse System 1834–1929: The history of an English social institution,* Methuen, London, 1983, pp. 118, 159–60, 216 and 241.

67. Beds. R.O. QSR 23/1818/528 and 529; QGV 10/4/128.

68. U.C.L. Chadwick MSS 16 'Police Memoranda etc. (1855–69)'. Printed return of cases of embezzlement and default by Poor Law administrators in the Metropolis 1853–59.

69. Davis, 'Law breaking and law enforcement', chaps. 3 and 5.

Chapter 6

A MID-POINT ASSESSMENT: THE CRIMINAL CLASS AND PROFESSIONAL CRIMINALS

The use of the term the 'criminal class' was probably at its most common during the 1860s,[1] but the idea of a criminal class and of professional criminals living, at least partly, by the proceeds of criminal behaviour was popular throughout the period. It has also informed the work of several historians of nineteenth-century criminality. 'Entry into the criminal class was a means of finding support', wrote J. J. Tobias:

> it was entry into an association, informal but none the less real, members of which could be found almost everywhere. In gaol or lodging-house or on the road, criminals could find companions in like situation, could exchange experiences and discover common acquaintanceships.[2]

While dubious about Engel's romantic notion that the most courageous members of the very poor became 'thieves and murderers' and waged 'open war against the middle classes', Kellow Chesney drew heavily on the work of investigators like Mayhew and revelled in the underworld slang of Victorian England to give his readers a glimpse of 'gonolphs, footpads and the swell mob' and 'magsmen, macers and shofulmen'.[3]

A few men did get a lot of money from criminal behaviour, but those who made the greatest financial hauls were white-collar offenders who were never considered to be part of a criminal class; and while 'William Smith' of Baring Brothers' Liverpool house, or the embezzling nephew of the Mathesons, may have been considered as professional gentlemen, they were never considered as professional thieves. Similarly, fraudsters like the Bidwell brothers who, in January and February 1873, tricked the Bank of England out of £100,405..7s..3d, and who attracted enormous crowds on their arrest and removal to London, were rarely considered in the same breath as Bill Sikes.[4]

Others who enjoyed the larger profits from criminal activity were receivers: men like Ikey Solomons, Jonathan Wild, or Jonathan Field. The latter was alleged to have had a headquarters in Barbican and branches in Bermondsey and Whitechapel.[5] But it is doubtful whether any receivers achieved the financial success of the Bidwells or 'Smith'; it is also doubtful whether many large-scale receivers existed. Policemen were always concerned about pawnbrokers acting as receivers.[6] Some unquestionably did, though many more, probably, simply preferred not to ask questions, and others must have received stolen goods unknowingly. Pawnbrokers and, lower down the social scale, the proprietors of 'dolly shops' or 'leaving shops' were important figures to the urban working-class communities of the eighteenth and nineteenth centuries; they provided a vital financial service within these communities, and not simply to the casual labourers. Sometimes certain kinds of goods were left with the pawnbroker on a regular weekly basis – good clothes could be pawned during the week and redeemed for weekends after pay day. Many of the articles of clothing, bed linen, table linen and cutlery taken in a petty theft were hastened to a pawnbroker; but as several divisions of the Metropolitan Police reported to Chadwick and the Constabulary Commissioners, some petty thieves were caught precisely because of the vigilance of pawnbrokers.[7]

A variety of other kinds of dealer and retailer made profits from receiving. There were butchers and poulterers who received game from poachers and who sometimes organised the poaching gangs. Old clothes dealers were suspect in the same way that pawnbrokers were; so too were the owners of chandler's shops who might receive and resell whatever was purloined from ships by dockers, ships crews or ship builders. There were scrap-metal dealers who asked no questions about small quantities offered to them for sale; and there were the grocers, like Harding's Aunt Liza, who received, repackaged and resold. It is, of course, most unlikely that many of these receivers made significant profits from such activities or that many of them could, in any meaningful way, be considered as professional criminals.

From Elizabethan times at least there was concern that children were being taught to be professional criminals. Fagin's school for pickpockets appears to have had some basis in fact and it was confidently asserted that a child starting out as a 'gonolph' street thief, if adept and well-trained, could rise to be a member of the exclusive group of professional pickpockets known as the 'swell mob'.[8] But several points need to be made about pickpockets and their trade. First, different styles of nineteenth-century fashion much aided such offenders: a handkerchief poking from the back-pocket of a fashionable mid-century tailed coat was easy pickings; Arthur Harding noted how the bustle, which came in and out of women's fashion in the second half of the century, could have been designed with the thief's requirements in mind. Pickpockets worked best in crowds. Harding and his mates worked fairs, markets and races and moved round the country where their work took them.[9] What appears to have been a gang of travelling pickpockets was apprehended in Bedfordshire in October 1860 after Mary Mayne was robbed of one promissory note, value £5, two sovereigns and one half sovereign. The gang consisted of George Brown, a twenty-one year old hair-brush stainer born in Leicester, Henry James Green, alias James Middleton, aged twenty-three, a stocking weaver born in Dublin whose last residence was in Nottingham, his wife Jane Green, alias Elizabeth Lockery, aged twenty, also a stocking weaver born in Coventry, and William Jones, alias William Johnson, alias David Dunn, a twenty-four-year old labourer from London. Both Henry Green and William Jones had previous convictions for picking pockets; Jones had been sentenced to seven years' transportation for such an offence at the Old Bailey in 1851 and had been released on licence in 1854.[10] The haul from Mary Mayne, split four ways, assuming it could be matched with similar hauls from the same crowd, may have provided the gang with a modest living. But it was estimated earlier in the century that a pocket-handkerchief thief would have to steal between twenty and thirty handkerchiefs in a week to be able to live off the booty.[11]

Burglary was another crime which most Hanoverian and Victorian commentators considered as a skill, the perpetrators of which were regarded as professional criminals. Burglars, it was alleged, set out armed with jemmies and false keys; at least as early as 1783 it was being described in parliament as a 'science' with specially made instruments available for the practitioners. Detailed sketches of such instruments made their way into the pages of Victorian magazines, though whether certain tools were indeed 'house-breaking implements' or simply a carpenter's brace and bit may have been purely within the perception of an arresting constable.[12] One or two burglars, however, equipped themselves with weapons which had only one use; press outrage and panic about armed burglars in the 1880s led to a revolver issue to metropolitan policemen on their beats.[13]

Interestingly, during the 1860s when reviewing the working of the old Marlborough Street Police Office, W. H. Watts could write:

> There are now no professional highwaymen; there are no professional burglars; there are no localities given over absolutely to the outcasts of society; there are now no colonies of thieves who only live by thieving; no burglars or highwaymen who support existence solely by following out their penal trade. The old haunts of vice are broken up, and the old gangs of offenders have either died off or been utterly dispersed. If you see in the papers that 'burglars' have been captured, you will find, on enquiry, the culprits have mostly trades of their own; if a batch of pickpockets is taken, the chances are that you will discover they have a 'calling' besides that of picking pockets, at which they are able to, and do, maintain themselves when the 'honest fit' is upon them.[14]

Whether Watts was correct in his assessment of the end of an old kind of full-time criminal is difficult to assess. Probably the new police had cleared some petty offenders from the streets, though these would not appear to have been the variety of criminals to whom he was referring. Moreover it is worth noting that he was writing in the immediate aftermath of the publications of Mayhew and others who wrote in terms of a 'criminal class'. Of course it is most unlikely that anyone who went before the Fieldings, or before Colquhoun or any of his contemporaries who served at the Marlborough Street Police Office, ever gave their trade or calling as burglar, highwaymen or pickpocket. But Watts's comments point to the key questions which have to be posed about the eighteenth and nineteenth-century professional criminal and criminal classes: how much crime were these professionals and/or this class responsible for? How many professionals were there? How big was the criminal class?

The statistics and the court records suggest that the overwhelming majority of thefts reported and prosecuted were opportunist and petty; most incidents of violence against the person involved people who were either related or who were known to each other. Professional criminals, in the sense of men who went out armed with tools for housebreaking and weapons and who committed more than one offence, might well have carried out the bigger robberies. Probably they committed these robberies as 'professionals' taking precautions and planning carefully, rather than yielding to momentary temptations; possibly fewer of them were arrested and prosecuted. Perhaps, as the new police grew in numbers and gained more experience petty street thieves and opportunist thieves were at greater risk; this may have contributed to the proportionate increase in burglaries during the second half of the nineteenth century as those who were determined to profit from criminal behaviour recognised a need for better planning and organisation, though the problem here is that 'burglary' itself is an elastic term which could be stretched or slackened according to the discretion of prosecutor and/or police. In general, it would be impossible to prove that most thefts and most violence was the work of persons who indulged in criminal behaviour as a way of life.

The notion of a criminal class poses a rather different problem. As was argued earlier the criminal class described by Victorian commentators was largely synonymous with the poorer working class, particularly those who existed by casual labour. Tobias followed this definition, and Chesney's Victorian underworld embraced the same groups, as well as travelling showmen, the organisers of prize fights and so forth. Certainly some people in these social groups committed crimes: families, peer-group gangs – usually of young men – sometimes whole streets or villages had negative attitudes towards some aspects of the law, and towards the police in particular. James Waring, a sixteen-year old sweep convicted, with two younger boys, of burglary at the Old Bailey in January 1797 used to pass his booty on to his mother who then took it to the pawn shop.[15] Listing the cases heard at the local Summer Assize in 1843 the *Bedford Mercury* singled out for comment the family of Thomas Smith, a seventeen-year old stocking maker from Biggleswade who pleaded guilty to stealing a parcel from a coach:

The father of the prisoner has just completed his term of transportation; his mother has been in prison for a considerable time; his brother is transported; and three years ago the prisoner was also ordered to be transported, but was respited on account of his youth.[16]

The Redman gang of Houghton Conquest has already been described. In eighteenth-century London there appear to have been gangs of, perhaps, four or five men who joined with each other to commit burglaries and highway robberies; but these gangs were not long-lived and their membership was never rigid. At the end of the nineteenth and beginning of the twentieth centuries Arthur Harding's East End gang picked pockets around the country and then began passing counterfeit money; subsequently they were available for hire as a gang of toughs and were, on one occasion, recruited to terrorise 'blackleg' printers.[17] Merthyr Tydfil's 'China' seems to have remained a criminal Alsatia for many years; and within the transient districts of other towns and cities could be found isolated invividuals – wandering labourers, sometimes genuine vagrants who moved from cheap lodging-house to cheap lodging house, and if the worst came to the worst to street or hedgerow, or if apprehended, to workhouse or prison. Sometimes these individuals acquired exotic names like the 'Wolds Rangers' of the East Riding or the 'Rodneys' of South Staffordshire 'who go about without any settled residence, and who never work, but live by robbery, and sleep by the coke and engine fires which are numerous in this mining district'.[18] These people were looked upon with suspicion by the respectable inhabitants whose streets or villages they dared to enter. The management of such people was increasingly taken over by the police; they were, in the modern sociological sense, 'police property'. Sometimes the wanderers and vagrants could be dangerous, sometimes they might steal, but it is not particularly helpful to lump them together with the Hardings, the Redmans, the population of 'China' and the few criminal families and to conclude that, together, they all constitute a criminal class since the only common denominator is the breaking of, often very different, laws.

The notion of a criminal class was, indeed remains, a convenient one for insisting that most crime is something committed on law-abiding citizens by an alien group. The more historians probe the notion, the more it is revealed to be spurious. Among the main findings of both David Philips's detailed study of crime in the Black Country and Jennifer Davis's work on mid-Victorian London, is the conclusion that no clear distinction can be made between a dishonest criminal class and a poor but honest working class.[19] Simon Stevenson's analysis of those subject to the 'habitual criminals' legislation of 1869 and 1871 reveals how small the number of 'habituals' was; perhaps no more than 4,000 a year throughout the 1870s. Furthermore he suggests that it is very difficult to conceive of these individuals as either a class or a group of professionals readily and continually identifiable by their behaviour and intergrating within some deviant familial lore. A few offenders adopted romantic names and posturings, but there does not appear to have been any specifically 'criminal' argot or practice of tatooing; most of the larcenies committed by these individuals involved goods of paltry value and criminal 'tools' were rarely used in the execution of their crimes. Lastly, if the 'habitual criminal' did have unsavoury friends and acquaintances, often drawn from his peer group, he was also equally likely to have family support of a rather different kind with parents and sometimes wives urging him to more law abiding and 'moral' behaviour.[20]

Tobias portrays the women of the criminal class as, primarily, the aiders and abettors of their menfolk. Prostitutes he perceives as central, starting trouble in pubs 'to draw the police away from the scene of an intended burglary' and being 'in league with pickpockets'. In addition there were 'prostitute-thieves' acting on their own account.[21] Some prostitutes did rob their clients, though the reluctance of victims to come forward in such circumstances is notorious[22]; possibly equally numerous were brutal physical assaults inflicted on prostitutes by their clients, often the worse for drink, or by their pimps, very few of which were reported. Prostitutes tended to be catalogued with the criminal classes as part of the detritus of a society eager to portray itself as a rock of morality. Dickens described the life of Sikes's Nancy as 'squandered in the streets and among the most noisome stews and dens of London'. She was '[t]he miserable companion of thieves and ruffians, the fallen outcast of low haunts, the associate of the scourings of the jails and hulks'.[23] As noted earlier 'abandoned prostitute' and 'hardened offender' were almost synonymous for women transported for theft, while policemen arresting drunken women invariably catalogued them as 'prostitutes'.[24] Prostitution as such was not a criminal offence; the prostitution offences were specifically soliciting, living off immoral earnings and running 'houses of ill fame', but these were enforced selectively. The elegant London brothels like the Argyll Rooms, Kate Hamilton's and Mott's were largely ignored by the police. Manifestly neither the proprietors, nor the expensive women of these establishments, were perceived of as members of the criminal class or professional criminals; and at this end of the market the profits were handsome. The less salubrious 'houses of ill fame' were more vulnerable, though even in some of the poorest districts the police did not interfere with them.[25] The woman soliciting on the streets appears to have been the most vulnerable to prosecution, and during the period that the Contagious Diseases Acts remained on the statute book, large numbers of young, quite innocent working-class women became 'police property' and the objects of police suspicion and surveillance. In the same way that the 'criminal class' became synonymous for the poorer sections of the working class, so 'prostitute' became, in many instances, the noun to describe the women of this class.

One last point needs to be made here: a criminal record led some men to be treated by the police as their property and, in many instances, men with criminal records had difficulty in finding work. The formal creation of the category of 'habitual criminals' by the Act of 1869 and the Prevention of Crimes Act 1871 probably contributed to such difficulties. Colquhoun highlighted the problem of the newly released prisoner when he asked: '*Without friends, without character, and without the means of subsistence*, what are these unhappy mortals to do?'.[26] The Victorians also recognised the problem. James Greenwood expressed his doubts about the police supervision of ticket-of-leave men for this reason:

> There are hundreds and thousands of men in London, and indeed in all great cities, who 'pick-up' a living somehow – anyhow, and who, though they all the time are honest fellows, would find it difficult to account for, and bring forward evidence to show, how they were engaged last Monday, and again on Wednesday, and what they earned, and whom they earned it of. Such men 'job about', very often in localities that, in the case of a man under police supervision, to be seen there would be to rouse suspicions as to his intentions. For instance, many a shilling or sixpence is 'picked up' by men who have nothing better to do, by hanging round railway stations and steamboat wharves, and looking out for passengers who have luggage they wish carried. But supposing that a man, a 'ticket-of-leave', was to resort to such a means of obtaining a livelihood, and that he was seen 'hanging about' such places day after day by a watchful detective who knew who and what he was, – with what amount of credibility would the authorities receive his statement that he was 'looking out for a chance to carry somebody's trunk or carpet-bag'![27]

The attempts of London's stipendiary magistrates to frustrate the supervision of habitual criminals by the Metropolitan Police may have stemmed partly from such a recognition. The various other attempts at a solution, such as the discharged Prisoners' Aid Society established in 1857,[28] were not especially successful. Yet here again it must be emphasised that the largest numbers of offenders arrested and imprisoned were always drawn from the ranks of young men; clearly not all young men arrested for crimes in their teens and twenties carried on with a criminal career into their thirties and forties. Parent-Duchâtelet and William Acton noted, probably correctly, that prostitution was a transitory stage for most women who followed the 'profession' during the nineteenth century; women became prostitutes because of temporary economic hardship. Probably the same was true for those who committed the bulk of petty thefts brought before the courts during the eighteenth and nineteenth centuries; criminality, in the forms of thefts committed by men from the poorer sections of the working class was transitory behaviour, possibly fostered by economic hardship, probably encouraged by opportunity. Most thefts, and most crimes of violence, cannot be attributed to professional criminals; nor is it helpful to think

Crime and society in England, 1750–1900

of these offences as committed by a group which can, in any meaningful sense, be described as a class.

REFERENCES AND NOTES

1. S. J. Stevenson, 'The "criminal class" in the mid-Victorian city: A study of policy conducted with special reference to the provisions of 34 and 35 Vict., c.112 (1871) in Birmingham and East London in the early years of registration and supervision', unpublished D.Phil Oxford University, 1983, p. 32 note 4.
2. J. J. Tobias, *Crime and Industrial Society in the Nineteenth Century*, Harmondsworth, Penguin, 1972, p. 108.
3. Kellow Chesney, *The Victorian Underworld*, Harmondsworth, Penguin, 1970; the quotation from Engels', *The Condition of the Working Class in England in 1844* is on p. 99.
4. For the Bidwells see their autobiographies, Austin Bidwell, *From Wall Street to Newgate*, Hartford, Conn., 1895 and George Bidwell, *Forging His Chains: The autobiography of George Bidwell*, Hartford, Conn., 1888. Both are discussed in Philip Priestley, *Victorian Prison Lives: English prison biography 1830–1914*, Methuen, London, 1985.
5. W. H. Watts, 'Records of an old police court', *St. James's Magazine*, x (1864), pp. 458–65 (at p. 460). I am tempted to believe that the 'Field' in Watt's account is a printing error and should read 'Wild'.
6. Patrick Colquhoun, *A Treatise on the Police of the Metropolis*, 3rd edn. London, 1796, p. 13 and chap. 8 *passim*. Colquhoun even proposed an act of parliament to control and supervise pawnbrokers and dealers in second-hand goods, see Sir Leon Radzinowicz, *A History of English Criminal Law*, 5 vols, Stevens, London, 1948–68, iii, Appendix 5.
7. U. C. L. Chadwick MSS 11 f.23: E division response to qu.11; f.25: R. division response to qu.11. For the importance of the nineteenth-century pawnbroker in working-class communities see Melanie Tebbutt, *Making Ends Meet: Pawnbroking and working-class credit*, Leicester University Press, 1983; for pawnbrokers as receivers and police informants see especially pp. 70 and 95–99. The fullest discussion of 'receiving' by pawnbrokers, 'dolly-shops', second-hand dealers as well as ordinary, legitimate tradesmen (like butchers or fishmongers buying pilfered paper to wrap their wares) is to be found in Jennifer Davis, 'Law breaking and law enforcement: The creation of a criminal class in mid-Victorian London', unpublished Ph.D. Boston College, 1984, chap. 2.
8. Chesney, *Victorian Underworld*, chap. 5 *passim*. For reference to a similar 'school' in Elizabethan London see J. A. Sharpe, *Crime in Early Modern England 1550–1750*, Longman, London, 1984, p. 114.
9. Raphael Samuel (ed.), *East-End Underworld: Chapters in the life of Arthur Harding*, RKP, London, 1981, p. 78.
10. Beds. R.O. QGV 10/4/23–26.
11. Charles M. De Motte, 'The dark side of town: Crime in Manchester and Salford 1815–75', Ph.D. University of Kansas, 1977, p. 247.

A mid-point assessment: the criminal class and professional criminals

12. *Gentleman's Magazine* liii (1783), pp. 740–41; Davis, 'Law breaking and law enforcement', p. 146. Several of the Victorian illustrations of housebreaking equipment are reproduced in Chesney, *Victorian Underworld*.
13. **Clive Emsley**, ' "The thump of wood on a swede turnip": Police violence in nineteenth-century England', *Criminal Justice History*, VI (1985), pp. 125–49 (at pp. 136–41).
14. Watts, 'Records of an old police court', xi (1864) pp. 444–52 (at p. 448).
15. *O.B.S.P. 1796–97*, nos. 70–71. In her excellent study of the low life of eighteenth-century Paris Arlette Farge notes several petty offenders working in family groups. **Arlette Farge**, *La vie fragile: Violence, pouvoirs et solidarités à Paris au XVIIIe siecle*, Hachette, Paris, 1986, pp. 176–78.
16. *Bedford Mercury*, 22 July 1843.
17. J. M. Beattie, *Crime and the Courts in England*, Oxford U.P., 1986, pp. 252–63. Samuel (ed.), *East End Underworld*, pp. 78–80 and 121.
18. *The Times* 16 November 1850, quoting the *Derby Mercury*.
19. **David Philips**, *Crime and Authority in Victorian England*, Croom Helm, London, 1977; Jennifer Davis, 'Law breaking and law enforcement: The creation of a criminal class in mid-Victorian London', unpublished Ph.D. Boston College, 1984.
20. Stevenson, 'The "Criminal Class" in the mid-Victorian city,' especially pp. 280, 284, 309, 311–31 and 355–61.
21. Tobias, *Crime and Industrial Society*, pp. 103–7.
22. See, for example, **Frances Finnegan**, *Poverty and Prostitution: A study of Victorian prostitutes in York*, Cambridge U.P., 1979, pp. 117–24.
23. Charles Dickens, *Oliver Twist*, chap. XL.
24. See above p. 67; **Clive Emsley**, *Policing and its Context 1750–1870*, Macmillan, London, 1983, p. 122.
25. Chesney, *Victorian Underworld*, pp. 365–67; Emsley, *Policing and its Context*, p. 140.
26. Colquhoun, *Treatise on the Police*, p. 91.
27. **James Greenwood**, *The Seven Curses of London*, London, 1869, p. 125.
28. Priestley, *Victorian Prison Lives*, pp. 283 and 286 for prisoners' attitudes to the discharged Prisoners' Aid Society.

Chapter 7

PROSECUTORS AND THE COURTS

There were significant changes in prosecution and court practice during the period 1750 to 1900. There were also significant changes in the kind of court environments in which criminal cases were heard. On occasions it was an act of parliament which heralded a change; sometimes, however, legislation simply formalised and sanctioned what had come to be existing practice; and many changes were gradual, almost imperceptible except over a long period.

The English legal system provides for any private citizen to initiate a prosecution. During the eighteenth century a few prosecutions were directed by the Treasury Solicitor, notably in coining offences. Some were conducted by the Attorney General, principally cases of treason or sedition; but again the numbers remained small and during the 1790s, the period of the English 'reign of terror', the Crown Law Officers regularly refused to finance prosecutions for sedition and urged magistrates – not always successfully – to organise these locally. The overwhelming majority of criminal prosecutions, more than eighty per cent, were conducted by the victims of crimes or, rather less frequently, by private individuals acting on the victim's behalf; and, reflecting the dominance of the male in eighteenth and nineteenth-century society, most prosecutors were men.[1]

Victims of a criminal offence had a variety of choices. They could, for example, let the matter drop regarding it as too insignificant or unimportant for a criminal prosecution. Sometimes, and especially in the earlier part of the period under consideration, an offender was dealt with by community action rather than by recourse to the law: a Jewish hawker, caught attempting to steal a ring from a young woman at Huntingdon races in 1753, was seized by a crowd and ducked in a horse pond.[2] However crowds, and individuals, could not be relied upon always to help a victim. Stories were reported in the courts of victims, in hot pursuit of thieves, being deliberately impeded either by individuals or by crowds.[3] Probably what happened in these instances was that the activist individuals or crowds took the part of the person who appeared to be the underdog. Arthur Harding recalled crowds taking the part of children at the end of the nineteenth century who, well aware of what they were doing and certain of getting popular support because of their tender years, openly stole from traders' carts and barrows or from shops and stalls.[4]

The occasional attack on, or 'rough musicing' of, a prosecutor is suggestive of communities which felt that certain offenders should not have been prosecuted, or at least should have been proceeded against on a lesser charge. In the summer of 1763 Mrs White, a Spitalfields victualler, prosecuted her servant, Cornelius Saunders, for theft after he had stumbled across her savings in her basement and decked himself out in new clothes. Saunders was found guilty and executed. Many inhabitants of Spitalfields were incensed; Saunders was well-known in the neighbourhood primarily, perhaps, because he had been blind from birth. Mrs White's house was attacked by large crowds; her furniture and possessions were thrown out into the street and burned.[5] A rather more complex affair occurred in Bedfordshire half a century later. At the 1817 Summer Assizes, Thomas Flemings was prosecuted for raping fifteen-year old Sarah Gardener. The latter had been visiting her sister at Tingrith village feast; on the way home she was frightened by a group of Irishmen and, in consequence, her sister asked Flemings to accompany her. It was during the two mile walk to her parents' house in Ampthill that Flemings raped her. Flemings was found guilty and executed. He went to his death, according to the local newspaper, a true penitent:

> he said he had never been guilty of any crime before, nor even summoned before a Magistrate on any occasion whatever; but he had neglected a place of worship and his Maker, which had brought him to that untimely end.

Sarah Gardener's parents then found themselves the objects of popular abuse; crowds of up to 200 gathered outside their house throwing stones, exhibiting effigies:

> one dressed as a man another as a woman and another as a child [and] hallowing and charging the family with having hung the man and that they ought to be hung themselves.[6]

There is nothing in the surviving details of the Flemings-Gardener case to suggest why the prosecutors were so unpopular, but possibly there was a feeling that the charge of rape was being used rather too freely in Bedfordshire on flimsy evidence. Three rape cases had been brought before the Summer Assizes in 1815; one was thrown out by the Grand Jury, the other two resulted in acquittal. One of these acquittals led to a prosecution for conspiracy at the 1817 Lent Assizes, just five months before the Flemings-Gardener case: the Reverend Robert Woodward and his daughters Sarah and Susannah were indicted for conspiring to prosecute James Harris on a charge of rape and making Susannah pregnant. The Woodwards were found guilty; the daughters were each sentenced to one year's imprisonment and the Reverend Woodward was compelled by the bishop to resign his living – 'a degree of punishment' which, he believed to be 'beyond what was in the contemplation of the Judge who passed sentence on him'.[7]

Violent hostility towards prosecutors and their witnesses in unpopular cases was not confined to the Georgian period. In Blackburn in November 1862, after the prosecution of four men for night poaching on the land of J. Butler Bowden, crowds turned on the gamekeepers who had given evidence as they left the town hall escorted by eight men from the Lancashire Constabulary. An estimated 400 people then marched on Bowden's house, Pleasington Hall, which they proceeded to stone until driven off by Bowden and his servants firing two or three shots over their heads. A troop of the 16th Lancers and squads of the county constabulary were rushed into Blackburn to maintain order.[8] Traditional rough musicing, with all of its folkloric paraphernalia, tended to fade away during the nineteenth century, though its Welsh variant, *ceffyl pren*, has been noted as being deployed against unpopular offenders and prosecutors in the Victorian period, and manifestations were not unknown in the great cities of mid nineteenth-century England.[9]

If the offender was known to, or instantly apprehended by, the victim, some personal retribution or private settlement could be sought, or offered, to avoid recourse to the law. Though it must be noted that this was not always the case, no matter how close the bonds between individuals. There are, for example, court records of children stealing from their parents, and being prosecuted for it. There are also examples of parents urging the prosecution of their offspring by those who had been their victims; thus the law could be brought into play as a means of discipline within the family.[10] An agreement to come to some private settlement over a theft was compounding a felony and was itself against the law. In October 1794 Richard Wadeson, a tallow chandler of Worksop was indicted before the Nottinghamshire quarter sessions for a misdemeanour 'in compounding a felony with Marmaduke Littleover for feloniously stealing, taking and carrying away two pounds weight of candles the goods and chattles of the said Richard Wadeson'. The following January Wadeson appeared before the Court, submitted to the charge and was fined twenty shillings.[11] Offenders brought to court sometimes protested that the prosecutor had agreed to let matters be after a financial settlement. There are similarly occasional statements recorded in court proceedings or depositions that the offender offered money to avoid prosecution. Thomas Richardson, a publican of Carnaby Street, prosecuted John Wilson at the Old Bailey in 1796 for the theft of two quart pewter pots and three pint pewter pots. Richardson testified in court that, when he confronted Wilson at the local watch-house after his arrest:

he made towards me, and said, I will give you ten or twenty pounds if you will not appear against me; I told him to offer me no money for I have suffered so much by pot stealers.[12]

George Burridge told the Bedfordshire quarter sessions in 1832:

> I left my watch ... hanging on the nail over the mantlepiece in my father's house at Steppingly between 7 and 8 in the morning. When I went home at 10 o'clock my watch was gone I have not seen it again. D[efendan]t when he was taken up said he would pay me for the watch and all expenses if I would settle it. I said I would if the magistrate would allow it.[13]

Other alternatives to prosecution continued to be exploited throughout the nineteenth century. Employers could, and often did, simply dismiss pilfering workmen; this, together with the threat that the offender would never be employed again was a tougher sanction than many courts could impose. Many victims were often satisfied with the return of their stolen property and/or with the scare which they gave the accused by the very fact of involving the police; once property had been restored and the offender had been warned by police involvement, some victims declined to press ahead with prosecutions, or else simply did not turn up for the trials.[14]

Legally assaults were different from thefts in that they were not necessarily felonious. During the eighteenth century many cases of assault were settled with a financial payment being made by the assailant to the victim. Magistrates could be involved in such settlements at petty sessions. At quarter sessions, if it was noted that agreement had been reached between the parties, the punishment imposed by the court could be nominal. In January 1766, for example, William Wesson prosecuted Thomas Turner, a grocer of Derby at the Nottinghamshire Sessions for assault; 'it appearing to the court that [the] prosecutor was satisfied', Turner was fined one penny and discharged.[15] But alleged agreements to make amends with a money payment could be as fraught with difficulties in assault cases as in larceny cases. At the Easter Sessions for Bedfordshire in 1833 Emily Crossley prosecuted Robert Wells for an assault after which she had suffered a miscarriage. Wells complained that 'the woman offered to make it up and did for 5/-'.[16] Again alternative settlements to prosecution continued to be sought and found in cases of assault throughout the nineteenth century. Moreover it would seem that many working-class prosecutions for assault were part of continuing feuds between families or groups, with the law being employed as one way of the complainant achieving a measure of what he or she considered to be justice, but certainly not bringing the affair to an end.[17]

Some victims of theft who reported their loss to constables or thief takers, were prepared to pay a reward for the return of their property and to ignore the prosecution of the offender; corrupt and unscrupulous constables and thief takers, working in league with thieves, were happy

Crime and society in England, 1750–1900

to fall in with these wishes splitting the rewards with the offender.[18] Newspaper advertisements or handbills describing the stolen property and offering a reward were regularly employed by victims and not without success in both the recovery of goods, the identification of the offender and thus in his or her prosecution and conviction; the circulation of information about offences became central to the Fielding's proposals for improving the system of policing.[19] Some victims went to considerable personal lengths to pursue offenders and regain their property. In the summer of 1769 Richard Wallis, a baker, and William Thornton, a tallow chandler spent several days chasing the men who had stolen their horses around the southern environs of London. After the theft of ten ferrets, a box, a spud, a dog and a gun John Jeffries and Thomas Asplen of Thurleigh pursued Samuel Colgrave for two days through the villages surrounding Bedford; subsequently they continued their pursuit into Huntingdonshire and Cambridgeshire, eventually running their quarry to earth in a Cambridge pub.[20] It was also possible for the victim to apply to a magistrate for a warrant to search a suspect's house or lodgings.[21] When an individual had gone to the effort and, like as not, the expense of an advertisement, of finding a constable or thief taker, or of a personal pursuit, he or she was less likely to balk at the effort and expense of a prosecution. Once judicial agents, particularly magistrates, were involved there was less likelihood of crime not being heard in court; and a warrant for an arrest, generally entrusted to a constable meant, at least, a hearing before a magistrate once the suspect was apprehended.[22]

The number of offences which could be heard and resolved summarily before a single magistrate sitting informally in his parlour or in a local tavern, or before one or two magistrates sitting with rather more formality in petty sessions, increased during the eighteenth century as legislation altered penalties and consolidated existing laws. Summary offences included specific minor thefts such as embezzlement by textile workers, stealing wood or vegetables, as well as, most notoriously, certain poaching offences and, by the Combination Acts, trade union activity. The prosecutor had the opportunity to decide whether he wished to have the accused tried summarily or before a higher court; summary justice was prompt, but the penalties were less severe involving only a fine or a short period of imprisonment. If the prosecutor was determined to make an example he probably would opt for a higher court and it was also possible for magistrates to advise victims to prosecute in a higher court so as to make an example. In 1792 a Bedfordshire magistrate urged a draper of Biggleswade to prosecute the draper's servant at quarter sessions rather than letting the matter be resolved summarily; he explained to the clerk of the peace that it would have been possible to send the offending youth to the Bridewell for ten or fourteen days 'but as the practice of infidelity in servants is become so General and ought to be discountenanced as much as possible' he had recommended the draper 'to prosecute him as a Thief and if convicted to

142

have him well flogged at Biggleswade Market with leave of the Court'.[23]

The legal guides for magistrates, like Richard Burn's *The Justice of the Peace and Parish Officer*, which went through thirty editions between 1755 and 1845, stated that, unless the offence brought before him was one that could be tried summarily in cases of felony, the magistrate had no alternative to committing the offender for trial in a higher court. In practice, however, often in consultation with the prosecutor, the magistrates employed wide discretion. Sometimes the accused was discharged for lack of evidence. Occasionally some prosecutions, particularly some assault charges, seem to have been brought out of spite, in which case magistrates rejected the complaints. Richard Wyatt threw out Richard Wells's accusation that James Britton had threatened him with violence on the grounds that it was 'litigious, vexatious and frivolous'.[24] But even if there did seem a felony case to answer, magistrates often encouraged reconciliation and interpreted some theft accusations as disputes over ownership. During the 1740s William Hunt studiously avoided the word 'theft' when noting certain cases in his justice book.[25] Samuel Whitbread's notebooks, kept seventy years later, reveal him occasionally seeking to settle matters by correspondence, threats, and bringing parties together, rather than simply committing an offender to trial.[26] In those instances where magistrates persuaded the accuser to drop a charge they were not, at least in their own eyes, compounding the offence, rather they were effectively establishing that there had not been a criminal offence in the first place. Some cases, especially assault cases might be settled with a monetary payment from the accused to the victim; in poaching cases the accused could have proceedings against him dropped if he entered into a bond not to poach on the victim's land again; in other instances an apology inserted in a newspaper might suffice.[27] In wartime the accused could be recruited into the army or navy without the case going beyond the magistrate; this saved the accused from a possibly lengthy pre-trial imprisonment, and it saved the accuser the expense of a prosecution. In eighteenth-century Essex, at least, such a policy was also pursued in peacetime with the accused being encouraged to enlist in the East India Company's service.[28] Finally it is apparent that magistrates used their wide powers over vagrants, servants, or those who could be described as 'idle and disorderly' to imprison, or otherwise punish offenders guilty of petty crimes, particularly petty theft.

If it was resolved to take the accused to a higher court the magistrate committed him, or her for trial; bail was very rarely given in larceny cases and committal generally meant the accused being put in gaol, often for several months before appearing in court – after all, with the exception of London and its environs, there were only four quarter sessions and only two assizes each year for the eighteenth and much of the nineteenth centuries. The magistrate also bound over the prosecutor and any witnesses to attend at the higher court. Still the prosecutor's discretion was not at an end. An indictment had to be prepared for the court; this was then submitted to the grand jury, together with any depositions, for a decision on whether or not there was sufficient cause for the case to proceed to a hearing before magistrates and a petty jury at quarter sessions, or judge and jury at assizes. The bill of indictment was generally prepared by the clerk of the peace, for quarter sessions, or the clerk of assizes. These clerks were solicitors, but very often in cases of theft their task was no more than taking a printed bill and filling in the names of the accused, the victim, and the details of the offence; these details sometimes simply involved writing the word 'larceny' or 'felony'. A particularly determined, or particularly wealthy prosecutor, might employ his own, independent solicitor to prepare the bill of indictment in which case the bill could incorporate several separate counts to ensure that, if the accused escaped on one charge, he could be caught by another. Following an attempted robbery of his Soho Works in 1800 Matthew Boulton was determined to have the four accused executed on a charge of burglary. Boulton's son was most impressed with the eight-count indictment prepared by his father's solicitors: 'it appears to be formed like a swivel gun and may be directed to all points as circumstances require'.[29] Yet, during the eighteenth and early nineteenth centuries, prosecutorial discretion in the bill of indictment could also lead to an offence being downgraded so as to ensure that the accused did not face the most serious, generally capital, charge available. Joseph Stenson, a hatter, was prosecuted for theft at the Borough Sessions in Leeds in January 1801: he was accused of taking one canvas bag value two pence, 500 shilling pieces value three pence, 500 sixpenny pieces value two pence and one gold half guinea value one penny.[30] The total value of the money which Stenson was accused of stealing was £38.0.6d. but by downgrading its value to a mere six pence he could be tried before the borough magistrates on a non-capital charge.

It should be noted in passing that some of the procedures outlined above could be bypassed. A prosecutor could decide to proceed with a voluntary bill whereby a hearing before a magistrate and the entering into recognisances to appear and prosecute were avoided. In such a case the prosecutor went directly to the grand jury, and it was possible for all of the initial steps to be taken without the accused being aware of what was going on. The accused was even more disadvantaged by an *ex-officio* information which was filed by the Attorney General in the Court of King's Bench. This avoided both an initial hearing before a magistrate and the hearing before a grand jury. *Ex-officio* information gave the Attorney General the opportunity of having the case heard before a carefully selected special jury, and even if the defendant was acquitted he could still be saddled with costs. Both voluntary bills and *ex-officio* informations were the exception rather than the rule; the latter, in particular, were rarely used and were confined to serious misdemeanours, often involving some form of sedition.[31]

The pursuit of offenders, going before magistrates and subsequent court appearances were time-consuming – there was no indication given beforehand of the point at which a trial would be heard at either quarter sessions or assizes and, in consequence, the prosecutor and his witnesses, after having travelled to the county town where a particular court was sitting, could have to wait for several days before their case was heard[32]; for members of the lower classes time was money. Henry Fielding believed that the poor were often discouraged from prosecuting because of the expense. Besides the loss of a day or two's pay, there were also the fees: it cost two shillings for an indictment to be drawn up by the clerk of the court in Fielding's London,[33] and there was, in addition, the recognizance bond to appear in court. Local prosecution associations had been formed from the late seventeenth century. There was, perhaps, as many as a thousand of these societies at any one time, though the numbers would appear to increase from about 1780. Membership of the associations was generally in the region of twenty to fifty, with gentlemen and farmers predominating in rural areas, and tradesmen and small businesses in urban districts. The members paid a subscription to finance the pursuit and prosecution of anyone offending against one of their number; but they rarely assisted anyone who was not a paid up member of the association and the poor man thus continued to remain largely dependent on his own resources.[34] Legislation of 1752 authorised the courts to pay expenses in felony cases if the prosecutor was poor and if the accused was convicted. An act of 1778 extended this provision to all prosecutors. Some courts, however, were prepared to pay expenses even if there was no conviction. In October 1785 the Nottinghamshire quarter sessions expressed concern that 'many felonies' were being compounded:

> and others not prosecuted for fear that the expenses of the prosecution should not be paid by the county, to prevent the like in future and for encouraging prosecutions against felons ... it was ordered by the Court that an advertisement be inserted in the Nottingham paper signifying that in all future prosecutions for felonies the reasonable charges of the prosecutors and their witnesses should be paid by the county.[35]

The Leeds Borough Sessions commonly paid expenses at the turn of the century when an accused was acquitted but when the court considered that 'there was reasonable ground of prosecution'. In Essex it was even known for the quarter sessions to award expenses after a bill of indictment had been rejected by the Grand Jury.[36] Unquestionably it was the less well-to-do prosecutors who profited most from this legislation and court practice. The knowledge that expenses were likely to be paid even if a good case failed before a petty jury may have encouraged poor men to prosecute, though the surviving evidence shows that poor men were not unwilling to seek redress for theft through the law. 'Labourers', servants, gardeners and husbandmen made up something like one-fifth of the prosecutors in larceny cases in the second half of the eighteenth century, with tradesmen and artisans accounting for about two-fifths.[37] Further legislation, culminating in Peel's Criminal Justice Act 1826, extended the provision of expenses to witnesses as well as prosecutors, and to certain misdemeanours (notably the more serious forms of assault) as well as felonies. Peel justified this extension on the grounds that, when expenses were not available 'you frequently close the avenues of justice in instances in which the poorest classes are the sufferers, and in which the public interest loudly demands reparation from the offender'.[38]

Besides the expense of, and time taken up by, a prosecution Henry Fielding believed that some victims did not prosecute because of a misplaced humanitarianism in not wanting to be the cause of someone being executed.[39] Sir Samuel Romilly, Sir James Mackintosh and other reformers urged this as a principal reason for bringing about a drastic reduction in the number of capital statutes which existed under the eighteenth-century Bloody Code. 'Numerous and respectable witnesses' testified to the 1819 Select Committee on Criminal Laws 'that a great reluctance prevail[ed] to prosecute' in some capital crimes and, unfortunately, this reluctance had 'had the effect of producing immunity to such a degree, that it may be considered as among the temptations to the commission of crimes'.[40] The influence of Mackintosh over this committee (he chaired most of its sessions) certainly coloured its conclusions, and unquestionably influenced the choice of witnesses and the way in which they were prodded for the kind of answers favourable to the reformers' code. There is other evidence, such as reducing the value of stolen property so as to reduce the charge, that some prosecutors thought very seriously about the likely outcome if they proceeded with a capital indictment.[41] Yet when, in 1811, the metropolitan stipendiary magistrates were asked a series of questions about the impact of Romilly's act removing capital punishment from the offence of stealing privately from a person (pocketpicking) the opinion was overwhelmingly that cost and inconvenience were much greater deterrents to the prosecutor than capital punishment. The Shadwell magistrates had noted a reluctance to prosecute but believed that this was because their jurisdiction bordered the Thames and victims in the area were 'seafaring people who cannot attend properly to the prosecution but are obliged to go to sea'. The Hatton Garden magistrates doubted whether there had been reluctance to prosecute on account of capital punishment 'but a great deal ... on account of the expense and trouble of prosecuting especially where the property to be recovered is of little value'. One of the stipendiaries from the Queen's Square office elaborated:

> The considerable sacrifice of time, the additional cost, nay the *heavy* load
> of expense, the tiresomeness of attendance, and keeping witnesses
> together, the too frequent petulancies etc etc in the many stages of
> Judicature, and the many painful mortifications frequently endured from
> examination, and the asperities of cross examination. But that the parties

are *often* deterred from the consideration of a higher description [?] of punishment is not true ... .[42]

These deterrents to prosecution continued well after the extension of expenses for prosecutors and witnesses and well after the reduction of capital statutes during the 1820s and 1830s. The Constabulary Commissioners were informed by the Metropolitan Police that 'the fear of ultimately having to prosecute deters many from giving information'.[43] Sometimes there was the problem of personal embarrassment as when clergymen or other gentlemen had their watches stolen while consorting with prostitutes[44]; and such embarrassment, particularly in the moral atmosphere of Victorian society, probably dissuaded women from prosecuting in cases of indecent assault, rape, or attempted rape.[45] A few individuals refused to prosecute from religious scruples,[46] or when they discovered that the offender was one of their own family, or a servant willing to make restitution.[47] Some victims were too frightened,[48] while others, together with their witnesses, were allegedly bribed:

> [N]o doubt it often happens that between the committal and the day of trial, the witness on whom the case rests is tampered with or for some pecuniary gain (and in some cases not a small amount) his testimony before the Grand Jury is quite different to what it was before the Magistrate. This is a common practice with old Thieves who say 'Smother it before the Grand Jury' as they know they would stand but little chance should it come into court. Hence the number of Bills ignored without any one knowing the cause, the Grand Jury excepted.[49]

On some occasions the reasons why victims refused to give information and to prosecute remained a mystery to the police but when the police felt that they could identify deterrents there were, overwhelmingly, loss of time, general inconvenience, and even expense:

> Mr Lawrence, New Cut, Lambeth prosecuted a person for felony and a short time afterwards another person robbed him. Mr L declined giving him in charge stating that it was such an annoyance to be detained for so long from business at the Police Office and again at the Sessions. Many instances might be given.[50]

> Many instances have occurred where parties have wished to decline prosecuting in consequence of loss of time. Many tradesmen preferring the infliction of a summary punishment rather than attend the sessions. Even after parties have been committed they have again been brought up and summarily convicted at the instance of the party robbed.[51]

> In the neighbourhood of Wandsworth, Battersea and Barnes, the market gardeners have declined prosecuting parties for robbing their grounds from the expense attending conviction before a magistrate at Wandsworth. Parties stealing fruit and vegetables are convicted in a small sum and the other expenses ... amounting sometimes altogether to 7s. or 8. the party convicted is frequently sent to prison in default and the expense falls upon the prosecutor besides his loss of time etc.[52]

Some nineteenth-century law reformers concluded from the reluctance to prosecute on the part of some victims that England needed some system of public prosecution similar to that in use in Scotland as well as elsewhere in Europe. In 1826 Peel expressed sympathy for the idea believing that it would ensure a prosecution when necessary and prevent frivolous or vexatious prosecutions; he suggested that much could be learned from Scottish practice.[53] During the following decade, and again in the 1850s and the 1870s proposals were brought forward, even to the extent of bills being introduced in the House of Commons, for such a system. Each time, for a variety of reasons, the proposals were rejected. There was opposition from a powerful vested interest in the shape of the growing profession of solicitors; they feared a significant loss of income should the state take over prosecutions. There was more general concern about the expense of a system of public prosecution and also of the growth of patronage that would accompanying it. Finally there was that uniquely English concern of an encroachment on personal and political liberty should the state become involved in prosecutions. A public prosecutor, declared the Clerk of the Peace of Wigan, in the mid 1840s:

> would have the power of refusing to proceed in cases where parties
> thought there ought to be a prosecution, and this power might (and
> particularly in cases of political excitement) cause a denial of justice. I
> think that in all cases any man who has sustained injury, ought to be at
> liberty to put the law in force, and not be deprived of his remedy through
> the malice or caprice of a public prosecutor refusing to proceed, and
> therefore leaving him without remedy. If this power is entrusted to a
> public prosecutor, it will be a greater encroachment upon the right of a
> trial by jury than any encroachment there has been, and these are not a
> few.[54]

As a result of such sentiments nineteenth-century legislation only marginally infringed on the rights of the private prosecutor. The Vexatious Indictments Act 1859 limited the opportunities for bringing voluntary bills for certain misdemeanours. A dozen or so other acts authorised only specific inspectors or local authorities to prosecute for certain infringements, and limited the independent civilian prosecutor's discretion in cases concerning excise offences, sedition, or other matters involving sensitive international or domestic affairs. A Director of Public Prosecutions was first appointed in 1879, but for nearly thirty years the function of the post was almost entirely advisory.[55]

Yet, while no nineteenth-century legislation had any dramatic impact on the system of prosecution by private individuals, there was a very significant, if gradual, change brought about with the development of the new police. In certain circumstances, before the establishment of police forces, it could be difficult to find a prosecutor. Joseph Radcliffe, a magistrate of the West Riding, was not prepared to finance the prosecution of Joseph Jubson for seditious words in 1803; after all, he protested to the Home Secretary, the offence was not personal to him. In 1824 Essex magistrates were unwilling to organise and finance the prosecution of people who had attacked an informer; they remembered an earlier prosecution which had resulted in them being saddled with a solicitor's bill for £200.[56] The new police could take on such prosecutions yet, gradually, they extended this role far beyond these instances.

The increasing role of the police as prosecutors from the middle of the nineteenth century has been largely ignored by police historians and there has been no detailed study, even on a regional basis, of precisely when, how and why the police came to predominate as prosecutors.[57] Constables and local law officers had always had a role in prosecuting misdemeanours such as vagrancy, and petty street offences. When the new police forces were established the incidence of arrest for these kinds of offences generally increased, at the same time acts of parliament relating to the police and local government bye-laws consolidated and extended this role. Private individuals could bring prosecutions under police acts, and Charles Dickens expressed satisfaction in having prosecuted a young woman for bad language in the street under a Metropolitan Police Act[58]; but overwhelmingly the police dominated the prosecution of offenders against public order, public decency and public safety. Such offenders were usually processed by the police courts or petty sessions. Probably the step from prosecuting these petty offenders to prosecuting petty thieves was not seen as a particularly marked one by the new police as they grew in confidence and professionalism. The central role of the new police was repeatedly emphasised to be the prevention of crime[59]; what better way to prevent crime than to arrest and to ensure the conviction of its perpetrators? Policemen did, after all, tend to think in terms of crime as something committed by a criminal class, a perception encouraged by the requirement that they submit annual statistics of known criminals in their district along with the figures of crimes reported and arrests made. At the same time it seems probable that the new police were sucked into acting as prosecutors in their early years because of the poverty of some victims of theft. The Superintendent of B Division of the Metropolitan Police explained to the Constabulary Commissioners that on one occasion arresting police constables had been obliged to pay for a bill of indictment since the two prosecutors in the case were too poor.[60] It may be significant that in several of the cases in mid nineteenth-century Bedfordshire in which the police acted as prosecutor, or joint prosecutor, the victim, or joint prosecutor, was a woman. Once the police began to step in as prosecutors in cases where the victim was poor or a 'weaker vessel', it was logical that they should step in on other occasions when the victim was simply reluctant. But it was not always the case that the new police were drawn in as prosecutors because of the poverty or the 'weakness' of the victims. In 1846 the Nottinghamshire

Constabulary preferred 3 out of 118 indictments at the quarter sessions; another one was preferred by an old-style parish constable. Ten years later they preferred 22 out of 116, with two other indictments preferred by parish constables. In 1866 there were 95 indictments at the quarter sessions, of which 47 were preferred by the police. But the cases which were prosecuted by the Nottinghamshire Police do not readily reveal much in the way of common characteristics suggesting why these, specifically, were taken on by the force. Nor was the increase in the number of cases prosecuted by the Nottinghamshire Police either a steady linear progression or precisely in parallel with the pattern elsewhere; in London, at least until the 1880s, the private prosecutor seems to have dominated.[61] For victims, however, when possible, it probably seemed logical to hand the whole matter over to the police who increasingly claimed to be the experts in the 'war' against crime; and it was especially preferable to hand over to the police when, even though the prosecutor's expenses might be reimbursed, he could still be out of pocket with some costs, or at least feared as much.[62] It was noted above that the market gardeners of south London were reluctant to prosecute for petty thefts of their produce in case they were saddled with costs when the convicted offender was too poor to pay these and his fine. In 1844 a poor man was charged before Oxfordshire magistrates with stealing turnips. He was found guilty and sentenced to pay a fine of two shillings, a further two shillings, being the value of the turnips, and eleven shillings being the costs of the magistrates' clerk. The man, who confessed that want had driven him to commit the theft in the first place, could not pay and was committed to prison. The magistrates then instructed the prosecutor to pay the clerk's costs. Naturally the man protested:

> [he] said he did not understand why he should be saddled with such
> expenses for merely discharging his duty towards himself and the public,
> and added something about its being much cheaper letting the thief off
> with his booty, than seek for punishment for the offence.

The newspaper reporting the case declared such instances to be commonplace.[63]

There was some hostility, especially during the middle years of the nineteenth century, to the police taking over the role of prosecutors; there were a few scandals and to those with an eye to preserving English liberties against what appeared to be foreign ideas and practices, policemen as prosecutors looked suspiciously like public prosecutors. But, in the long term, the police assumption of the role of prosecutor may have brought them closer to the working class – as much, if not more, the victims of petty crime – and helped to foster that police legitimacy which appeared unique to England from roughly the middle of the nineteenth century to the middle of the twentieth century.

Between 1750 and 1850 most of the criminal cases brought before assizes and quarter sessions were characterized by a face-to-face confrontation between the prosecutor and the accused. Occasionally the accused said nothing, or very little in response to the charge.[64] Sometimes he or she attempted to blacken the prosecutor's name: 'I hope your Lordships will examine this woman well', protested eighteen-year old James Angas when faced with his principal accuser at the Old Bailey in April 1797, 'for she has transported several, and wants to make a property of me; she transported her own son'. Sixty years later Mary Ann Harriet Forbes, aged sixteen, was prosecuted by her master for stealing his property after which, without notice, she had left his employ; in court she protested that she had left after he had seized her round the waist, kissed her and told her to 'pull the bed down'; unfortunately she had made no similar complaint to the arresting police constable, and the court did not believe her.[65] More often than not, however, the accused's defence depended on denying the charge and calling a succession of character witnesses. The confrontation between prosecutor and accused witnessed a change during the nineteenth century as, increasingly, it was replaced by a confrontation between lawyers acting for both the prosecution and the defence. Like other professions, the legal profession increased dramatically in numbers in the nineteenth century and while its standards of training remained minimal, legal practitioners of all types jealously preserved and advanced their boasted expertise. Part of this preservation of expertise involved a rigorous demarcation of their sphere of influence. The courts, with their ritual and tradition, were one such sphere; and as the century progressed the non-initiated public were required, more and more, to depend upon, and to pay for, the expert barrister and solicitor when they entered the courts. Like the increasing dominance of the police as prosecutors the increasing role of lawyers in adversarial confrontation in the courts has not been charted in detail, it has, rather, been indicated by historians looking at changing procedures in eighteenth-century courts and for their contrast with modern practice.[66]

During the seventeenth century prosecuting counsel rarely appeared in the courts, and then only in cases such as treason; defence counsel appeared even less, and only in complex misdemeanour cases, notably those involving civil or regulatory matters such as liability for the upkeep of roads. The assumption was that the accused had no need of counsel since the burden of proof was on the prosecution and the accused was a greater expert on the truth, or otherwise, of what was alleged against him than any lawyer; the trial judge was expected to assist the accused with legal counsel when necessary. Concern for the weakness of the accused's position began to be expressed with reference to treason prosecutions towards the end of the century and defence counsel were permitted by the Treason Act 1696. The *Old Bailey Sessions Papers* begin recording rare appearances by prosecution counsel in other criminal cases during the second decade of the eighteenth century, most notably in murder cases. By the end of the century such appearances were more common, but were by no means the rule; generally speaking prosecuting counsel appear to have been employed primarily in cases where the victims were particularly aggrieved, where the case was difficult, or where the defence was employing counsel and it was feared that this might lead to acquittal. The prosecutors who employed counsel were clearly going out of their way to ensure that the case was conducted correctly and that the verdict was satisfactory; associations for the prosecution of felons appear, perhaps understandably, to have been significant among the employers of counsel. By the 1840s the employment of such counsel seems to have been widespread, particularly at assizes, and was also to be found at quarter sessions. Indeed it was the lack of prosecution counsel at the Bedfordshire Lent Assizes for 1844 which prompted two outbursts from Sir John Pattison, the presiding judge. He interrupted one case to enquire:

> why there were no counsel for the prosecution, and observed that it was a disgrace to the county to impose upon the Judge the necessity of acting as a counsel against the prisoner ('an unseemly position' added his Lordship, with emphasis) besides the additional trouble which it entails upon the judge.

Then, when the case against a tramp for stealing a shawl was called, 'his lordship said "There is no counsel I suppose?" and upon the clerk of the arraigns replying in the negative, added, "Ah! Bedford's so poor it can't afford them".'[67]

Defence counsel, according to the evidence of the *Old Bailey Sessions Papers*, began to make very rare appearances in ordinary criminal trials during the 1730s, but for the eighteenth and the early part of the nineteenth centuries their role was not strictly defined and the extent of their participation seems to have varied from one assize circuit to another. Both the accused and his or her counsel could cross-examine witnesses; what defence counsel could not do, until legislation in 1836, was sum up the defence for the benefit of the jury. Judges may have begun to allow counsel to appear for the accused because of the concern about the weakness of the accused's position; this concern also led to a greater querying of hearsay and circumstantial evidence as the eighteenth century wore on, and confessions were often rejected, especially if there was the slightest hint of them being extracted under duress. At the same time, even during the reforming years of the 1830s, a Solicitor General could voice concern that 'improper acquittal' could result from a barrister's eloquence, while another M.P. feared:

> that if Counsel were allowed to both prisoner and prosecutor, it would have no better result than giving rise to trials of professional skill. The prosecutor in most cases being the richer, would have the advantage, since

it might naturally be supposed that he could obtain the best professional aid.[68]

Some contemporaries suggested that the Prisoner's Counsel Act 1836 favoured professional thieves who could afford counsel, at the expense of poor prosecutors who could not; J. J. Tobias has viewed this suggestion sympathetically.[69] Yet a limited analysis of the employment of counsel suggests that overwhelmingly it was prosecutors who hired counsel rather than defendants[70] and throughout the nineteenth century the accused probably remained at a disadvantage.

It was not until the end of the nineteenth century that the accused in criminal proceedings was allowed to give evidence on oath. Two decades of heated debate preceded the Criminal Evidence Act 1898: on one side it was insisted that the accused's ability to give sworn evidence on his own behalf would reduce the number of innocent persons convicted as well as abolish anomalies and bring criminal law in line with civil law; on the other side it was alleged that such a change would disadvantage the nervous, provoke an outbreak of perjury and, perhaps most serious, transform the judge from an impartial observer to a bullying French-style inquisitor.[71] It is, of course, impossible to assess how far the accused was disadvantaged by being unable to give sworn evidence, but financial considerations unquestionably limited his options. There were no expenses allowed for the accused; travelling to court as a witness for a defendant could cost an individual expenses for the journey; time spent in court, or waiting to be called, also cost money. Defence counsel cost money. Except in cases of murder there was no provision for legal aid for a defendant, otherwise the cheapest counsel available was through the system known as 'dock briefs' by which the defendant could pay one guinea, plus a clerk's fee, and obtain the service of a barrister without the mediation, and expense, of a solicitor. Barristers were obliged to accept 'dock briefs' but the overall standard of those who undertook criminal work was regarded as inferior. Money was one key incentive for the more able barristers to concentrate on civil business; in the 1840s it was estimated that earnings from the latter were ten times greater than earnings from criminal business. In 1851 it was argued in the *Law Times* that the state had a duty to allow or assign counsel to prisoners who could not afford them, but it was not until the Poor Prisoner's Defence Act 1903 that any significant move was made in this direction.[72]

As trials at assizes and quarter sessions increasingly became contests between lawyers, so judges and juries played less of a central role and, in addition, trials became much longer and much more formal. During the eighteenth and early nineteenth centuries most criminal trials were over in a matter of minutes; they rarely seem to have taken as long as an hour. Often the jurors did not leave the courtroom to deliberate, but simply went into a huddle, and not a particularly refined huddle. Towards the end of the eighteenth century Martin Madan condemned the practice of courts meeting during the afternoon following a lengthy break for food and drink. It was the drink which created the problems according to Madan; sometimes the judge had to spend an hour bringing the court to order:

> and when this is done, drunkeness is too frequently apparent, where it ought of all things to be avoided, I mean, in *jurymen* and *witnesses*. The heat of the court, joined to the fumes of the liquor, has laid many an *honest juryman* into a calm and profound sleep, and sometimes it has been no small trouble for his *fellows* to *jog* him into the verdict – even where the wretch's *life* has depended on the event!

Madan claimed to have witnessed such incidents personally. A press report of an 1844 assize graphically describes a jury huddling in the court to discuss the verdict.

> After a few minutes noisy consultation a portion of the jury turned round and said they were divided, as 'one or two old men wouldn't fall in with the others', whereupon the 'one or two old men' nodded their heads sagaciously, and in a manner to indicate that they had 'a reason for it'.[73]

Jurors served for an entire session of the court and were often drawn from men who had served before, even quite recently; jurors were thus often old hands who well understood the procedures and the tasks expected of them. The evidence of the *Old Bailey Sessions Papers* suggests, moreover, that while jurors were in harmony with, and deferential towards, the judge, they were not simply passive auditors but asked questions and, on occasions, stated their reasons for a verdict. In January 1766, for example, an Old Bailey jury acquitted Brian Swinney on a charge of highway robbery and 'declared that they had a very bad opinion of the prosecutor'.[74] Sometimes, during the supremacy of the Bloody Code, juries brought in verdicts reducing the value of property stolen to bring the accused out of range of a capital statute; such behaviour was connived at, or often directed, by the judge. There could be an exchange of views with the judge if he queried a jury's verdict, and it was not unknown for judges to reinstruct juries and request them to deliberate again should they have returned a verdict which the judge believed to be incorrect. Some judges exerted much greater influence over juries than others. Lord Mansfield drew the fire of John Wilkes's supporters for brow-beating and bullying juries; and this may further have disadvantaged the accused since it appears that when Mansfield was on the bench there were marginally more convictions than usual.[75] Interplay between the magistrates and the jurors at quarter sessions was probably much the same, but the paucity of evidence remaining for such proceedings probably makes any detailed analysis impossible.

The right to a trial by a jury of his peers was, indeed still is, lionised as one of the key rights of the free-born Englishman. Yet it is probably the case that, even during the eighteenth century, the most common experience of the law and of courts, for the bulk of the people, was the magistrate sitting alone, or with one or two colleagues more formally in petty sessions. Justice in these instances was administered summarily and while, during the eighteenth and nineteenth centuries, juries gradually became less and less active participants in the higher courts, so did new legislation bring more and more cases within the remit of the magistrates acting without a jury. Considerable concern was expressed about this development. Sir William Blackstone condemned summary jurisdiction as 'fundamentally opposed to the spirit of our constitution'. In 1772 the *London Chronicle* condemned a new Game Act which established summary jurisdiction in certain poaching offences and thus undermined 'the great Bulwark of an Englishman's Rights, the Trial by Jury'. Over half a century later *The Times* expressed similar regrets in a wide ranging review of the activities of magistrates.[76] But requirements that justice be speedy and that it put the minimum burden on the prosecutor's time and pocket, were paramount.

Technically summary jurisdiction in the eighteenth and early nineteenth centuries only covered misdemeanours; felonies had to be tried on indictment before a jury. The spread of summary jurisdiction, however, increasingly blurred the distinction as legislation gave the prosecutor greater discretion in how he wanted to proceed against an offender and also what kind of punishment he wanted; punishments under summary jurisdiction were limited to either a fine, a whipping, or, at most, a few months' imprisonment. An employer wanting to prosecute the organisers or perpetrators of industrial action could use summary jurisdiction; a variety of trades were covered by individual acts of parliament before the notorious Combination Acts which were in force between 1799 and 1824. But if he wanted to inflict a terrible example he could opt for a prosecution on indictment at a higher court on a charge of larceny, if the offence was the appropriation of materials, or on a charge of conspiracy, if the offence involved some kind of strike activity; in both instances punishment could amount to transportation. Similarly the increase of summary jurisdiction in poaching offences gave the prosecutor a wide choice: he could choose between the new summary jurisdiction, the more serious prosecution on indictment, and even a civil suit by which the plaintiff sued for half of the fine to be imposed and, if he won, he also collected twice the cost of the prosecution.[77]

As the examples of summary jurisdiction noted here suggest, certain of the increasing summary categories were delicate ones for the relationships between social groups. Of all others, from the late seventeenth until well into the nineteenth century, it was the Game Laws which provoked the greatest anxiety and outcry. These laws manifestly preserved the privileges of sporting gentlemen possessed of wealth and property. Many magistrates were such gentlemen, or were closely involved with such, and concern developed about the partiality of Game Law cases before summary tribunals. This concern culminated in the petition of John Deller which was presented to parliament in 1823 in the midst of the early nineteenth-century debates on law reform. Deller was a Hampshire farmer whose farm was bounded in part by land belonging to the Duke of Buckingham. He had been brought before the Duke on a complaint from two of the Duke's gamekeepers for coursing hares on his own farm. Deller protested that the hares had done between £30 and £60 damage, but this did not prevent the Duke from fining him £5 and warning him that any impertinence would lead to the stocks or to gaol. Subsequently Deller had brought a complaint against one of the Duke's servants for entering upon his land with three dogs, but two clerical justices had continually postponed the hearing while binding Deller over for assault:

> [Y]our humble petitioner has heard much talk about the liberty and property of Englishmen; but ... to his plain understanding, a state of slavery so complete as that in which he has the misfortune to live, cannot be found in any other country in the world.[78]

Yet, whatever the mythology and the occasional instance of cases like Deller's, Game Law offences do not seem to have dominated eighteenth-century summary tribunals; furthermore the most sober recent study of the workings of these laws concludes that, especially after the 1750s 'openly biased tribunals were less common than the game laws' critics have assumed'.[79]

The Combination Acts have a similar notoriety to the Game Laws, yet there has never been a detailed analysis of their use; indeed, given the paucity of evidence surviving from summary tribunals, probably there cannot be. Similarly the trade-specific predecessors of the Combination Acts have received little serious attention and, again the lack of evidence militates against detailed statistical assessments.[80] The poor man and the employee probably did have the cards stacked against them in eighteenth and early nineteenth-century summary tribunals; but there were magistrates who sympathised with them and who were especially critical of the employers who used illegal truck payments.[81] Furthermore partly through public pressure, but also no doubt because the ruling class believed the rhetoric of the law's impartiality, magistrates were keen to demonstrate their own impartiality. In 1824 the *Kent and Essex Mercury* condemned an Essex magistrate who prosecuted a waggoner for obstruction and inflicted an on-the-spot fine of ten shillings.[82] Ten years later west country newspapers were highly critical of a Devon magistrate who, after having been fined £5 for violently assaulting his children's nurse, went into an adjacent room to try another assault case.[83] But such incidents appear exceptional and the outcry which they provoked reinforces this assumption. There was a tradition, clearly apparent in the eighteenth century, that magistrates should not try cases in which they had a personal concern[84]; and when they stepped down from the bench they could not be sure that colleagues and friends would find in their favour.[85] The problem is, of course, assessing the extent to which economic and social and/or class prejudice displaced the desire of most magistrates to demonstrate the impartiality allowed within the framework of the law. In those instances where the partiality seems blatant the problem disappears. During the eighteenth century many magistrates enforcing labour legislation were employers in the industries concerned. This was especially true in big manufacturing boroughs, like Norwich, but could also be true in mid eighteenth-century rural manufacturing areas, like Wiltshire. In early nineteenth-century Wigan magistrates linked with local industry appear to have administered justice with relative impartiality, except in cases of industrial theft; after the Municipal Corporations Act this partiality took on party political and sectarian hues.[86] In the second quarter of the nineteenth century, as noted earlier, there was a change in the composition of the magistracy in the various jurisdictions of the Black Country as industrial entrepreneurs began to dominate over landowners; this change was accompanied by increasing activity in prosecuting for industrial theft and in seeking to control the workforce by means of the Master and Servant Act. It has been suggested that while, in comparison with the size of the labour force, prosecutions under the Master and Servant Act in the third quarter of the century were small in number, they were not confined to exceptional cases. In fact the Act appears to have been regarded as an essential weapon for controlling labour.[87] However changes in the magistracy were quite different in neighbouring Warwickshire where landed gentry displaced clergy on the bench to become the dominant group and where, during industrial troubles, notably those in the mines during the 1840s, most magistrates had no direct interest.[88] Finally it is also probable that the increasing appointment of professional lawyers as stipendiaries and as recorders to supervise the part-time magistrates, particularly at borough sessions, checked the most blatant abuses.

The relaxed, relatively informal magistrates' tribunals of the eighteenth century had little place in the increasingly urbanised England of the nineteenth century with its emphasis on decorum and bureaucratic formality. The system of magistrates sitting singly or in petty sessions was not spread uniformly throughout eighteenth-century England; while petty sessions met in Hampshire and Dorset for example, none appear to have met in Berkshire.[89] Populous urban districts had difficulty in finding gentlemen of the first rank to act as magistrates and 'trading justices' had begun to appear in and around the metropolis during the seventeenth century. These were gentlemen, generally of modest property, who could be relied upon to act in these urban districts for the sake of the fees which they could collect for resolving petty disputes and for granting and signing particular documents. The 'trading justices' of the Kent parishes bordering London were far busier than the justices of rural Kent from the very beginning of the eighteenth century; they were looked down upon by their country cousins because they took fees, and some of them became justifiably notorious, but manifestly they were fulfilling a need.[90] The Bow Street magistrates' office grew out of the trading justice system, though from the mid eighteenth century the magistrates here, notably Henry and later Sir John Fielding, received money from the Treasury rather than relying on fees. The system of stipendiary magistrates established for London in 1792, primarily as a police measure, created a more general, and more formal precedent for the way in which magistrates adjudicated lesser offences. In 1839, ten years after the creation of the Metropolitan Police, the stipendiary magistrates of London lost their police role and their offices were transformed into the Metropolitan Police Courts, vividly described for the *Illustrated London News* by Angus Reach:

> In Bagnigge Wells road ... that glaring and dusty summer thoroughfare, stands a large pile of buildings, generally ornamented by numerous lounging policemen, and further diversified and adorned by crowds of shabby-looking people, a vast proportion whereof may be observed to have their personal appearance improved by such additional attractions as are contributed by blackened eyes, plastered-up foreheads, and noses with broken bridges.

> The buildings form the Clerkenwell Police Court and its appurtenances; the lounging constables are the guardians of last night's peace, waiting to prefer charges against its disturbers; the maltreated gentry about are the sufferers – some of them, perhaps, the active, as well as passive partakers in the constant drunken rows which such districts as Clerkenwell – a favoured abode of those unfortunate helots of the hod, generally complimented as the 'low Irish' – naturally furnish, from day to day, for police adjudication.

> We enter – we traverse a long, dirty passage: the passages leading to Police Courts are always dirty – the walls are always greasy – glazed, so to speak, by the constant friction of frowsy rags. A turn to the left – a push at a swinging door – and we stand in the midst of a similar crowd to that which we left outside, to that which we passed in the lobby – the disreputable public of a Police Court.

> The room is a large one than most of the 'Worthy Magistrates' are blessed with – in fact, a handsome, airy, wainscotted apartment. You glance at once towards the judicial armchair, and see it faced and flanked by the usual Police Court arrangements – a square, open box in the centre, bounded, so to speak, on one side by the bench, on the others by the particular boxes occupied by Clerks, Police Inspectors, Reporters, Barristers, and last, not least, Culprits. The part of the room not taken up by these pens and boxes, forms the *locus standi* for that portion of the enlightened public who come to improve their tempers by the contemplation of the placid equanimity of a Greenwood – or to see how perfectly even the balance of justice, as between a private individual and a policeman, can be held by a Combe.[91]

By the middle of the century there were thirteen such courts in London with twenty-three magistrates like Messrs Combe and Greenwood, dispensing justice in cases of misdemeanours such as common assault, drunk and disorderly, gambling, suspicious behaviour, unlawful possession and vagrancy. Justice in these courts was speedy with little time available for deliberation; at the beginning of the twentieth century Edward Carpenter reckoned that cases took 'on an average say three minutes to dispose of'.[92] At the same time, and in keeping with the notion that the law was impartial, these magistrates were also charged with providing 'a system of poor man's justice' which could 'encourage in the common people a habit of looking to the law for protection'. There is no question but that many of them took this charge seriously, and that they sometimes used their power and authority to conform to popular conceptions of justice rather than the strict letter of the law.[93]

A few fast-growing provincial urban districts began contemplating the appointment of stipendiary magistrates from the moment they appeared in London; but the first such appointments were not made until the early nineteenth century and it was not until 1835 that legislation made it possible for any borough that so wished to appoint a stipendiary. The arguments in favour of stipendiaries were manifold. Many of the fastest growing urban-industrial sprawls had no resident magistrate since they were not incorporated boroughs and county magistrates, even with property in the town, were often reluctant to commit themselves to the time necessary for dispensing justice in such areas.[94] Concerns were raised by some individuals about the capabilities of the part-time gentleman magistrate and about the need for stricter regulation of the administration of justice. There was also a lobby calling for some kind of more professional tribunal to try cases not serious enough for quarter sessions or assizes, but too serious for the amateur magistrate sitting alone or in petty sessions. Lord Brougham, for example, expressed his concerns to parliament about both the constitution of the different tribunals of magistrates and the way in which they exercised their powers. *The Times*, in contrast, believed that while the system of unpaid magistrates had its faults:

> the interference of lawyers in the magisterial business of a county is often more mischievous than useful, and ... the love of justice, and the household common sense of country gentlemen, are more efficacious in the accomplishment of the ends of justice than the labours of professional magistrates.

Nevertheless the increase in summary jurisdiction was undesirable and there were cases which required 'a more skilful and practised tribunal'.[95] A Juvenile Offenders Bill discussed in parliament in 1840 contained a clause which would have done away with the 'evil' of petty sessions being held in public houses. The proposer wanted:

> to erect an intermediate tribunal between the magistrates and the superior courts, in order to prevent young persons of 12, 11, and 10 years of age,

and perhaps even younger children, from being sent to prison for first and trivial offences.[96]

Three years later, following an enquiry from the Buckinghamshire quarter sessions for clarification on the use of the magistrate's own home for the transaction of judicial business, the Home Office urged:

> that in any district in which there is a regular and fixed place for holding the petty sessions, to which the public have access, the most desirable course to adopt is that the cases which are to be brought before magistrates should be there heard and adjudicated, though, certainly, it is not illegal for the magistrates to hear cases at the office of their clerk.

The *Morning Herald* put a gloss on this emphasising that privacy was not a good thing; justice should be seen to be done in public.[97]

The middle years of the nineteenth century witnessed legislation which gave much greater organisation and formality to the summary courts and which brought more cases within their remit. A series of measures, known collectively as Jervis's Acts, were passed in 1848. These dealt generally with the judicial work of the magistrates, established stricter procedures for preliminary hearings, granted greater protection to magistrates for any innocent breach of the law which they might accidentally commit, and, perhaps most importantly, amended and consolidated existing legislation on summary jurisdiction. In February 1847 Sir John Packington, M.P. for Droitwich, requested leave to introduce a bill to permit the summary trial of juvenile offenders. Packington's intention was to ensure that such offenders did not spend days or weeks in prison awaiting assizes or quarter sessions; he feared that such a period could only expose them to the corrupting influence of hardened criminals. Furthermore he urged 'that good would result from young offenders being taught to feel that their crimes would be followed by immediate punishment'. Concern was initially expressed that such trials would be in secret; once again the requirement was that justice be seen to be done. There was also anxiety in some quarters about 'upsetting the great principle of trial by jury'.[98] Nevertheless Packington's Bill was eventually accepted. The Juvenile Offenders Act of 1847 empowered magistrates assembled in petty sessions to try juveniles under the age of fourteen years who were charged with simple larceny. A second Juvenile Offenders Act, passed in 1850, raised the age limit to sixteen.

During the second reading of Packington's Bill Robert Palmer, the member for Berkshire and a former chairman of quarter sessions, had suggested that the value of articles stolen would be a better criterion for deciding which offences should be subject to summary justice since 'not three-fourths of the criminal cases were, if they looked to the value of the articles stolen, worth the trouble of being brought into court'.[99] Palmer's suggestions was ignored in 1847 but eight years later the Lord Chancellor, Lord Cranworth, introduced a bill on this principle. The problem, as Cranworth saw it, was that the law was being dragged into disrepute by the spectacle of men, held in prison for a long time before assizes or quarter sessions came round, being prosecuted for trifling thefts; furthermore both the accused's time in prison before trial, and the trial itself, cost a great deal of money. Again concerns were expressed about the impact that an increase in summary jurisdiction would have on 'that great safeguard of our liberties – trial by jury'. There was also worry that the propŝed legislation would give new 'tyrannical' power to the police; and William Henry Watson, M.P. for Hull, a Q.C. and Bencher of Lincoln's Inn expressed the anxieties of his profession:

> although we were much indebted to the magistracy for the zealous and conscientious manner in which they discharged their duties, the country could scarcely have confidence in them as competent persons to be intrusted with summary jurisdiction in criminal cases.[100]

The Criminal Justice Act nevertheless passed into law much to the consternation of those barristers who specialised in criminal cases and who feared for their fees.[101] The Act empowered two magistrates meeting in petty sessions to try cases of theft or embezzlement of goods to the value of less than five shillings when the accused was agreeable to a summary trial; they were empowered also to hear cases where the value of expropriated goods exceeded five shillings, but only when the accused entered a plea of guilty. The results of all such proceedings had to be recorded at quarter sessions.

The extension of cheap and speedy summary justice, while it did nothing to check the growing dominance of the police as prosecutors, appears to have led to an increase in the actual number of larcenies prosecuted and, at the same time, to a marked decline in the number of cases brought before quarter sessions.[102] In 1879 summary justice was extended further, but the fear for English liberties with the removal of trial by jury from yet more cases was no longer an issue. Opposition in 1879 centred on the fear that magistrates might be able to throw out cases on the grounds that, regardless of what the law said, they personally did not regard a particular offence as a crime; and once again the perquisites of the legal profession were brought up. Two Liberal Q.C.s feared that the extension of summary trial would lead to a dramatic reduction in the emoluments of clerks of the peace, perhaps as much as £500 or £600 a year. However in the Lords, Lord Aberdare praised the magistracy:

> on the whole, considering that Justices of the Peace were qualified for their office more by social status than by legal knowledge, it was creditable to them that so few complaints were heard of their administration of the law.[103]

The 1879 Act raised from 5s. to £2 the value of goods, for the theft or embezzlement of which, offenders might be brought before the summary courts.

In 1857 the justices in petty sessions were estimated to be handling twenty times the number of cases dealt with by all the other criminal courts combined.[104] The rise of the summary courts led to questions being posed about assizes and quarter sessions. Many of the county towns where these courts were held were fast being superseded in size and importance by the newer commercial and industrial centres. More important, however, the speed of summary jurisdiction highlighted the long waits often forced upon those whose cases were to come before assizes or quarter sessions; this waiting could mean many weeks in prison before trial for the accused. Various means were proposed and tried in order to remedy the problem. Some old assize towns had their court abolished, and a few new assizes were established. During the 1820s Peel experimented with a third assize held in the winter in Essex, Kent, Hertfordshire, Surrey and Sussex.[105] The number of assizes was increased from two to three a year in the middle years of the century; then, in 1876–77, some counties were given a fourth assize. There was, however, insufficient business on either the criminal or the civil side of the assize courts to justify the increase and, in 1888, most counties had their assizes reduced to three a year. Some proposed that the problems of too little work for the assizes might be solved by handing over the bulk of the criminal work to quarter sessions; in 1857 quarter sessions were handling four times the criminal work of the assizes. The stumbling block to this proposal, at least as far as the legal profession was concerned, was that few magistrates were qualified in the law. They had the advice of their clerks, who were solicitors, in some instances they were bolstered by stipendiaries, who had legal training, or they might receive guidance from a recorder, who was a barrister; but there was no requirement that a magistrate, even the chairman of the bench at quarter sessions, should have any legal qualification. In the event no nineteenth-century government was prepared either to extend the powers of quarter sessions or to require legal qualifications for magistrates.[106]

The English system of criminal prosecutions and trials entered the twentieth century shot through with paradoxes though, interestingly few contemporaries appear to have been aware, or, at least, much concerned. There was no formal system of state prosecution run by state officials; the prosecution of a criminal offender was still perceived as the right of any individual, but, increasingly such prosecutions were being dominated by the professional police. Trial by jury continued to be trumpeted as one of the central pillars of English liberty and constitutionalism; yet, increasingly and overwhelmingly, criminal prosecutions were being brought before summary courts which conducted their business without juries. Finally, while the legal profession was advancing and consolidating its monopoly in civil law and in the higher criminal courts, most criminal business was being handled before tribunals composed of lay magistrates.

REFERENCES AND NOTES

. **Douglas Hay**, 'Controlling the English prosecutor', *Osgoode Hall Law Journal*, **21** (1983), pp. 165–86 (at p. 167); **Clive Emsley**, 'An aspect of Pitt's "Terror": Prosecutions for sedition during the 1790s', *Social History*, **6** (1981), pp. 155–84; idem, 'Repression, "terror" and the rule of law in England during the decade of the French Revolution,' *EHR* C (1985), pp. 801–25.

. *Northampton Mercury* 6 and 13 August 1753.

. **George Rudé**, *Criminal and Victim: Crime and society in early nineteenth-century England*, Clarendon Press, Oxford, 1985, pp. 59–60. Rudé cites four examples; the first three (from *O.B.S.P.* 1810, 1820 and 1830) were instances of the victim being impeded in his pursuit of the offender; in the fourth instance (from 1840) the victim was helped.

Rudé asks: 'does this denote a change in popular attitudes towards criminal and victim?' Obviously it will take far more than four examples to prove anything like this, and it should also be remembered that the hue and cry had a long pedigree.

. **Raphael Samuel** (ed.), *East End Underworld: Chapters in the life of Arthur Harding*, RKP, London, 1981, pp. 43–5.

. **Peter Linebaugh**, 'The Tyburn riot against the surgeons', in Douglas Hay, Peter Linebaugh *et al, Albion's Fatal Tree: Crime and society, in eighteenth-century England*, Allen Lane, 1975, pp. 107–8.

. *Huntingdon, Bedford and Cambridge Gazette* 2 and 16 August 1817; Beds. R.O. QSR 23/1817/230–31.

. *Huntingdon, Bedford and Cambridge Gazette*, 15 and 22 July 1815, 22 March 1817; Beds. R.O. QSR 23/1817/508.

. H.O. 45.7323. My thanks to Professor John Bohstedt for this reference.

. **David Jones**, 'The Welsh and crime, 1801–91', in **Clive Emsley** and **James Walvin** (eds.), *Artisans, Peasants and Proletarians 1760–1860*, Croom Helm, London, 1985, pp. 89–91; for an example of charivari or rough music in mid nineteenth-century Liverpool see *Liverpool Mercury*, 12 November 1855, though the cause appears to have been sexual transgression rather than crime.

10. In June 1847, for example, Ann Wood, a widow of Edingley, Nottinghamshire, left her house in the care of one of her daughters. In the mother's absence a second daughter stole several articles of clothing together with some money and then ran off. She was eventually arrested in Derbyshire by a police constable. Notts. R.O. QSD/1847. See also **Jennifer Davis**, 'Criminal prosecutions and their context in late Victorian London', paper presented to the Conference on the History of Law, Labour and Crime, at the University of Warwick, 15–18 September 1983, pp. 9–10.

This issue has been rarely noted with reference to England; recent research in France has shown that the law, the police and the infamous *lettre de cachet* were regularly used to discipline unruly children. See, inter alia **Claude Quétel**, *De Par Le Roy: Essai sur les lettres de cachet*, Privat, Toulouse, 1981, pp. 137–40 and 146–48; **Arlette Farge** and **Michel**

Foucault, *Le Désordre des Familles: Lettres de cachet des archives de la Bastille*, Gallimard Julliard, Paris, 1982, chap. 3.

11. Notts R.O. QSM 1788–96; East Retford 10 October 1794 and 16 January 1795.
12. *O.B.S.P. 1796–97* no. 43, p. 65.
13. Beds. R.O. PM 2629, Notebook of Francis Pym (1832–34); see also Beds R.O. QSR 1830/34.
14. Jennifer Davis, 'Law breaking and law enforcement: The creation of a criminal class in mid-Victorian London', unpublished Ph.D. Boston College, 1984, chap. 5 especially.
15. Notts. R.O. QSM 1761–67; Nottingham 13 January 1766.
16. Beds R.O. PM 2629, Notebook of Pym.
17. Davis, 'Law breaking and law enforcement', pp. 307–10.
18. See below pp. 175 and 177.
19. **John Styles**, 'Sir John Fielding and the problem of criminal investigation in eighteenth-century England', *T.R.H.S.* 5th series, **33** (1983), pp. 127–50; idem, 'Crime in the eighteenth-century provincial newspaper', unpublished paper, has estimated from depositions from the Northern Assize Circuit that certainly 25 per cent of arrests for horse stealing and perhaps as many as 43 per cent were, at least partially the result of advertisements in newspapers.
  In 1827 John Pilstow, a shopkeeper of Northampton stopped at a Woburn Inn on his way to London. During the night he was robbed. He promptly had some handbills printed offering a £1 reward for the arrest of a suspect; the handbills led directly to an arrest two days after the robbery, in Leicester. Beds R.O. 1827/295.
20. **Elizabeth Silverthorne** (ed.), *Deposition Book of Richard Wyatt J.P. 1767–76*, Surrey Records Society, vol. xxx (1978), nos. 64–67; Beds R.O. QSR 1830/495.
21. Wilts R.O. Stourhead Archive, 383/955 Justice Book of R. C. Hoare 1785–1815 has several examples of warrants issued on suspicion, for example: '21 Feby [1795] Granted a Warrant on Information of Giles Jupe of Mere to search the houses of Edmund Williams, Thomas Herridge, Hugh Deverill, Edward Mills, John Miles and Edward Avery, for wood stolen from the coppice of Deverill Longwood.'
  Wood was found in the possession of Herridge and Mills, and acting summarily Hoare fined them both 10s.
  For an example leading to a more serious charge see *O.B.S.P. 1800–01*, no. 99 for a warrant issued to Richard Jones, a soap and perfume manufacturer of Shoreditch, to search the lodgings of his former foreman whom he rightly suspected of pilfering large quantities of goods to set up in the trade on his own account.
22. Beds R.O. 25/1822/610 contains a letter from a magistrate, the Rev Orlebar Smith suggested that a certain Sinfield be indicted for felony. Sinfield had gone to Smith for a warrant accusing William Pilgrim of stealing his watch. He had then used the warrant to frighten Pilgrim into returning the watch and to paying Sinfield 30s. in compensation; the business completed to his satisfaction, Sinfield had then, illegally, destroyed the warrant.
23. Beds R.O. QSR 17/1792/119.

24. Silverthorne (ed.), *Deposition Book of Richard Wyatt*, no. 207.

25. **Elizabeth Crittal** (ed.), *The Justicing Notebook of William Hunt 1744–49*, Wiltshire Record Society, xxxvii (1982), pp. 13–14.

26. **Alan F. Cirket** (ed.), *Samuel Whitbread's Notebooks, 1810–11, 1813–14*, Bedfordshire Historical Records Society, vol. 50 (1971), nos. 210, 215, 224.

27. **P. B. Munsche**, *Gentlemen and Poachers: The English Game Laws 1671–1831*, Cambridge U.P., 1981, p. 92. The apology inserted in the newspaper could be used in assault cases (e.g. Beds R.O. QSR 16/1789/284), in seditious libel cases during the 1790s (Emsley, 'An aspect of Pitt's "Terror"', pp. 159–60) and even in poaching cases (e.g. *Sussex Weekly Advertiser*, 11 June 1796).

28. **P. J. R. King**, 'Crime, law and society in Essex 1740–1820, unpublished Ph.D. Cambridge University, 1984, p. 258.

29. Hay, 'Controlling the English prosecutor', p. 168; idem, 'Manufacturers and the criminal law in the later eighteenth century: Crime and "police" in South Staffordshire', *Past and Present Society Colloquium: Police and policing*, 1983, pp. 39–41.

30. Leeds City Archives, LC/QS 1/12, f.132; and for similar examples see ibid f.126 (William Hartley), f.175 (Thomas Brumfutt), and f.176 (Jesse Holmes).
This kind of downgrading the value of stolen property could also occur in the higher courts during trials. Catherine Hart was tried at the Old Bailey in December 1784 for stealing clothing from John Norfolk valued in total at £2. 17s. according to the indictment. The judge asked the prosecutor what was their value noting that 'if they are above forty shillings ... it will be a capital offence'. Norfolk then valued the goods at 30s. 'in order to save her life, because the wretch's life is no value to me'. *O.B.S.P. 1784–85* no. 124, p. 174.

31. Hay, 'Controlling the English prosecutor', pp. 168–69; Emsley, 'An aspect of Pitt's "terror"', p. 168; idem, 'Repression, "terror" and the rule of law', p. 819.

32. *P.P.* 1828 (533) vi, *Select Committee on Police of the Metropolis*, p. 83.

33. **Henry Fielding**, *An Enquiry into the Causes of the Late Increase of Robbers, with some Proposals for Remedying this Growing Evil*, 2nd. edn., London, 1751, pp. 168–71.

34. **Adrian Shubert**, 'Private initiative in law enforcement: Associations for the prosecution of felons, 1744–1856', in **Victor Bailey** (ed.), *Policing and Punishment in Nineteenth-Century Britain*, Croom Helm, London, 1981, now superseded by the research of Peter King and David Philips. **Peter King**, 'Prosecution associations, courts and community concerns in Essex 1740–1800' and **David Philips**, 'Good men to associate and bad men to conspire: Associations for the prosecution of felons in England 1770–1860', both papers presented to the Conference on History of law, Labour and Crime, at the University of Warwick, 15–18 September 1983.

35. Notts. R.O. WSM 1782–88; Nottingham 3 October 1785.

36. Leeds City Archives, LC/QS 1/12 f.36 and see also ff.82 and 88; King, 'Crime, law and society', pp. 172–77; **Janet Gyford**, ' "Men of bad character": Property crime in Essex in the 1820s', unpublished M.A., University of Essex, 1982, p. 22.

37. Peter King, 'Decision-makers and decision-making in the Englis|
    criminal law, 1750–1800', *H.J.* **27** (1984), pp. 26–58 (at p. 28). My ow|
    study of prosecutors at the Bedfordshire quarter sessions, based on th|
    indictments and recognizances every five years 1750 to 1810 gives |
    similar breakdown:

Gentry (esquires, yeomen)	34
Professionals (clergy, schoolmasters etc.)	4
Farmers	10
Tradesmen and artisans	45
Husbandmen and gardeners	11
Labourers and servants	10
Total	114

38. *Hansard* new series xiv (1826), col. 1230.
39. Fielding, *Enquiry*, p. 164.
40. *P.P.* 1819 viii, *Select Committee on Criminal Laws*, p. 8.
41. Hay, 'Controlling the English prosecutor', p. 170.
42. H.O. 42/114/182–84, reply from Shadwell, 27 February 1811; H.O|
    42/114/168–70, reply from Hatton Garden, 26 February 1811; H.O|
    42/114/172–73, reply from Mr Fielding, Queen's Square, 26 Februar|
    1811. (The reply from the other two magistrates of Queen's Square is i|
    H.O. 42/114/186–87, 27 February 1811; it is shorter, but not significantl|
    different.)
43. U.C.L. Chadwick MSS 11 f.35: T Division response to q.14.
44. H.O. 42/114/151–56, reply from Worships St. 25 February 1811; *Th|
    Times* 26 July 1847, for the case of the Rev Ridley Bray.
45. In June 1824 parliament discussed the use of summary punishment fo|
    men 'lewdly and obscenely exposing the person'.
    T. G. B. Estcourt reported the opinion of magistrates 'that the offence wa|
    so frequent, and it was so difficult to prevail upon females to overcom|
    their natural delicacy, and prosecute the offender in a court of justice, tha|
    some summary punishment was almost indispensable'. (*Hansard* nev|
    series xi (1824), col. 1082)
    In September 1857 Ann Spowage a spinster and maidservant was rescuec|
    from an attempted rape by a neighbour. She finally gave a deposition o|
    the incident eleven days after it had occurred: 'I complained about it to m|
    mistress on the Thursday after. I was so shy I hardly dare mention it'|
    (Notts R.O. QSD 1857).
46. Gyford, ' "Men of Bad Character" ', p. 15; U.C.L. Chadwick MSS 11 f.38|
    D division response to q.16.
    Committed 'evangelical' atheists during the Victorian period refused tc|
    swear oaths and therefore could not commence proceedings. G. J|
    Holyoake was prevented in this way from swearing a writ against the cal|
    driver who, while drunk, ran over and mortally injured his son. (**F. B|
    Smith**, 'The atheist mission, 1840–1900', in **Robert Robinson** (ed.), *Idea|
    and Institutions of Victorian Britain*, Bell, London 1967, p. 233).
47. U.C.L. Chadwick MSS 11 f.36: responses of E and M divisions to q.15|
    f.38: responses of B and H divisions.
48. Fielding, *Enquiry*, p. 164; U.C.L. Chadwick MSS 11 f.42: H divisior|
    response to q.18.

49. U.C.L. Chadwick MSS 11 ff.50–51: G division response to q.22, and see also ff.47–48 responses to q.21.

50. U.C.L. Chadwick MSS 11 f.41: C division response to q.17; there were similar responses from other divisions.

51. U.C.L. Chadwick MSS 11 f.39: L division response to q.16.

52. U.C.L. Chadwick MSS 11 f.44: V division response to q.19. As late as the 1880s many of the same reasons were being given as detering prosecutions in Wales, even in cases of arson. (Jones, 'Welsh and crime', p. 88 and note 22).

53. *Hansard* new series xiv (1826), col. 1232.

54. Quoted in Hay, 'Controlling the English prosecutor', p. 176.

55. Hay, 'Controlling the English prosecutor', pp. 178–79 lists fourteen acts, excluding the Vexatious Indictments Act, passed between 1791 and 1888 which infringed the discretion of the private prosecutor.

56. Emsley, 'Aspect of Pitt's "terror" ', pp. 161–62; Gyford, ' "Men of Bad Character" ', pp. 18–19.

57. **David Philips**, *Crime and Authority in Victorian England*, Croom Helm, London, 1977, pp. 101 and 123–24 notes the increasing importance of the police as prosecutors especially in the Staffordshire part of the Black Country between 1836 and 1851. By 1847 the Staffordshire Constabulary was handling nearly 36 per cent of the prosecutions in the district. My own, more limited work on Bedfordshire, suggests that the county force there was responsible for a much smaller percentage of prosecutions during the 1850s: of the 109 indictments brought before the quarter sessions in 1850, only three originated with the police; of the 124 indictments brought before quarter sessions in 1855, only 12 were brought directly by, or were assisted by the police.

58. **Charles Dickens**, 'The ruffian', in *The Uncommercial Traveller*; also idem, footnote to 'Stories for the first of April', *Miscellaneous Papers* (first published in *Household Words*).

59. See below, p. 187.

60. U.C.L. Chadwick MSS 11 f.36.

61. In 1859, for example, of the 92 indictments brought before the Nottinghamshire quarter sessions, the police preferred only 14 and a parish constable one. For the limited number of prosecutions by police in London see Davis, 'Law breaking and law enforcement', p. 195.

62. *The Times* 11 September 1856, for a letter from a Cornish attorney (following similar complaints from Devon and Yorkshire), critical of the paucity of costs allowed by Cornish magistrates and instancing a respectable tradesman who, in order to prosecute a serious case of felony, had to travel 50 miles and spend three nights in a hotel, for all of which he was allowed one guinea expenses.

63. *Bedford Mercury* 30 March 1844, quoting *The Globe*.

64. In six of the twelve criminal cases brought before the Bedfordshire Epiphany Sessions for 1832 the chairman of the bench noted 'Defence says nothing'. Beds. R.O. PM 2629, Notebook of Pym.

65. *O.B.S.P. 1796–97*, no. 302, p. 291; *C.C.C.S.P. 1856–57*, no. 600, pp. 58–59; see also Rudé, *Criminal and Victim*, pp. 58–59.

66. **J. M. Beattie**, 'Crime and the courts in Surrey 1736–53' in **J. S. Cockburn** (ed.), *Crime in England 1500–1800*, Methuen, London, 1977; idem, *Crime*

and the Courts in England 1660–1800, Oxford U.P. 1986; chap. 7; **John H. Langbein**, 'The criminal trial before the lawyers, '*University of Chicago Law Review*, **45** (1978), pp. 263–316; idem, 'Shaping the eighteenth-century criminal trial: A view from the Ryder Sources', *University of Chicago Law Review*, **50** (1983), pp. 1–136. The discussion of the lawyers and the courts during the eighteenth century is based largely on these sources.

For the development of the legal profession see **Brian Abel-Smith** and **Robert Stevens**, *Lawyers and the Courts: A sociological study of the English legal system 1750–1965*, Heinemann, London, 1967, pp. 19–27.

67.   *Bedford Mercury* 23 March 1844.

68.   *Hansard* 3rd series xvi (1833), cols. 1202–3.

69.   **J. J. Tobias,** *Crime and Industrial Society in the Nineteenth Century*, Penguin, Harmondsworth, 1972, p. 267.

70.   Philips, *Crime and Authority*, pp. 104–5.

71.   **Graham Parker**, 'The prisoner in the box – The making of the Criminal Evidence Act', in **J. A. Guy** and **H. G. Beale** (eds.), *Law and Social Change in British History*, Royal Historical Society, London, 1984.

72.   **A. H. Manchester**, *A Modern Legal History of England and Wales 1750–1950*, Butterworths, London, 1980, p. 100; Abel-Smith and Stevens, *Lawyers and the Courts*, pp. 32 and 135–36.

It is worth noting that a form of legal aid had existed for the accused in Scotland since the late Middle Ages.

73.   **Martin Madan**, *Thoughts on Executive Justice*, London 1785, pp. 143–44; *Bedford Mercury*, 23 March 1844.

74.   *O.B.S.P., 1765–66*, no. 73, p. 55.

75.   King, 'Crime, law and society', pp. 299–300.

76.   For Blackstone and the eighteenth-century debate on summary jurisdiction see **Norma Landau**, *The Justices of the Peace 1679–1760*, University of California Press, Berkeley and Los Angeles, 1984, pp. 343–45; *London Chronicle* 12 March 1772; *The Times* 4 May 1829.

77.   Munsche, *Gentlemen and Poachers*, chaps. 1 and 4 passim.

78.   *Hansard* new series viii (1823), cols. 1292–98.

79.   Munsche, *Gentlemen and Poachers*, p. 162; while noting that game offenders were probably punished more severely, King has discovered a far greater incidence of wood, fruit and vegetable theft brought before summary jurisdiction in eighteenth-century Essex ('Crime, law and society', pp. 266–69).

80.   **John Styles**, 'Embezzlement, industry and the law in England 1500–1800', in **Maxine Berg, Pat Hudson** and **Michael Sonenscher** (eds.), *Manufacture in Town and Country before the Factory*, Cambridge U.P., 1983, pp. 200–4.

81.   **R. E. Swift**, 'Crime, law and order in two English towns during the early nineteenth century: The experience of Exeter and Wolverhampton 1815–56', unpublished Ph.D. University of Birmingham, 1981, pp. 329–30.

82.   *Kent and Essex Mercury*, 27 January 1824, quoted in Gyford, ' "Men of Bad Character" ', p. 24.

83.   Swift, 'Crime, law and order', pp. 125–26.

84.   Landau, *Justices of the Peace*, pp. 356–58; Silverthorne (ed.), *Deposition Book of Richard Wyatt*, p. x and nos. 108–10.

85.   Francis Pym recorded stepping down from chairmanship of the

Bedfordshire bench at the Midsummer Sessions in 1833 when Samuel Barnes was tried for a larceny in stealing wood from Pym's land. He also recorded 'verdict of *acquitted* on the ground that it was trespass and not a felony'. Beds R.O. PM2629.

86. **P. C. Barrett**, 'Crime and punishment in a Lancashire industrial town: Law and social change in the borough of Wigan, 1800–50', unpublished M.Phil, Liverpool Polytechnic, 1980, pp. 84–86 and 88–98.

87. **D. C. Woods**, 'The operation of the Master and Servants Act in the Black Country 1858–75', *Midland History*, vii (1982), pp. 93–115.

88. **R. Quinault**, 'The Warwickshire country magistracy and public order, c.1830–70', in **John Stevenson** and **Roland Quinault** (eds.), *Popular Protest and Public Order: Six studies in British history, 1790–1820*, Allen and Unwin, London, 1974, pp. 189, 207.

89. **Olwen Hufton**, 'Crime in pre-industrial Europe', *Newsletter of the International Association for the History of Crime and Criminal Justice*, **4** (1981), p. 15.

90. Landau, *Justices of the Peace*, chap. 6.

91. *Illustrated London News*, 22 May 1847, p. 322. Charles Dickens gave a far less attractive picture with his portrayal of Mr Fang (based on the notorious Mr Laing of Hatton Garden) in *Oliver Twist*, chap. xi.

92. **Edward Carpenter**, *Prisons, Police and Punishment*, London, 1905, p. 70.

93. Jennifer Davis, ' "A poor man's system of justice": The London police courts in the second half of the nineteenth century', *H.J.* **27** (1984), pp. 309–35: quotations at p. 315. See also idem, 'Law breaking and law enforcement', pp. 297–98.

94. **Clive Emsley**, *Policing and its Context 1750–1870*, Macmillan, London, 1983, pp. 22 and 47–48; Tobias, *Crime and Industrial Society*, p. 265.

95. *Hansard* new series xviii (1828), cols. 166–67; *The Times*, 4 May 1829.

96. *Hansard* 3rd series lii (1840), col. 652.

97. *Bedford Mercury*, 11 February 1843.

98. *Hansard* 3rd series xc (1847), cols. 430–38, and xcii (1847), col. 38.

99. *Hansard* 3rd series xcii (1847), col. 46.

100. *Hansard* 3rd series cxxxvi (1855), col. 1871, cxxxvii (1855), col. 1168, and cxxxix (1855), cols. 1867, 2018.

101. Abel-Smith and Stevens, *Lawyers and the Courts*, p. 31.

102. Philips, *Crime and Authority*, pp. 132–34.
Reference to the quarter sessions minute books of both Beds and Notts shows the dramatic decline in cases brought before these courts in the second half of the century. At the Epiphany Sessions in the middle years of the century, for example, the counties were hearing, on average about 20 and between 30 and 40 cases respectively; by the late 1890s these numbers had fallen, generally, to less than half a dozen in both instances. At the same time the number of cases heard summarily, was soaring; at the Epiphany Sessions by the mid 1860s Beds was recording around 50 and Notts around 100 cases under the Criminal Justice Act, with another half dozen or so under the Juvenile Offenders Act. In addition they were also filing, respectively, around 150 and around 300 other summary convictions for assault, drink offences, malicious damage, game offences, highway offences, vagrancy, etc.

103. *Hansard* 3rd series ccxliii (1879), cols. 1099 and 110–03, and ccxlvii (1879), col. 1703.
104. Abel-Smith and Stevens, *Lawyers and the Courts*, pp. 31–32.
105. *Hansard* new series vi (1822), col. 1320.
106. Abel-Smith and Stevens, *Lawyers and the Courts*, pp. 31–32.

Chapter 8

DETECTION AND PREVENTION: THE OLD POLICE AND THE NEW

The period 1750–1900 witnessed a marked increase in the number of professionals employed in England and Wales to combat crime. The old police system, generally dependent on part-time constables and watchmen was being condemned as inadequate in the metropolis well before the close of the eighteenth century. The first manifestation of the new police were the 3,000 uniformed constables of the Metropolitan Police who began their beat patrols in London between September 1829 and May 1830. The Municipal Corporations Act 1835, in theory, spread the new police into provincial boroughs. The Rural Constabulary Act 1839 enabled counties, or parts of counties, to establish police forces. The County and Borough Police Act 1856 capped this legislation making the new police obligatory for all local authorities. The arguments and assessments of the late eighteenth and nineteenth-century police reformers were, generally speaking, accepted by historians of the English police well into the second half of the twentieth century. They insisted that the old system of policing was inefficient, that offenders tended to be caught more as a result of luck than anything else. The new system of uniformed beat policemen, in contrast, helped to prevent crime and made the arrest of offenders much more certain. Many of the Whig historians of the new police have tended to look back from an idealised contemporary model, to assume that there was no alternative and that this was the model which the far-sighted reformers and policitians of the late eighteenth and nineteenth centuries had in mind. The new system of police thus fitted precisely with the requirements of society. Many of the recent critics of this 'Whig' view have also perceived a fit. They have emphasised the public order role of the new police development and the control requirements of capitalism.[1]

For most of the eighteenth century in England, as elsewhere in Europe, the word 'police' had the general meaning of the management and government of a particular piece of territory, particularly a town or city. In England the idea of a uniformed body of policemen patrolling the streets to prevent crime and disorder was anathema. Such a force smacked of the absolutism of continental states. The models for such police forces were to be found in the organisation commanded by the *lieutenant général de police* in Paris, and in the military police, the *maréchaussée*, which patrolled the main roads of provincial France. The fact that these models were French, in itself, was sufficient to make most eighteenth-century English gentlemen conceive of a police force as something inimical to English liberty. Policing in eighteenth-century England was perceived as a local government task, and like other areas of local government it depended upon local men being selected, or voluntarily coming forward, to serve in an official capacity, but generally for a limited period, part-time, and usually unpaid.[2]

Essentially the constables of eighteenth-century England were neither a preventive nor a detective police force. The high constables of counties were often men of some social standing. These were selected in a variety of ways, depending on traditional local practice. They had a variety of tasks; the most important of which was supervision of the collection of the county rates. In respect of crime, they had an obligation to pursue any felonies reported to them, and this might involve primitive detective work as when, in 1818, John Shaw, high constable of the hundred of Redbornstoke in Bedfordshire found a footprint near the hiding place of some stolen wine and was subsequently able to fit a shoe to it.[3] The high constables had supervision of the petty constables. The latter were men of less social significance; again they were selected in a variety of ways depending upon local custom. Their tasks were many and varied, and they were allowed expenses and fees. The pursuit of offenders was often undertaken by victims, as described in the preceding chapter; but the constable was charged with making arrests. They were also required to serve warrants, to move offenders from place to place – either transporting a vagrant out of the parish, or taking an accused party to court; they might even have to accommodate offenders, temporarily, in their homes. Such tasks were burdensome; if a man had a trade, any time spent on constable's duties could cost him business. Occasionally the tasks brought threats of violence; Edward Wright, constable of the parish of Egham, Surrey, deposed:

> When he served a summons on Samuel Smith younger of Chertsey who stands charged with getting a bastard child on the body of Ann Jacob, Samuel Smith the elder swore that if ever he came to his house after his son he would do for him. Informant now has a warrant to apprehend Samuel Smith the younger which he is afraid to execute, Samuel Smith the elder having sworn that he would do him some bodily harm.

Hostility to constables in the execution of their duty did not always stop at verbal threats and abuse as a glance at any eighteenth or early nineteenth-century newspaper or run of quarter sessions indictments will show. In 1817 Constable Henry Thompson of Ruardean in Gloucestershire was shot dead by William Turner after he had arrested the latter's wife in possession of stolen wheat. A more typical example of violence towards constables occurred one Saturday evening in the late summer of 1827. Thomas Franklin, the constable of Leighton Buzzard, was called to a public house where a quarrel was leading to blows. William Smith, a butcher, who was to go to Franklin's aid, described what happened as he was walking past the pub:

> I saw Thomas Franklin ... coming out ... backwards. John Brandon ... was opposite and close to the constable. I saw the said John Brandon strike the said constable twice 'bang full in the face' the blows knocked the constable down on his back John Brandon fell down with him. Sarah Adams ... got on top of the constable and jostled his head against the ground ... The constable appeared very much hurt and his face was all over blood.[4]

Brandon and Adams were both indicted for assault. Yet some men were prepared to take on the post of constable full-time; in return for an initial payment they agreed to act in place of the man selected and then sought to earn their living through the fees. There was nothing especially new in this as Elbow, the simple constable in Shakespeare's *Measure for Measure*, had also acted in this way:

> Escalus: Come hither to me, Master Elbow; come hither Master Constable. How long have you been in this place of constable?
>
> Elbow: Seven year and a half, sir.
>
> Escalus: I thought by your readiness in the office, you had continued in it some time. You say seven years together?
>
> Elbow: And a half, sir.
>
> Escalus: Alas! it hath been great pains to you! – They do you wrong to put you so oft upon't. Are there not men in your ward sufficient to serve it?
>
> Elbow: Faith, sir, few of any wit in such matters; as they are chosen, they are glad to choose me for them; I do it for some piece of money, and go through with all. (Act II, scene 2)

Of course the fact that some men were prepared to take on the tasks of constable full-time does not mean that they were, necessarily, any good at the job. Many parish constables probably were as bad and as uncommitted to their tasks as the police reformers made out. But others could be and were relied upon;[5] a serious analysis of the men who fulfilled this role during the eighteenth and early nineteenth centuries is long overdue and it may well prompt a major revision of the traditional picture.

Preventive policing in eighteenth-century England was largely confined to urban areas where watches patrolled the streets after dark. Again for the Tudor period Shakespeare provided a comic example with the watchmen who act under the bumbling Dogberry and Verges in *Much*

Ado About Nothing. The problem is that too often these fictional, comic characters have been taken as representatives of a reality spanning the period from the Tudors to the late Hanoverians because they fit so well with the police reformers' condemnations of the old system of policing.[6] In fact eighteenth and early nineteenth-century watchmen have been subject to even less serious study than constables. It is, however, clear that at least in some metropolitan parishes there were determined attempts to ensure that the night watch was competent and capable a hundred years before the Metropolitan Police took to the streets.[7] Some watchmen were fully prepared to stop men on suspicion, and their suspicions could prove valid: one night towards the end of 1796 John Wilson was picked up on suspicion by two London watchmen; he was taken to the Hanover Square parish watch-house where he was searched by a constable and found to have five pewter pots concealed about his person; the pots had been taken from a pub in Carnaby Street and Wilson was subsequently tried and convicted at the Old Bailey. The evidence given in an Old Bailey burglary trial twenty years later suggests a watch system functioning in some parts of the metropolis which possessed men behaving in the active and observant way which according to the Whig historians, was introduced only with the new Metropolitan Police:

> On the night of the 12th December, I was calling four o'clock in the morning; I came by Mr. Levy's house, in Wentworth-street; I saw the prisoner standing in the court there; I did not know him before, I thought he might live in the court; I went up the court, and took particular notice of his dress, as I passed him; I went on, and returned again; I missed him; I went up the court, and saw Levy's side door was open, it is in the court; I returned to my box, and in a few minutes, the prisoner came by my box; I stepped out, and called to him, he stopped, and I crossed over to him, and asked him what he did at the house round the corner - he said 'what house', and seemed strange. I asked him, what he had got upon him, his pockets appeared full, and bulky – he said, 'nothing at all', and that he was a different character to what I took him to be ... Levy's house is considered a receiving house. I have been on that beat fifteen months ...

The watchman found stolen lace hidden in the prisoner's hat, and took him into custody.[8] The Select Committee enquiring into the police of the metropolis in 1828 heard largely complimentary comments on the watches in Marylebone, St James's, and St George's Hanover Square; the majority of these watchmen appear to have been ex soldiers 'stout tall fellows', according to the inspector in St James's 'not exceeding forty years of age'.[9] This is not to argue that the watch was not in need of reform, but simply that the traditional image of the 'Charlie' as old, decrepit and, like as not drunk or asleep when needed, is a generalisation not always borne out by the evidence.

Occasionally a provincial magistrate might be found who was interested in solving a crime and detecting offenders, and he could go to considerable trouble and expense in so doing.[10] But if a victim could not follow up an offence in person, with friends, or by advertisement, the only other recourse – apart from a visit in rural areas to the cunning man – was to a thief-taker. Until the establishment of a special group of thief takers in the office of the Bow Street magistrates in the middle of the eighteenth century, the thief-takers were private individuals. They lived off the rewards from the courts for bringing offenders to justice,[11] and the rewards from victims who paid to get property returned. Both kinds of reward were liable to abuse. The reputation of the thief-takers is low primarily because of the notorious career of Jonathan Wild the self-appointed 'Thief-taker General of Great Britain and Ireland' who was exposed, in 1725, as a leading receiver of stolen goods who kept himself in the thief-taking business by the occasional sacrifice of a thief on the gallows. The Stephen Macdaniel affair which blew up some thirty years later was less far-reaching, but re-emphasised the dangers of rewarding thief-takers by results when the result, as like as not, was an innocent body swinging from the gallows.[12] Not all pre-police thief-takers were like Wild and Macdaniel, especially the semi-official detectives like Richard Green who combined his detective work with being keeper of the lock-up at Knott Hill, Manchester, and John and Daniel Forrester who worked in the City of London from 1817 to 1857.[13]

It was the metropolis which witnessed the major developments and the major proposals for police reform during the eighteenth century; not the square mile of the City of London proper, which had its own police system organised under the Lord Mayor and the City Marshals, but the sprawls of the City of Westminster, urban Middlesex and, south of the Thames, urban Surrey. The architects of these developments and proposals were the Fieldings who established the group of paid thief-takers – the celebrated Runners – in the 1750s and, after some abortive starts, who organised paid patrols of part-time constables circulating the central thoroughfares and the main roads into the metropolis from evening until midnight. By the end of the century the Bow Street Patrol consisted of sixty-eight men divided into thirteen parties. Sir John Fielding drew up plans for a centralised police for London with five or six separate police offices under the overall supervision of Bow Street. This central office, he argued, could act as a clearing house for information about different crimes and different offenders; detailed information and descriptions, readily available to different peace officers, were regarded by the Fieldings as central in the 'war' against crime. Sir John's proposals for a systematised and centralised police in London came to nothing during his lifetime, but they influenced the abortive legislation of the 1780s and the Middlesex Justice Act 1792.

In 1772 and 1773 Sir John circulated the clerks of the peace of all the English and Welsh counties with his General Preventative Plan. His idea was to make the Bow Street Office a central clearing house for information about serious crimes and offenders encompassing the whole country; he wanted provincial magistrates to supply Bow Street with details of offenders and offences, goalers to supply descriptions of those committed to their custody via the assize calendars already received in his office, and both officials and members of the public to give descriptions of stolen horses. The proposal was well received and, from the autumn of 1773 with government backing to the tune of £400 per annum, this information was collected in Bow Street, collated and circulated in the form of a newspaper, *The Hue and Cry*. The extent to which the circulation of information in this way improved the clear-up rate cannot be ascertained, for one thing there is no data on which to base a measurement of the situation beforehand, yet it does appear to have contributed to several arrests. But Fielding's subsequent proposals, circulated in February 1775, were scarcely responded to. They were far more radical, recommending what would have amounted to a system of paid professional policemen. Fielding wanted high constables to be resident on the main roads for at least one hundred miles distance from London; they were to display a board announcing their office outside their home, they were to undertake the pursuit of offenders, and to be paid a salary for keeping a horse for these pursuits. In addition the numbers of petty constables were to be increased. The cool reaction to these proposals probably stemmed partly from a reluctance on the part of the county benches to reorganise the tasks of their constables, especially when high constables were men of some standing who would have balked at being simply the pursuers of common felons. Probably also the magistrates could see little value in the proposals for their own localities; provincial England was not London with its urban sprawl and its apparently disproportionate amount of serious crime. Local constables could handle the vagrants on the roads; there were few highway robberies in the provinces and seemingly few fugitives moving along the roads from one district to another. What appeared of value from the centre of London to suppress the city's unique crime problem, had little value outside.[14]

Yet whatever the concerns of men like Fielding about crime in eighteenth-century London, the fear of a French system of police was greater. A bill brought before parliament in 1785 proposed dividing the entire metropolis into nine police divisions each with three stipendiary magistrates and twenty-five constables; it foundered partly on the fear that a system of regular police was alien to England, and partly because of the hostility of the City of London which brought its powerful parliamentary lobby into play to protect its independent jurisdiction. When, seven years later, the Middlesex Justice Bill was introduced, the territory of the Lord Mayor and his Marshals was studiously omitted from the proposal. The legislation of 1792 established seven police offices, six north of the Thames – Queen's Square, Westminster; Great Marlborough Street; Hatton Garden, Shoreditch; Whitechapel; Shadwell – and one south of the river in Southwark. Each office had three stipendiary magistrates and six constables. Among the first of the magistrates was Colquhoun who poured a steady stream of voluminous letters in miniscule writing in the direction of different offices of state; many of these letters urged various reforms and improvements.[15] Attempts to spread the system failed, probably because of expense, but in 1798 Colquhoun was instrumental in the creation of the Thames Police Office at Wapping with, ultimately, three stipendiaries and 100 constables to police the river. The system of stipendiary magistrates and their constables working alongside the Bow Street Patrol, and the various parish constables and watches (Table 8.1), with the City jealously guarding its separate jurisdiction, saw London into the new century. The stipendiary magistrates and some of their constables rapidly assumed the role of experts on crime to be consulted when ministers or parliament, pressurised by reformers like Romilly and Mackintosh or by events like the Ratcliffe Highway murders, mounted enquiries into aspects of crime and policing in London. In February 1811 a circular was sent to the police offices requesting the magistrates' opinions on whether the recent abolition of the death penalty for picking pockets had led to any change in the incidence of the crime, of prosecutions for the crime, or convictions.[16] Magistrates and constables became regular witnesses before parliamentary committees. Some of the constables, like George Ruthven and John Townsend of Bow Street, acquired formidable reputations as detectives and the apprehenders of offenders; the assistance of such Bow Street officers was often sought by provincial authorities faced with a spate of robberies, a gang of poachers or a difficult murder. Yet the concerns about 'blood money' continued. Most of the constables had underworld informants known as 'Noses',[17] and on occasions links with the underworld became rather too friendly. Even Bow Street officers were suspended and occasionally prosecuted for compounding, or for conspiring with offenders whom they subsequently brought before the courts on capital charges so as to claim the reward.[18]

The revelations of corruption, the scare created by the Ratcliffe Highway murders, the publication of statistics giving a public picture of crime, the reports of crowd behaviour in revolutionary Paris aggravating fearful recollections of the Gordon Riots, combined with the writings of men like Colquhoun to make gentlemen of property concerned about the policing of London. Yet parliamentary committee after parliamentary committee was reluctant to recommend a completely new police system; a centralised system still appeared inimicable to English liberty, it was something peculiarly French, and under Napoleon the police system of the old enemy had achieved an authoritarian model of even more alarming proportions.

Early in 1822 Robert Peel took over as Home Secretary. He was determined to reform and revise the criminal code and he considered the establishment of a preventive police as integral to this. His involvement

TABLE 8.1 Watchmen, patrols, superintendents and beadles acting in the jurisdiction of the Police Magistrates, Union Hall, Southwark, 1 January, 1812*

Parish or district	Population	Number of beadles/ superintendents	Number of watchmen	Number of 'patrols'	Total police
Christchurch, Southwark	11,050	1	23	—	24
St George, Southwark	27,967	1	17	2	20
St John, Southwark	8,370	1	14	—	15
St Olave, Southwark	7,917	1	16	—	17
St Thomas, Southwark	1,466†	—	2 (private watch)	—	2
St Saviour's Southwark	15,349	1	11	—	12
St Saviour's Clink Libery		2	—	14	16
Manor of Hatcham			Patrolled by Bow Street Patrol		
Bermondsey	19,530	1	13	—	14
Camberwell		1	16	3	20
Dulwich	11,309‡	—	2	1 (horseman paid by subscription)	3
Peckham		1	7	2	10
Clapham Town	5,083§	1	14	2	17
Clapham Road		—	10	2	12

TABLE 8.1 (cont.)

Parish or district	Population	Number of beadles/ superintendents	Number of watchmen	Number of 'patrols'	Total police
Lambeth	41,644		Patrolled by Surrey Watch, some private watchmen, numbers unknown.		—
Newington	23,853	1	24	2	27
Rotherhithe	12,114	1	14	6	21
Streatham	2,729	1	2	6	9
Surrey Watch	—	1	42	2 (horsemen)	45

*Based on information in H.O.42.114.29, and population statistics drawn from the 1811 census.
  The area of urban Surrey covered by the magistrates at Union Hall was the largest jurisdiction of the seven police offices established in 1792; from the centre in the borough of Southwark it ran about five miles south-west up the Thames to Clapham, four miles east down stream to Rotherhithe, and six miles due south to Streatham.
†Includes the 'population' of St Thomas's and Guy's Hospitals.
‡Population of the Parish of Camberwell, which included Dulwich and Peckham.
§Population of Clapham Parish.

in the creation of the Police Preservation Force when Chief Secretary for Ireland during the preceding decade had convinced him of the utility of police reform, and he was assured that police were no threat to liberty as he and other liberal, reforming Tories perceived it. Peel's police reforms were centred on London and, initially, on the expanding Bow Street establishment; in 1805 a horse patrol had been established and in 1821 a dismounted night patrol. In the summer of 1822 Peel set up a force of twenty-four men as the Bow Street day patrol. Wearing a uniform of blue coat and red waistcoat – hence their nickname of 'redbreasts' – these men, mainly ex-soldiers, patrolled the main streets of the centre of the metropolis between 9 a.m. and 7 p.m. In 1828 Peel was successful in getting a new parliamentary enquiry into the police of London; he was equally successful in getting men appointed to the committee who shared some of his ideas. The committee recommended the creation of a centralised, uniformed, preventive police for London, and in the following year Peel skillfully guided the legislation establishing the Metropolitan Police through parliament; he carefully avoided a confrontation with the City by omitting the Lord Mayor's square mile from the jurisdiction of the new force.

The view of the Whig historians of the English police is that 1829 was the turning point: the new Metropolitan Police, by its example of checking crime and disorder, provided a model for the rest of the country, indeed, for the rest of the world. The reformers, from the Fieldings to Colquhoun, and on to Peel and the first two commissioners of the Metropolitan Police, Colonel Charles Rowan and Richard Mayne, thus became far-sighted men; those who opposed the reforms as un-English or who criticised the police as a military body, as 'gendarmes', thus became myopic, foolish, or worse. The creation of a police force of 3,000 uniformed men answerable directly to a minister of state was, indeed, something new and something possibly deserving the adjective 'revolutionary' in the English context. But whether this police force provided, overnight, a new level of efficiency in the struggle against crime is debatable, and the point noted above with reference to provincial magistrates' relucance to adopt Fielding's proposal in 1775, might also be raised in explanation of the opposition to police reform in the provinces over the next few decades: what relevance did this metropolitan model have for the rest of the country?

The police reform clauses of the Municipal Corporations Act 1835 appear to have been included, not so much from any recognised success of the metropolitan model, but because municipal policing had always been the preserve of local government, and if the entire system of municipal government was to be reformed and rationalised, then it was logical, indeed necessary, to include municipal policing. Some boroughs appear to have had disciplined and fairly efficient police systems at their disposal before the act,[19] what was singularly absent was any degree of uniformity. The act required boroughs to establish Watch Committees which, in turn, were to appoint police forces. Yet while Watch Committees generally appear to have been set up fairly quickly, many boroughs were dilatory in fulfilling the statutory obligations relating to police forces; of the 178 boroughs mentioned in the 1835 act, only 100 could claim to have police forces by the beginning of 1838, and fifteen years later at least six still had no force.[20] In some boroughs the creation of police merely meant that various town functionaries like the sword bearer, the beadle, and the watch simply donned uniforms and began to be called policemen. The nine policemen of the borough of Bedford appointed in January 1836 included the mayor's serjeant, the bellman and the beadle; and the old system of one group of men to patrol by day and another by night was maintained into the 1850s. The division of day and night police was similarly maintained in Exeter and Nottingham where the new police were also largely recruited from the old.[21] In towns without charters local worthies had long been developing police systems to their own needs. Some had their own lighting and watching committees established through private acts of parliament. The Lighting and Watching Act passed by parliament in 1833 provided an umbrella under which urban districts could set up such committees without any special legislation. A private town act had enabled Wolverhampton to establish a watch in 1814; a police force was established in the town in 1837, eleven years before incorporation. The worthies of Wolverhampton recruited Richard Castle, a sergeant of the Metropolitan Police, to command their new force; but half of the twelve-man force were veterans of the watch.[22] In 1838 the leading residents of Horncastle in Lincolnshire, with a population of just under 4,500, determined to establish a police force under the terms provided by the Lighting and Watching Act 1833. They approached the commissioners of the Metropolitan Police for a possible chief policeman, but were informed that no member of that force would go to Horncastle for less than 30s. a week. In the event they were lucky enough to find a local man who had served in London and who was willing to act for 16s. a week. The new police of Horncastle consisted of two men.[23]

This desire for men from the Metropolitan Police to command the new borough forces has been interpreted as a desire to follow the London model. Up to a point this may be true: the municipal authorites of early nineteenth-century England wanted value for money; the Metropolitan Police had acquired a reputation for efficiency and consequently a chief policeman with experience of London policing was to be valued precisely because of this experience. But the actual practices of policing did not always owe much to a metropolitan model; the division between day police and night police, which continued well into the 1850s in some areas, was a legacy of traditional policing. The relationship between policemen and the municipal authorities was also different. The Metropolitan Police were responsible directly to the Home Secretary. This was a matter of concern and annoyance to metropolitan parishes during the early years of the police, and the issue was raised again towards the end of the century; after all local ratepayers contributed directly, and significantly, to the force.[24] Municipal ratepayers financed municipal police forces in nineteenth-century England, and they had no intention of letting anybody give them orders or instructions other than the municipality. Municipal governments, through their watch committees, kept firm control of their policemen, and the relationship was very much that of master and servant with the policemen occasionally required to perform tasks which would never have been required of any metropolitan police constable.[25] Again this reflected the continuation of 'pre-police' traditions and by no means the triumph of any new model.

Lord Melbourne's Whig government had been contemplating some kind of police reform for the counties before the establishment of the Royal Commission on the Rural Constabulary in 1836. Three men served as commissioners: Edwin Chadwick, Colonel Charles Rowan of the Metropolitan Police, and Charles Shaw Lefevre. Chadwick was largely responsible for writing the report, but his Benthamite notions of centralisation and his desire for close links between rural police and the new poor law organisation were not shared by his fellow commissioners. Nevertheless such aspects of centralisation as were recommended in the report, published in March 1839, provoked hostility and disquiet. Rowan was amazed and suggested to Chadwick that one way of avoiding the supposed:

> danger to the liberties of the country would be to give the power
> *absolutely* of dismissal to the magistrates. Thus if the Secretary of State
> should take it into his head to endeavour to enslave a whole country
> (which is not at all [illegible] likely, after paying 20 million to enfranchise
> the *niggers*) by sending six or seven additional Police Constables 'armed
> with a bare bodkin' into that county, the magistrates might, seeing the
> immency [sic] of the danger, immediately dismiss the said six dangerous
> individuals and thus frustrate the base attempt. It is impossible to
> maintain gravity on the subject.

He concluded with a sentence prefiguring the thinking of Whig historians of the police 'What a pity it is that all men who are not Rogues should be fools'.[26]

Melbourne's government was too weak to push through parliament such a contentious reform as a national constabulary even if it had so wished. Moreover it seems that the Home Secretary, Lord John Russell, and interested cabinet colleagues never contemplated anything other than permissive legislation with the new county forces firmly under local control. The Royal Commission's recommendation that the Treasury pay one quarter of the cost of rural constabularies and that the Metropolitan Police train and appoint their members was not included in the Rural Constabulary Bill which swept through parliament in the summer of 1839 alongside bills to establish police forces in Birmingham,

Bolton and Manchester. Chartist activity was as much a spur to this spate of legislation, particularly in the case of the urban acts, as the report of the Royal Commission. The Rural Constabulary Act enabled any county that so wished to authorise the appropriate rate and to establish its own police force. Two crucial points in the origins and early workings of this legislation have been too little emphasised. First, the Royal Commission's investigations revealed that provincial England during the 1830s was not unpoliced, and that such policing as there was did not always depend upon the old constable system. In 1829 parliament had authorised the creation of a county police system in Cheshire. The Cheshire Police were not centralised under a single chief constable but were based on the hundred or petty sessional division; each hundred was supervised by a paid high constable who maintained close communication with the local magistrates. The system was amended slightly by act of parliament in 1852. Edwin Corbett, the vice-chairman of the Cheshire quarter sessions, informed the 1853 Select Committee on Police that he did 'not think it possible for any police force to work better than it does' and that the London Metropolitan Police was 'more completely organised than we should be able to establish in the rural districts'.[27] Elsewhere, sometimes established under the Lighting and Watching Act 1833, there were a variety of small, professional police forces functioning under local magistrates and/or local gentlemen. In some places they were financed out of a local rate, elsewhere by subscription. Second, the quarter sessions' debates over whether or not to implement the legislation in 1839 and 1840 did not divide simply into those who wanted a county force similar to that recommended by the Royal Commission but under the county bench, and those who wanted to maintain the old system. Some conservative backwoodsmen could be found to demand the preservation of the old parish system, but these were a minority. Some could also be found who condemned the idea of a uniformed constabulary as un-English. More concern, however, was expressed about cost. Some magistrates were uneasy about the power to raise new rates which the legislation gave them; unlike the borough magistrates, those in the counties were unelected and unrepresentative. There were others who felt that police reform was desirable, but they preferred smaller forces under immediate local control, rather than constabularies which would cover whole counties.[28] There is discrepancy in the figures, but of the fifty-four provincial counties in England and Wales (that is excluding Middlesex and dividing Yorkshire into its three constituent ridings) only about one half had established constabularies under the 1839 act by the mid 1850s, and in about three or four instances these 'county' forces were confined to one or two divisions or hundreds within the county.[29]

The forces established under the 1839 act were not based on any one simple model drawn from the London experience. Men who had served in new police forces were recruited by the counties, particularly for the more senior positions. But men were also recruited from the old police: Henry Goddard, the first chief constable of Northamptonshire, was a former Bow Street officer; two long-serving constables from the old police, William Craig from Stowbridge and James Kings from Bromsgrove, were appointed superintendents in the new Worcestershire Force.[30] Gloucestershire magistrates had employed Metropolitan Police officers for temporary emergencies during the 1830s, but when it came to establishing a county force in 1839, they turned to the Irish model; the first chief constable, Anthony Lefroy brought thirteen men with him from Ireland as a cadre for the 250-man Gloucestershire force. Other counties also looked to Ireland.[31] Like the borough police, the new county constabularies remained firmly under local control; but the relationship between the magistrates on the police committees and their police forces was not so obviously the master-servant relationship of most boroughs. The chief constables of the counties were, generally speaking, of more genteel origin than their borough counter-parts. There was, in addition, a significant presence of military officers among them, and this presence increased as the century wore on: seven out of the twenty-three chief constables appointed to English counties before 1856 had army or naval experience; twenty-two out of the twenty-four appointed between 1856 and 1880 had such experience.[32] The perception of the police as a kind of soldiery informed much of the thinking behind the County and Borough Police Act 1856 and, both before and after this legislation, several chief constables were eager for their men to receive military training so that they might act as auxiliaries to the army in case of invasion. Many magistrates perceived their county constabularies as the first line of defence against an internal enemy which, in cases of popular disorder, led to them being deployed in a military fashion.[33]

Those counties which did not take advantage of the 1839 act did not always leave their police systems unchanged. Some districts organised patrols under the Lighting and Watching Act 1833, some utilised the enabling legislation of the Parish Constables Act 1842. The latter reaffirmed the old system of local policing and selection of parish constables, it also authorised the recruitment of paid, superintending constables to oversee the parish constables of a petty sessional division. For many, including persons in those counties where rural constabularies had been established, the act was a godsend. It offered a policing system which was cheaper and which was better suited to the needs of a rural society. In Nottinghamshire, for example, the quarter sessions received 224 petitions from different groups of ratepayers urging that the new constabulary be disbanded. Among these petitions was one from the parish of Harworth which expresses clearly and fully the sentiments of the dissatisfied ratepayers:

> The parish of Harworth has paid during the last year upwards of 21 .. 9 ..
> 2 pounds [sic] as their quota of the expenses incurred by the maintenance
> of [the County Constabulary], without discovering they have received any

benefit whatever. And legislation has provided for a considerable increase of parish constables (men who know all the suspicious characters in the neighbourhood and who are specially interested in keeping a good look-out and in whom their neighbours can place implicit confidence) the Ratepayers and other Inhabitants of the Parish of Harworth respectfully request the Magistrates will take their case into their most serious consideration.[34]

In the event none of the new constabularies were disbanded, though many were reduced in size and the old parish constable system continued to be developed and refined. In 1850 amending legislation extended the provisions of the 1842 act and in all provisions were adopted by fourteen counties. The new lease of life injected into the old system was popular not only because it was cheaper than a full-blown county constabulary but also because it kept control of the police within the smaller, traditional units of parishes and petty sessional divisions.

Even the most thoughtful of the Whig historians of the police have written off the superintending constables as a failure, yet the evidence given to the 1853 Select Committee on Police suggests that in counties where they were established there was no serious dissatisfaction with the system. Lieutenant Colonel Henry Morgan Clifford M.P., chairman of the Herefordshire quarter sessions insisted that they were 'quite sufficient; the diminution of crime is very great'. Sir Robert Sheffield Bart., chairman of the quarter sessions for the parts of Lindsey, Lincolnshire, believed that the new system was working well; he was not sure what the long-term impact was going to be on crime, but 'certainly the county looks to the superintendents very much as protectors', and they had reduced the number of vagrants. Richard Healey, the Chief Constable of the Hundred of Aveland in the parts of Kesteven, Lincolnshire, was of the opinion that the creation of a rural constabulary would be very unpopular in his district: 'the farmers ... and the ratepayers are exceedingly well satisfied with things as they are'. Maurice Sawbey, a former police magistrate, and a county magistrate for Buckinghamshire, Middlesex and Surrey, urged that a rural constabulary be established in Buckinghamshire, but he had to admit that the ratepayers did not complain about any threat to their property and seemed satisfied with the protection which they received from the superintending constable system. William Hamilton, one of the superintending constables in Buckinghamshire and a veteran of sixteen years' service in the Royal Irish Constabulary and the Lancashire and the Essex constabularies, was highly critical of the superintending constable system, and particularly of the parish constables who served under him; David Smith, another veteran of the Essex force and a superintending constable in Oxfordshire was similarly critical. But George Carrington, a Buckinghamshire magistrate, was not surprised:

> I think those men naturally wish for the discipline of a regular force; but
> that is their opinion, and I am only giving mine. The man who was

examined from our county gave me a general idea, before he came to the Committee, what he was going to say; he came to me afterwards, and told me that he was asked whether he could say it was efficient; he said, he thought he could not say so. He has told me that some of the [parish] constables are efficient men, and ready to act with him; of course not so ready to act as men whom he might dismiss at a moment's notice. What he said was, 'I can lead them, but I cannot drive them'.

Carrington wished to see how the system developed in Buckinghamshire, but he felt that it would be perfectly adequate for the preservation of the peace and the protection of property.[35] The superintending constables, however, were swept away by the County and Borough Police Act 1856 which made the new, uniformed police obligatory.

The County and Borough Police Act stemmed from a variety of beliefs and concerns. Palmerston, briefly Home Secretary in 1852 and 1853, was convinced of the necessity for reform; he was apparently moved by the criticisms of the patchwork system of policing in the early 1850s which prompted logical demands for uniformity and rationalisation. The Select Committee which he established, and which met in 1853, lacked the reforming fervour of a Chadwick at the helm, but, nevertheless, stacked the evidence in favour of consolidation and a uniform system across the country. The desire for new legislation was also fostered by the belief that a reformed police would assume some kind of auxiliary military rôle; in addition there were fears brought about first, by the virtual end of transportation, which threatened persons of property with having more 'habitual criminals' discharged from prison on to the highways and byways, and second, by the prospective demobilisation of brutalised soldiery from the Crimean campaign. Yet the legislation eventually steered through parliament by Palmerston's successor at the Home Office, Sir George Grey, was a compromise. The initial plans to amalgamate the smaller borough forces and five small county forces with their larger neighbours provoked an outcry and were dropped. The police forces of provincial England and Wales remained under local control, but the new legislation imposed some basic standards and uniformity, notably with the creation of a national system of supervision by the three Inspectors of Constabulary; and there was also a greater degree of central government involvement with the different forces thanks to the Treasury's agreement to pay one-quarter the cost of pay and clothing for forces declared 'efficient' by the inspectors. Twenty years later the grant was increased to one-half and greater pressure was put on the smaller boroughs to amalgamate with their surrounding county force.

In spite of the urgings of reformers and chief constables, notably Admiral MacHardy the Chief Constable of Essex, the police were not trained as military auxiliaries. Their tasks, however, were many and varied. The continuing 'servant' role of many borough policemen led to them acting as collectors of market tolls, poor law relieving officers, and the local fire brigade. Emergencies stretched manpower; following disorders and an alleged spate of pocketpicking in the summer of 1867, the Home Secretary lamented to the Commons that some 300-400 members of the Metropolitan Police were having to be employed to keep cattle plague out of the city.[36] The Metropolitan Police, county forces and the largest urban forces were often called upon as riot squads to assist outside their districts; the smaller borough forces were too small to cope with large crowds. But the maintenance of public order did not just mean riot control; from their creation the new police were employed to clamp down on those working-class leisure activities which offended middle-class sensibility.[37] Order, in its broadest sense, also meant keeping the traffic moving and keeping the streets tidy and safe: in October 1841 the Bedford Watch Committee expressed its concern to the Chief Constable about harrows, ploughs and other articles exposed for sale on Market Hill, and left there after dark when they became a danger to pedestrians. In Manchester during the 1890s the Watch Committee and Chief Constable were vexed by the traffic problems ranging from ice-cream stalls to 'scorching' cyclists, and to school children throwing fireworks near horses on the run-up to Guy Fawkes' Day.[38]

Yet in spite of this variety of tasks, crime was perceived as the key *raison d'être* for the new police. The Fieldings, Colquhoun and Peel had all argued that a preventive police was essential in the struggle to combat crime in the metropolis. The *New Police Instructions* published in September 1829 announced: 'It should be understood at the outset, that the object to be attained is "the prevention of crime".'[39] It was crime – its amount and its seriousness – rather than any of the other tasks that subsequently fell to policemen, which dominated the debates in quarter sessions over whether or not to establish a constabulary during 1839 and 1840. Once formed, the county forces had their preventive role emphasised in the instructions drafted by chief constables: Lefroy in Gloucestershire used, word for word, the London formulation quoted above; Gilbert Hogg, in Staffordshire, informed his men that: 'It should be understood that the principal object to be attained is the *prevention of crime.*'[40] The reformers had great hopes of prevention; the regular patrols of the police constable, the impersonal agent of the law, would, it was hoped, deter potential malefactors. So confident of success was Sir Richard Mayne, Rowan's fellow commissioner, that in 1834 he suggested to a parliamentary committee the possibility of reducing the number of police in London in one or two years when 'the present race of thieves, who may be called the schoolmasters, are sent abroad, as we hope they soon will be, and the rising generation will become better'. Almost forty years later the Chief Constable of Chester boasted that, in just under a decade, he had successfully removed from his district the forty-seven known thieves and depredators:

> There is, I am afraid, a widely spread feeling that, as there always have
> been criminals in society, so there always must be. I am not entirely of
> that opinion. Given the power, I really see no great difficulty, if not in
> stamping out professional criminals, at least in reducing their numbers
> very materially, especially in a comparatively small place such as
> Chester.[41]

It is difficult to measure the effectiveness of prevention. Whig historians of
the police, like the police reformers, lauded the new system and asserted
its success. But contemporary newspapers often carried complaints that
the police were not around when they were needed either to prevent
crime or to help victims seize offenders. One night in April 1844 William
Radley Mott had his pocket picked in Brighton and the *Brighton Gazette*
reported that 'he searched the town from Steyne to Ship Street without
being able to find a single policeman to take the rascal into custody'.
Twenty-four years later, worthies of the East End of London were
protesting that metropolitan policemen were spending too much time
warning children not to play with their hoops in the street and protecting
the wealthy of the West End. According to the *East London Observer*: 'In
the leading thoroughfares outrages of all kinds are perpetrated –
frequently in broad daylight – and to look for a policeman is out of the
question.' 'Where are the Police?' demanded *The Times* after a
warehouse robbery in High Holborn in 1875 which must have taken the
perpetrators two or three hours. On the other hand some petty offenders
were foolish enough to attempt crimes under the eyes of watchful
uniformed policemen – like John Mason and Richard Kidd who, in
November 1836, tried to pick a pocket in Blackfriars in full view of P.C.
Charles Goff; and some street robberies were committed within calling
distance of the beat policeman who was able to assist the victim and
catch an offender – as when P.C. William Cottle caught James Adam
running away after the attack on a merchant seaman in Shadwell in
April 1857.[42] The more critical and thoughtful among the historians of
crime and policing have suggested that the new police contributed to the
statistical decline of theft and violence in the second half of the
nineteenth century.[43] It seems reasonable to acknowledge that the
physical presence of the uniformed policeman on the streets did deter
some petty theft from shops, stalls or individuals. But empirical
evidence of the situation with and without police is impossible to come
by. The proposal of a Bedfordshire magistrate in 1844 to remove the
county force from two divisions of the county and to measure the result
was rejected by his fellows on the county bench; contemporary
experiments and research suggests that the removal of police patrols
makes little difference to the level of reported crime yet it is probably
equally true to say that policing does have some impact in keeping crime
to a certain base-line level.[44]

A police constable could not report to his superiors and, at the top of
the hierarchy, a chief constable could not report to his Watch

Committee or County Police Committee, that their activities had prevented a particular number of crimes over a given period. However the new police could demonstrate their worth by publishing the statistics of arrests. The easiest arrests to make, except where there was a positive identification of a thief or of a violent offender, were those for petty public order offences. Such offences as begging, drunk and disorderly, drunk and incapable, illegal street selling, soliciting, were generally committed in the street and were often readily observable by the beat policeman. Moreover the removal of the drunk, the nomadic street seller, the prostitute or the vagrant was popular with the respectable Victorians who perceived these individuals as members of the dangerous or criminal classes. The creation of new police forces saw an increase in the statistics for these offences.

Yet if success could be claimed for the new police in dealing with some of the behaviour of the criminal class, there were crimes about which a uniformed constable patrolling an urban or a rural beat could do little. After all individual beats could be large; in London, in 1870, the average day-time beat was seven-and-a-half miles, the average night-time beat was about two miles[45]; in rural districts beats could be very much larger and villages without a resident constable might rarely see one. Major crimes in urban areas often, if not generally, took place behind closed doors and closed windows. If, for example, burglars could observe a police constable pass on his beat and then enter a property, especially when the house-holder of factory-owner was away, then there was little that the police could do other than record the offence when reported, and then seek and to detect the offenders. Following the conviction of several burglars in London early in 1865 the Commissioner of the City of London Force urged businessmen and property owners not to leave external fastenings unsecured, to replace those which were defective and not to leave 'shops and warehouses stored with goods of great value entirely unattended at night, and throughout the whole of Sunday'. *The Times* quoted him as emphasising that a policeman's beat:

> was on the street. They were bound to see that no house was *broken into*, but they could not guard equally against operations conducted by thieves left snugly locked up in houses by their occupiers, and indulged with six-and-thirty hours of licence.[46]

Other senior policemen were sometimes quite candid about the difficulties of catching determined thieves while patrolling in uniform on the beat. A year before one select committee heard Mayne look forward to a reduction in police numbers, another committee heard one of his superintendents report that '[a] man in uniform will hardly ever take a thief'. Indeed Rowan and Mayne confessed to the committee that they were informed that most felons were arrested by men in plain-clothes; and according to the Earl of Chichester, Rowan was later to suggest that the beat system could not really work in the countryside: 'a rural police was rather to prevent crime by detecting offenders rather than to prevent it by their actual presence in every village'. Edwin Corbett, lauding the Cheshire system of police before the 1853 Select Committee stated:

> There is one objection, I think, to the Rural Police Act, namely, that the policemen should be in uniform. It may be very useful in towns, where there a great number of police always parading about [sic], but in the country where they are only moving about the country, and particularly when they have an object in view, they should pass unobserved, which at other times they would not. I know several instances in which constables have gone to watch at night, when a burglary has been suspected, and where they have been successful in apprehending the burglars; if two or three policemen had been found coming to a given point, there would have been an alarm raised, but a man in coloured clothes could come without exciting any observation.[47]

Both Rowan and Mayne were reluctant to employ their men in plain-clothes, and not simply because of their faith in uniformed, preventive patrols. There was concern that the new police should not be reminiscent of a 'Continental Spy system', and the recollection of the spies and secret agents employed against English Jacobins and Regency Radicals remained painful. For the first decade of their existence the Metropolitan Police functioned side by side with the old London Police Offices each with its complement of plain-clothes constables; indeed, some men left the Metropolitan Police to take up the better-paid position of constable under the stipendiary magistrates.[48] The policing tasks of the stipendiaries' offices, together with their constables, were abolished in 1839. Three years later, with some reluctance, Rowan and Mayne were forced to admit the need for, and to appoint, a small group of full-time detectives. Concerns about European spy systems, together with fears that men in plain-clothes were much more susceptible to corruption, meant that this body was increased only slowly over the next twenty-five years – from eight men to fifteen. Even those who praised the old police office constables to the detriment of the new police could unwittingly indicate dangers inherent in the detective system. W. H. Watts, for example, argued during the 1860s that the new police had been singularly unsuccessful against burglars and robbers, and while the developing detective system was an improvement on uniformed constables periodically adopting disguises. It remained inferior:

> One reason is, that the old officers were generally of a better class, had more general experience, possessed larger funds, and were permitted a wider field of action, being sure to have the protection of their own magistrates if, in the capturing or ferreting out of offenders, they overstepped those strict limits which it might be conceived were proper for a police officer to observe.[49]

Following hard on the failure of the Metropolitan Police in intelligence gathering during the Fenian outrages of 1867, full-time divisional detectives were established in 1869. Nine years later, after the exposure of four detective inspectors for involvement in an international swindling racket the divisional detectives were centralised into the Criminal Investigation Department under a barrister, Howard Vincent, who had studied the detectives of the Paris Police. By the mid 1880s Vincent's department had grown from 250 to 800 men.[50]

The *modus operandi* of the new detectives, indeed of the new police in general, when it came to investigating offences and pursuing offenders, does not appear to have been greatly different from the more conscientious and determined of their predecessors. Policemen in plain-clothes watched and followed suspicious characters, sometimes with reward as when constables George Legge and Samuel Evans followed two young men who were gazing into jewellers' shops in Cheapside; the suspects 'watched the [uniformed] policeman on the beat away', and then attempted a smash-and-grab raid.[51] Policemen in uniform on their beats stopped suspicious characters, as the best of the old watchmen had done, again sometimes with success[52]; and until the developments of fingerprinting and forensic science, detection still often simply involved matching a suspect's shoes to footprints at the scene of the crime, perhaps with the occasional refinement of digging such footprints up, preserving them between boards and presenting them in court as evidence.[53] The telegraphic communications, photographic records of offenders and centralised record-keeping all of which were utilised and developed by the new police can be seen as technical aids to the kind of information gathering, circulation and storage urged by Sir John Fielding. Finally the occasional revelations of both uniformed and detective policemen profiting from links with a criminal underworld demonstrate that the new police did not sweep away all the abuses of the old.[54]

The uniformed police constable received only a modicum of training – much of it military-style drill – before being put on his beat. Few of the early recruits seem to have conceived of the police as a career; many appear to have volunteered to tide themselves over a period of unemployment. Of course some stayed in the police, sometimes transferring to different forces to gain promotion; and some prospered. But while the pay may have been regular, unlike the pay in many working-class occupations, it was not high. Moreover there were niggling restrictions on the constables' ability to make money on the side. A constable in Northamptonshire protested to a local M.P. in 1880 that his pay was less than that of a farm labourer; in addition there was:

the ban on police keeping dogs, fowls, or more than two pigs, neither of which must be a brood sow. To supplement the family income I am not permitted to take in a lodger; nor can I sell the produce from my garden ...

191

Others protested that, unlike the wife of an rural worker, the country policeman's wife was forbidden to keep a cow, and unlike the wife of an urban worker, the urban policeman's wife could not run a small shop.[55] Even if a man was eligible, before 1887 policemen were denied the vote for fear of political partiality.[56] The constables worked long hours in all weathers; chest and rheumatic complaints accounted for more than one-quarter of the men pensioned for disability from the Metropolitan Police between 1840 and 1860.[57] Discipline was harsh and enforced by fine, demotion or dismissal. These conditions and regulations led to an enormous turnover of manpower. They also provoked dissatisfaction leading to petitions and strikes within some forces.[58] The complaints found a national focus in the *Police Service Advertiser* first published in February 1866 which urged improvements in pay, conditions and pensions. 'Probably', it lamented, 'no public servant is so ill-used by his employer as the policeman'.[59]

The *Police Service Advertiser* helped to develop the idea of the ordinary policeman as a professional, yet the idea of police as professionals and, consequently, as experts in the war against crime was fostered early on by the demands of the government and the legislature. Like the magistrates and constables from the London Police Offices, senior officers, first from the Metropolitan Police and then from other forces, were called upon to give evidence to committees and commissions. As noted earlier the Royal Commission on a Rural Constabulary received and published lists of known criminals prepared by local forces, and from 1857 all forces were required to prepare such details for the annual Judicial Statistics; the definition of known criminals was left to the discretion of the individual police forces. This requirement fed upon itself to reinforce the perception amongst policemen, their political masters and commentators on criminality, that a criminal class existed. At the same time the labelling of individuals as criminals, and of the districts in which they lived as criminal, could become self-fulfilling by propelling first-time offenders into further crime since they were now stigmatised, and by urging any 'respectable' families to do their best to move out of a stigmatised neighbourhood. Labelling as a 'criminal' might not even have occurred as the result of an initial offence. Gilbert Hogg advised his men that arrest on suspicion was one means of ensuring the principal object – prevention; the constable could, therefore, arrest an individual:

> whom, from his situation and character, the law judges to be likely to commit some felony, and whom [the constable] has just cause to suspect is about to do so ... Though no charge be made, yet if the constable suspect a person to have committed a felony, he should arrest him; and if he have reasonable grounds, founded on fact, for his suspicion, he will be justified, even though it should afterwards appear that no felony was committed.[60]

Woolly directives of this sort were open to abuse, and not always deliberately, given that the constable on the beat had so little training.

Occasionally constables were criticised by magistrates and the objects of their suspicion were promptly released, but this was not always the case. Two men were arrested and charged with the garotte robbery of Hugh Pilkington M.P. The police had no direct evidence against them other than information which they claim to have received; but the accused, both ex ticket-of-leave holders, were sentenced to three months' imprisonment each as suspicious characters.[61] Perhaps the labelling process only affected a minority of offenders in the nineteenth century turning but a few into recidivists or 'professional' criminals, but it gradually enhanced the professionalism of the police by giving them an identifiable enemy to observe, catalogue and, when appropriate, to arrest for the good of society.

Rowan put it to a select committee that 'we look upon it that we are watching St James's and other places while we are watching St Giles and bad places in general'.[62] It was in these 'bad places' among the poorer working class that persons were to be found indulging in the boisterous popular culture which so offended Victorian sensibilities and which the police were directed to control. In the same places, and from the same groups, were to be found the street-traders who were 'moved on', the men on the tramp and the seasonal workers suspected of being criminals because they were on the roads; Chadwick, and several other witnesses to the Select Committee of 1853 urged the value of a centralised, uniformed constabulary for bringing about a significant decline in vagrancy – 'a great source of crime .... they begin by being vagrants, and they end by becoming thieves'.[63] It was from among these groups in general that, it appears, the police found 'suspicious persons'; and in garrison towns from the mid 1860s to the mid 1880s it was young women from the working class who were stopped and questioned on suspicion of being prostitutes under the Contagious Diseases Acts. The new police might also be felt as a pressure by members of the working class who broke their contracts and thus, under the provision of the master and servant legislation, were subject to criminal prosecution, as well as by workers taking strike action who sought to dissuade police-protected 'blacklegs' from working. Yet the new police were not simply a pressure on the working class. Police constables knocked men up in the morning to enable them to get to work on time or to be first in the queue for the distribution of casual work. They could be called in or used as a potential threat against an obstreperous neighbour even in a notoriously 'criminal' quarter like Jennings Buildings in Kensington. When all else had failed a distraught parent might summon a constable to deal with a difficult child; thus in March 1871 P.C. Alexander Hennessy of the Metropolitan Police was called upon to arrest Catherine Driscol, aged fourteen and a half, charged with stealing clothing by her mother.[64] Lost children were also reported to, and found by, the new police; indeed some children from the poorer districts may deliberately have got themselves lost, or been encouraged so to do by their parents, since they enjoyed a period of play with a few toys and bread and jam supplied in the police station.[65] Moreover the working class were as much, if not more, the victims of theft and they could, and did use the police in precisely the same way that middle-class victims did. Assisting in the domestication and disciplining of the working class may have been one role imposed upon the police – both old and new – but it must not be forgotten, first that many radical working-class activists were sympathetic to such domestication and discipline, and second, that the system of beat policing, which was central to the new police, was designed for the prevention of crime – and what men understood by crime was essentially theft and, to a lesser extent, assault.

REFERENCES AND NOTES

1. Among the most significant of the Whig police histories and **Charles Reith**, *The Police Idea*, Oxford University Press 1938; *British Police and the Democratic Ideal*, Oxford U.P., 1943; **Sir Leon Radzinowicz**, *A History of English Criminal Law*, 5 vols. Stevens, London, 1948–69; **T. A. Critchley**, *A History of Police In England and Wales*, 2nd. edn. Constable, London, 1978.
    Critics of the Whig interpretation include most notably **Allan Silver**, 'The demand for order in civil society' in **D. J. Bordua** (ed.), *The Police: Six sociological essays*, Wiley, New York, 1967; **Robert D. Storch**, 'The policeman as domestic missionary: Urban discipline and popular culture in Northern England, 1850–80', *Journal of Social History* (Summer 1976), pp.481–509; 'The plague of blue locusts: Police reform and popular resistance in Northern England, 1840–57', *International Review of Social History* xx (1975), pp.61–90.
    For a valuable introduction to the debate over the origins of the New Police see **Robert Reiner**, *The Politics of the Police*, Wheatsheaf Books, Brighton, 1985, chap. 1 *passim*

2. For the contrast with France see **Clive Emsley**, *Policing and its Context 1750–1870*, Macmillan, London, 1983, chap. 2 *passim*

3. Beds. R.O. QSR 23/299; for a similar 'detection' by the Constable of Ampthill see ibid, QSR 1827/316.

4. **Elizabeth Silverthorne**, (ed.), *The Deposition Book of Richard Wyatt J. P. 1767–76*, Surrey Records Society, vol. xxx, 1978, no 154, 10 Mar. 1772; **Bryan Jerrard**, 'Early policing methods in Gloucestershire', *Transactions of the Bristol and Gloucestershire Archaeological Society*, c (1982), pp. 221–40 (at p. 227): Beds R. O. QSR 1827/338.

5. In August 1838, for example, when Henry Towlson a cordwainer of Mansfield was robbed of a silk handkerchief he went to Thomas Meltham the local constable. Meltham set off in pursuit of two suspects: 'I traced (them) on the Worksop Road and at last found them in a house at Mansfield Woodhouse. I immediately charged them with the robbery and on searching them I found the handkerchief ... in the prisoner

Dennington's hat'. Notts R. O. QSD 1838, deposition of Meltham 8 August 1838.

6. **J. A. Sharpe,** 'Policing the parish in early modern England', *Police and Policing: Past and present society colloquium*, 1983. The point generally ignored in Whig police history about Dogberry, Verges and their watchmen is that they do catch the villains.

7. **J. J. Tobias,** 'Police and public in the United Kingdom', *Journal of contemporary History*, vii, 1972, pp. 201–19, draws attention to the Metropolitan Watch legislation of 1735.

8. *O.B.S.P. 1796–97* no. 43, p. 65. Patrick McCarty (apparently a watchman, though this is not stated) was less fortunate than the men who detained Wilson when, a few months after their success, he stopped William Gore who had 37lbs of lead in his possession. Gore was indicted but was acquitted at the Old Bailey as no one knew to whom the lead belonged. Ibid, no. 166, p. 244. *OBSP 1816–17* no. 224, pp. 94–95.

9. *PP*1828 (533), vi, *Police of the Metropolis* pp. 25–6, 60, 92–3, 123–4, 126.

10. **John Styles,** 'An eighteenth-century magistrate as detective', *Bradford Antiquary* new series, vol. 47, 1982.

11. An act of 1692 was the first significant reward statute promising £40 to anyone apprehending and successfully prosecuting a highwayman. This was followed over the next half century by a series of statutes promising similar financial reward or sometimes 'Tyburn Tickets' which exempted their holders from parish or ward office. See **John H. Langbein**, 'Shaping the eighteenth-century criminal trial: a view from the Ryder sources', *University of Chicago Law Review* **50** (1983), pp. 1–136; (at pp. 106–110);, Radzinowicz *Criminal Law* ii, 155–61 especially.

12. **Gerald Howson,** *Thief-Taker General: The rise and fall of Jonathan Wild*, Hutchinson, London, 1970; **R. Leslie-Melville,** *The Life and Work of Sir John Fielding*, London, 1934, chap. 5 *passim*.

13. J. J. Tobias, *Crime and Police in England 1700–1900*, Gill and Macmillan, Dublin, 1979, pp. 54–6; idem, *Prince of Fences: The life and times of Ikey Solomons*, Vallentine Mitchell, London, 1974, p.31.

14. **John Styles,** 'Sir John Fielding and the problem of criminal investigation in eighteenth-century England', *T.R.H.S.*, 5th series, vol.33 (1983), pp.127–49.

15. Radzinowicz, *Criminal Law* has references to Colquhoun's letters in the Home Office files. The abortive London Police Bill 1786 was taken over and modified by the Irish Law Officers and, as a result, professional magistrates and police were established in Dublin in 1786. Six years later, as the new London stipendiaries were being appointed, a campaign against the Dublin Police was gaining momentum. The Dublin Police system was condemned as expensive and inefficient, and the policemen themselves were criticised as brutal and oppressive. In 1795 the system was dismantled and magistrates elected by the Lord Mayor and the Corporation replaced the stipendiaries. See **Kevin Boyle,** 'Police in Ireland Before the Union, Part II', *Irish Jurist* **8** (1973), pp. 90–116 and 'Part III' ibid, pp. 323–48. Policing in Edinburgh developed under a series of acts of parliament establishing lighting and watching commissioners. By the early nineteenth century the Edinburgh Police – one superintendent, or captain-lieutenant, three lieutenants, a sergeant-major, two dozen

195

sergeants and about two hundred watchmen – seem closer to a Parisian-style police than anything English. The lieutenants, for example, took turns at supervising night duty and had strict instructions on day-time tasks which began before breakfast with the supervision of scavengers, and involved checking streets and lanes, inspecting pavements, removing 'nuisances', ordering repairs to unsafe structures and visiting lodging houses on the look-out for suspicious characters. (See Edinburgh R.O. Minute Book of Watching Committee March 1820 to February 1827, ff.25–32.) However when the force was reorganised in 1843 William Haining, the Superintendent, applied to the Commissioners of the Metropolitan Police for a man to serve as one of the Lieutenants and to assist in the reorganisation. W.F.N. Smith, from the Greenwich Division, subsequently moved to Edinburgh (Edinburgh R.O. Minute Book of Watching Committee Apr 1839 to June 1844 ff 172–3). There is no detailed modern study of how, what appears by 1900 to be a largely English model of police, came to predominate in Scotland.

16.   H. O. 42. 114.

17.   **W. H. Watts,** 'Records of an old police court', *St James's Magazine*, x (1864), pp.353–60 and 458–65 (at p.463); xi (1864), pp.444–52; xii (1865), pp.232–41 and 499–506.

18.   See e.g. *The Times* 23 and 25 September 1816 for the affair of Constable George Vaughan; *The Times* 24,27 February and 30 Mar 1818 for the affair of Constable Thomas Limbrick; Tobias, *Prince of Fences*, pp. 53–4 for the affair of Bow Street Constable Bishop who, in 1828, agreed, for a reward, to get back property stolen from a jeweller, and eventually, returned the property less £50-worth of jewels.

19.   Newcastle-upon-Tyne, for example, had a system of town sergeants, constables and watchmen. Extracts from the *Tyne Mercury* for the years 1829–30 reveal Mayor George Shadforth instructing his sergeants on the enforcement of street regulations and requiring them (in French style) to collect weekly lists of the lodgers and inmates of both the lodging houses and the 'houses of ill fame' in their districts. Shadforth weeded out constables who were infirm or who did not live within their district and issued them with detailed instructions on their duties. Lax and corrupt watchmen were removed and this may, in turn, have prompted others to an excess of zeal. On 30 October 1829 Watchman Whittingham brought Mary Bateman before Alderman Reed in the Mayor's court charged with being disorderly. 'It appeared that when taken she was doing nothing, but the watchman said she used bad language, and *she had been* just before quarrelling in the street'. Reed released Bateman and advised Whittingham: 'You are not to take people into custody for using bad language. Persons are not to be imprisoned for nothing'. **H. A. Mitchell,** (ed.), *A Report of the Proceedings in the Mayor's chamber, Newcastle-upon-Tyne, during the Mayoralty of Geo. Shadforth, Esq. 1829–30*, Newcastle, no date. For a similar excess of zeal among early members of the Metropolitan Police in London see Emsley, *Policing and its Context*, p.140.

20.   **Jenifer Hart,** 'Reform of the borough police, 1835–56', *EHR* LXX (1955), pp. 411–27 (at pp. 414–16).

21.   Beds R.O. Bedford Borough Records: Watch Committee Minutes B 3/1 fol. 3; **R. E. Swift,** 'Crime, law and order in two English towns during the

early nineteenth century: the experience of Exeter and Wolverhampton 1815–56', unpublished Ph.D., University of Birmingham, 1981, p.142; **Geoffry G. Everitt**, 'The development of law and order in Nottingham', unpublished M.A., University of Sussex, 1971, copy in Notts R.O. at M24,550; see also **John Field**, 'Police, power and community, in a provincial English town: Portsmouth, 1815–75', in **Victor Bailey**, (ed.) *Policing and Punishment in Nineteenth-Century Britain*, Croom Helm, London, 1981, pp. 48–9; **B. C. Jerrard**,'The Gloucestershire constabulary in the nineteenth century', unpublished M.Litt, University of Bristol, 1977, pp.40–2.

22.   Swift, 'Crime, law and order', pp. 358, 368, 381.

23.   **B. J. Davey**, *Lawless and Immoral: Policing a country town 1838–57*, Leicester University Press, 1983, p.55.

24.   Reith, *British Police*, pp. 64–8 has some useful detail on metropolitan vestries and the police during the 1830s; U.C.L. Chadwick MSS 16, Police Memoranda etc. (1880–90) for a draft 'Bill for Placing the Police of the Metropolis under the Control of the Ratepayers, February 1889'.

25.   **Carolyn Steedman**, *Policing and the Victorian Community: The formation of English provincial police forces 1856–80*, RKP, London, 1984, pp.15–16, 39, 53–55; Emsley, *Policing and its Context*, p.81.

26.   U.C.L. Chadwick MSS 1722/70-1, Rowan to Chadwick 26 May 1839. The government had emancipated slaves in the British Empire, with £20 million paid in compensation to slave owners, in 1833.
       For a detailed analysis of the background to the 1839 legislation see **Anthony Brundage**, 'Minister, magistrates and reformers: The genesis of the Rural Constabulary Act 1839', *Parliamentary History Yearbook*, 1986.

27.   *P.P.* 1852–53 (71) XXXVI, *Select Committee on Police* qq.2235 and 2257. The Cheshire Police Act (10 Geo IV cap. 97) and its workings would probably repay serious study.

28.   **Robert D. Storch**, 'Policing rural England before the police, 1830–56', paper presented to the Conference on the History of Law, Labour and Crime at the University of Warwick, 15–18 September 1983; Clive Emsley, 'The Bedfordshire Police 1840–56: A case study in the working of the Rural Constabulary Act', *Midland History* vii, (1982), pp.73–92 (at p.74).

29.   Critchley, *History of Police*, p.89; Emsley, *Policing and its Context*, p.72

30.   **Henry Goddard**, *Memoirs of a Bow Street Runner*, London, 1956; I am grateful to Elizabeth Lally, the curator and archivist of the West Mercia Constabulary, for information on Craig and Kings.

31.   Jerrard, 'Gloucestershire Constabulary', pp.61–2; **David Philips**, *Crime and Authority in Victorian England*, Croom Helm, London, 1977, p.65. Of the forty-seven chief constables appointed to English county forces between 1839 and 1880 fourteen had experience in the Royal Irish Constabulary as opposed to three with the Metropolitan Police and one with a borough force. Steedman, *Policing the Victorian Community*, p.48.

32.   Ibid.

33.   *P.P.* 1852–53 (71) XXXVI, *Select Committee on Police* qq.166–8, 212–27, 231–2 and Appendix 1 no. 7; Steedman, *Policing the Victorian Community*, pp. 21–5 and 32–8; Clive Emsley, 'The thump of wood on a swede turnip': Police violence in nineteenth-century England', *Criminal Justice History*, VI 1985, pp.125–49, (at pp.135, 136).

34. Notts R.O. QAC 2/1 Petition from Harworth, 26 June 1843. The petitions are to be found in QAC 2/1-6 and appear to have been prompted initially by a proposal at the Michaelmas Sessions 1842 to increase the new county force.

35. *P.P.* 1852-53 (71) XXXVI, *Select Committe on Police*, quotations respectively, at qq. 3833, 610, 641, 3444, 855-6, and 3228
A detailed study of the superintending constable system would be useful. Critchley, *History of Police* pp. 92-4, notes the criticism of the system by those superintending constables called before the Select Committee in 1853. But Critchley's paragraphs contain the usual Whig references to 'discredited ideas' and 'far-seeing' magistrates who persevered with the new police in spite of the opposition.

36. *Hansard*, 3rd series clxxxvii, 6 June 1867, cols. 1664-6.

37. Storch, 'The policeman as domestic missionary', idem, 'The plague of blue locusts'; Emsley, *Policing and its context*, pp.66 and 137-38.

38. Beds. R. O. Bedford Borough Records: Watch Committee Minutes B 3/1 13 Oct. 1841; Manchester Police Museum, Manchester Watch Committee Minutes 1895 onwards, vol. 2, ff. 113-6 and 152, vol.3, f.,97; *Manchester Police Instruction Book* (1908 edn.), p.113.

39. *The Times* 25 Sep. 1829.

40. Gloucs. R.O. Q.Y2.1.1, Chief Constable's General Order Book, 1840; Staffs. R.O. C. PC Box VI, *Rules and Regulations for the Government and Guidance of the Staffordshire Constabulary*, 1859, p.3.

41. *P.P.*1834 (600) XVI, *Select Committee on the Police of the Metropolis* q. 433; U.C.L. Chadwick MSS 16 Police Memoranda etc. (1880-90), MS extract from the *Guardian* 17 Dec. 1873.
Not everyone was as sanguine see e.g. U.C.L. Chadwick MSS 1017/3-13 M.D. Hill to Chadwick 12 Jan 1868; and Rowan, in an undated memorandum to Chadwick lamented 'we have used out best exertions and we find that crime and depredation are reduced to a certain extent, but there is still a good deal which we appear to be unable to reach, as our monthly returns for a year past both of the number of crimes and the value of property [stolen?] is wonderfully near one month to the other'. (Chadwick MSS 1722/130).

42. *Brighton Gazette*, 25 April 1844; *East London Observer*, 5 December 1868; *The Times*, 24 March 1875; *C.C.C.S.P., 1836-37*, no. 71, p. 83; *C.C.C.S.P., 1836-37*, no. 71,, p.83; *C.C.C.S.P.m, 1856-57* no. 560, p. 30; for a similar example to the arrest of Adams see *C.C.C.S.P., 1865-66* no. 157, pp. 212-3 when, again, the victim was a merchant seaman.

43. **V.A.C. Gatrell**, 'The decline of theft and violence in Victorian and Edwardian England', in **V.A.C. Gatrell, Bruce Lenman** and **Geoffrey Parker**, (eds.), *Crime and the Law: The social history of crime in Western Europe since 1500*, Europa, London, 1980, pp. 277-78; **D. J. V. Jones,** 'The new police, crime and people in England and Wales, 1829-88, *T.R.H.S.,* 5th series, vol. 33 (1983), pp. 151-68; (at pp. 162-3).

44. Emsley, 'Bedfordshire Police', pp. 87-88; for an introduction to the contemporary research see Reiner, *The Politics of the Police*, pp. 117-19 and 218, n.4.

45. 'The police of London', *Quarterly Review* CXXXIX (1870), pp. 87-129; (at p. 100); U.C.L. Chadwick MSS 16, Police Memoranda etc. (1855-69)

contains a printed report on the Metropolitan Police Superannuation Fund by William Farr M.D., F.R.S. (April 1862) which gives the average day beat as 376 acres or .542 square miles, and the average night beat as 160 acres or .2495 square miles.

46. *The Times* 1 and 25 March 1865.

47. *P.P.* 1833 (627) XIII, *Report from the Select Committee on the Petition of Frederick Young, and others ... complaining that Policemen are employed as Spies,* q. 1127; *Times* 15 October 1850; *P.P.* 1852–53 (71) XXXVI, *Select Committee on Police,* q. 2276.

48. *P.P.* 1834 (600) XVI, *Select Committee on the Police of the Metropolis,* qq. 2156, 2165 and 1446–8.

49. Watts, 'Records of an old police court', xii, 505.

50. For the development of the detective police in London see **Phillip Thurmond Smith**, *Policing Victorian London: Political policing, public order, and the London Metropolitan Police*, Greenwood Press, Westport Connecticut, 1985, chap. 3 *passim*; **Wilbur R. Miller**, *Cops and Bobbies: police authority in New York and London, 1830–70*, University of Chicago Press, 1977, pp.33–4.

51. *C.C.C.S.P.*, *1856–57* no. 6, p.13; for a similar example see *C.C.C.S.P.*, *1898–99* no. 114, p. 128 when P.C.s Stainton and Longridge, in plain clothes, foiled an attempted street robbery in Shoreditch.

52. *C.C.C.S.P.*, *1836–37* no.4, p.11 and no.68, p.82.

53. *Bedford Mercury* 23 March 1844; and see for other examples: Notts R.O. QSD 1847. Statement of Police Superintendent Frederick Willis about checking the blood and fat-stained boots of a suspect with footprints in a field where sheep had been feloniously killed (10 May 1847); see also *C.C.C.S.P.*, *1856–57* no.79, 54.

54. See above p. 123. Also for police negotiating with offenders for the return of stolen property see *P.P.* 1844 (549) XVI, *Select Committee on Dog Stealing (Metropolis)* q.196.

55. 'Life on a Labourer's Wage', *Police Review* 29 March 1985 pp.651–2; see also *Police Service Advertiser*, 27 April 1867 and, for the counter case, 11 May 1867.

56. The constables of some boroughs do appear to have had the vote, and to have used it before 1856.*P.P.*1852–53 (71) XXXVI; *Select Committee on Police,* qq.2028–30 and 2127. for discussions among policemen over whether or not they should be enfranchised during debate on the Second Reform Bill see *Police Service Advertiser* 30 March and 6 April 1867.

57. U.C.L. Chadwick MSS 16. Police Memoranda, etc. (1855–69), Report to the Secretary of State on the Metropolitan Police Superannuation Fund by William Farr M.D., F.R.S., April 1862.

58. Emsley, *Policing and its Context*, pp.82–5.

59. *Police Service Advertiser*, 26 January 1867.

60. Staffs. R.O. C.PC Box VI, *Rules and Regulations*, pp.39–41.

61. **Jennifer Davis**, 'The London Garotting Panic of 1862' in **Gatrell, Lenman and Parker**, (eds.), *Crime and the Law*, p.204.

62. *P.P.* 1834 (600) XVI, *Select Committee on the Police of the Metropolis,* q.166.

63. *P.P.* 1852–53 (71) XXXVI, *Select Committee on Police,* q.844; see also qq. 3575–79 and 3653.

64. P.C.Hennessy's notebook is in the Metropolitan Police Museum. For Jennings Buildings, five courts of narrow, slum tenements in the middle of fashionable Kensington, and how they were policed, see Jennifer Davis, 'Law breaking and law enforcement: The creation of a criminal class in mid victorian London', unpublished Ph.D, Boston College, 1984, chap.6.
65. **Raphael Samuel**, (ed.), *East End Underworld: Chapters in the life of Arthur Harding*, R.K.P. London, 1981, p.36. For an assessment of the role of U.S. police forces in the care of lost children, and the impact on police/public relations see **Eric H. Monkkonen**, *Police in Urban America, 1860–1920*, Cambridge University Press, 1981, pp.109–28.

Chapter 9

PUNISHMENT AND REFORMATION

The treatment of convicted offenders during the years 1750 to 1900 saw a shift from death or transportation being considered as the predominant punishments for felony to incarceration. At the same time there was a shift, admittedly less marked, from the personnel of the courts making all the key decisions about the offender to the experts in the new prison system making some of these decisions. Finally, once it was generally accepted that most offenders should be sent to prison, the crucial arguments centred on to what extent the prison was a place for punishment or for reformation.

The histories concerned with these changes in the treatment of the offender divide in a similar way to histories of the police. The traditional Whig interpretation largely accepts the case argued by eighteenth and nineteenth-century reformers that the 'Bloody Code' was arbitrary and savage, and that the reformers' stance was morally and rationally unassailable. Penal reform thus begins with the abolition of capital statutes urged by Romilly and Mackintosh and largely carried out by Peel and Russell; it develops and gathers pace as the government takes an increasing role in the organisation and supervision of prisons with the opening of Millbank in 1816 and Pentonville in 1842, with the creation of a prison inspectorate in 1835 and, ultimately, with the centralisation of the entire system under the Home Office in 1877. Revisionist historians have accepted the savagery of the 'Bloody Code' but they have been more subtle in assessing its 'arbitrariness', furthermore in relating penal reforms to changing economic and social structures they have emphasised the parallels between the new prisons and other developing institutions in the late eighteenth and nineteenth centuries, most notably the workhouse established under the New Poor Law; the new prison thus becomes another institution concerned with discipline and social control.[1] In many respects the arguments of traditionalists and revisionists are the mirror image of each other. In the Whig interpretation the humanitarian and progressive nature of penal reform fits with the humanitarian and progressive requirements of the liberal-democratic society which emerged in the early nineteenth century. In the revisionist account there is a fit between the new system of prison and punishment and the control requirements of the developing capitalist system.

There was a range of punishments available to judges and magistrates when they passed sentence during the eighteenth century. The most serious offences against persons and property tried at assizes or at the Old Bailey were punishable by death; the legacy of the Middle Ages left one or two borough sessions with the authority to impose a capital sentence[2] but county quarter sessions had no such power. Execution was usually by hanging; the more grisly punishments inflicted on the offender's body were rarely used in the mid eighteenth century though traitors could still be sentenced to death by beheading, drawing and quartering, and until 1790, women found guilty of high or petty treason, (which included coining), could be burned at the stake. The lesser forms of mutilation which were not part of a capital sentence, such as burning in the hand, were also declining. Indeed, apart from the severity of its statute law with the celebrated 200 or so capital offences, the actual level of punishment inflicted on an offender's body during a capital sentence in eighteenth-century England was far milder than in many other parts of Europe, notably France, the centre of both absolutism and the Enlightenment.[3] Individuals convicted of some capital offences could escape the death penalty by pleading benefit of clergy; this was a left-over from the right of clerics to be tried before ecclesiastical courts alone which, by the mid seventeenth century, had been extended to men and women who were not clerics but who could demonstrate basic literacy. The courts had begun to clamp down on benefit of clergy in the early eighteenth century and many of the capital statutes passed during the century were specifically declared to be non-clergiable, however the right to plead benefit of clergy in some offences remained until Peel's rationalisation of the criminal law in the 1820s. Conviction on a capital charge did not automatically lead to a death sentence, or, at least did not automatically lead to an execution. Even though in the century following the Glorious Revolution of 1688 many more capital statutes found their way on the statute book, there was considerable debate about, and interest in, secondary punishments. Two alternatives dominated this debate: prison and transportation.

Custodial confinement in some form of institution went back at least to the Middle Ages and was always available as an option for eighteenth-century judges and magistrates. Eighteenth-century gaols held the accused before trial; some petty offenders were sentenced to short periods in gaol, in particular those who were perceived to be on the slippery slope to perdition and therefore in need of correction – the disorderly, the idle, the vagrant, and even some described simply as 'pilfering persons'. The more well-to-do among the lesser offenders might be punished with a fine, the less well-to-do with a whipping sometimes, to give maximum emphasis to the punishment, at the scene of the offence.[4] Both the pillory and the stocks also remained available: the pillory for serious public crimes such as fraud, cheating, some sexual offences, sedition and libel; the stocks for petty local offences, indeed the use of the stocks continued at least until the middle of the nineteenth century.[5] No-one seriously suggested extending the use of the pillory or the stocks, but perceived crime waves did prompt suggestions for the more severe physical punishment of offenders. More importantly in the late seventeenth and early eighteenth centuries the various merits of prison and transportation were rehearsed and experiments were made in the desire to find a satisfactory secondary punishment. The Transportation Act 1718 more or less resolved the matter for roughly fifty years. Transportation provided for the removal out of the Kingdom of those offenders who, for a variety of reasons – their youth, the actual nature of their offence, the fact that it was a first-time offence – were not considered to be deserving of the death penalty but to be deserving of something more than a whipping and a discharge. The sentence was generally for periods of seven or fourteen years; sometimes it was for life. Transportation across the Atlantic began to lose favour in the middle years of the century and was effectively ended by the outbreak of the war for American independence, however the courts continued to pass sentences of transportation and some expedient had to be found to cope with the offenders so sentenced. In 1751 a committee of the House of Commons had proposed hard labour in the Royal Dockyards as a suitable alternative to transportation, but the proposal had not been taken up. The difficulties created by the American war led parliament to adopt a temporary solution along these lines however. In the years between the Declaration of Independence and the departure, in 1787, of the first 778 convicts for the new penal colony of Botany Bay, the government took over itself the management and organisation of a large number of convicted felons within the kingdom as those sentenced to transportation were incarcerated in old, rotting ships – the hulks – and set to work dredging rivers or labouring in the naval dockyards. The appalling state of the hulks gave the reformers yet more ammunition in their campaign to establish well regulated prisons, designed to reform offenders, as the principal, and much expanded secondary punishment in the criminal justice system.[6]

One of the key errors of many historians, both Whig and revisionist, has been to take the eighteenth-century 'Bloody Code' at a face value based on modern perceptions of the law; thus they have assumed that the increase in capital statutes during the eighteenth century was a meaningful one. In reality the new capital legislation of the eighteenth century generally defined offences in a very narrow way and often made reference to a specific institution or piece of property only; as a consequence the number of prosecutions likely to follow the passing of a capital statute was tiny. Destroying Westminster Bridge was the same kind of offence as destroying Fulham Bridge, but each offence had its own capital statute. Peel made much of such legislation when, in 1826, he proposed his rationalization of the law relating to felony. There were, he explained, twenty statutes concerning the protection of trees from theft and wilful damage; the legislation for the prevention of stealing or destroying madder roots and for the preservation of hollies, thorns and quicksets in forests was tacked on, respectively, to acts relating first, primarily to sugar brought from the Americas and second, to customs duties. 'If an offence were committed in some corner of the land,' protested Peel;

> a law sprang up to prevent the repetition, not of the species of crime to which it belonged, but of the single and specific act of which there had been reason to complain.[7]

As was noted in the introduction with reference to Henry Banke's bill to prevent the invasion of mines, matters were rarely that simple. Nevertheless Peel was right in drawing attention to the fact that eighteenth-century parliaments did not legislate for species of crime; while there were efforts to consolidate the vagrancy laws and the game laws, eighteenth-century legislators never attempted to codify capital legislation, indeed they did not think in terms of general codification or going back to first principles.

More important, perhaps, in any assessment of the 'Bloody Code' is to recognize that the majority of those executed during the eighteenth century were prosecuted under legislation which went back to the Tudors and Stuarts. Furthermore there were far more executions during the late sixteenth and early seventeenth centuries than during the eighteenth; and one or two offences ceased to be capital: at least two Jacobite pamphleteers were executed for sedition, but at the end of the eighteenth century Jacobin pamphleteers, if convicted, even at worst were rarely sentenced to more than two years in gaol.[8] Figure 9.1 shows the pattern of capital convictions and actual executions based on figures in the appendices of the *Report from the Select Committee on Criminal Laws 1819*. Convictions and executions follow roughly the same pattern with marked increases in the aftermath of the American War of Independence, when gentlemen were expressing concern about a crimewave, and in the famine year of 1801, though, interestingly, London and Middlesex saw no marked increase on this occasion. Equally noticeable is the widening gap between capital convictions and actual executions in the aftermath of the Napoleonic Wars; possibly the promptings of reformers against the Bloody Code were having an impact on the courts, but equally by this time alternatives of transportation and the penitentiary were more readily available. Within this pattern it is instructive to see what were the principal offences for which persons were executed (Table 9.1) and what percentage of capital convictions were carried out for the major offences (Table 9.2). It is clear

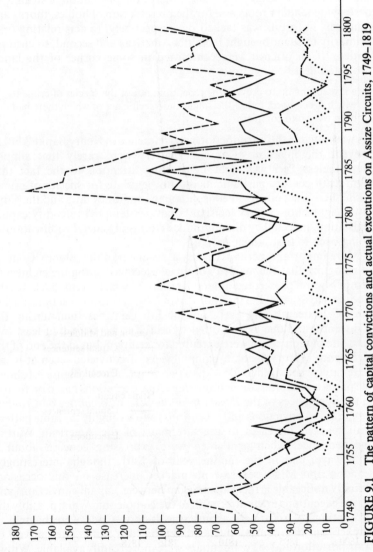

FIGURE 9.1   The pattern of capital convictions and actual executions on Assize Circuits, 1749–1819

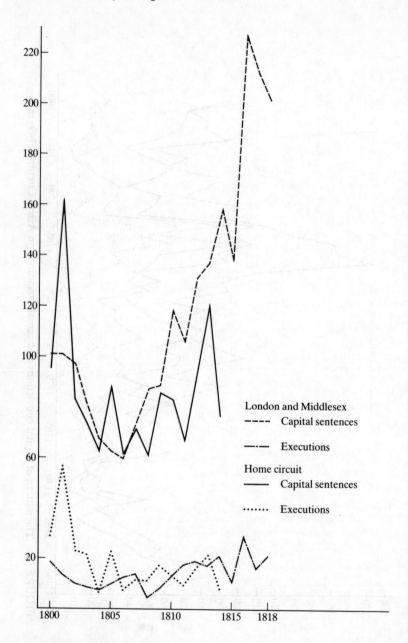

FIGURE 9.1   (*cont.*)

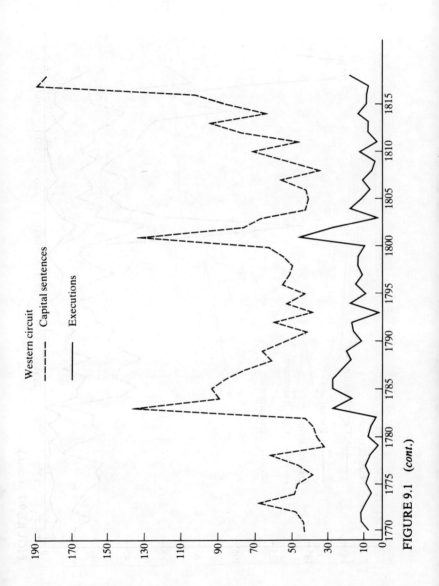

FIGURE 9.1 *(cont.)*

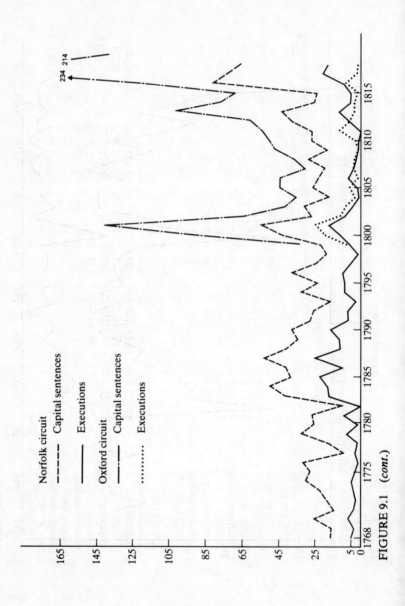

FIGURE 9.1 (cont.)

TABLE 9.1 Principal offences for which persons were executed, 1755–1814

	London and Middlesex*		Home circuit	Western circuit	Norfolk circuit
	(a)	(b)			
1755–1814					
Total executed	162	191	96		
Burglary	18 (11.1%)	23 (12%)	17 (17.7%)		
Forgery	24 (14.8%)	28 (14.6%)	4 (4.1%)		
Highway robbery	58 (35.8%)	65 (34%)	28 (29.1%)		
Murder	17 (10.4%)	26 (13.6%)	23 (23.9%)		
Horse stealing	6 (3.7%)		6 (6.2%)		
House breaking			1 (1%)		
Sheep stealing			3 (3.1%)		
1765–1774					
Total executed	278	303	139	43†	33‡
Burglary	86 (30.9%)	53 (17.4%)	24 (17.2%)	8 (18.6%)	14 (42.4%)
Forgery	20 (7.1%)	19 (6.2%)	3 (2.1%)	1 (2.3%)	1 (3%)
Highway robbery	79 (28.4%)	57 (18.8%)	63 (45.3%)	11 (25.5%)	7 (21.2%)
Murder	29 (10.4%)	30 (9.9%)	14 (10%)	14 (32.5%)	
Horse stealing	2 (1%)		7 (5%)	1 (2.3%)	1 (3%)
House breaking	3 (1%)		6 (4.3%)		1 (3%)
Sheep stealing			1 (0.7%)	2 (4.6%)	1 (3%)

209

TABLE 9.1 (cont.)

	London and Middlesex* (a)	London and Middlesex* (b)	Home circuit	Western circuit	Norfolk circuit
1775–1784					
Total executed	414		197	85	67
Burglary	108 (26%)		56 (28.4%)	18 (21.1%)	30 (44.7%)
Forgery	21 (5%)		3 (1.5%)		4 (5.9%)
Highway robbery	124 (29.9%)		87 (44.1%)	29 (34.1%)	12 (17.9%)
Murder	17 (4.1%)		20 (10.1%)	23 (27%)	4 (5.9%)
Horse stealing	1 (0.2%)		9 (4.5%)	3 (3.5%)	3 (4.4%)
House breaking			5 (2.5%)	2 (2.3%)	2 (2.9%)
Sheep stealing	6 (1.4%)		2 (1%)	5 (5.8%)	5 (7.4%)
1785–1794					
Total executed	375	404	234	180	126
Burglary	103 (27.4%)	154 (38.1%)	54 (23%)	30 (23.8%)	
Forgery	27 (7.2%)	24 (5.9%)	1 (0.4%)	3 (1.6%)	3 (2.3%)
Highway robbery	121 (32.2%)	122 (30.1%)		96 (41%)	36 (20%)
Murder	18 (4.8%)	22 (5.4%)	9 (3.8%)	24 (13.3%)	23 (18.2%)
Horse stealing	12 (3.2%)		23 (9.8%)	27 (15%)	14 (11.1%)
House breaking	12 (3.2%)		12 (5.1%)	10 (5.5%)	4 (3.1%)
Sheep stealing	2 (0.5%)		6 (2.5%)	12 (6.6%)	6 (4.7%)

TABLE 9.1 (cont.)

| | London and Middlesex* | | Home circuit | Western circuit | Norfolk circuit |
	(a)	(b)			
1795–1804					
Total executed	142	166	217	160	78
Burglary	23 (16.1%)	29 (17.4%)	48 (22.1%)	34 (21.2%)	16 (20.5%)
Forgery	40 (28.1%)	46 (27.7%)	4 (1.8%)	11 (6.8%)	2 (2.5%)
Highway robbery	22 (15.4%)	29 (17.4%)	58 (26.7%)	25 (15.6%)	15 (19.2%)
Murder	18 (12.6%)	23 (13.8%)	14 (6.4%)	25 (15.6%)	4 (5.1%)
Horse stealing	3 (2.1%)		17 (7.8%)	15 (9.3%)	15 (19.2%)
House breaking	2 (1.4%)		8 (3.6%)	4 (2.5%)	1 (1.2%)
Sheep stealing			10 (4.6%)	19 (11.8%)	9 (11.5%)
1805–1814					
Total executed	137		142	82	39
Burglary	24 (17.5%)		30 (21.1%)	13 (15.8%)	6 (15.3%)
Forgery	44 (32.1%)		13 (9.1%)	22 (26.8%)	3 (7.6%)
Highway robbery	13 (9.4%)		12 (8.4%)	7 (8.5%)	1 (2.5%)
Murder	21 (15.3%)		21 (14.7%)	20 (24.3%)	9 (23%)
Horse stealing			11 (7.7%)	4 (4.8%)	6 (15.3%)
House breaking			8 (5.6%)		
Sheep stealing			13 (9.1%)	5 (6%)	2 (5.1%)

*There are two separate returns for London and Middlesex in the appendices for the 1819 Report from the Select Committee on Criminal Laws. Column (a) is based on the more detailed figures in Appendix No. 5; column (b) is based upon Appendix No. 2.
†Figures for 1770 to 1774 only.
‡Figures for 1768 to 1774 only.

TABLE 9.2 Capital convictions and executions for principal offences, 1775–1815

	London and Middx			Home Circuit		Western Circuit			Norfolk Circuit		
	cvr'd	ext'd	ext'd as % of cvr'd	cvr'd	ext'd as % of ext'dcvr'd	cvr'd	ext'd	ext'd as % of cvr'd	cvr'd	ext'd	ext'd as % of cvr'd
1775–1784											
Burglary	185	108	58.3%	115	5648.6%	99	18	18%	73	30	41%
Forgery	37	21	57.7%	4	375%	14	—	—	4	4	100%
Highway robbery	318	124	38.9%	227	8738.3%	158	29	18.3%	35	12	34.2%
Murder	18	17	94.4%	25	2080%	30	23	76.6%	4	4	100%
1785–1794											
Burglary	220	103	44.2%	120	5445%	139	51	36.6%	79	30	37.9%
Forgery	38	27	71%	2	150%	32	3	9.3%	3	3	100%
Highway robbery	309	121	39.1%	224	9642.8%	111	36	32.4%	50	31	62%
Murder	19	18	94.7%	11	981.8%	25	24	96%	23	23	100%
1795–1804											
Burglary	168	23	13.6%	176	4827.2%	130	34	26.1%	56	16	28.5%
Forgery	61	40	65.5%	9	444.4%	20	11	55%	2	2	100%
Highway robbery	127	22	17.3%	134	5843.2%	84	25	29.7%	42	15	35.7%
Murder	20	18	90%	17	1482.3%	26	25	96.1%	4	4	100%
1804–1815*											
Burglary	226	18	7.9%	158	3018.9%	118	13	11%	53	6	11.3%
Forgery	84	47	55.9%	17	1376.4%	30	22	73.3%	9	3	33.3%
Highway robbery	196	17	8.6%	62	1219.3%	39	7	17.9%	16	1	6.2%
Murder	26	26	100%	26	2180.7%	28	20	71.4%	9	9	100%

*London and Middlesex figures 1812–18

from these figures that the largest number of capital sentences were passed on those convicted of the more serious kinds of theft, namely burglary and highway robbery. The theft of various animals – cattle, horses and sheep – could bring a capital sentence, but it was also more likely to bring a reprieve (Table 9.3). It is equally noticeable that, while the numbers capitally convicted on charges of burglary and, to a lesser extent, highway robbery remained high into the early years of the nineteenth century, the percentage of executions which were actually carried out fell. The capital offences for which reprieves were most rarely given were, first and foremost, violent offences against the person, notably murder but also sexual offences (Table 9.4). If, as has been argued, the threat of the gallows was employed during the eighteenth century to enforce an unequal division of property, it must, nevertheless, be recognised that the offenders least likely to escape the gallows were those guilty of offences against the persons of others. There is one significant exception to this; to modern eyes the most startling figures are probably those of the percentage executed out of those convicted of forgery. Sir William Blackstone explained the growth of capital sanctions for forgery as the result of banking and commercial interests

TABLE 9.3   Capital convictions for animal theft

	Convictions	Executions	Executions as a percentage of convictions
Home Circuit 1755–1814			
Cattle theft	42	7	16.6%
Horse theft	549	73	13.2%
Sheep theft	381	35	9.1%
Norfolk Circuit 1768–1818			
Cattle theft	37	4	10.8%
Horse theft	267	36	13.4%
Sheep theft	278	25	8.9%
Western Circuit 1770–1818			
Cattle theft	98	15	15.3%
Horse theft	355	50	14%
Sheep theft	457	48	10.5%

It is probably significant that the peak year for convictions for sheep stealing on all three circuits was the famine year of 1801: 44 convicted, of whom 3 were executed on the Home Circuit; 24 convicted, of whom 4 were executed on the Norfolk Circuit; and 40 convicted, of whom 16 were executed on the Western Circuit.

Crime and society in England, 1750–1900

TABLE 9.4   Capital convictions for sexual offences

	Convictions	Executions	Executions as a percentage of Convictions
London and Middlesex			
1756–1804			
Rape	19	11	57.8%
Sodomy	9	5	55.5%
1812–1818			
Rape	3	2	66.6%
Sodomy	4	4	100%
Home Circuit			
1755–1814			
Rape	38	18	47.3%
Buggery	14	12	85.7%
Norfolk Circuit			
1768–1818			
Rape*	15	11	73.3%
Buggery and sodomy	4	3	75%
Western Circuit			
1770–1818			
Rape†	29	20	68.9%
Carnally knowing an infant under 10 years	4	3	75%
Sodomy	7	4	57%

*Includes two cases of rape committed on infants.
†There is a discrepancy in the figures between the annual totals for the Western Circuit and the overall figures for particular offences given in Appendix 9 and Appendix 10 of the 1819 Report. The figures given here are for the offence totals in Appendix 10; the annual figures, given in Appendix 9 when totalled come to 26 convictions and 17 executions. The discrepancy appears to be for the period 1810–18.

seeking protection for paper credit and exchange in the developing national market. When the capital legislation respecting forgery was passed in the early eighteenth century there is no evidence from the courts that forgery was perceived as a major and increasing problem.[9] However the evidence of the sentences and executions in the late eighteenth and early nineteenth centuries suggest that, by this time, the judiciary had accepted the need to protect commercial interests with a rigorous deployment of the law.

Crowds massed around pillories and gallows in both London and the assize towns. Public punishment was theatre. In as much as the ruling

214

class or the state had devised such punishment it was didactic theatre: the gallows and the pillory were to provide lessons and warnings for other would-be transgressors of the law. But for the crowds, drawn from all social groups, the proceedings appear to have been rather melodrama of the rudest sort: there were villains who might be abused and unfortunate heroes who might be cheered and cherished. Those to whom the crowds had taken a dislike, most probably because of their offence, were cruelly treated whilst in the pillory. One of the most celebrated victims was Charles Hitchen, a former Marshal of the City of London, convicted in 1727 of an assault with attempt to commit sodomy. Hitchen took the precaution of wearing armour, yet he still had to be rescued by the authorities after only half of his allotted hour in the pillory.[10] John Williams, in contrast, was a popular hero. Williams, a bookseller, fell foul of authority for selling prints which ridiculed the Earl of Bute, and a reprint of John Wilkes' *North Briton*: but his hour in the pillory in February 1765 only aggravated the government's discomfiture – rather than pelting him with anything that came to hand the crowd cheered him and raised a collection for him amounting to £200.[11] Executions could elicit similar extremes of behaviour. On occasions the condemned behaved with the kind of penetential decorum suited to the requirements of the didactic theatre of punishment; they ascribed their ruin to drink or 'to the Association of lewd Women, who drove them to unlawful Courses, in order to support the Extravagances of these Daughters of Plunder'.[12] Invariably, even if the accused was not penitent, enterprising printers and hawkers provided cheap handbills with appropriate 'last-dying words' or doggerels illustrating the offender's moral decline. But often the performance of the condemned was itself better suited to melodrama than didactic theatre and the situation backfired on the authorities. Some offenders insisted that they did not deserve death:

> James Holt, the Smuggler, behaved very penitently, but did not seem
> convinced that his Sentence was just, or that Smuggling merited Death.
> Amongst his last words were, '*It is very hard* to be hanged for
> Smuggling'.[13]

Others struggled with the executioner or, probably fortified with strong drink, affected an air of heroic nochalance. Penitence, protest and/or nonchalance might win the commiseration and/or acclamation of the crowds who admired those making 'a good end'. The crowds could object violently to attempts to convey the body of an executed felon to a surgeon for dissection, particularly when the man had made 'a good end' or when the popular feeling was that he had not deserved death. At the same time, whatever their performance on the way to execution and on the scaffold, a few of the condemned were execrated by the crowds because of their offences. In August 1754 Mary Smith was executed at Tyburn for robbing a three-year old girl. The *General Evening Post* reported that:

> The Mob, who generally lose the Sense of the Crime in its Punishment, in respect to this Woman, acted the contrary Part: for, instead of Pity and Prayers, generally used on these Occasions, they, especially the Females, vented bitter Execrations as the Cart went along; particularly a poor Woman in Oxford Road, who, to show her Indignation to the Criminal, held up a Child in her Arms, which this Wretch had stripped, rejoiced in her Punishment, and seemed pleased to exhibit a remarkable Proof of her offence.[14]

Concern about the baccanalia surrounding public punishment and demands for better regulated systems of intermediary punishment were being voiced by men like the Fieldings in the mid eighteenth century. These concerns received a tremendous boost with the publication of two books: in 1767 came the first English translation of Cesare Beccaria's *Dei Delitti e delle Pene*; in 1777 John Howard published *The State of the Prisons in England and Wales*.

Beccaria's treatise, originally appearing in Italy in 1764, was seized upon by progressive thinkers throughout Europe as proposing, in the most succinct way, the kind of system of punishment best in keeping with the ideas of the Enlightenment. Existing punishments, he insisted, were arbitrary and barbaric, and they did not diminish crime. Punishment should have aims which were explicable and rational; it should be the certain outcome of any lawbreaking; it should suit the offence; it should prevent the culprit from offending again; it should deter potential offenders. Rather than relying upon the death penalty for many offences it would be more salutary, Beccaria believed, to deprive offenders of their liberty, and to compel them to recompense society for their transgressions with a period of hard labour visible to the public. In November 1770 Sir William Meredith, the Rockinghamite M.P. for Liverpool, urged the commons to mount an enquiry into the criminal law; his speech was suffused with Beccarian ideas. He was concerned:

> that a man, who has privately picked a pocket of a handkerchief worth thirteen pence, is punished with the same severity, as if he had murdered a whole family of benefactors.

Such punishment, Meredith maintained, only served to make the petty thief worse and more dangerous and, he went on:

> none should be punished with death, but those who could not be made safely useful, except in cases of murder, where a capital punishment, as it would be less common, would operate more forcibly *in terrorem*, and consequently more effectually answer its end.[15]

The following year William Eden published the influential *Principles of Penal Law* rejecting the existing system centred on capital punishment, querying the value of transportation and, on Beccarian lines, recommending some kind of continuing public display of useful punishment. Eden was also doubtful about the value of prison sentences; he believed that confinement often made offenders worse, however, within a decade he was helping to draft new penitentiary legislation. Eden's conversion to the idea of putting offenders into regulated, orderly prisons, like the similar conversion of other reformers, was largely through the work of John Howard.

Howard, a philanthropic, nonconformist gentleman with an estate at Cardington in Bedfordshire, had become county sheriff in 1773. He was appalled by the squalor of the county gaol which his new post led him to visit; he was also shocked by the plight of the prisoners, notably those who, although acquitted by the courts, were compelled to remain incarcerated because they could not pay the discharge fee required by the gaoler. These problems and abuses were not unique to Bedfordshire nor were they unknown before Howard's publications. The office of gaoler was typical of other petty offices during the eighteenth century; the holder was expected to be an entrepreneur who augmented such wage as he might receive with fees and the sale or rent of goods to those in his charge. What impressed the public about *The State of the Prisons* was certainly Howard's moral fervour but, perhaps more important, the systematic way in which he had gone about categorising every imaginable detail from diet to size of cell in every prison in England and Wales; more than this, he had contrasted the squalor of these gaols with in particular, the Rasp Houses of Amsterdam and Rotterdam and the Maison de Force in Ghent. The book was an indictment of the administration of those local justices who rarely took seriously their responsibilities in supervising their local gaols and gaolers; yet, as Michael Ignatieff emphasises, the book was not couched as an indictment but rather as 'a confrontation with Evil in the abstract'. Magistrates could therefore accept the conclusion without feeling that they themselves were being condemned.[16] Further editions of the book were brought out in 1780 and 1783, and Howard expanded his empirical research in Europe publishing, in 1789, *An Account of the Principal Lazarettos in Europe* which was itself reprinted in 1791, the year after his death.

Yet in spite of the enthusiastic reception given to the work of Beccaria and Howard and the boost which they gave to reformers, change remained slow and continued to depend on the zeal and initiative of private individuals rather than on any government direction. In 1779 parliament passed the Penitentiary Act; drafted by Blackstone, Eden and Howard, this provided for the construction of two penitentiaries in the metropolis, one for 600 men, the other for 300 women. Here offenders, otherwise liable for transportation, could be imprisoned for up to two years. They were to be uniformed, kept to hard labour in association with each other by day and shut in solitary confinement by night. Section 5 of the act emphasised the reforming intention of the penitentiaries: inmates were to be inured 'to Habits of Industry'. But conscious of complaints that some of the poor might prefer the clothing, diet and lodging of the penitentiaries to their hard life outside, the legislators were determined to make confinement sufficiently hard, rigorous and disagreeable to deter any such preference. In the event, these penitentiaries were never built. Death and resignation broke up the original board of commissioners established to oversee implementation of the act. There were problems over the purchase of land. But, probably most important, none of the ministries between 1779 and 1785, when plans finally lapsed, had the building of the penitentiaries among their prime concerns even though the end of the American War initially threatened, and then statistically showed, an increase in prosecutions. Ministers had to busy themselves with concluding the war and struggling for the continuance of their shaky administrations.[17] The hulks were accepted as 'temporary expedients' and for the government to take on the expense of permanent structures would not have been popular in years when economic reform and retrenchment were watchwords. Such a reform, even though it had passed through parliament, might also have been condemned as enlarging the patronage of the Crown and encroaching on the rights of local boroughs and counties to administer gaols. Furthermore the belief continued that prisons, and the hulks, by throwing first offenders together with recidivists, only served to make all offenders worse. Jonas Hanway, an advocate of solitary confinement from the early 1770s, branded the London Bridewell as 'a nursery for thieves and prostitutes'.[18] The House of Commons Committee on Transportation argued similarly in 1784 and went on to explain that, while prisoners released from the gaols and the hulks could get neither work nor parish relief and consequently returned to crime, transportation to America had 'tended directly to reclaim the Objects on which it was inflicted, and to render them good Citizens'.[19] The Transportation Act 1784 signalled a continuing preference in central government circles for removing offenders overseas, even though the site for a new penal colony was still to be found. Nor was it only among government circles that such sentiments existed. In March 1786 the Lord Mayor and Aldermen of the City of London petitioned George III about 'the rapid and alarming increase of crimes and depredations in this city and its neighbourhood, especially within the last three years'. The petitioners asserted that the end of transportation and the release of offenders back into English society was 'alone sufficient to account for all the evils that are so heavily felt and so justly complained of'. The only punishments mentioned in the petition were death and transportation, 'without which all other regulations must prove nugatory and abortive'.[20] In the closing decades of the eighteenth century it was influential figures in county administrations who organised the building of new gaols or the refurbishing of old ones, and who introduced new regimes of regular work, solitary confinement, and the separation of different classes of offender – men from women, first-time offenders from recidivists, those convicted from those awaiting trial. Notable among these reformers were the Duke of

Richmond in Sussex, Sir George Onesiphorus Paul in Gloucestershire, and Thomas Butterworth Bayley in Salford.

By the decade of the French Revolution the exertions of local reformers together with the steady stream of printed propaganda were beginning to make the penitentiary a viable alternative punishment. Furthermore it was a punishment with the added advantage, according to its advocates, of reforming the prisoner for the benefit of English, as opposed to a colonial, society. Those released from the rigours of the penitentiary would be accustomed to hard work, instead of idleness, while religious teaching and periods of solitary confinement would have helped the offender to contemplate the evils of wrong doing thus inculcating morality and virtue. But there was no steady triumph of a single penitentiary idea. Reformers themselves were divided about the kind of work and about the role and effect of solitary confinement. In 1791 Jeremy Bentham threw his intellectual weight behind prison reform with his own plan, *Panopticon*. The panopticon structure was to enable the constant supervision of convicts working, and thus reforming, for perhaps as many as sixteen hours a day; it also provided for the supervision of the prison guards, for here Bentham parted company with other reformers in suggesting that the custodians themselves might need watching. Bentham's principal gaoler – Bentham himself – was to be the entrepreneurial gaoler *par excellence* running the panopticon as a profitable commercial enterprise and selling the products of the convicts' labour; the need to have a fit and healthy workforce would, according to Bentham, ensure that the convicts were looked after. In 1794 legislation provided for the construction of the panopticon and Bentham acquired a site at Millbank, but the Treasury never released the money for construction. In addition to their differences over the best system, the prison reformers received setbacks from the criticisms levied at the realities even of new gaols by political radicals. The English Jacobins who spent time in prison for sedition or under the suspension of the Habeas Corpus Act were few in number, but they were articulate and able publicists. Paul's Gloucester Penitentiary and, more especially the House of Correction in Coldbath Fields were the focus of this criticism. Coldbath Fields had been opened in 1794, designed with Howard's principles in mind, but it was unfortunate in acquiring as its first governor a former baker, Thomas Aris, who turned out to be precisely the kind of grasping gaoler of whom Howard was critical; the problem was compounded by the Middlesex justices giving Aris a free hand in the administration of the gaol.[21]

The wars against Revolutionary and Napoleonic France again involved government departments in the organisation and administration of large numbers of prisoners on British soil. The wars created problems in transportation, not the least of which was the higher cost of freight; this led to more and more convicts being incarcerated on the hulks, and while contemporaries did not really do the sums, those lodged in this way, were less costly than those shipped to Botany Bay and their labour on public works, notably for military purposes, proved valuable.[22] But prisoners in the government's charge during these years were not simply convicts; there were also prisoners of war in unprecedented numbers who, because of the duration and new style of war, had to be kept over a longer period than in previous conflicts. It is impossible to measure the precise impact on penal policy of keeping large numbers of convicts on the hulks and enemy servicemen in prisoner of war camps, but in 1816, the year following the battle of Waterloo, the first national penitentiary was opened at Millbank. The go-ahead for the penitentiary was the result of the report of a parliamentary committee appointed in 1810 under the chairmanship of George Holford. This committee, packed with keen advocates of the penitentiary idea, was primarily concerned with choosing between different forms of penal discipline: that exemplified by the Gloucester Penitentiary where solitary confinement was given a key role in an attempt to change the offender's character by bringing him, through religion, to an awareness of his wrong-doing; and that which gave offenders incentives to work in association with each other in the belief that instilling habits of work would drive out the bad habit of idleness which led to crime. Holford's committee came up with an amalgam of the two; the first part of a convict's sentence was to be spent in separation, the second part in association. It rejected Bentham's plans for running the prison like a factory as well as his elaborate panopticon structure, though elements of Bentham's structural ideas for supervision were incorporated into Millbank's seven massive pentagons. Bentham himself was compensated financially for his efforts spread over the preceding two decades. The construction of Millbank was begun in 1812 and eventually cost the enormous and quite unexpected sum of £450,000. It was the largest prison in Europe when it opened and marked a significant step in the state taking on the management of convicts in an institution on native soil.

But while the government was sucked more deeply into penal administration and reform, the running for the changes in penal policy continued to be made by a small group of M.P.s passionate in their philanthropy and politically tending towards the opposition Whigs. The Gaol Fees Abolition Act 1815 which signalled the beginning of the end for the entrepreneurial gaoler was introduced into parliament by one of these reformers, Henry Grey Bennet. But most notable among this group was Sir Samuel Romilly. Prison improvement was just one element of Romilly's campaign to mitigate and rationalise the Bloody Code. From the early years of the new century he campaigned vigorously for a reduction in the number of capital statutes. He protested that there was a 'lottery of justice' in that there was uncertainty about the punishment for different offences; even when a capital sentence was passed it was far from certain that it would be carried out and consequently there was no lesson for the public. Judges, he feared, had too much potentially tyrannical discretion; furthermore they responded to different offences in their own individual ways.

Romilly and reformers like him have been lionised by the Whig historians of criminal justice; they have been portrayed as far-sighted humanitarians beset on all sides by die-hard reaction. Humanitarians they certainly were, yet whether their achievements were as great and whether the issues were as clear-cut as Whig history would suggest, is a moot point. It was emphasised earlier that there were never 200 or so separate and completely different offences which were liable to a capital sentence while the graphs and tables at the beginning of this chapter reveal a proportional decline in the numbers executed for property crime. '[T]he legal massacres ... when "the prisons of the metropolis are emptied into the grave" '[23] were being queried long before Romilly began his campaign: it was in 1783 that the procession to Tyburn was abolished and, in the hope of limiting the crowd bacchanalia, public executions in the metropolis began to be sited outside Newgate Gaol. Put in the context of a growing unease about the Bloody Code and its ritual paraphernalia the role of Romilly as a courageous initiator of reform is less pronounced. Rather he, and other early nineteenth-century law reformers, were able to get things done because parliamentary opinion, across the political spectrum, was already beginning to line up behind the arguments that they were employing. In his *Memoirs* Romilly protested that the French Revolution had made it exceedingly difficult to get 'legislative reform on humane and liberal principles' and he cited the abuse which his 1808 bill to abolish the death penalty for pickpockets had prompted from the younger brother of a peer. What he does not mention is the fact that his bill went through parliament without a division and received the royal assent less than six weeks after its introduction.[24] Admittedly other bills were less successful: in 1810, 1811, 1813, 1816 and 1818 the commons passed bills to abolish capital punishment for stealing from a shop to the value of five shillings; on each occasion the Lords rejected the bill. But the statistics collected by the government revealed that between 1805 and 1820, when the Stealing in Shops Act was passed, no one was executed for the offence.[25]

As with the opponents of police reform, the early nineteenth-century opponents of reform of the criminal law had a coherent and logical case, though few historians have given them credit for such. Anti-reformers insisted that justice was not a lottery and that judicial discretion was sensibly and conscientiously practised; as the reformers could point to cases of injustice so their opponents could point to examples which showed the system working with mercy and moderation – no one was executed for stealing from a shop goods worth under five shillings, but the potential was there if a sufficiently evil character did face such a charge and if an example was required *pour décourager les autres*. Probably the strongest plank in the platform of the traditionalists was

221

their doubt that there could ever be a significant measure of certainty in the way that a punishment was meted out to fit a particular crime. The Criminal Law Commissioners who were appointed in 1833 ran into major difficulties when they sought to establish a rational system of punishment: in their second report, in 1836, they specified four overall classes of crime each with two alternative penalties; in their fourth report, three years later, there were fifteen overall classes of crime, each with a far greater range of penalties; by 1843, and their seventh report, the scale of penalties had reached forty-five, more than double the number of twenty which they had initially specified as the absolute maximum. The attempts of the commission to establish precise penalties for precise offences eventually foundered.[26] Randall McGowan has argued, persuasively, that the issue in dispute between traditionalists and legal reformers in the early nineteenth century:

> was not how to secure the greater efficiency of the criminal justice system, but how to present a more pleasing image of justice. The desire was not just to reduce crime but to secure wider support for the legal order.[27]

The traditionalists were defending an aristocratic and paternalistic image of justice and focussed on the practice of the courts and the use of mercy; the reformers focussed on existing severity and proposed an image of impersonal justice in which the law was above the suspicion of dependence on any personal discretion. The problem for the opponents of reform was that moderate and often influential Tories, like Peel, were sympathetic to the reformers' image of justice. Whether this sympathy was simply because of a combination of philanthropic humanitarianism and rationalist ideas rooted in the Enlightenment together with a larding of evangelicalism and Benthamite utilitarianism, or whether beneath this, as McGowan argues, there were in addition the deeper structures of developing class alliances in a fast-changing society, is a moot point. What has to be recognised is the logic of the traditionalists' case; what has to be rejected is the notion that the reformers had a far-sighted vision of nineteenth-century progress which would culminate in the modern legal system.[28]

It was under Peel's reformist régime at the Home Office during the 1820s that the first significant moves were made by a government to rationalize the criminal justice system. Prompted by the energetic philanthropists of the Prison Discipline Society, as well as by his own reformist inclinations, Peel sponsored a Gaol Act in 1823, and amending legislation in the following year, which sought to establish a measure of uniformity throughout the prisons of England and Wales. The legislation was informed by the idea of the penitentiary: it spelled out health regulations and religious regulations; it required the separation of different categories of prisoner and facilities for hard labour; it directed magistrates to inspect their local gaols three times a quarter, and demanded that annual reports be sent from each gaol to the

Secretary of State. Many local gaols ignored at least some of these regulations, including the requirement for an annual report. Peel was reluctant to antagonize local sensibilities about independence and consequently made no attempt to impose sanctions in the legislation or a national system of inspection. It was not until 1835 that the reforming Whig government of Melbourne, with Lord John Russell at the Home Office, established a prison inspectorate of five. Yet from Peel's time onward, home secretaries were interventionist and every government had to develop some sort of policy on the punishment of criminal offenders.

The death penalty began to lose its central role in the criminal justice system with Peel's rationalization of the law even though the numbers capitally convicted continued to rise roughly in line with the rise in criminal statistics during the 1820s and early 1830s. Nevertheless, following on from Peel's reforms, the number of capital offences continued to be reduced throughout the 1830s and early 1840s.[29] By the late 1830s it was rare for anyone to be executed for any offence other than murder (Table 9.5), and by the mid 1840s a significant movement had developed for the total abolition of the death penalty.[30] With the decline in the use of the death penalty prisons of different varieties had more of a central role to play in the criminal justice system, but until the middle of the century transportation also remained an option for the courts when dealing with those deemed serious offenders.

The numbers transported began to increase from about 1,000 to about 2,500 a year with the perceived crime wave at the end of the Napoleonic Wars. They increased further during the 1820s and reached a peak in the early 1830s with about 5,000 convicts being shipped to Australia each year from Great Britain and Ireland; the numbers transported from England and Wales constituted roughly two-thirds of the total. From the beginning of the second decade of the nineteenth century until the mid 1830s, about one-third of all those convicted at assizes or quarter sessions were either sentenced, or had a death sentence

TABLE 9.5 Capital sentences, number executed and number executed for murder, 1805–54 (based on figures given in Parliamentary Reports)

Ten-year period	Average number capitally convicted per ann.	Average number executed per ann.	Average number executed for murder per ann.
1805–14	443	66	13
1815–24	1073	89	16
1825–34	1218	53	12
1835–44	199	13	10
1845–54	57	9	9

commuted, to transportation. This fraction began to fall rapidly over the subsequent decade to about one-seventh. Except for the early years and the very last years of the system, between two-thirds and three-quarters of those sentenced to transportation were actually shipped to Australia.[31]

During the eighteenth century doubts had been expressed about the extent to which transportation was a punishment; one penal reformer, writing in the aftermath of the loss of the American colonies, suggested that those who had been transported had actually been given the opportunity to become 'profitable members of another state'.[32] Similar doubts were raised about conditions in Australia. The relatively liberal and reforming régime of Governor Lachlan Macquarie in New South Wales was criticised in J. T. Bigge's official enquiry into the conduct of the colony published in 1822. As a result of Bigge's report restrictions were put on the governors of the colonies and policies of greater severity were applied towards convicts. Even so in 1826 the Reverend Sydney Smith could write to Peel satirising a sentence of transportation as follows:

> translated into common sense [it] is this: 'Because you have committed this offence, the sentence of the Court is that you shall no longer be burdened with the support of your wife and family. You shall be immediately removed from a very bad climate and a country over burdened with people to one of the finest regions of the earth, where the demand for human labour is every hour increasing, and where it is highly probable you may ultimately gain your character and improve your future. The Court have been induced to pass this sentence upon you in consequence of the many aggravating circumstances of your case, and they hope your fate will be a warning to others.'[33]

Stories circulated of men committing crimes simply to get transported.[34] Yet the treatment of many convicts in Australia was appalling and some of this was brought out in evidence to the Select Committee on Transportation which met between 1837 and 1838 under the chairmanship of Sir William Molesworth. The problem was, as the committee rightly pointed out, the penal colonies were so far away that people in England were unaware of the severity of the life and, consequently, there was no deterrence.[35] The committee condemned the existing system of transportation and favoured the building of penitentiaries; the majority proposed penitentiaries in both Britain and the colonies but Molesworth himself opposed their establishment in the colonies on the grounds that this simply perpetuated transportation under another name. The report did ultimately lead to changes in the system of convict labour and to experiments aimed particularly at the reformation of convicts, but the practice of shipping abroad the more serious offenders was not abolished as a judicial sentence until 1857 and for ten years after that a few offenders continued to be sent to Western Australia. It was as much pressure from the colonists, increasingly proud of their new land, as any growing faith in prisons as the best means of punishment which finally brought about the demise of transportation in the British penal system.[36]

As the wave of colonial opposition to transportation built up during the 1830s and 1840s so a particular concept of prison discipline began to dominate from Westminster. The Select Committee of the House of Lords whose report, in 1835, recommended the appointment of a government inspectorate of prisons, also advocated a common system of discipline for all prisons based on silence. Wakefield Gaol and Coldbath Fields had adopted the silent system the preceding year; overnight, recalled the governor of the latter institution, 'all inter-communication by word, gesture or sign was prohibited'.[37] But a different group of experts advocated the separate system in preference to silence; notable among these were William Crawford, a leading figure in the Prison Discipline Society, and the Reverend Whitworth Russell, a former chaplain at Millbank; both men were among the first five appointees to the prison inspectorate. Separation, or solitary confinement, had been central to the thought of many early advocates of the penitentiary. A visit to the United States by Crawford convinced him of the superiority of the separate over the silent system and on his return he published a massive study of American prisons explaining his conclusions. More importantly, while there was no unanimity among the prison inspectorate, both Crawford and Whitworth Russell took every opportunity to urge their preference in their inspectors' reports. Somewhat hesitantly Lord John Russell authorised the construction of a new national penitentiary in London and Captain Joshua Jebb of the Royal Engineers was entrusted with the design. Jebb, subsequently appointed Surveyor-General of Prisons, was favourable towards the separate system himself, but his evidence to a parliamentary committee in 1850 suggests that the leading advocates of the system were not averse to a bit of blackmail:

> I was requested by ... Mr Crawford and Mr Russell ... to allow them to be associated with me in the consideration of the plans, and they urged this reason: they said,'We do not wish to control your professional opinion; but if you erect a prison which we do not consider to be adapted for the enforcement of the system which we advocate, we will not certify the cells, and the prison will be useless.[38]

Pentonville, the end product of Jebb's designs and Crawford's and Whitworth Russell's urgings, was opened in 1842.

The inmates of Pentonville were kept in solitary cells. They wore a mask, the 'beak', when they were moved around the building so that anonymity was preserved. At the required church parades each convict was confined to a separate box so that communication with his fellows was all but impossible. The plan was for the solitary confinement and anonymity of Pentonville to last for eighteen months before a man was transported. It was believed that, thrown in upon themselves, in the quiet, contemplative state of the solitary cell, convicts, assisted by their bibles and the exhortations of the chaplain, would come to a realisation and repentance of their wrong doing. The Reverend John Clay, another ardent supporter of the separate system recorded how:

> a few months in the solitary cell renders a prisoner strangely impressible. The chaplain can then make the brawny navvy cry like a child; he can work on his feelings in almost any way he pleases; he can, so to speak, photograph his thoughts, wishes and opinions on his patient's mind, and fill his mouth with his own phrases and language.[39]

The problem was that not every convict was quite as malleable; some abused and assaulted warders, others developed serious psychological disorders or attempted suicide. Before the end of the 1840s even the annual reports of the prison's commissioners were compelled to admit that there were difficulties with the system.[40]

The initial, optimistic logic of the separate system, together with increasing pressure from the Home Office for national uniformity, led to some county and borough authorities establishing a cellular system in existing or in purpose-built prisons. But, as with policing, developments in provincial gaols were limited by cost. The Bedfordshire justices ruled out the construction of a miniature Pentonville for their county on the grounds that it could not be done for less than £25,000. When, in 1848, they did embark on a rebuilding programme on a tender of just over £17,000 they faced a vociferous protest from ratepayers. Northernhay Gaol in Exeter was completed in 1819; by the 1830s it was insufficient for the number of prisoners sent to it but, primarily because of the expense, there was no new gaol and no provision for the separate system. The Lancashire magistrates, partly at the prompting of Clay, were committed to the separate system by the middle of the century, but a ratepayers' revolt helped to put the brakes on any successful implementation.[41]

Religion was central to the convict's reformation in the eyes of the experts who advocated the separate system. This led to the eclipse of the idea that useful and profitable labour could be an element in reformation. Preston Gaol had provided the model for the industrial prison with its inmates sub-contracted by three local textile firms and being allowed a proportion of the monetary value of their work. The practice was vehemently condemned by Sydney Smith in a celebrated article for the *Edinburgh Review*. In Preston itself the practice received little support from Clay, while Crawford objected that prisons were not intended as training schools for artisans. Work had a place, but only as a privilege, and to prevent the convict from dwelling too much on his previous evil way of life.[42] As a consequence labour in prisons from the 1820s tended to be increasingly pointless marching on the treadmill, turning a handcrank or picking oakum in the solitude of a cell, or shifting cannonballs along a line of men from point A to point B and back.[43] But, again, whatever the theories of the influential experts some local gaols continued to go their own way. During the 1840s the inmates of Durham Gaol were producing cloth, mats, nets and rugs for sale in nearby markets; indeed one of the prison inspectors even suggested employing a tailor to teach his trade to the prisoners and replacing a treadmill with a smithy and a workshop.[44]

To a lesser extent the arguments over work in prisons were replicated in arguments over education. Moral reformation did not necessarily require the development of basic skills in literacy and numeracy; and, it was argued, prison should punish offenders not reward them with educational advancement. Nevertheless some prisons did offer such opportunities to their inmates,[45] and few seriously questioned the necessity of educating, and thus reforming and rescuing, juvenile offenders. Here again institutional developments began primarily through the efforts of enthusiastic philanthropists.

The need to separate young offenders and thus prevent their total corruption by hardened recidivists had been urged for generations. As early as 1818 magistrates in Birmingham were sentencing some juveniles to short periods in a local reformatory financed by private subscription.[46] Melbourne's government took a positive step towards separating the juvenile offender in 1838 when a former military hospital on the Isle of Wight, Parkhurst, was opened with a reformatory régime for convicts under the age of eighteen prior to their transportation. The experiment was short-lived. During the 1850s a band of indefatigable reformers including Mary Carpenter and Matthew Davenport Hill proselytised in favour of reformatories and industrial schools while private organisations, like the Philanthropic Society, established such institutions on an independent basis to reform and educate juvenile delinquents. In 1853 a Select Committee on Criminal and Destitute Children recommended a degree of state assistance for reformatory schools and the Youthful Offenders Act 1854 provided for persons under sixteen years to be sent to such schools for from two to five years following a prison sentence. Three years later legislation sanctioned the sending to industrial schools of children between the ages of seven and fourteen who had been committed for vagrancy. A perceived decline in juvenile crime during the second half of the nineteenth century was often attributed by the reformers to the reformatory and industrial schools; though they also insisted that a lack of trained staff and a reluctance on the part of magistrates to use the provisions were unnecessarily limiting the success of the schools.[47] It is, of course, unlikely that a decline in juvenile crime can be put down to one single element and taking the country as a whole it is clear that there was no common sentencing policy with reference to juveniles, the number of places available in these schools varied from locality to locality,[48] and the majority of convicted juveniles continued to be sent to ordinary gaols.

The deaths of both Crawford and Whitworth Russell in 1847 removed the two most ardent advocates of the separate system at the centre of national prison administration. The system had never been implemented across the nation with the uniformity and rigour that they had wished for; and within a decade of their deaths the debates about the penal system had shifted from whether that system should be separate or silent to other questions: how to handle convicts who, because of the end of transportation, were now released into the home community; and was the whole penal system sufficiently severe? Furthermore the deaths of Crawford and Whitworth Russell contributed to the balance of the system swinging away from the idea of religion as a central and significant aspect in the convict's reformation and towards a more rigorous application of the idea of prison as punishment.

The ticket-of-leave, introduced by the Penal Servitude Act 1853, was not entirely new.[49] Releasing convicts on licence following good behaviour had become a feature of the system in the penal colonies; moreover large numbers of persons sentenced to transportation were, for a variety of reasons, never shipped abroad and were released in Britain after a term in gaol. The virtual end of transportation in the early 1850s required that something be done for those convicts in the national penitentiaries who were expecting a release on licence at some stage after they reached Australia. Jebb warned the Home Office of a build-up of tension among frustrated convicts and while there were considerable qualms expressed by both the Home Secretary, Lord Palmerston, and his civil servants, the ticket-of-leave seemed to offer an answer. The ticket-of-leave was a conditional pardon with remission granted towards the end of a sentence to any convict not guilty of idleness or misconduct. Initially the press and members of parliament appear to have been sympathetic to convicts released on licence in this way, particularly when they seemed unable to get work or seemed to be the objects of police harassment.[50] But there was the major problem of a lack of an administrative bureaucracy organised and primed to cope with the ticket-of-leave system. Furthermore by the mid 1850s both sections of the press and some members of parliament had become vociferously hostile linking a perceived rise in violent crime with ticket-of-leave men now prowling the English streets rather than those of the antipodes. Probably also the suspicions about ticket-of-leave men were linked with the perceptions of criminals as a group. While Mayhew himself was sympathetic to the plight of ticket-of-leave men, the picture that he, and others, sketched of criminals as a class apart brought up to their own, skilled criminal trades, was not conducive to the ex-convict being accepted and re-assimilated as an unfortunate, *former* offender who had paid his debt to society. Amending legislation in 1857 tightened up the system and extended prison sentences so that seven, rather than four years' penal servitude in England, became the equivalent of seven years' transportation to Australia. Momentarily, the concerns subsided, but they erupted again with the garotting panic of 1862. Garotting was seen in many quarters as the work of ticket-of-leave men; it was defined as a 'science' along with housebreaking.[51] Parliament responded with the 'Garotters' Act', which authorised up to fifty strokes of corporal punishment in addition to any other punishment inflicted on those guilty of armed or violent robbery, and a Royal Commission was appointed to investigate the legislation relating to transportation and penal servitude. The report of the Royal Commission resulted in a new Penal Servitude Act 1864 which required police supervision of ticket-of-leave men and specified minimum sentences of penal servitude: five years for a first offence, seven years for any subsequent.

There was doubt about the precise meaning of the term 'penal servitude' when it was first enshrined in law in 1853; the doubt continued. Even though the Home Office was increasingly responsible for, and issuing directions about, prison administration, no government was prepared to commit itself as to whether the penal system as a whole, and penal servitude in particular, was designed to deter, to punish, or to reform. The Penal Servitude Acts were *ad hoc* legislation rather than the product of any consistent, reasoned policy. The initial legislation established 'penal servitude' (whatever it was) to balance the declining use of transportation, with those sentences which were served at home to be marginally less than those in the colonies. The amending legislation ironed out the problems which emerged, but also generally made penal servitude sentences longer in response to concerns about the end of transportation, the ticket-of-leave system and the garotting scares of 1856 and 1862.[52]

1863 can be singled out as a key year for the increasing severity of the penal system, though primarily through coincidence. In addition to the Garotters' Act it was in that year that Joshua Jebb died. Knighted and promoted to a major-general Jebb nevertheless died with the régime which he had administered as Director of Convict Prisons coming increasingly under attack for being too soft on dangerous men. That same year Edmund Du Cane, another officer of the Royal Engineers and a strict disciplinarian who was ultimately to take over the directorship, was appointed an Assistant Director of Convict Prisons. Finally, but by no means least, a Select Committee of the House of Lords, chaired by the Earl of Carnarvon, presented its report on Gaol Discipline. The Carnarvon Committee disputed the suggestion that moral reformation was more important than punishment and urged greater severity with the prisons extolling the virtues of the crank, the treadmill and shot drill. The Committee also urged the closure of small prisons and the withdrawal of Treasury support from any local gaol which did not conform to Home Office regulations. Many of the recommendations, particularly those advocating greater severity, were incorporated in the third Penal Servitude Act. The results were not always what was intended. While the crank and the treadmill were recommended for those sentenced to penal servitude, they seem to have been more likely the lot of the short-term prisoner confined to a local gaol for a petty offence, and often a first time offence. After nine months of solitary confinement in Millbank or Pentonville, where they generally picked oakum or sewed, long-term penal servitude convicts were removed to the public works prisons of Chatham, Dartmoor, Portland or Portsmouth where, often at great risk to life and limb, they generally quarried stone or constructed fortifications and dockyard facilities.[53] Some of the smaller local prisons also continued to go their own way and it was not until 1877 that all prisons were brought under central control, which in practice then meant the strict supervision of Du Cane.

The hardening attitude towards prison discipline coincided with further legal limitations on capital punishment and the final shift of physical punishment away from public view. While in practice since the 1840s no one had been executed for any crime other than murder it was not until the Offences Against the Person Act 1861 that parliament finally abolished the death penalty for all crimes other than murder and high treason. In 1856 a Select Committee recommended the ending of public executions. A Royal Commission made the same recommendation ten years later. The deterrent effect of a public execution was perceived as negligible and far outweighed by the problems and dangers created by the large crowds which such executions attracted. The last public execution took place outside Newgate on 26 May 1868. Except for the occasional glimpse of a convict gang in the vicinity of a public works prison or the possible sight of a convict being escorted by guards by rail the penal system was now completely private. After sentencing in court – justice as personified by the courts still had to be *seen* to be done – the convict was not seen again by the public until release; the capitally convicted person was never seen again in public, unless subsequently reprieved and released.

The removal of the convict and of punishment from public gaze robbed the felon of any moment of glory or martyrdom. It was also in keeping with notions of dignity and decorum so important to Victorian sensibility, but which certainly pre-dated Victoria's reign.[54] Whether the mystery of punishment increased its deterrence is a moot point.[55] Whether the dramatic reduction of the number of capital offences together with the bringing down of the curtain on the theatre of public executions produced a qualitatively more humanitarian penal system is also open to debate. Of course convicted criminals were no longer executed, or at least sentenced to be executed, in large numbers. The early reformers like Howard and then the gaol inspectorate led to prisons being better regulated and cleaner; the chance of death from that variety of typhus known as gaol fever was all but removed. The replacement of the entrepreneurial gaoler with an increasingly centralised and regulated system also meant a common diet for all prisoners whatever their financial situation. Yet whatever the boasts of the experts the diet was not particularly nourishing and regularly brought on the most unpleasant and painful stomach complaints. If public spectacle had gone, brutal punishment still remained with the added variant of electric shock treatment – 'galvanising' – for convicts suspected of malingering. In addition to the official brutality of the birch, the crank, the electric shock and the treadmill, there was the psychological suffering brought about by solitary confinement and enforced silence. Warders, like policemen, had discretion and were not always under the eyes of upright superiors; some showed kindness and generosity towards those in their charge; others were noted for lashing out unofficially with boot, club and fist. Convicts responded in kind.[56]

Entrepreneurial gaolers and the officials responsible for penal colonies could coerce their charges, but once the notion of reformation came in sanctions became necessary to make the recalcitrant conform even if they did not intend to reform; if one or two convicts were allowed to set bad examples the system would be undermined. By the same token rewards were gradually introduced to encourage compliance and to reward the well behaved. Ferocious abuse from a warder, a bread and water diet, solitary confinement, or a flogging provided the stick; gratuities for good conduct and industry among long-term prisoners, and the ability to work time off the end of a long sentence by collecting high 'marks', provided the carrot. The 'marks' system was finalised to mechanical perfection under Du Cane and, at the same time, different uniforms were designed to denote at what stage a convict was at in his sentence, and whether his behaviour had been good or bad.[57]

The increasing role of prison staff in deciding the punishment or treatment of convicts in their charge developed as arguments and unease continued about sentencing policy in the courts. While some late eighteenth and early nineteenth-century reformers had sought particular punishments to fit particular crimes, the improved bureaucracy and record-keeping at both national and local level meant that previous convictions could more easily be brought to a court's attention before sentence was passed.[58] For some offenders a criminal record became a veritable millstone around their necks; being 'known to the police' and being found in suspicious circumstances could lead in itself to magistrates inflicting a short sentence as a suspicious person. As noted in the previous chapter there was insufficient evidence to convict the two ex ticket-of-leave men charged with garotting Hugh Pilkington M.P., but the police magistrate nevertheless sentenced them to three months' imprisonment as suspicious persons.[59] Liberal public concern centred on the discretion and veracity of the police. In 1866, following proven corrupt evidence by police in a burglary trial and a magistrate's initial refusal to hear evidence for the defence, *Fun* ridiculed the Metropolitan Police Courts with a cartoon of a magistrate rejecting a ragged boy while a smug policeman looked on:

> *Learned Magistrate*:—Hear the evidence for the defence? Nonsense! I
> won't hear a word of it! What's the use? I could not think of doubting a
> policeman's word.[60]

The sentence of penal servitude gave magistrates and judges the
opportunity to inflict ferocious sentences on persons who, while
undoutedly pests in that they were continually being brought before
different courts, never carried out any particularly serious offence. The
prosecution and sentences of Crowsley, Hudson and Taverner offer
examples of this (Table 9.6); it is worth noting, in passing, the three-
month sentence imposed on Taverner in March 1861 for being a
suspicious person. But again it must be stressed that the use of this
legislation varied from place to place. The magistrates in the industrial
districts of the north west used the legislation more than those in
London or in rural counties; and Gloucestershire and Hampshire stand
out among the rural counties for their use of the Penal Servitude Acts,
almost certainly because of the influence of T. B. Lloyd Baker and the
Earl of Carnavon on their respective county benches.[61]

Sentences of this sort on relatively minor, if persistent and infuriating
offenders, brought forth criticism from liberal-minded reformers.[62]
Concern was also expressed that sentences for property offences often
seemed excessive in comparison to those meted out to violent offenders.
But, as in the case of prison policy, no consensus could be reached on
how to improve the sentencing system. There was a basic conservatism
in the legal profession and especially amongst the judiciary which
worked against proposals for a codification of the law. Codification was
a foreign route; and while it was a last resort, Francophobia could
always be enlisted to bolster arguments that, whatever the merits of the
Code Napoleon, the reasons for its creation were not relevant to
England, and the means by which it was established were alien to the
English constitution. When even Du Cane criticised the system of
sentencing, his comments served, not to foster change, but to reveal a
division within the Home Office over whether government should
appear to give directives to judges and magistrates. Throughout the
century judges and magistrates continued to use their discretion and to
be swayed by influences external to the case before them when they came
to pass sentence; and while reformers and codifiers might lament it,
others boasted, in contrast, that herein lay one of the strengths of the
system. 'It seems to me', remarked Baron Alderson in 1854:

> a very unwise thing to abolish the common law principles of decision,
> which can accommodate themselves to the varying circumstances of the
> times, and thus, as it were, to stereotype them by Act of Parliament in
> verbal definitions, *many of them inaccurate*. This will leave the courts only
> to construe precise words, instead of adapting old principles to new cases
> as they arise.[63]

Yet if controversy continued to remain about sentencing policy a

TABLE 9.6 'Penal servitude' for petty recidivists*

(a) Prosecutions and convictions of William Henry Crosley, born c.1849, labourer.

Offence	Court*	Date	Sentence
Stealing provisions	Bedford Borough	7 July 1862	1 calendar month
Stealing bread		Easter 1863	Acquitted
Stealing tares		1 June 1863	1 calendar month
Assault		4 July 1864	1 calendar month
Wilful Damage		5 Sept. 1865	1 calendar month
Stealing potatoes	Bedford Borough	Midsummer 1866	12 calendar months
Stealing growing crops		4 May 1868	2 calendar months
Using Insulting Words		7 Jan. 1870	7 days
Riot	Bedford Borough	Epiphany 1871	acquitted
Stealing 2½ pecks potatoes	Bedford Borough	Easter 1872	7 years penal servitude and 7 years police supervision

(b) Prosecutions and convictions of William Hudson, born c. 1808, labourer.

Offence	Court*	Date	Sentence
Sheep stealing	Beds Quarter Sessions	Midsummer 1838	Acquitted
Stealing a spade	Beds Quarter Sessions	Midsummer 1838	6 weeks
Stealing a fowl	Beds Assizes	Lent 1839	1 year
Game Laws		Feb. 1844	6 weeks
Stealing hen and chickens	Beds Quarter Sessions	Epiphany 1845	acquitted

Crime and society in England, 1750–1900

TABLE 9.6 (cont.)

(b) Prosecutions and convictions of Hudson (cont.)

Offence	Court*	Date	Sentence
Sheep stealing	Beds Quarter Sessions	Epiphany 1845	Transported 15 years
Stealing potatoes		Aug 1854	1 calendar month
Stealing hay	Beds Quarter Sessions	Midsummer 1860	7 days
Stealing meat	Beds Assizes	Lent 1867	3 calendar months
Stealing sickles, basket and other articles	Beds Quarter Sessions	Michaelmas 1868	7 years penal servitude

(c) Prosecutions and Convictions of Samuel Taverner, born c. 1839, labourer.

Offence	Court*	Date	Sentence
Stealing fowls	Beds Quarter Sessions	Michaelmas 1855	3 calendar months
Stealing iron		25 Mar 1856	3 calendar months
Wilful damage		17 Nov 1857	6 weeks
Stealing barley	Beds Quarter Sessions	Epiphany 1858	No true bill
Assault		8 June 1858	1 calendar month
Wilful damage		14 Sep 1858	21 days
Stealing barley		14 Sep 1858	21 days
Stealing a rat trap		31 Jan 1860	1 calendar month
Suspicious person		5 Mar 1861	3 calendar months
Drunk and riotous		21 Oct 1861	21 days

TABLE 9.6 (cont.)

(c) Prosecutions and convictions of Taverner (cont.)

Offence	Court*	Date	Sentence
Stealing manure bags	Beds Quarter Sessions	Epiphany 1862	3 years penal servitude
Drunk and riotous		27 Sep 1864	7 days
Stealing cabbages		10 June 1865	1 calendar month
Game Laws		19 Dec 1865	2 calendar months or £3.8 fine
Game Laws		18 Sep 1866	1 calendar month or £2.14 fine
Stealing barrow wheel and some iron (value 3s.)	Beds Quarter Sessions	Michaelmas 1867	7 years penal servitude
Stealing 5 pieces of Lindsey (value £1)	Beds Quarter Sessions	Epiphany 1874	10 years penal servitude and 7 years police supervision

*Based on details in Beds R.O. QGV 10/4
†Where the court is unspecified in the records it was almost certainly petty sessions.

significant change had taken place. In the space of 100 years a custodial
sentence had become virtually the only punishment that the courts could
award; fines continued to be imposed for many petty offences, but with
the proviso that failure to pay would lead to imprisonment. These
changes in the system of punishment have been related to the great
changes taking place in society, implicitly by the Whig historians who
thought in terms of progress with the past developing towards a more
enlightened future, and explicitly by Marxists, and others, who have
explained the development of the prison in terms of the control needs of
bourgeois captialism. The old notion of the 'truth' lying somewhere
between the extremes will not do; why should the 'truth' necessarily be
found between just two world views?

Humanitarianism counted in the reform of punishment. Whatever
the psychological make-up of late eighteenth and early nineteenth-
century reformers which fostered their ideas of prison discipline,[64] they
drew considerable inspiration from the humanitarian and rational
elements within the Enlightenment. Brutal punishments, suffering in
unregulated gaols, the apparent lottery of who was executed and who
was not, all mattered to these reformers; they also convinced others that
these things mattered, and notably they convinced men at the centre of
government. The state played an important role in the changes in
punishment. It was a capitalist state and, arguably, increasingly a
bourgeois state. Anglo-Saxon historians have, perhaps, been too timid
in acknowledging the role of the state in pushing ahead with many
reforms in the nineteenth century. Albeit piecemeal and, at times,
reluctantly governments sponsored legislation which reduced capital
punishment and were prepared to become involved in the administration
of convicts and prisons; once involved it was probably impossible for the
state to extricate itself as bureaucratic machinery spawned and renewed
itself. But, at the same time, it is difficult to detect a 'state' or a 'class' line
on punishment developing consistently during these years.[65] Serious
divisions remained and at the beginning of the twentieth century Sir
Robert Anderson lamented the way that punishment continued to swing
between extremes:

> Let anyone propose, for example, that a 'hooligan' shall receive the sort of
> punishment which at a public school would be meted out to the son of a
> duke for gross misconduct, and they will raise such an outcry as will stifle
> legislation to that end. Another minority, equally small in numbers, will
> always protest against any amelioration of the prisoner's lot. And thus the
> pendulum is kept swinging, while an easy going public remains perplexed
> and passive.[66]

Much of the legislation – the Penal Servitude Acts for example – was
ad hoc; and when parliament legislated, or when the Home Office issued
directives, many localities were reluctant to act promptly and
thoroughly in accordance with the new law or the new directive, partly

because of local pride but more often perhaps because of the expense. If the bourgeois capitalist state wanted a new system of punishment to help control the new and growing proletariat, the provincial bourgeois capitalists – even in the heartlands of the industrial revolution – may have been notably keen to see the Penal Servitude and Habitual Criminals legislation enforced, but they were most reluctant to pay increased rates to finance changes in policing and prisons:

> 'Prisons' (according to one author) ... like the workhouse under the New
> Poor Law, were not primarily for locking people up, but about
> disciplining those who were not in prison. So, although convicts might
> resist and obstruct prison discipline, their role in social control was
> assured simply by their existence.[67]

The fact that the new prison was developed at roughly the same time as the workhouse under the New Poor Law makes this equation appealing; the parallel with the control system of the new factory can also be drawn.[68] Clearly there are similarities: closed institutions are going to resemble each other from the very fact of being closed institutions, though this does not necessarily prove similar motives for their creation. Vagrancy and idleness were faults which reformers like Chadwick perceived as rampant in sections of the working class; these faults had to be eradicated and the threat of the workhouse was a means to this end. In this perception of the world vagrancy and idleness also led to crime, which gives further underpinning to the equation. But the equation requires some qualification; there were also considerable differences in intention between the two institutions, and considerable differences in perception which it would be difficult to put down simply to bourgeois hegemony. Provision for the very old, the very young, and the infirm was also supposed to be a part of the new workhouse; and the debate over whether prisons were meant to reform and inculcate good habits, or simply to punish, was never resolved. But perhaps most important is to look at the two institutions from the bottom up. There was no working-class sanction for the workhouse as the disorders of the 1830s and 1840s, and the continuing hostility throughout the nineteenth century demonstrates. The workhouse hung over sections of the poorer working class like a sword of Damocles in a way that the prison never did. The workhouse was more visible; several of the great convict prisons were constructed well away from centres of population and what went on inside them was increasingly private – one reason perhaps for the apparent popularity of prison biographies which revealed this secret world for the vicarious pleasure of the nineteenth-century reader.[69] Groups of workers who profited from illegal fiddles and perks did not regard as 'criminals' those of their workmates who were caught, convicted and imprisoned for such offences. Yet other former convicts from the working class did find it hard to get accepted, not simply by employers, but also by some working-class communities after a prison sentence.[70] Since the working class were often the victims of crimes it is scarcely surprising if they had little time for many former offenders. The popular abuse heaped on certain unpopular offenders as they were conveyed to Tyburn Tree in the eighteenth century should warn against any notion of the working class automatically siding with convicted criminals against a common class enemy. There is no reason to suppose anything other than that, in the popular mind, the prison was accepted as being designed not as an encouragement to them to behave, but as a place where genuine offenders were to be punished.

REFERENCES AND NOTES

1. The most detailed and subtle of the Whig studies in **Leon Radzinowicz**, *A History of English Criminal Law*, vol 1, Stevens, London, 1948; for a Whig view of the abolition of the death penalty see **David D. Cooper**, *The Lesson of the Scaffold*, Allen Lane, London, 1974. The most vivid of the revisionists is **Michael Ignatieff**, *A Just Measure of Pain: the penitentiary in the Industrial Revolution 1750–1850*, Macmillan, London, 1978. Ignatieff has now back-tracked to some degree; see his autocritique 'State, civil society and total institutions: a critique of recent social histories of punishment', in **S. Cohen and A. Scull** (eds.), *Social Control and the State*, Oxford University Press, 1983.

2. *P.P.* 1833 (344) xiii, *Select Committee on Municipal Corporations* pp. 2730, 3088–89 and 6388–90; **R. E. Swift**, 'Crime law and order in two English towns during the early nineteenth century: the experience of Exeter and Wolverhampton 1815–56', unpublished Ph.D. University of Birmingham, 1981, pp. 82–83.

3. **Michel Foucault**, *Discipline and Punish: the birth of the prison*, Allen Lane, London, 1977, makes much of the gruesome execution of the attempted regicide, Damiens. For French executions see, inter alia, **Nicole Castan**, *Justice et Repression en Languedoc à l'Epoque des Lumières*, Flammarion, Paris, 1980, especially pp. 278–89; **Julius R. Ruff**, *Crime, Justice and Public Order in Old Régime France*, Croom Helm, London, 1984, pp. 58–66; **Arlette Farge**, *La Vie Fragile: Violence, pouvoirs et solidarités à Paris au XVIIIe siecle*, Hachette, Paris, 1986, pp. 206–34.

4. For example at the Old Bailey Sessions in January 1801 George Mell was convicted of stealing indigo from an East India Company warehouse in Billiter Lane; he was sentenced to six months in Newgate and a public whipping to be conducted for a distance of 100 yards in Billiter Lane. At the same sessions Richard Cain was convicted of stealing coal from a barge at Queenhithe; he was sentenced to twelve months in Newgate and a public whipping from Queenhithe to Queen Street. *O.B.S.P. 1800–1*, nos. 111 and 112.

5. For the use of the stocks in the mid nineteenth century see **Clive Emsley**, 'The Bedfordshire Police 1840–56: A case study in the working of the Rural Constabulary Act', *Midland History*, vii (1982), pp. 73–92 (at pp.

84–85); **B. J. Davey**, *Lawless and Immoral: Policing a country town 1838–57*, Leicester U.P. 1983, pp. 44, 143, 147, 162 and 164.

6. For the best survey of eighteenth-century punishment and the contemporary debate see **J. M. Beattie**, *Crime and the Courts in England 1660–1800*, Oxford U.P, 1986, chaps 9 and 10. Beattie argues, convincingly, that the 1718 Transportation Act constituted a fundamental break with the practices and intentions of the penal policy of the past, and that it was, in consequence, as significant as the establishment of prisons in the last decades of the eighteenth century.

7. *Hansard*, new series, xiv, col. 1220.

8. **J. A. Sharpe**, *Crime in Early Modern England 1550–1750*, Longman, 1984, pp. 63–66; Clive Emsley, 'Repression, "terror" and the rule of law in England during the decade of the French Revolution', *E.H.R.* c (1985), pp. 801–25 (at pp. 822–23).

9. Ignatieff, *Just Measure of Pain*, p. 17; Sharpe, *Crime in Early Modern England*, pp. 177–78.

10. **Gerald Howson**, *Thief-Taker General: The rise and fall of Jonathan Wild*, Hutchinson, London, 1970, p. 288.

11. **John Wardroper**, *Kings, Lords and Wicked Libellers: Satire and protest 1760–1837*, John Murray, London, 1973, pp. 48–49 and plate 9.

12. *Northampton Mercury*, 20 July 1752, quoting the *London Evening Post*.

13. Ibid. See also *Sussex Weekly Advertiser* 30 August 1819 for the following: 'Upon arrival of the cart under the fatal tree the Rev Mr Noyce, the clergyman in attendance, ascended it and began to pray ... requesting the unhappy man to join him, but this Piper refused to do, saying that he was a murdered man and that Pearce was perjured and that he never snapped a pistol at him ... he went on to observe that there was no law for a poor man, and referred to a case at our last Assize wherein one prisoner was condemned to death and another, charged with a similar crime, was sentenced to two months imprisonment, and called down heavy vengeance on the heads of his prosecutors.'
    Martin Madan urged the following story on assize judges faced with such pleas: 'It was worthy the understanding and policy of a low thief to say to *Judge Burnett*, once, at *Hertford* assizes – 'My lord, it is very hard to hang me for *only* stealing a horse'. – It was worthy the good sense and wisdom of that learned Judge, to answer – 'Man, thou art not to be hanged *only* for stealing a horse, but that horses might not be stolen'. **Martin Madan**, *Thoughts on Executive Justice*, London, 1785, p. 105.

14. *Northampton Mercury*, 12 August 1754.

15. *Gentleman's Magazine*, xli (1771) p. 147.

16. Ignatieff, *Just Measure of Pain*, p. 57.

17. Lord North's government finally collapsed in March 1782; the second Rockingham administration lasted only till July 1782 and Lord Shelburne's administration, which followed it, fell in April 1783. The Fox-North coalition lasted from April to December 1783, and while the younger Pitt ultimately brought stability, he had to fight a general election in December 1784.

18. **Jonas Hanway**, *The defects of police, the cause of immorality and the continual robberies committed, particularly in the metropolis*, London, 1775, p. 72; for similar criticism of the hulks see Madan, *Thoughts on Executive Justice*, pp. 74–76.

19. *Journals of the House of Commons*, xl, pp. 1161–64.
20. *Gentleman's Magazine*, lvi (1786) pp. 263–64.
21. Ignatieff, *Just Measure of Pain*, pp. 128–42.
22. **A. G. L. Shaw**, *Convicts and the Colonies: A study of penal transportation from Great Britain and Ireland to Australia and other parts of the British Empire*, Faber and Faber, London, 1966, p. 59.
23. *Gentleman's Magazine*, lvi (1786) p. 102.
24. **John Cannon**, *Parliamentary Reform 1640–1832*, Cambridge University Press, 1973, p. 140 note 3.
25. Cooper, *The Lesson of the Scaffold*, p. 33 states that the 1820 legislation failed, but see **K. K. Macnab**, 'Aspects of the History of Crime in England and Wales between 1850–60', unpublished Ph.D. University of Sussex 1965, appendices pp. 22 and 24.
26. **Sir Leon Radzinowicz** and **Roger Hood**, 'Judicial discretion and sentencing standards: Victorian attempts to solve a perennial problem', *University of Pennsylvania Law Review*, **127** (1779), pp. 1288–1349 (at pp. 1290–99).
27. **Randall McGowan**, 'The image of justice and reform of the criminal law in early nineteenth-century England', *Buffalo Law Review*, **32** (1983), pp. 89–125 (at p. 96).
28. Of course no sensible historian has argued simply and explicitly that Romilly, Mackintosh and other reformers had a contemporary legal system in mind as the model toward which they aspired; yet this view often implicitly informs the work of the Whig historians. McGowan highlights this in his excellent critique of Radzinowicz: 'His volume on the death penalty is informed by one idea – that the gallows represented an inefficient and inhumane form of punishment. This observation is so obvious to him that he pauses to wonder before thinkers and politicians who for so long resisted the 'truth'. The opponents of change are portrayed as simple reactionaries, blinded by self-interest or prejudice from seeing the value of new institutional forms'. Ibid., p. 94.
29. Macnab, 'Aspects of . . . crime', appendix 3, pp. 13–14 lists 26 acts of parliament removing capital punishment from particular offences between 1808 and 1835; subsequent legislation, in 1837, removed the death penalty from such offences as assembling with arms to assist smugglers, abortion, forging wills and power of attorney for the transfer of stock, attempted murder, burglary, piracy, arson of buildings or ships; and legislation of 1841 abolished the death penalty for rape, carnally abusing girls aged under ten, riot, and embezzlement by Bank of England servants. Following the Offences Against the Person Act 1861 the death penalty remained only for murder and high treason.
30. Cooper, *Lesson of the Scaffold*, pp. 45–53 and chap. 3 *passim*.
31. Shaw, *Convicts and the Colonies*, pp. 147–50; **L. L. Robson**, *The Convict Settlers of Australia*, Melbourne University Press, 1965, p. 9. Unless otherwise stated the discussion of transportation is based on the work of Robson and Shaw.
32. *Gentleman's Magazine*, lvi (1786) p. 103.
33. **Charles Stuart Parker**, (ed.), *Sir Robert Peel: From his private papers*, 3 vols., London, 1891, i, 400–1.
34. **J. J. Tobias**, *Crime and Industrial Society in the Nineteenth Century*, Penguin, Harmondsworth, 1972, p. 246.

35. *P.P.* 1837–38 (669) xxii, *Select Committee on Transportation*, p. 20.

36. The end of transportation as a sentence in the British courts coincided with its increased use by the French and, in spite of the fact that the British were questioning their system French politicians continued to use it as a model. **Patricia O'Brien**, *The Promise of Punishment: Prisons in nineteenth-century France*, Princeton University Press, 1982, pp. 259–87; **Gordon Wright**, *Between the Guillotine and Liberty: Two centuries of the crime problem in France*, Oxford University Press, 1983, pp. 105–8 and 132–35.

37. Quoted in **Philip Priestley**, *Victorian Prison Lives: English prison biography 1830–1914*, Methuen, London, 1985, pp. 35–36.

38. Quoted in **Christopher Harding**, *et al. Imprisonment in England and Wales: A concise history*, Croom Helm, London, 1985, p. 152. There was little love lost between Jebb and these two inspectors, see **Eric Stockdale**, 'The rise of Joshua Jebb, 1837–50', *British Journal of Criminology*, **16** (1976).

39. **W. L. Clay**, *The Prison Chaplain: A memoir of the Rev John Clay*, London, 1861, p. 386.

40. Ignatieff, *Just Measure of Pain*, pp. 9–10; Priestley, *Victorian Prison Lives*, p. 38.

41. **Eric Stockdale**, *A Study of Bedford Prison 1660–1877*, Phillimore, London, 1977, pp. 165 and 176; Swift, 'Crime, law and order', pp. 87–88; **Margaret E. DeLacy**, 'Grinding Men Good? Lancashire's prisons at mid century', in **Victor Bailey**, (ed.), *Policing and Punishment in Nineteenth-Century Britain*, Croom Helm, London, 1981, pp. 209–11.

42. **Sydney Smith**, 'Prisons', *Edinburgh Review* xxxvi (1822); DeLacy, 'Grinding Men Good?', pp. 200–2.

43. Priestley, *Victorian prison Lives*, pp. 121–31; Harding, *et al., Imprisonment*, appendix 3.

44. **James C. Burke**, 'Crime and criminality in County Durham 1840–55', unpublished M.A. University of Durham, 1980, p. 91.

45. Priestley, *Victorian Prison Lives*, pp. 108–11; Burke, 'Crime and Criminality', pp. 93–96.

46. **Barbara Weinberger**, 'Law breakers and law enforcers in the late victorian city: Birmingham 1867–77', unpublished Ph.D. University of Birmingham, 1981, p. 116.

47. **Jelinger C. Symons**, *Special Report on Reformatories in Gloucs., Shropshire, Worcs., Herefordshire and Monmouthshire, and in Wales*, (Printed in *P.P.* 1857–1858 [2315] xlvi *Minutes of the Committee of the Council on Education*); **John Trevarthen**, 'Hooliganism', *Nineteenth Century*, xlix (1901), pp. 84–89.

Weinberger, 'Law breakers and law enforcers', pp. 130–31 notes that in the Birmingham area, which figured prominently in the movement for the reform of juvenile offenders, there was no proportionate decline in the number of juveniles in prison between 1861 and 1881, in contrast to the national figures.

The question of juvenile delinquency in general is explored in **Susan Magarey**, 'The invention of juvenile delinquency in early nineteenth-century England', *Labour History*, **34** (1978), pp. 11–27; though whether the policitians of the early nineteenth century can, as Magarey argues, be held to have 'invented' the notion of juvenile delinquency is open to debate. See above p. 74 n. 40.

48. Stockdale, *Bedford Prison*, p. 153.
49. Unless otherwise stated what follows is drawn largely from **Peter W. J. Bartrip**, 'Public opinion and law enforcement: The ticket-of-leave scares in mid victorian Britain', in Bailey, (ed.), *Policing and Punishment*.
50. Of course police harassment could be, and was used as a defence in court by former convicts who insisted that because of the police they were unable to get a steady job. For example in November 1856 Charles Hunter, accused of robbery with violence at the Old Bailey protested: 'When I came home from transportation, I obtained a situation at a beer house in the Waterloo Road, where I was getting a comfortable living, and supporting my wife and aged mother; I had been there a few weeks when sergeant Broad came and told the landlord that I was a ticket-of-leave man, and if he allowed such characters in his house he should indict it; he told me to go; after that I drove a costermonger barrow, and he followed me about the streets, telling my customers to see that their change was good, for I was a ticket-of-leave man; I was compelled to give that up; I went to live with my parents, and worked at tailoring, and every time I came in or out of the court where I lived, he would stop and search me, if any of the neighbours or their children were about; so that at last I could get nobody to trust me with anything; what had I to do? I would work if they would let me, but they will not.' *C.C.C.S.P. 1856–57*, no. 87, pp. 102–3.
51. **H. W. Holland**, 'The science of garotting and housebreaking', *Cornhill Magazine*, vii (1863), pp. 79–92.
52. **M. Heather Tomlinson**, 'Penal servitude 1846–65: A system in evolution', in Bailey, (ed.), *Policing and Punishment*.; see also Bartrip, 'Public Opinion and Law Enforcement'.
53. Priestley, *Victorian Prison Lives*, pp. 131–34.
54. In March 1825 for example during discussions on a bill dealing with the punishment for sending threatening letters and a Felonies Pardon Bill, Ralph Bernal condemned the 'most unbecoming' practice employed at some of the London Police Offices 'of passing the prisoners, many of whom stood charged with common assaults, manacled through the streets from the offices to the prison'. Peel agreed about the 'indecency' though he considered that it would be too expensive to provide transport; he had advised the magistrates to use hackney carriages. *Hansard*, new series xii (1825), col. 1167.
55. **Henry Fielding**, *An Enquiry into the Causes of the Late Increase of Robbers*, 2nd edn., London, 1751, was critical of the Tyburn executions and urged privacy drawing a theatrical parallel. 'Foreigners have found fault with the Cruelty of the English Drama, in representing frequent Murders upon the Stage. In fact, this is not only cruel, but highly injudicious: A Murder behind the Scenes, if the Poet knows how to manage it, will affect the Audience with greater Terror than if it was acted before their eyes.' He instanced Macbeth's murder of Duncan as performed by David Garrick, p. 193.
56. Priestley, *Victorian Prison Lives*, especially chaps. 7 and 9.
57. Harding, *et al., Imprisonment in England and Wales*, p. 229.
58. During the 1830s local gaolers kept the Bedfordshire Clerk of the Peace informed of men awaiting trial who had faced previous prosecutions. See, for example, Beds. R.O. 1834/634–35, 640 and 644–45.

59. See above p. 193.
60. *Fun* 13 Oct. 1866, p. 51; the case which prompted the cartoon is reported on p. 49.
61. S. J. Stevenson, 'The 'Criminal Class' in the mid-victorian city: A study of policy conducted with special reference to the provision of 34 and 35 Vict., c. 112 (1871) in Birmingham and East London in the early years of registration and supervision', unpublished D.Phil. Oxford University, 1983.
62. Radzinowicz and Hood, 'Judicial discretion and sentencing standards', pp. 1310–11; Sir James Fitzjames Stephen argued in his *A History of the Criminal Law of England* (vol. 1., p. 479) that there could be some justification for bringing back the death penalty not only for brutal violence, but also for someone who, it was proved, was totally irredeemable. See the discussion in Robert Anderson, 'Our absurd system of punishing crime', *Nineteenth Century*, xlix (1901), pp. 268–84.
63. Quoted in ibid, pp. 1302–3 (emphasis in original).
64. Ignatieff, *Just measure of Pain*, is excellent on the psychology of reformers like John Howard.
65. Simon Stevenson suggests, persuasively, a pendulum effect in the final third of the nineteenth century with the authoritarian side of Benthamite liberalism dominant among legislators from the mid 1860s to the mid 1870s, a swing to a more liberal intellectual outlook during the 1880s, with a swing back towards coercive solutions in the 1890s. Stevenson, 'The Criminal Class' in the mid-victorian city', pp. 389–422.
66. Anderson, 'Our absurd system of punishing crime', p. 278.
67. Philip Rawlings in Harding, *et al., Imprisonment in England and Wales*, p. 278.
68. See, for example, D. Melossi and M. Pavarini, *The Prison and the Factory: Origins of the penitentiary system*, Macmillan, London, 1980.
69. See the bibliography in Priestley, *Victorian Prison Lives*.
70. Weinberger, 'Law breakers and law enforcers', p. 156.

Chapter 10
CONCLUDING REMARKS

In the last analysis it has to be acknowledged that the law defines crime and that legislators can criminalise or decriminalise activities. But criminal behaviour also adapts to other changes: a lasting alteration in fashion meant that the cutpurse had to metamorphose into the pickpocket; the development of the internal combustion engine and the decline of horse-drawn transport made 'van-dragging', whereby goods could be lifted from a moving vehicle, an extremely hazardous undertaking.[1] The key question, however, is what impact did the enormous economic and social changes of the eighteenth and nineteenth century have on crime as practised by offenders, as defined by legislators, and as enforced by state agents?

On one level there is a clear answer to the impact of these changes on criminal behaviour, though it would be impossible to quantify it. Increasing wealth, more goods in shops and warehouses, more moveable property in people's homes and, possibly also at the workplace, provided greater opportunities and greater temptation. Similarly the extension of the business and commercial worlds provided greater opportunities for embezzlement, fraud and financial corruption, offences which, generally speaking, were far more difficult to uncover and prosecute than the straightforward theft of small, moveable property. These offences were generally linked with the workplace and thus make workplace crime too complex and varied to be explained solely in terms of an employer's determination to maximise his profits and an employee's desire to hang on to customary practices and perks; indeed it would seem that in some instances the employees preferred regular wage payment to old customary practices.[2]

Monocausal explanations of property crime cannot cope with John Waldon's decision to sell his master's stool and the nephew of the Matheson's who calmly removed '*over* a million in sterling' from the strongroom of Matheson and Jardine. Whatever prompted the latter's actions it can hardly have been economic necessity; there is, however, some justification for accepting Waldron's plea of poverty. The increase in property crime recorded by the admittedly imperfect statistics during the serious economic slumps of the first period of industrialization, does appear significant. But the equation that poverty led to theft remains too simple. Most offenders were young. There was, perhaps, a degree of alienation among them: some suffered a marginal existence, they had no responsibilities, and no way of making their voice heard within society; in addition there were the pressures of the peer group to enjoy communal leisure activities, activities which generally cost money. Any or all of these elements could combine, perhaps also with the thrill of breaking the law, to encourage breaking of the law when an opportunity arose or was perceived. Economic hardship brought about by a slump merely exacerbated the situation and spread temptation further.

But if there is a correlation between the peaks of property crime and the troughs of the business cycle it is also apparent that the steepest overall increase in the criminal statistics during the period 1750 to 1900 coincides with fears for the social order, the fear of 'the mob', the fear of revolution and, during the 'hungry forties', the identification of and anxiety about 'the dangerous classes'. Jim Sharpe had identified a similar statistical peak in crime coinciding with fears for the social order two centuries before.[3] The problem is explaining why these two should coincide. Was it that people were more aware of their vulnerability to thieves and therefore more inclined to report offences and to prosecute if an offender could be identified? Was it also that an apparently shaky social order encouraged more people to reject accepted morality and to steal when the opportunity presented itself?

In his excellent study of the 'respectable fears' about street crime and disorder during the nineteenth and twentieth centuries Geoffrey Pearson has suggested that such fears seem 'to serve a specific ideological function within British public life, as a convenient metaphor for wider social tensions which attend the advance of democratisation'.[4] The difficulty here is that some of the short-term panics which he identifies are well and truly 'out-of-synch' with concerns about the social order and democratisation, most obviously the mid-nineteenth-century garotting panic. Chartism was scarcely perceived as a threat after 1848 and three years later the Great Exhibition ushered in a period of relative social peace and satisfaction; yet it was the ten years immediately following the Great Exhibition which were punctuated by the garotting 'outbreaks'.

Crime is rarely something that people experience regularly as victims and their perceptions of crime therefore depend largely on what they are told about it. When they are informed, authoritatively, that crime is a serious problem, and when this is reiterated and backed up with statistics and graphic instances, they will probably believe it. It seems clear that 'crime waves' and 'moral panics' could be accelerated, perhaps even generated, during the eighteenth and nineteenth centuries by newspapers eager to boost their sales or crusading for changes in the penal system.[5] The publication of national crime statistics, together with faith in the new science of statistics, the fearful example of European revolutions together with reports of riots and disorders at home, and the repetition of notions like the concept of the 'dangerous classes', possibly served to foster the perception of a longer-term crime wave in the first half of the nineteenth century; as people's concern about crime was heightened so, arguably, more crime was reported and prosecuted. This would not be to deny that necessity and need did prompt more people to steal simply to exist in the early nineteenth century, but, rather, to re-emphasise that the increase in the statistics was not just the result of more crime. By the same token the general stability of the Victorian social order in the second half of the nineteenth century, the faith in progress, and the belief that, in spite of one or two spectacular failures, the police and the courts were improving and winning the war against crime, may have contributed to a decline in the reporting and prosecution of the lesser and smaller offences.

Before moving on to look at the question of legislation it is worth underlining two points. First, while the collective noun 'crime' encompasses a variety of activities from murder and rape to petty theft, some of which are the result of careful planning and premeditation, and some of which are perpetrated largely because the opportunity presents itself, during the eighteenth and nineteenth centuries it was the small, opportunist theft which was statistically the most common. Secondly this fact was, indeed still is, often obscured by the vicarious appetite for violence fed by sections of the newspaper press as well as by much popular literature which implied that violence was part of crime *per se*. Violent crime was what worried people; it was central to the moral panics and crime waves; it provided good copy. But the incidence of serious inter-personal violence committed by thieves in the process of a robbery was rare within the statistics of crime. Crime waves did not centre on the fear of being murdered or assaulted by spouse, parent, child, other relation or acquaintance; statistically, except possibly for policemen, perhaps they should have.

It would probably be true to argue that the state has yet to be established in which the law treats those lacking power and influence in precisely the same way as those possessing power and influence. The law, and the police, tend to reinforce divisions and inequalities; yet often they seek also to overcome divisions and inequalities. Both the courts and legislators, recognising that the poor victims were disadvantaged in prosecuting offenders, sought to remedy the situation in the late eighteenth and early nineteenth centuries. It is surely just too cynical to suggest that this was done purely out of self interest and to bolster the confidence trick of equality before the law. The main argument put forward for establishing the new police was that they could prevent crime. From the moment that they took to the streets and country lanes most of the new police forces were also deployed to enforce new concepts of order on the working class, but police aid was demanded by, and rendered to, working-class communities and individuals; to date the social welfare role of the police has been largely ignored by historians.

The arguments for establishing the new police were firmly rooted in the problem of how to prevent crime; the arguments for a new punishment system were rooted in the Enlightenment's humanitarianism and rationalism. Of course hidden agendas can be identified, but sometimes their identification obscures the public agendas. There was heightened concern about order in late eighteenth and early nineteenth-century England which led to the use of the new police in enforcing particular concepts of decorum and respectability. But then again 'enforcing order' was generally easier than 'preventing' or 'detecting' crime, and by emphasising their order role, the new police could demonstrate an efficiency and effectiveness which was nowhere near as apparent in their crime prevention role. The gospel of work was central to Victorian ideology; instilling habits of work and morality on the convict who was perceived, very often, to have taken the short step from idleness to crime was regarded as being beneficial both to society and to the offender. Yet to conclude from this that the prison system which developed in the late eighteenth and nineteenth centuries, together with the new police, stemmed essentially from the control requirements of a new bourgeois capitalism is to short-circuit a variety of processes and to obliterate many nuances in, and impediments to, these new systems.

In sum during the period 1750 to 1900 the opportunities for criminal behaviour changed, probably increasing markedly. As in other periods the statistical pattern of crime appears to follow concerns about social order though the coincidence between the troughs of the business cycle and the peaks of crime in the first half of the nineteenth century would suggest some links between economic necessity, and petty theft. The reorganisation and rationalisation of the criminal law, the changes in punishment, and the creation of new organs of containment and control all linked with the changing economic and social order. These developments also needed, and benefited from, a state which was increasingly prepared to be interventionist. The rhetoric of English rights and liberties contributed to the shape and extent of change in the criminal justice system. Finally, the extensive range of people who participated in this system, often with considerable discretion, militates against any simple equation of either a ruling class making and administering the law for its own benefit, or a system steadily ironing out problems and abuses and developing towards a modern system somehow legitimated by the concept of the rational march of progress.

REFERENCES AND NOTES

1. For 'van-dragging' see **Raphael Samuel** (ed.), *East End Underworld: Chapters in the life of Arthur Harding*, RKP, London, 1981, pp. 70–71, 284.
    There is an example in *C.C.C.S.P. 1898–99* no. 106, the case of Michael William Hickey, aged 21 who was sentenced to nine months' hard labour for endeavouring to pull a post packet and seventeen postal orders off the back of a mail van. He was apprehended by the driver of the following van.

2. **Joanna Innes** and **John Styles**, 'The crime wave: Recent writing on crime and criminal justice in eighteenth-century England', *Journal of British Studies*, xxv (1986).

3. **J. A. Sharpe**, *Crime in Early Modern England 1550–1750*, Longman, London, 1984, pp. 183–87.

4. **Geoffrey Pearson**, *Hooligan: A history of respectable fears*, Macmillan, London, 1983, p. 230.

5. **Peter King**, 'Newspaper reporting, prosecution practice and urban crime. The Colchester crime wave of 1765', unpublished paper presented to Urban History Group Conference, College of St Paul and St Mary, Cheltenham 3-4 April 1986; **R. S. Sindall**, 'Street violence in the second half of the nineteenth century', unpublished Ph.D. University of Leicester, 1984, especially chaps. 3 and 4 and pp. 298–99.

FURTHER READING: FURTHER RESEARCH.

I have endeavoured to make the notes to each chapter as detailed as possible, not to obviate the need for a bibliography, but rather to supply a guide to further reading and to current debates and controversies under the relevant headings. What follows is simply to point up the most significant and useful texts and where more research might be usefully undertaken.

The starting point for eighteenth-century crime must remain **Douglas Hay, Peter Linebaugh, E. P. Thompson,** *et al., Albion's Fatal Tree: Crime and society in eighteenth-century England* (Allen Lane, London, 1975) with its challenging essays, in particular Hay's 'Property, authority and the criminal law'. The subsequent collection, **John Brewer** and **John Styles**, (eds.), *An Ungovernable People: The English and their law in the seventeenth and eighteenth centuries* (Hutchinson, London, 1980) is also invaluable with its rather different angle of vision. The outstanding monograph on eighteenth-century crime is **J. M. Beattie**, *Crime and the Courts in England 1660–1800* (Oxford U.P., 1986) which is based largely on material relating to Surrey. Peter King's study of crime in southern England, working outwards from his thesis on Essex, is in an advanced stage of preparation. For a critical assessment of the debates and subsequent research generated by *Albion's Fatal Tree*, see **Joanna Innes** and **John Styles**, 'The crime wave: Recent writing on crime and criminal Justice in eighteenth-century England', *Journal of British Studies*, xxv, 1986.

The pioneering academic study of nineteenth-century crime is **J. J. Tobias,** *Crime and Industrial Society in the Nineteenth Century* (Batsford, London, 1967;

Concluding remarks

Penguin, Harmondsworth, 1972). The book remains useful for its survey of the contemporary literature, but subsequent research has challenged many of its basic assumptions and conclusions. **V. A. C. Gatrell** has produced cogent arguments for the use of nineteenth-century criminal statistics in (with **T. B. Hadden**) 'Nineteenth-century criminal statistics and their interpretation' in E. A. Wrigley, (ed.), *Nineteenth-century Society: Essays in the use of quantitative methods for the study of social data* (Cambridge U.P., 1972), and 'The decline of theft and violence in Victorian and Edwardian England' in **V. A. C. Gatrell, Bruce Lenman** and **Geoffrey Parker** (eds.), *Crime and the Law: The social history of crime in Western Europe since 1500* (Europa, London, 1980). The former essay draws significantly on the crime statistics for Lancashire as well as the national figures. There are several nineteenth-century regional studies in thesis form, most of which show the influence of **David Philip's** excellent study of the Black Country, *Crime and Authority in Victorian England: The Black Country 1835–60* (Croom Helm, London, 1977). **Victor Bailey,** (ed.), *Policing and Punishment in Nineteenth-century Britain* (Croom Helm, London, 1981) and **David Jones,** *Crime, Protest, Community and Police in Nineteenth-century Britain* (RKP, London, 1982) are both useful collections of thematic and regional essays. For crime in London see **Jennifer Davis,** 'Law breaking and law enforcement: The creation of a criminal class in mid-Victorian London', Ph.D, Boston College, 1984; while for valuable insights into the 'criminal class', how it was perceived and treated during the nineteenth century, see **S. J. Stevenson,** 'The "criminal class" in the mid-Victorian City: A study of policy conducted with special reference to those made subject to the provisions of 34 & 35 Vict., c. 112 (1871) in Birmingham and East London in the early years of registration and supervision', D.Phil., Oxford, 1983. Some of Stevenson's general conclusions may be found in his essay 'The "habitual criminal" in nineteenth-century England: some observations on the figures', *Urban History Yearbook*, 1986. The fullest, critical bibliographical essay, though ranging well beyond the nineteenth century, is **Victor Bailey,** 'Bibliographical essay: crime, criminal justice and authority in England', *Bulletin of the Society for the Study of Labour History*, 40, Spring 1980.

No one interested in the legal, penal and police reforms of the eighteenth and nineteenth centuries can afford to ignore **Michel Foucault,** *Discipline and Punish: The birth of the prison* (Allen Lane, London, 1977); while the bulk of the illustrative material here is French, the argument ranges far wider. These reforms, as they occurred in England, provide the focus for **Sir Leon Radzinowicz's** exhaustive *A History of English Criminal Law* (Stevens, London, 5 vols. 1948–86). Alternative interpretations to Radzinowicz's fundamentally 'Whiggish' approach can be found in **Michael Ignatieff,** *A Just Measure of Pain: The penitentiary in the Industrial Revolution 1750–1850* (Macmillan, London, 1978) and **David Philips** 'A new engine of power and authority': The institutionalization of law-enforcement in England 1780–1830', in Gatrell, Lenman and Parker, (eds.), *Crime and the Law*. A useful introduction to legal institutions and to developments in the law since the middle of the eighteenth century is **A. H. Manchester,** *A Modern Legal History of England and Wales 1750–1950* (Butterworths, London, 1980).

The opportunities for archival research remain legion. Eighteenth- and nineteenth-century quarter sessions records provide one rich mine; the county material is probably more detailed than that for the boroughs. Assize records in the Public Records Office and petty sessions records in local archives are rather more fragmentary, but there is profit to be found in their exploitation. Statistical surveys have probably been taken to their limit, but much more use could be made of depositions than has hitherto been the case. A detailed exploration of crime in some eighteenth-century northern counties, well away from the pull of the metropolis, would be useful to set alongside the work of Beattie and King; and they, together with David Philips, provide the models for such research. It would also be useful to know more about the functioning of the old system of police, and the extent to which the old system survived in the guise of something new. Lastly, Simon Stevenson's use of the documentation on the 'habitual criminals' suggests that there is much more to be made of the material in the Public Records Office which emanated from the Home Office and the prisons, and that much more could be done in exploring how different local authorities enforced legislation.

Index